Essays on Islam and
Indian History

Essays on Islam and
Indian History

Richard M. Eaton

OXFORD
UNIVERSITY PRESS

OXFORD
UNIVERSITY PRESS

YMCA Library Building, Jai Singh Road, New Delhi 110 001

Oxford University Press is a department of the University of Oxford. It furthers the
University's objective of excellence in research, scholarship, and education
by publishing worldwide in

Oxford   New York

Auckland   Bangkok   Buenos Aires   Cape Town   Chennai
Dar es Salaam   Delhi   Hong Kong   Istanbul   Karachi   Kolkata
Kuala Lumpur   Madrid   Melbourne   Mexico City   Mumbai   Nairobi
São Paulo   Shanghai   Singapore   Taipei   Tokyo   Toronto

with an associated company in Berlin

Oxford is a registered trade mark of Oxford University Press
in the UK and in certain other countries

Published in India
By Oxford University Press, New Delhi

First published 2000
Second impression 2001
Oxford India Paperbacks 2002

ISBN 019 566 2652

Typeset by Printline, New Delhi
Printed at Saurabh Print-o-Pack, Noida
Published by Manzar Khan, Oxford University Press
YMCA Library Building, Jai Singh Road, New Delhi 110 001

To my many former teachers, including

> Philip D. Curtin
> Robert E. Frykenberg
> John F. Richards
> John R.W. Smail

and in fond memory,

> Philip Rhys Adams
> Johnny Myers
> Lucy Reed

Contents

List of Maps

Acknowledgements

I would like to acknowledge the following works where my essays were first published:

'Islamic History as World History', reprinted in Michael Adas, ed., *Islamic and European Expansion: The Forging of a Global Order* (Philadelphia: Temple University Press, 1993), 1–36.
'Comparative History as World History: Religious Conversion in Modern India', in *Journal of World History* 8, no. 2 (Fall, 1997), 243–71.
'Multiple Lenses: Differing Perspectives of Fifteenth-Century Calicut', in Laurie J. Sears, ed., *Autonomous Histories, Particular Truths: Essays in Honor of Prof. John R. W. Smail* (Madison: University of Wisconsin Southeast Asia Monographs, 1993), 71–86.
'Temple Desecration and Indo-Muslim States', in David Gilmartin and Bruce B. Lawrence, eds, *Beyond Turk and Hindu: Rethinking Religious Identities in Islamicate South Asia* (Gainesville: University Press of Florida, 2000).
'(Re)imag(in)ing Other²ness: A Postmortem for the Postmodern in India', in *Journal of World History* 11, no. 1 (Spring, 2000).
'The Articulation of Islamic Space in the Medieval Deccan', in Irene A. Bierman, ed., *Islam on the Margins* (Los Angeles: Center for Near Eastern Studies, UCLA, 2000).
'Historical Introduction', George Michell and Richard Eaton, *Firuzabad: Palace City of the Deccan* (Oxford: Oxford University Press, 1992), 9–19.
'Sufi Folk Literature and the Expansion of Indian Islam', in *History of Religions* 14, no. 2 (November 1974), 117–27.
'The Political and Religious Authority of the Shrine of Bābā Farīd in Pakpattan, Punjab', in Barbara Metcalf, ed., *Moral Conduct and Authority: The Place of 'Adab' in South Asian Islam* (Berkeley: University of California Press, 1982), 333–56.
'Court of Man, Court of God: Local Perceptions of the Shrine of Bābā Farīd, Pakpattan, Punjab', in Richard C. Martin, ed., *Islam in Local Contexts*, vol. 17 of *Contributions to Asian Studies* (Leiden: Brill, 1982), 44–61.

'Who are the Bengal Muslims? Conversion and Islamization in Bengal', in Rafiuddin Ahmed, ed., *Understanding Bengali Muslims: Interpretive Essays* (New Delhi: Oxford University Press, 2000).

I wish to thank Joan Dayan for the valuable conversations we had concerning the drafting of various passages in this volume. Thanks also go to Dr Bertram H. Schaffner, owner of the miniature painting reproduced on the book jacket, for permission to reproduce it here.

Introduction

I made my first trip to South Asia in the mid-1960s, travelling by train from Iran across the Baluchistan desert and Sulaiman Mountains, down through the Bolan Pass until the fertile, green strip of the Indus Valley hove into view. Karachi, Bombay, Hyderabad, Madras, Calcutta, Benares, Delhi, Lahore—at first these great cities seemed utterly unfamiliar. But gradually, perhaps because I had spent the previous year living in Iran, I began to recognize much of what I found in the subcontinent. Persian architectural forms, seventeenth century miniature paintings, qawwali music, the Urdu language, Islamic tomb-cults—all of these appeared refracted through the prism of Iran, brushed with the turquoise patina of Perso-Islamic civilization. After all, how can anyone who has visited Shiraz or Isfahan see the Taj Mahal without feeling a shock of recognition? Similarly, a glance at the family names listed in a Delhi telephone directory at once reveals deep connections, whether real or imagined, between north India and the peoples and cultures of Central Asia and the Iranian Plateau.

The long encounter between Islamic and Indic civilizations, I came to realize, had stirred remarkably creative energies among peoples of the subcontinent, producing one of the most vital centres of Islamic culture in the world. But how did this happen? Why did the Perso-Islamic encounter with India give rise to such greater cultural florescence than, say, the Arab-Islamic encounter with Europe? How did it happen that, worldwide, more Muslims came to live east of Karachi, than west of that city? Even within South Asia, how can one explain the extraordinarily uneven distribution of Muslims, where their numbers would dominate in some regions but not in others?

The essays in the present volume address these and related issues and are subdivided into two categories: historiographical essays, which examine how historians structure and answer the questions they choose to ask of the past, and case studies on the history of particular Indian communities. The case studies are drawn from research done over the course of twenty-five years on regions that were in some sense peripheral to upper India's imperial heartland, that is, the Delhi Doab, with its associations with Mughal grandeur. Explicit or implicit in these essays, then, is a concern with the dynamics of metropolis-frontier relations. For example, a glance at a map of South Asia's religious demography shows that Islam took root much more readily in Bengal or the Punjab than in upper India, the area with the deepest traditions of Indo-Muslim rule and patronage.

The essays also challenge the image of Islam or of any religion as a fixed or monolithic essence. In South Asia as elsewhere, religious traditions have been continuously redefined, reinterpreted, and contested, as competing social groups have risen or fallen in prominence and influence. For me, therefore, the challenge has been to identify those groups and, by situating them in their historical contexts, to determine how and why they constructed their religious culture in the particular way they did. In this light, it becomes unproductive, or flatly wrong, to speak of one group as 'orthodox' and another as 'unorthodox', or of one religious variant as 'fundamentalist' and another as, for example, 'syncretic'. As rhetorical clubs, these labels might help identify competing social classes or factions in a given historical situation. But as analytical tools, they are quite useless. Moreover, if religions are understood in terms of fixed or monolithic essences, then a phenomenon like religious conversion—a theme that runs through many essays in this volume—can be seen only in terms of a tradition's one-way movement from a 'heartland' to a 'periphery'. Such thinking has given rise to the flawed notion of the 'spread' or 'expansion' of Islam and other religions in India, as though South Asia were an inert soil that only passively received the active seed of a religion imported from elsewhere.

The first group of essays places the study of Islam and Indian history in larger historiographical frameworks. Chapter One attempts to situate Islam in the context of world history, while at the same time exploring the changing ways in which Western historians, between the eighteenth and twentieth centuries, thought about Orientalism, Islam, and Islamic history. In view of the global demographics of Islam, the question here is not whether South Asia can be considered as any sort of periphery, but rather, how this region became a cultural and demographic epicenter for the entire Muslim world.

Though concerned not with Islam but with Christianity in India, Chapter Two offers a model for explaining religious conversion. Arguing for a more nuanced and reciprocal understanding of cultural change, I choose the theme of religious conversion as proof of how people reinterpret and reconstruct their cultures. I also plead for the comparative method as a means of solving historical problems and propose that social processes can be a more fruitful category of historical analysis than geographical entities. The problem with using the latter as 'natural' units of historical inquiry is further illustrated in Chapter Three, which examines the different ways that fifteenth-century visitors from China, Portugal, Russia, and Central Asia constructed their images of the Malabar coastal city of Calicut. Inasmuch as each image was shaped by the visitor's particular cultural background, 'Calicut' as an objective place virtually dissolves before our eyes, leaving only the cultural screens or lenses through which outsiders perceived the famous city.

Few issues in current public discourse are more controversial than that of the political status of religious monuments. The 1992 destruction of the Baburi Masjid by a frenzied mob of Hindu activists raised a number of urgent questions. Some of those that are historical in nature, addressed in Chapter Four, were prompted by the belief that the Baburi Masjid had been built on the site of a former temple. What temples were in fact desecrated in India's pre-modern history? When and by whom? How and for what purpose? What role did the desecration of temples play in the legitimization or delegitimization of royal power in pre-modern India? Were mosques and temples functionally equivalent as religious and political monuments? In short, the essay explores the basis for the view, currently much in vogue, of wholesale temple destruction by Muslims in pre-modern India.

The essay '(Re)imag(in)ing Other²ness' shifts the historiographical focus to recent scholarly trends both within and beyond India, while at the same time indicating something of my own preferences in the way of historical methods and approaches. The 1980s and 1990s saw the rise of the Subaltern Studies project and the transformations this movement experienced as it encountered literary theory, post-modernism, and 'cultural studies'. Concerning these developments, I ask two questions. First, what have been the implications of placing the British Raj at the centre of Indian time, such that the Orientalists' tripartite formulation of India's historical periods—'Hindu-Muslim-British'—became effectively replaced by the formulation 'Precolonial-Colonial-Postcolonial'? And second, connecting this essay to the preceding one, how did the destruction of the Baburi Masjid affect the way Subalternist, post-modernist, or postcolonialist historians thought about the history of premodern India?

The essays in Part Two are all case studies that explore permutations of Islamic history and society in three regions of South Asia: the Deccan,

Punjab, and Bengal. Chapter Six examines the cultural construction of sacred space deep in India's pre-modern era, taking as its starting point the twentieth century conception of the Krishna River as constituting a sort of 'Maginot Line' that divided an 'Islamic' northern from a 'Hindu' southern Deccan. How, I ask, was sacred space constructed by people living when this line was said to have been established, that is, in the fourteenth century, with the launching of the Bahmani and Vijayanagara kingdoms? Chapter Seven shifts the focus from sacred space to political space. Here I try to locate the palace-city of Firuzabad, an early fifteenth-century site hitherto neglected by historians and archaeologists, in the context of the great conflicts between the Bahmani and Vijayanagara kingdoms.

The remaining essays address Islamization in South Asia, a process in which the secondary literature identifies Sufis as principal agents. Few scholars, however, have specified the precise mechanisms by which a small number of mystics or holymen might have effected such dramatic social transformations as the wholesale conversion of entire populations. Nor have scholars considered how an elite body of literate mystics could have influenced, or even cared about, the non-literate masses they are said to have converted. Chapter Eight, 'Sufi Folk Literature and the Expansion of Indian Islam,' addresses this issue by attempting to bridge the gap between the 'mystical' and 'folk' literature produced by Sufis of the medieval Deccan. It also advocates a gendered understanding of India's pre-modern social history, highlighting the role of rural women in the diffusion of Islamic culture in the region.

The mechanisms by which Sufis contributed to the Islamization of large sections of Indian society are also probed in Chapter Nine, which shifts attention from the Deccan to the Punjab, and from Sufi literature to the cults that coalesced around Sufi tomb-shrines. Concentrating on perhaps the most famous such tomb-shrine in the Punjab, that of Farid al-Din Ganj-i Shakar (d. 1265), popularly known as 'Bābā Farīd', the essay seeks connections between the processes of Islamization and peasantization in the western Punjab. Specifically, I ask why and how it was that Jat tribesmen, as they abandoned pastoral nomadism for settled agriculture between the thirteenth and nineteenth centuries, gradually took on an Islamic identity. Chapter Ten, based on legal depositions given in the context of a 1938 court dispute over the rightful control of the same shrine, probes the ways in which twentieth century devotees understand Bābā Farīd and his shrine. How, I ask, has Islam, a religion par excellence 'of the Book,' been mediated among illiterate

villagers, and how has the shrine served to promote a conceptual con-
flation of Heaven and Earth among Muslims of rural Punjab?

The great Bengal delta, which contains the world's second-largest
ethnic group of Muslims, has long posed a challenge to explaining
Islamization in terms that might go beyond the simplistic notion, found
repeatedly in the secondary literature, of pious Sufis preaching love
and equality among an underclass oppressed by Brahmanical Hinduism.
No contemporary evidence supports this facile and somewhat roman-
ticized view of India's past. By pursuing a theme sketched out in Chapter
Nine in the context of the Punjab, however, Chapter Eleven explores
linkages between peasantization and Islamization in the Bengal delta
during the sixteenth to eighteenth centuries, a period that also saw the
ascendance of Mughal power in the region. The essay contrasts the
style of Islamic piety imported by the imperial Mughals with that of
a new Muslim peasantry, a class then forming in the eastern delta from
amongst tribal groups that had been at best only partially integrated
into the values of caste Hinduism. The essay then goes on to argue
how indigenous Bengalis reinterpreted and adapted elements of the
Islamic tradition to the dynamic civilization then developing along the
delta's expanding agrarian frontier.

In Bengal, as in the subcontinent generally, Islam and Islamic culture
became closely integrated with indigenous cultures and local societies.
Indeed, by the eighteenth century Islam in this part of the world had
in many respects become as thoroughly Indian as any other religion
of South Asia. The essays in this volume are contributions to understanding how this might have happened.

SECTION 1
HISTORIOGRAPHY

1

Islamic History as World History[*]

THE LEGACY OF EUROPE'S ENCOUNTER WITH ISLAM

Some years ago, Harold Isaacs wrote *Scratches on Our Minds*, a book probing the images that ordinary Americans held about China and India. Subjecting his informants to the techniques of psychoanalysis, the author also wanted to learn where, when, and how such images as 'inferior' Chinese and 'fabulous' Indians had been formed. If Isaacs had written another book scratching American minds respecting Islam or Islamic history, one suspects he would have uncovered some fairly lurid images: of grim fanatical clerics seizing political power in contemporary West Asia, of generals amputating the hands of thieves in the name of religion, or of women held in a state of permanent, domestic bondage. Had he scratched a bit more, he might have found images, informed perhaps by youthful readings of *The Arabian Nights*, of Arab princes lavishly entertained by sensuous women, of sumptuous banquets, or of genies and lamps—all set in an atmosphere of Oriental splendour and decadence. He might also have dredged up from the minds of his informants images of medieval violence: of fierce warriors on horseback wielding broad scimitars, or of caliphs delivering swift and arbitrary justice via the executioner. Finally, well embedded in the subconscious of his hypothetical subjects, Isaacs may also have found some hazy notion of Islam as a religious heresy, or of Muhammad as a false prophet.

Such images are part of the legacy of Europe's long and often hostile encounter with Muslim societies. For here was a religion that affirmed the one God of the Jews and Christians yet denied the Trinity; that accepted Jesus as sent to humankind and born of the Virgin Mary,

* Reprinted from Michael Adas, ed., *Islamic and European Expansion: The Forging of a Global Order* (Philadelphia: Temple University Press, 1993), 1–36.

yet rejected his divinity; that accepted the Torah and the Gospels and their adherents, the Jews and Christians, as 'People of the Book,' yet rejected the claims to exclusivity made by the former and the worship of Jesus as practiced by the latter. Unlike Hinduism or Buddhism, which were rendered relatively innocuous by their geographical and theological distance from Europe and Christianity, Islam was simply too close to Europe—both geographically and theologically—to be treated with anything like equanimity. Hence the Crusades: the Europeans' forcible attempt to reconquer Palestine for the Cross and, by extension, to uproot the so-called heresy that Arabo-Islamic civilization was taken to represent. Contemporary impressions of Arab Muslims are vividly reflected in the *Chanson de Roland*, the French epic poem that crystallized in the eleventh century and which depicts Muslims as idolaters, polytheists, and, above all, as the arch-villians of Christendom; while the Emperor Charlemagne is portrayed as the snowy-bearded defender of Christendom who leads the French into a mighty struggle waged in the name of, and on behalf of, the Christian God.[1] The poem thus expresses a worldview rigidly split into a we–they opposition that is about as absolute as any to be found in Western literature.

Since the eleventh century, it was the fate of Islamic civilization to serve in the European imagination as a wholly alien 'other,' a historic and cultural foil in opposition to which Europeans came to define their own collective identity as a world civilization. Gradually, however, Western scholars became aware of the primary textual sources on which Islamic civilization was built. Beginning with the Crusades and continuing throughout Europe's medieval period, a handful of scholars learned Arabic and began editing, translating, interpreting, and publishing the immense corpus of primary texts that had accumulated during the rise and expansion of Islamic civilization. Some wished to refute the religious claims of what they saw as a Christian heresy; others sought to recover for classical scholarship those texts translated into Arabic by Muslims that had been lost in the Greek original. Then in the late eighteenth century, when much of the Muslim world began falling under European colonial rule, institutional foundations such as the Asiatic Society of Bengal or the French Asiatic Society were established for the serious study of Islamic civilization, while in European universities chairs in Arabic language and literature were founded. The fruit of these developments was the emergence of a new cadre of scholars in the nineteenth and early twentieth centuries—like Ignaz Goldziher,

---

[1] See Dorothy L. Sayers, trans., *The Song of Roland* (Baltimore: Penguin Books, 1957), 175–76.

D.B. McDonald, J. Wellhausen, Carl Brockelmann, C. H. Becker, Theodor Nöldeke, Louis Massignon, Edward G. Brown, and Reynold Nicholson—who studied Islamic civilization as their primary field of study and not just as a subject ancillary to some other discipline.

These scholars' strength was their mastery of philology and the principal languages of Islam: Arabic, Persian, and Turkish. Many were veritable pioneers who ransacked obscure private collections all over Europe and Asia in search of original manuscripts that were then edited, collated, or translated. Those who analysed and published these texts more or less consciously endeavored to give definition to Islam as a civilization, that is, as a unified body of beliefs, ideas and values elaborated and transmitted in literature. And perhaps somewhat less consciously, they saw themselves as interpreters of that civilization to 'the West,' their home audience. But there was a darker side to this intellectual enterprise. In their attempt to give definition to Muslim civilization, many tended to present Islam as a 'tradition' that was static, timeless, and uniform, and by implication, impervious to the dynamics of change or of historical process. Moreover, recent critics have sensed in much of this scholarship a political motive. Scholarly concentration on the classical texts of Islam, and especially on those produced during the formative eighth-to-eleventh centuries, encouraged the belief that this particular period represented some sort of 'golden age', after which Islamic civilization was doomed to a slow and painful decline. And the notion of a declining Islamic civilization suggested, in turn, that Europe's relatively easy conquest of Muslim societies in the eighteenth and nineteenth centuries, and the continued European domination over them into the twentieth, had been not only inevitable but justified.

THE RISE AND GROWTH OF ISLAM, AND ITS HISTORIANS

For most Europeans and North Americans, the vision of Islam as a static monolith, or as a mysterious, exotic 'other' remained dominant until the mid-twentieth century. In the decades after World War II, however, and especially since the 1960s, American and European universities experienced a historiographical revolution that considerably expanded the conceptual framework within which Islamic history was studied. Whereas classical Islamicists had asked the question 'What can the *text* tell us of the *civilization*?' a new generation of historians began asking, 'What can the *data* tell us of the *societies*?' Implicit in these very different questions was a whole range of issues, both conceptual and methodological, asked not only by historians of Muslim civilization, but by historians throughout the profession who had been influenced by new intellectual currents, particularly the pioneering work of Marc Bloch and the *Annales* school of historical scholarship in post-World War I France. The new approach also signalled the influence of anthropology on history and all the social sciences.

To say that societies replaced civilization as the principal object of study implied a shift in focus from the literate elite classes from whose milieu the authors of the classical texts usually came, to those many other communities whom Eric Wolf has called the 'people without history.' The new emphasis also recognized that Islamic civilization was not the monolithic entity that many had thought it to be but that, on closer examination, it broke down into a diffuse plurality of communities that differed vastly over time and space. Many, in fact, rejected the concept of civilization altogether as a useful category in social analysis, since any reconstruction of Islamic history based primarily on the Muslim literary tradition will likely give undue importance to the normative social vision conveyed by Muslim literate elites. Furthermore, as the object of historical analysis changed, so also did the questions asked. Earlier Islamicists had concentrated on political and intellectual history largely because classical Islamic texts were themselves preoccupied with these topics. But the new generation of historians began asking questions that ranged considerably beyond the political or intellectual, embracing such sub-disciplines as economic history, the history of technology, historical demography, urban history, social history, political economy, nomadic history, micro-history, and historical linguistics.

The methodological techniques employed for addressing these questions also expanded. True, the immense corpus of Arabic or Persian texts on which older generations of Islamicists relied almost exclusively will remain indispensable for any sort of inquiry into Muslim history. But such texts were frequently formal works written by Muslim chroniclers—many of them in the pay of political leaders—who were self-consciously writing about their own present or recent past with a view to posterity. Hence the texts such authors produced were deliberate constructions or reconstructions of people or events, carrying with them the same risks of bias, judgment, perspective, or interest that can accompany the endeavor of any scholar. What the new historians wanted to do was to supplement such texts with information that had not already been self-consciously packaged for them as 'history' by intermediaries, that is, by the authors of the texts who stood between them and the events or processes they wished to describe. Once the principle of paying attention to sources other than primary texts was accepted, as increasingly has been the case among historians working since the

1950s, the search was on for contemporary literary sources generated outside the Islamic corpus, or for *any* sort of contemporary artifact that happened to be produced by the society in question and which had survived into our own times. The new generation of historians thus dredged up an impressive variety of source materials: commercial documents, tax registers, official land grants, administrative seals, census records, coins, gravestones, magical incantations written on bowls, memoirs of pilgrims, archaeological and architectural data, biographical dictionaries, inscriptional evidence, and most recently, oral history.

We may illustrate some of the new questions and techniques for addressing them by examining specific issues that have occupied modern historians. These issues include some of the most remarkable movements in Islamic history and indeed in world history: the rise of Islam among the tribes of seventh century Arabia; the eruption of Arab Muslims out of the Arabian peninsula and their defeat of the two largest and culturally most advanced empires in Western Asia, Sasanian Persia and Byzantine Rome, and the integration of most of the population of West Asia into a newly constituted Islamic society that had become by the tenth century a world civilization.

The Rise of the Islamic Religion in Arabia

There is a cliché that Islam, because it appeared in the seventh century, long after the other world religions, arose 'in the full light of history,' as if news reporters were on hand to record for posterity exactly what happened. But the widely differing historical interpretations of this event would suggest more obscurity than light, at least as concerns the earliest phase of Islamic history. In our day, three principal kinds of interpretations prevail: the traditional Muslim account based on Arabic sources that appeared in the early centuries of Islam; modern Western accounts that tease sociologically rational explanations out of those same materials; and modern Western accounts that look outside the corpus of Arabic sources.

Traditional Muslim accounts of Islamic history generally commence with the Prophet of Islam, Muhammad ibn Abdullah, whose prophetic career began in the early decades of the seventh century. A west Arabian belonging to a mercantile clan, Muhammad had been in the habit of retreating to meditate on a mountain near his native city of Mecca. On one such occasion he was startled to hear a voice identified as that of the angel Gabriel, who addressed him with the command, 'Recite!' Muhammad soon realized that he had in fact received a command from God:

Read: In the name of thy Lord Who createth,
        Createth man from a clot.
Read: And thy Lord is the Most Bounteous,
        Who teacheth by the pen,
Teacheth man that which he knew not.[2]

On subsequent occasions Muhammad received further revelations that were committed to memory by the small band of followers to whom he began preaching in Mecca and who were known later as Muslims, meaning those who had 'submitted' to God. Several decades later Uthman (644–56), the third 'successor' or caliph (*khalīfa*) to Muhammad as leader of the growing community of believers, ordered that these verses be collected into the canonical scripture that constitutes the Qur'an. For Muslims, these revelations represent the last of several occasions on which God, through the medium of successive prophets, had broken through from the divine realm, where he alone resides, to the human realm. Thus Muhammad is connected prophetically with Abraham, Moses, Jesus, and other prophets, yet because he came *after* the Hebrew prophets, his revelation was believed to have superseded those of his predecessors.

Initially, according to traditional accounts, the oligarchs who dominated Mecca rejected Muhammad's prophecy as a threat to their position. On the other hand the nearby city of Medina, which was at that time split into contentious factions, invited Muhammad to come and arbitrate their internal disputes. In the end they accepted not only Muhammad the arbiter but Muhammad the Prophet of God, and thus the first Muslim community emerged in Medina in the year 622. That Muslims date the beginning of Islam from this event indicates that it was not so much God's breakthrough to humankind that marked off Islam from other world events. Rather, the year 622 was significant because it represented humanity's *response* to God's message, humanity's willingness to undertake the moral obligation of obeying God by forming a new human society—the community of believers called the *umma*—constructed around the divine message.

Since the late nineteenth century, Western scholars have developed interpretations of the rise of Islam using the same body of classical Arabic texts as those used by Muslim traditionalists, but they have done so with a view to finding in those texts explanations that conform to Western models of social development. Thus scholars like Montgomery Watt or M.A. Shaban, current representatives of this trend,

---

[2] Marmaduke Pickthall, trans., *The Glorious Koran* (London: Allen & Unwin, 1976), Sura 96: verses 1–5, p. 813.

have viewed the emergence of the new religion as a function of deeper socio-economic changes held to have been occurring in sixth- and seventh-century western Arabia. During the half century or so before the emergence of Muhammad, Meccan merchants are said to have become long-distance traders who entered and even dominated international trade routes connecting Yemen to the south with Syria to the north, and ultimately, India with Europe. The rise of Mecca as the hub of an expanding international trade network, according to this view, was the cause of any number of social problems for Mecca and western Arabia generally: greater social stratification, greater social inequities, greater dependence of poorer clans on wealthier ones, general social disruption, and even spiritual malaise. In this situation the Prophet Muhammad emerged proclaiming a message intended to dissolve the tribal units altogether and replace them with a single pan-Arab community to be guided by a new and much higher authority—God. Since the new movement declared all people to be equal before God, converted communities whose aspirations had previously been blocked by social inequities now acquired, or expected to acquire, much greater socio-economic mobility. Likewise, the movement's heavy emphasis on social justice and its rejection of all forms of hierarchy or privilege is said to have found a receptive audience among the disenfranchised classes of Arab society, especially the poor, slaves, and women—Muhammad himself had been an orphan—for whom the message guaranteed specific rights and forms of protection.

Thus the emergence of Muhammad and the success of his preaching is interpreted in terms of the Prophet's solutions to specific, contemporary socio-economic problems. But the premise upon which these arguments rest—that the problems of Muhammad's day arose from the rapid wealth that accrued to Mecca as a result of its rise in international trade—has been seriously challenged by several scholars. In particular, Patricia Crone has recently published considerable evidence showing that far from occupying the hub of a vast and expanding commercial network, Mecca at the time of Muhammad was quite peripheral to world trade, and in fact occupied an economic backwater on the fringes of the world's two superpowers, Sasanian Persia and Byzantine Rome. If Mecca was not the thriving commercial centre that most social historians had alleged it to be, then the entire sequence of sociological arguments that rest on that assumption, and which are used to explain the rise of Islam, collapses.

A third cluster of scholars has sought to move beyond exclusive reliance on the vast corpus of Arabic texts (commentaries, histories, biographies, etc.) that developed within the early tradition of Islamic scholarship, and to study early Islamic history on the basis of contemporary literary materials written by non-Muslims in Greek, Hebrew, Syriac, Coptic or Armenian.[3] The discovery and use of such literary sources have truly revolutionized the field. The editor of a volume arising from a 1975 conference on early Islam that included a paper on Syriac sources wrote: 'For the first time in our lives many of us became acquainted with the outlook of non-Arab, non-Muslim historians on the conquests and [their] perpetrators.'[4] By comparing the non-Arabic with the Arabic sources, or by combining both, scholars are now beginning to replace earlier, over-simplified views with more refined interpretations of early Islamic social history. It is as though a generation of World War Two historians who had previously used only German sources for writing about the War suddenly discovered the mountains of wartime sources written in English, Russian, Japanese, and French.

If some historians wish merely to supplement Arabic sources with non-Arabic ones for the study of early Islam, others, such as Patricia Crone and Michael Cook, are more skeptical of the reliability of the Arabic sources altogether. For, apart from the Qur'an itself, these sources did not begin to appear until several centuries after the death of Muhammad, meaning that the primary materials historians had been using for writing the early history of Islam are far from contemporary. On crucial issues, moreover, they are ambiguous or even self-contradictory. On the other hand, many non-Arabic sources were contemporary, or nearly contemporary, with the events they described, though as outside sources they also carried the possibility of anti-Muslim bias. It is hardly surprising, then, that scholars who have been most skeptical of the Arabic literary tradition and most receptive to using non-Arabic sources have reached extremely controversial conclusions—for example, that the earliest Muslims considered themselves descendants of Abraham through Hagar and Ishmael, that the movement originated in northern Arabia and not Mecca, or that Palestine and not Medina was the movement's principal focus.[5] Moreover, whereas the traditional Muslim position

---

[3] Among these are Claude Cahen, Michael Morony, J. Wansbrough, Elton Daniel, S. P. Brock, G. R. Hawting, Patricia Crone, and Michael Cook. While all these authors have utilized literary materials beyond the Arabic sources, they nonetheless differ sharply on points of interpretation.

[4] G.H.A. Juynboll, ed., *Studies on the First Century of Islamic Society* (Carbondale: Southern Illinois University Press, 1982), 2.

[5] For example, a fifth-century Greek source, written two hundred years before Muhammad, reported Arab communities in northern Arabia practicing a primitive form of monotheism, which, though corrupted by the influence of their pagan neighbors, was identical to that practiced by the Hebrews up to the days of Moses.

sees Islam as having appeared fully developed in the form of Muhammad's revelations in Mecca and Medina, contemporary non-Muslim sources depict the slow evolution, in the centuries before Muhammad, of a monotheistic cult that, heavily influenced by Jewish practice and Jewish apocalyptic thought, absorbed neighbouring pagan cults in Arabia in the time of Muhammad.[6]

In sum, the Muslim scholarly tradition generally postulates a dramatic break between the age of pre-Islam (the *jāhilīya*, or 'age of ignorance') and that of Islam. In contrast, modern Western interpretations, influenced by nineteenth-century European notions of social evolution, have come to regard the origins of Muslim history in distinctly organic terms, that is, as having logically grown out of earlier socio-religious structures. The important division among Western historians is between those whose work is confined to the traditional Arabic sources, and those who have begun tapping into the contemporary non-Muslim sources, resulting in interpretations of Islam's origins and early development that are more complex, and in some instances far more controversial, than earlier understandings.

The same source added that these Arabs had come into contact with Jews from whom they learned of their descent from Abraham through Ishmael and Hagar. Syriac sources dating from the 640s, which were contemporary with the Arab conquests, identified Arab Muslims as 'descendants of Hagar'; while the earliest biography of Muhammad, an Armenian chronicle dating from the 660s, described the Arabian Prophet as a merchant who had restored the religion of Abraham among his people and had led his believers into Palestine to recover the land God had promised them as descendants of Abraham.

[6] Such an evolutionary interpretation is consonant with the growth of Allah from the particular deity of a second-century Arab tribe to, in Muhammad's day, the high God of all Arabs as well as the God of Abraham. From the Qur'an itself we know that before Muhammad's mission the tribes of western Arabia had already acknowledged Allah as their high god and were paying increasing attention to him at the expense of lesser divinities or tribal deities. At the time Muhammad began to preach, Allah was already identified as the 'Lord of the Ka'ba' (Qur'an 106:3), and hence the chief god of the pagan divinities whose idols were housed there. In some Qur'anic passages the existence of lesser divinities and angels is affirmed, but their effectiveness as intercessors with Allah is denied (36:23, 43:86, 53:26); while in another passage Arab deities are specifically dismissed as nothing 'but names which ye have named, ye and your fathers, for which Allah hath revealed no warrant' (53:23). This would indicate that these gods were altogether nonexistent, a position consonant with the first half of the Muslim credo, 'There is no god but Allah, and Muhammad is his Prophet.'

The Early Conquests in the Middle East

During the ten years immediately following the Prophet's death, from 632 to 642, Arab Muslims erupted out of the Arabian peninsula and conquered Iraq, Syria, Palestine, Egypt, and western Iran. Nor did the movement stop there. To the west, Arab ships sailed into the Mediterranean Sea, previously a 'Roman lake,' taking Cyprus (649), Carthage (698), Tunis (700), and Gibraltar (711), before conquering Spain (711–16) and raiding southern France (720). Sicily, Corsica, and Sardinia suffered repeated pillaging during those years. Meanwhile, Arab armies during the 650s marched eastward across the Iranian Plateau and completed the destruction of the Sasanian Empire, forcing the son of the Persian 'king of kings' to flee to the T'ang court in China. By 712 they had seized strategic oases towns of Central Asia—Balkh, Samarqand, Bukhara, and Ferghana—and would soon be meeting Chinese armies face to face. To the south, Muslim navies sailed to the coasts of western India where in 711 they conquered and occupied the densely-populated Hindu–Buddhist society of Sind. Thus began the long and eventful encounter between Islamic and Indic civilizations, during which time Islamic culture would penetrate deep into India's economy, her political systems, and her religious structure.

While Arab rule in Sind was being consolidated, other Arab armies continued the overland drive eastward. Requested by Turkish tribes to intervene in conflicts with their Chinese overlords, Arab armies in 751 marched to the westernmost fringes of the T'ang Empire and engaged Chinese forces on the banks of the Talas River. The Arabs' crushing victory there, one of the most important battles in the history of Central Asia, probably determined the subsequent cultural evolution of the Turkish peoples of that region, who thereafter adopted Muslim and not Chinese civilization. Although Muslims would never dominate the heartland of China or penetrate Chinese civilization as they would India, their influence in Central Asia gave them access to the Silk Road, which for centuries to come served as a conduit for Chinese civilization into the Muslim world. Moreover, Muslim Arabs had already established maritime contact with China, having begun trading along the Chinese coast from the late seventh century.

Thus, within 130 years of Islam's birth, Arab armies and navies had conquered a broad swath of the known world from Gibraltar to the Indus delta, and had penetrated both China and Europe by land and sea. But how to explain it? Whence came the energy that had propelled Arab Muslims out of the Arabian peninsula, laying the groundwork for the establishment first of an Arab empire and then of a world civilization? Traditionalist Muslim sources generally accounted for these momentous events in terms of a miraculous manifestation of Allah's favour with his community, an interpretation consonant with Islamic understandings of the relationship between divine will and the historical process, but one that tells us more of Islamic theology than of Islamic history.

Theories of the Muslim conquests advanced by many nineteenth- and early twentieth-century European Islamicists are hardly more helpful. The general tone is captured in the following lines penned in 1898 by the Scotsman, Sir William Muir, whose interpretation of the Arab conquests sounds rather like the screenplay for a Cecil B. De Mille film, complete with technicolor, panoramic vision, and stereophonic soundtrack:

It was the scent of war that now turned the sullen temper of the Arab tribes into eager loyalty. . . . Warrior after warrior, column after column, whole tribes in endless succession with their women and children, issued forth to fight. And ever, at the marvellous tale of cities conquered; of rapine rich beyond compute; of maidens parted on the very field of battle 'to every man a damsel or two' . . . fresh tribes arose and went. Onward and still onward, like swarms from the hive, or flights of locusts darkening the land, tribe after tribe issued forth and hastening northward, spread in great masses to the East and to the West.[7]

In the end, though, after the thundering hooves have passed and the dust has settled, in attempting to explain the conquests, Muir leaves us with little of substance, apart from simply asserting the Arabs' fondness for the 'scent of war,' their love of 'rapine,' or the promise of 'a damsel or two.' Muir's vision of a militant, resurgent Islam gone berserk reflected, in addition to the old European stereotypes, colonial fears that Europe's own Muslim subjects might, in just such a locust-like manner, rise up in revolt and drive the Europeans back to Europe. Sir William, after all, was himself a senior British official in India as well as an aggressive activist for the Christian mission. But his was no fringe school concerning the rise of Islam or the subsequent conquests; indeed, his understanding dominated for decades to follow and, like the traditionalist Muslim interpretation, tells us more about the narrator than the subject.

In the early twentieth century, scholars introduced the thesis that around the time of the Prophet's death, Arabia's grazing lands had suffered from a severe, short-term desiccation that drove the nomadic Arabs to search, literally, for greener pastures. Although it lacked convincing

[7] William Muir, *The Caliphate, Its Rise, Decline, and Fall* (London, 1898; reprinted Beirut: Khayats, 1963), 45.

evidence, this theory found plenty of advocates, and still does today. Variations on the desiccation theory, also lacking firm evidence, held that poverty, over-population, or other such social miseries had driven the Arabs out of their homeland. Still other historians shifted attention from the Arabs themselves to Byzantine Rome and Sasanian Persia, the two great empires of western Asia, whose domains included, respectively, Syria and Iraq. These empires were portrayed as 'exhausted' from several hundred years of mutual warfare, thus enabling the more 'vigorous' Arabs to walk over both with ease. But this thesis likewise lacked empirical evidence, and, above all, failed to account for the Arabs' continued expansion into lands far beyond the domain of either empire. Meanwhile, the notion of the Arabs' supposed militancy, legitimized by the religious doctrine of *jihâd*, or holy war, still informs popular sentiment about Muslims and has continued to find its way into history textbooks down to the present day, though in a somewhat less lurid version than Muir's portrayal.

Whereas older theories saw the invasions as a random or unorganized influx of rag-tag hordes pushed out of the peninsula by population pressure or drawn by the love of rapine, recent research has revealed methodically planned and well-executed military manoeuvres, directed by a central command in Medina and undertaken for quite rational purposes. There was the economic need to provide the growing community with material support—accomplished by the movement's capture of lucrative trade-routes and new surplus-producing regions—which the relatively meagre economic resources of Arabia could not provide. And there was the political need to contain and channel the tremendous energies released by the Prophet's socio-religious revolution. In this sense, the initial Arab conquests resemble the French or Russian revolutions, in which socio-ideological energies generated in the process of consolidating the original movement proved so intense that they could not be contained geographically and spilled over into adjacent regions.

Above all, what is missing from earlier explanations is any mention of Islam itself. One does occasionally come across references to the lure of an Islamic paradise filled with dark-eyed beauties awaiting the frenzied believer who would martyr himself in battle, but such romantic allusions appear to be holdovers from older stereotypes associating Islam with sex and violence. By and large, Western historians of the nineteenth and early twentieth centuries displayed a chronic inability to accept the possibility that the religion itself could have played a fundamental, as opposed to supportive, role in the movement. In recent years, however, there has been an effort to bring religion back into the discussion by focusing on the Muslim community's social fragility during the earliest years of its formation, and especially the volatility of divine revelation as the basis of its authority. Thus the death of Muhammad in 632 confronted the community of believers, then confined to the population of western Arabia, with their first genuine crisis: How would the charismatic authority of the Prophet, who for ten years had provided both spiritual and political leadership to the growing umma, be sustained or chanelled when he was no longer present? Some tribes, apparently supposing that with the loss of the Prophet the continuing authority of revelation had ended, simply withdrew from the community altogether. Others began following rival prophets—at least two men and one woman sprang up in the Arabian interior—who claimed to be receiving continuing revelations from God.

With both the political and the religious basis of the fledgling community thus threatened, Muhammad's first successor as leader of the community, Abu Bakr, moved vigorously to hold the volatile movement together. First, he forbade any tribe to leave the community once having joined; and second, in order to prevent the movement from splintering into rival communities around rival prophets, he declared that Muhammad had been the last prophet of God. These moves amounted, in effect, to a declaration of war against those tribes who had abandoned the umma or subscribed to other self-proclaimed prophets. Thus the initial burst of Muslim expansion after the Prophet's death was directed not against non-Muslims, but against just such Arab tribes within the peninsula. In the process of suppressing these rebellions, however, Abu Bakr made alliances with tribes on the southern fringes of Iraq and Syria, and as the circle of such alliances widened, Muslim Arabs soon clashed with client tribes of the Sasanians and Byzantines, and eventually with Sasanian and Byzantine imperial forces themselves.

Once launched, the movement continued to be driven by powerful religious forces. Islam had derived its initial power from Muhammad's ability to articulate the collectivization of Arabia's deities into a single supreme God, together with the collectivization of its tribes into the single, corporate umma under the direct authority of God. After the Prophet's death, these movements gained momentum as the masses of the Arab soldiery participating in the expansion came to regard the movement's social ideals as immediately attainable. Hence, for them the distribution of the riches of conquered lands among members of the community, which looked to the rest of the world like senseless plunder, served to actualize the ideal, preached by the Prophet, of attaining socio-economic equality among all believers. The importance of this factor is underscored by the fact that one of the first and most serious dissident movements in Islam, the Kharajite movement, was spearheaded in conquered Iraq by men of piety whose military stipends had just been reduced. Leaders of the revolt, which resulted in the assassination of the Caliph Uthman in 656, justified their actions by emphasizing the radical egalitarianism, including social equality for women, that had been preached by the Prophet. In short, recent explanations of the early Arab conquests, unlike earlier European theories, have focused on social processes rather than social stereotypes, and on the internal dynamics of early Muslim society and religion.

EARLY ISLAMIC CIVILIZATION AND WORLD HISTORY

From the perspective of world history, perhaps the most significant theme of early Islam is the evolution of a relatively parochial Arab cult into a world civilization, indeed history's first truly global civilization. For the Arab conquests inaugurated a thousand-year era, lasting from the seventh to the seventeenth century, when all the major civilizations of the Old World—Greco-Roman, Irano-Semitic, Sanskritic, Malay-Javanese, and Chinese—were for the first time brought into contact by, and within, a single overarching civilization. What is more, Muslims synthesized elements from those other civilizations—especially the Greek, Persian, and Indian—with those of their Arabian heritage to evolve a distinctive civilization that proved one of the most vital and durable the world has ever seen. At work here were several factors: the emergence of state institutions and urban centres that provided foci for the growth of Islamic civilization; the conversion of subject populations to Islam; the ability of Muslim culture to absorb, adapt, and transmit culture from neighbouring civilizations; and the elaboration of socio-religious institutions that enabled Islamic civilization to survive, and even flourish, following the decline of centralized political authority.

Islamic States and Islamic Cities

In the early years of the Islamic venture, the community had been ruled from Medina by an Arab merchant aristocracy led by four consecutive successors to Muhammad. By the second half of the seventh century, however, political power had shifted outside Arabia and into the hands of two successive imperial dynasties—the Umayyad, which governed a de facto Arab empire from Damascus between 661 and 750; and the Abbasid, which overthrew the Umayyads and reigned, if not always ruled, from its splendid capital city of Baghdad until 1258. Thus while Mecca and Medina remained the spiritual hubs of Islamic civilization, reinforced by the annual pilgrimage to the Ka'ba shrine, the Arab rulers in Syria and Iraq inherited from the Persian and Roman empires traditions and structures that facilitated their own transition to imperial rule. These included notions of absolute kingship, courtly rituals and styles, an efficient bureaucratic administration, a functioning mint and coinage system, a standing army, a postal service, and the kind of land revenue system on which the political economies of all great empires of the Fertile Crescent had rested. Even the Iwan Kisra, the famous royal palace of the Persians on the banks of the Tigris River, had been conveniently vacated by the last Sasanian emperor, Yazdegird III, as if to beckon its new Arab occupants to embark on and fulfil their own imperial destiny.

This they certainly did. Earlier historians, writing under the spell of Arabic narratives that dwelt on the swiftness and thoroughness of the conquests, emphasized the sense of discontinuity between the old order and the new order. More recent historians, however, especially those drawing on non-Arabic as well as Arabic sources, have tended to see more continuity between the two orders. In fact, recent research suggests that the Arabs' rapid transition from a life of desert nomadism to one of imperial rule resulted largely from the expectations of their non-Muslim subjects. In Egypt, the earliest Arab governor ratified the appointment of Church patriarchs just as Byzantine governors had done, and in Iraq they adjudicated disputes among Nestorian Christians at the insistence of the Nestorians themselves, for that was what the Sasanian government had done. For the first fifty years of their rule, the Arabs even continued to mint coins in the fashion of the Sasanians, complete with a portrait of the Persian Shah on one side. The Persian office of *wazîr*, or chief minister of state, was carried over into Abbasid government. And the caliphs, though technically the successors (*khalîfa*) to the Prophet's leadership, adopted the regalia, the majestic court ceremonies, and the mystique of absolutism of their Sasanian predecessors, even adopting the titles 'Deputy of God' and 'Shadow of God on Earth.' The caliphs also carried over the Sasanian practice of patronizing a state religion, substituting Islam for Zoroastrianism. They appointed *qâḍîs*, or Muslim judges, and promoted the construction of mosques, just as the Persian Shahs had appointed Zoroastrian priests and built fire temples. Moreover, having acquired the taste for urban life that their Sasanian predecessors had cultivated, the caliphs lavishly supported the whole gamut of arts and crafts that subsequently became associated with Islamic culture: bookmaking, carpet weaving, pottery, calligraphy, ivory carving, wood carving, glassware, and tapestry, among others. Thus the centralized, imperial caliphate, though strictly speaking a violation of Islamic notions of the equality of believers, served as a vehicle for the growth of Islamic civilization in its widest sense.

As the social historian Ira Lapidus has shown, all of this growth took place in the context of the extraordinary urbanization that soon followed the conquests. While older cities like Damascus, Jerusalem, Isfahan, Merv, or Cordova were simply occupied, others, like Cairo or Basra, began as garrison cities for Arab soldiers, a development resulting in part from a policy of settling and urbanizing otherwise potentially turbulent nomads. Cities, both new and old, also grew in response to the Caliphate's need for administrative centres, and these, once in place, drew in and absorbed the surrounding population as urban proletariat classes. The most spectacular such case was that of Baghdad. Established in 756, the new Abbasid capital rapidly swelled to a population of about half a million, or ten times the size of nearby Ctesiphon, the former Sasanian capital. Everywhere from Cordova to Delhi there sprang up great cities which, stimulated by the appetite of the ruling classes for luxury goods, became burgeoning centres and markets for the production and consumption of numerous crafts and industries. Also, by spatially dividing functionally autonomous communities into separate quarters, these cities projected a social vision, inherited ultimately from the Sasanians' policy toward their own minority communities, whereby the Islamic ruler extended to the communities recognition, tolerance, and protection in return for political loyalty and taxes. By virtue of such arrangements a Muslim city like eleventh century Toledo, in Spain, could absorb a community of 10,000 Jews without experiencing the sort of anti-Semitic hostility typical of Christian cities of late medieval Europe.

Conversion to Islam

Another dimension to the entry of Islamic civilization into world history was the mass conversion of West Asian sedentary communities to Islam. Unlike other great conquests in which the foreign conqueror merely came and went—or perhaps came and assimilated—by the tenth and eleventh centuries Islam was well on its way to becoming the dominant religion in West Asia. The dynamics of this movement have been fruitfully explored in Richard Bulliet's *Conversion to Islam in the Medieval Period: An Essay in Quantitative History*, a book whose subtitle illustrates the entry of new social science techniques into a field that had formerly been the exclusive preserve of classical, textual scholarship. Bulliet's concern was to plot the pace and direction of conversion by tabulating the patterns of change in personal names recorded in biographical dictionaries for selected West Asian communities.

Other recent studies have emphasized the striking extent of cultural continuity amidst the conversion process. In an important study of the cultural effects of the conquests in Iraq, Michael Morony argued that non-Muslims found it easier to accept Islam when ideas, attitudes, or institutions already present in their own cultures shared affinities with those imported from Arabia. For example, the Muslims shared animal sacrifice with pagans and Zoroastrians and ritual slaughter with Jews; they shared circumcision with Jews and Christians; they institutionalized charity, like Jews and Christians; they covered their heads during worship, like Jews; they had a month-long fast followed by a festival, like many other groups; they practiced ritual ablutions, as did Zoroastrians; and their ritual prayer resembled that of Nestorian Christians. Studies like Bulliet's and Morony's thus show a distinct shift away from earlier and cruder models of religious conversion, which, in the tradition of William Muir, tended to conflate the conquests and the conversion of non-Muslims into a single process, thereby reducing Islam to a 'religion of the sword.'

Moreover, we are now beginning to see that already by the late seventh century Muslims were regarding themselves as carriers of a global civilization and not just members of an Arab cult. In their newly-won empire they found themselves ruling over a plurality of autonomous and self-regulating religious communities—Greek Orthodox Christians, Monophysites, Nestorians, Copts, Zoroastrians, Manichaeans, Jews—as well as a plurality of linguistic and literary traditions, including Greek, Coptic, Syriac, Armenian, Middle Persian, and various dialects of Aramaic. In forging an independent Islamic identity amidst these older religious communities, Muslims faced a critical choice: Either they could constitute themselves as one more autonomous community modeled on those they ruled—thereby preserving Allah as an Arab deity, Islam as an Arab cult, and Arabic as the language of the ruling class—or they could try to bring all these diverse communities and traditions together into a new cultural synthesis. During the initial decades after their conquest of the Fertile Crescent and Egypt, Muslim rulers generally opted for the former alternative, as Islam remained the proud emblem of the Arab ruling elite. But by the eighth century they had turned to the latter alternative, a move that may have been decided as much on practical as on religious grounds. Convinced of the political imprudence of a tiny ethnic minority ruling indefinitely over an enormous non-Muslim majority, the Caliphs openly encouraged their non-Arab subjects to convert. Henceforth the Arabic language and the Islamic religion would provide a sense of civilizational coherence by uniting hitherto separate religious and linguistic communities into a single ethno-religious identity, initially transcending and ultimately supplanting all other such identities. Because Muslims chose this second option, Islam became a world civilization, and not just one more parochial, ethnic cult.

That Muslims quite self-consciously saw themselves as playing this unifying role seems to be the import of the Qur'an's passages exhorting Jews and Christians to leave aside their differences and return to the pure, unadulterated monotheism of Abraham, their common ancestor. Verses to this effect were inscribed around Islam's earliest surviving monument, Jerusalem's magnificent Dome of the Rock, built in 691:

O mankind! The messenger hath come unto you with the Truth from your Lord. Therefor believe; (it is) better for you. . . .

O People of the Scripture! Do not exaggerate in your religion nor utter aught concerning Allah save the truth. The Messiah, Jesus son of Mary, was only a messenger of Allah, and His word which He conveyed unto Mary, and a spirit from Him. So believe in Allah and his messengers, and say not 'Three'—Cease! (it is) better for you!—Allah is only One God. Far is it removed from His Transcendent Majesty that He should have a son. His is all that is in the heavens and all that is in the earth. And Allah is sufficient as Defender.[8]

As an invitation clearly intended for the Jews and Christians of Jerusalem, and of Palestine generally, these words point to the unifying, integrative role that Muslims saw themselves as playing amidst the older religious traditions of the Middle East.

Islamic Civilization and Cultural Diffusion

Islamic civilization also became a global civilization in its capacity to receive and absorb culture from one end of the world and then pass it on to other parts of the world. Consider, for example, the art of papermaking. The Islamization of Central Asia was only one consequence of the Arabs' defeat of Chinese armies in the mid-eighth century. The other was that the victors learned from their Chinese prisoners of war the technology of papermaking, which then rapidly diffused throughout the Abbasid Empire. By the end of the eighth century Baghdad had its first paper mill; by 900 Egypt had one, and by the twelfth century paper was manufactured in Morocco and Spain, whence it spread to Europe. Papermaking technology also travelled southeastward. Having learned the technology from the Abbasids, Turks introduced it in north India in the thirteenth century, and for the next several centuries it gradually spread throughout the subcontinent, everywhere replacing the much less efficient palm leaf, just as in Europe paper replaced the Egyptian papyrus. Moreover, since paper is the bureaucrat's stock-in-

---

[8] Pickthall, *Glorious Koran*, Sura 4: verses 170–1, 131.

trade, papermaking technology greatly contributed to the expansion and consolidation of Indo-Muslim bureaucratic states from the fifteenth century onward.

The diffusion of paper technology would have religious as well as political consequences. Since Muslims believe that the Qur'an—every syllable of it—is the actual Word of God, the diffusion of that scripture, vastly accelerated by the new technology, contributed to the growth of the religion as well. Indeed, when one considers the power of literacy and the role of literate communities in articulating and preserving the substance of law, religion, or education, the spread of papermaking technology must have played an enormously important role in the post-eighth-century history of the globe, and especially in the expansion of Islamic civilization with which the initial diffusion of paper was clearly associated.

One of the most exciting areas of recent research is the study of the world-wide diffusion of agricultural products to, through, and from the early Muslim world. In terms of the number of species and the geographical scope involved, this was probably the most dramatic agricultural event in world history prior to the meeting of the peoples of the Western and Eastern Hemispheres in the fifteenth century. In a superbly documented study, Andrew Watson has recently laid to rest the myths that the Arabs, because of their desert, pastoral background, were somehow disinclined to agrarian life and that early Islamic times had witnessed a decline in agriculture. Watson shows, to the contrary, that between the eighth and thirteenth centuries, while Europeans remained un-receptive to agricultural innovation, Muslims both actively promoted such innovations and vastly expanded agricultural production everywhere they went.

A key event in Watson's analysis was the Arab conquest of Sind in 711, which established a direct and regular contact between India and the Fertile Crescent, the heartland of the Umayyad and Abbasid governments. This conquest in turn threw open western Asia, Africa, and Europe to the agricultural treasures of India, effectively incorporating all these regions for the first time into a single agricultural universe. Between the eighth and tenth centuries Arabs had brought back from India and successfully begun cultivating staples such as hard wheat, rice, sugar-cane, and new varieties of sorghum; fruits such as banana, sour orange, lemon, lime, mango, watermelon, and the coconut palm; vegetables such as spinach, artichoke, and eggplant; and the key industrial crop, cotton. From Iraq, these crops (except the mango and coconut) then spread westward all the way to Muslim Spain, which was transformed into a veritable garden under Muslim rule. Other crops passed by ship from southern Arabia to East Africa, and reached as far south as Madagascar, while still others moved by caravan from northwest Africa across the Sahara to tropical West Africa. This was especially true for cotton, whose diffusion in Africa directly paralleled the spread of Islam itself. Finally, from the thirteenth century, most of these crops were introduced into Europe via Spain, Sicily, and Cyprus, but at a comparatively slow rate owing to the Europeans' inferior agricultural skills, their more limited irrigation technology, and their lower population density, which made it unnecessary to maximize their soil productivity.

Everywhere they were cultivated, the new crops contributed to fundamental social changes. Since the traditional crops of the pre-Islamic West Asia and Mediterranean area had been winter crops, the fields of those regions generally lay fallow in the summertime. But as most of the newly-introduced crops were summer crops, adapted to India's hot, monsoon climate, their spread into western Asia vastly increased agricultural productivity by adding, in effect, another growing season for each calendar year. Moreover, since the Indian crops were adapted to high rainfall regions, they required more water than could be provided by the irrigation systems already present in the pre-Islamic Western world. Hence the Arabs' successful diffusion of the Indian crops also involved an intensification of existing irrigation technology (e.g., underground water canals, water-lifting devices), and the invention of still others (e.g., certain types of cisterns). All these innovations, in addition to systems of land tenure and taxation that encouraged land reclamation and a more intensified use of older fields, contributed to a significant increase in food production in the eighth to eleventh centuries, making possible the population increases and urbanization so characteristic of Muslim societies in this period.

Just as they had borrowed, assimilated, and diffused Indian agriculture, Muslims did the same with Greek and Indian knowledge. By the seventh century the Byzantine Greeks had long neglected the classical intellectual tradition of Aristotle, Ptolemy, and Galen, the cultivation of which migrated eastward when religious persecution drove Syriac-speaking Nestorian Christians into Iran. There the Nestorians continued to teach Greek sciences under the late Sasanians. In the eighth and ninth centuries this submerged intellectual tradition resurfaced when the Abbasids established their capital, Baghdad, in the heart of the old Sasanian Empire. Eager for what they deemed practical knowledge—for example, keeping themselves physically well, measuring the fields, predicting the agricultural seasons from heavenly bodies—the caliphs opened a 'house of wisdom' that sponsored the translation into Arabic of Greek, Syriac, Sanskrit, and Persian works dealing with a broad spectrum of foreign thought, especially medicine, astronomy and mathematics. By the ninth, tenth, and eleventh centuries, Muslim scientists, most of whom were Arabic-writing Iranians, were no longer merely translating, but were now creatively assimilating this foreign knowledge. From the Greeks they accepted the notion that behind the apparent chaos of reality lay an underlying order run by laws that could be understood by human reason. In addition to this imported rationalist tradition, scholars evolved their own empiricist tradition that developed especially rich knowledge in the field of medicine. Representing the more mature phase of Muslim knowledge, both al-Razi (d. 925) and Ibn Sina (d. 1037) compared and contrasted what the Greeks had written about certain medical problems with what they had learned directly from their own medical observations. The resulting syntheses were translated into Latin in the twelfth century and remained major medical texts in Europe for the next five hundred years.

We also see this combining of various intellectual traditions in mathematics and astronomy. Around 770, Indian scholars brought to Baghdad treatises on astronomy, which the caliph promptly ordered translated into Arabic. Some decades later, the translations fell into the hands of Khwarizmi (d. ca. 850), the famous astronomer and mathematician, who then combined and harmonized Greek, Iranian, and Indian systems with astronomical findings of his own. The Indians had also brought works on mathematics to Baghdad, and it was from these that Muslim scientists assimilated what was to them, and would be for the rest of the world, a revolutionary system of denoting numbers, including the concept of zero. Called by Muslims 'Indian (Hindi) numerals', they were known as 'Arabic numerals' when subsequently received by Europeans via Spanish Arabs. Building on this knowledge, Khwarizmi combined principles of Greek geometry and Indian arithmetic to evolve a system of mathematics known as algebra, itself an Arabic word taken by Europeans from the title of one of his works, *Hisâb al-Jabr wa'l-Muqâbala.*

The accumulation of this sort of knowledge had a compounding effect that moved Islamic science considerably beyond the merely imitative or eclectic. Indeed, one may rightly challenge the popular contention that in the eleventh century Christian Europe 'rediscovered' classical Greek knowledge in the libraries of Toledo or Granada in conquered Muslim Spain. This is in reality a Eurocentric view, as it implies that Muslims played a strictly passive role, in which their historic destiny was to put early European knowledge into cold storage until such time as it could be reclaimed by subsequent Europeans. With greater truth one could say it was Indian thought that Christian Europeans discovered in those Spanish libraries; or more correctly still, an integrated alloy of Greek, Indian, and Iranian knowledge.

Islamic Socio-religious Institutions

Between the tenth and thirteenth centuries, the Abbasid caliphs began to lose their grip on power as Turkish military slaves, recruited to guard the caliphs and the empire, began taking control into their own hands. The caliphate was thus reduced to a mere figurehead office while real power devolved among various sultanates throughout the Muslim world. The final blow came in 1258 when Mongol armies, having moved from East to Southwest Asia in the early thirteenth century, entered, sacked, and destroyed the Abbasid capital of Baghdad. What is more, they executed the last Abbasid Caliph and abolished his office, thus severely undermining the symbolic unity of the Muslim world. In recent centuries many Western scholars came to understand these events as signaling the beginning of a protracted period of decline for Islamic civilization. But it now seems apparent that such an interpretation of gloom and decline confused the destiny of Islamic civilization as a whole with that of Muslim rulers and their states—a perception that in turn reflects an earlier historiographical emphasis on dynastic and political–military history.

Over the past several decades, historians have cast their vision far beyond the political careers of the caliphs, sultans, shahs, and amirs that had figured so prominently in earlier studies of Islamic history. In part, this shift in emphasis reflects a more general trend, prevalent throughout the historical profession, from political to social history. Moreover, students of Islamic history had to address an apparent contradiction that political history could not resolve: in the post-thirteenth-century period, the very time that it fragmented politically, Islamic civilization not only maintained its internal cohesiveness but achieved its highest cultural florescence. Moreover, at that time, it also embarked upon a career of world-wide diffusion even more impressive in scope than the Arab conquests of the seventh and eighth centuries. Hence, much recent scholarship has focused on the social groups and classes that provided Muslim societies with internal cohesion and spiritual direction when Islamic civilization lost its political coherence. These included, above all, the scholars, saints, and mystics who, from the eighth century forward, elaborated an immense corpus of rituals, dogmas, legal structures, social forms, mystical traditions, modes of piety, aesthetic sensitivities, styles of scholarship, and schools of philosophy that collectively defined and stabilized the substance of Islamic civilization. Because of its vitality, this civilization was able to survive and even expand amid adverse political fortunes.

The role played by scholars, or the *'ulamâ*, in Muslim societies came from basic religious assumptions. Since Muslims have always understood Islam as the response of the community of believers to divine command, it became essential that ordinary Muslims know exactly how they should act both toward their fellow humans and toward God. This entailed the elaboration of the *Sharî'a*, or Islamic Law, and hence the emergence of specialists to interpret and implement that law. Based mainly on the Qur'an and the remembered words and deeds of the Prophet, the Sharî'a is understood as a comprehensive guide to life. Not at all priests, the 'ulamâ constituted a class that included judges, interpreters for judges, Qur'an reciters, prayer-leaders, and preachers. For their training, there were of course formal colleges and state-supported theological schools, but most 'ulamâ were trained through informal networks of teachers whose competence was certified not by any government board of education but by the more personalized means of popular acclaim. Hence Muslims placed especially high value on a peripatetic tradition of education, whereby people seeking knowledge would travel from one renowned *shaikh* to another, studying until given 'permission' (*ijâzat*) to teach by their shaikh. In this way, informal schools of law and scholarship grew up around especially famous teachers, and in time, informal schools crystallized into formal schools. Yet the tradition of informal scholarly networks has persisted throughout the history of Islam, providing the community of believers with remarkable cohesion and stability whatever the fortunes of the rulers and their armies.

If it was the vocation of the 'ulamâ to inform ordinary Muslims how to live their lives before God and men, it was the calling of mystics, known as Sufis, to know God in their hearts and to assist others in doing so. Although it grew alongside Islamic legal and scholastic traditions, Sufism addressed a different, and complementary, side of human consciousness. Like many scholars, Sufis often lived itinerant lives searching for renowned masters who could help in their personal quest for God. There also emerged various schools of mysticism oriented around particular modes of spiritual discipline. Named after their founders, these schools soon coalesced into stable organizations, or orders, whose networks criss-crossed the Muslim world and beyond, knitting together widely scattered communities with shared literatures and spiritual genealogies. Significantly, the great Sufi orders appeared in the thirteenth and fourteenth centuries, precisely at the time when the community's political unity had shattered, suggesting that the loss of political unity prompted Muslim communities to seek legal and spiritual direction closer to home.

Pioneered by J.S. Trimingham's *Sufi Orders in Islam* (1971), a growing literature has appeared in recent years analysing the rise and growth of institutionalized Sufism, focusing on the role that the orders and individual Sufis played in the growth of the global Muslim community. In fact, in areas far from the reaches of Muslim states the first seeds of new Muslim communities often began with the appearance of anonymous, itinerant holy men whom the local population might associate with miraculous powers. Typical is the following extract from the medieval folk literature of eastern Bengal:

At that time there came a Mahomedan *pîr* [Sufi] to that village. He built a mosque in its outskirts, and for the whole day sat under a fig tree. . . . His fame soon spread far and wide. Everybody talked of the occult powers that he possessed. If a sick man called on him he would cure him at once by dust or some trifle touched by him. He read and spoke the innermost thoughts of a man before he opened his mouth. . . . Hundreds of men and women came every day to pay him their respects. Whatever they wanted they miraculously got from this saint. Presents of rice, fruits, and other delicious food, goats, chickens, and fowls came in large quantities to his doors. Of these offerings the *pîr* did not touch a bit but freely distributed all among the poor.[9]

It is apparent here that the Sufi's widespread popularity rested on his perceived supernatural, healing, and psychic powers, and the simple generosity he displayed to the poor. Moreover, we can detect here an early phase of Islamization. The humane qualities of the Sufi would be associated with his mosque, which would remain after the Sufi's departure and continue to provide the local community, at this point not yet formally Muslim, with some rudimentary religious focus. What was happening in Bengal was occurring in many corners of the globe, a theme to which we now direct closer attention.

ISLAM IN THE WIDER WORLD

As the accompanying table illustrates, more than two-thirds of the world's one billion Muslims live outside West Asia. Furthermore, over four-fifths of all Muslims are non-Arabs, with the majority of the worldwide community living in South and Southeast Asia. Indonesia has the largest Muslim population in any country in the world, followed by Pakistan, Bangladesh,

[9] D. C. Sen, trans. and ed., *Eastern Bengal Ballads.* 3 vols. (Calcutta, 1923), 1: 219–20.

Worldwide Distribution of Muslims, 1983

Country or Region	Percentage of Worldwide Total (country)	Percentage of Worldwide Total (region)
China		2(?)
Southeast Asia		17
Indonesia	15	
Malaysia, Philippines, and mainland countries	2	
South Asia		30
Pakistan	11	
Bangladesh	10	
India	9	
Central Asia		6
West Asia		32
Turkey	6	
Iran	5	
Afghanistan	2	
Egypt	5	
North Africa and Sudan	8	
Arabian Peninsula and Fertile Crescent	6	
West Africa		9
Nigeria	5	
Remaining West Africa	4	
East Africa		3
Ethiopia	1	
Remaining East Africa	2	
Balkans		1

Source: Richard V. Weekes, *Muslim Peoples: A World Ethnographic Survey*, 2nd ed. (Westport, Conn.: Greenwood Press, 1984). Compiled from data in Appendix 1.

and India. Yet scholarly work on Islamic history in Asia or Africa has lagged far behind that done in West Asia. As recently as 1976 a college-level textbook entitled *Introduction to Islamic Civilization* neglected to discuss—citing 'practical reasons'—the two-thirds of the Muslim world that resides beyond the Middle East.[10] The reason for this unfortunate blindness probably lies in Europe's historic confrontation with its neighbours across the Mediterranean Sea, as a consequence of which

[10] R.M. Savory, ed. (New York: Cambridge University Press, 1976).

the Muslim world *is* the Arab world for many European Islamicists. It is an association that dies very hard.[11]

Research in the past several decades, however, has gone far in redressing this scholarly imbalance. Especially noteworthy is Marshall Hodgson's three volume *The Venture of Islam* (1974), which remains today the most sympathetic and comprehensive history of Islam on the market. In three important respects—conceptual, geographical, and chronological—Hodgson's work broke decisively with most earlier scholarship. First, he endeavoured to understand Islamic history on its own terms and not view it through the tinted lenses of European bias. Even before Hodgson wrote, the era had passed when the caliph was casually termed Islam's pope, the Qur'an its Bible, the mosque its church, or Shi'ism its Protestant sect. But *The Venture of Islam* goes further and persistently challenges the reader's unconscious terminological assumptions, themselves legacies of a thousand years of Europe's mystification of the Islamic 'other'. Second, Hodgson refused to confine his study geographically to West Asia or ethnically to the Arabs but insisted instead that the only proper unit for the study of Islamic history is the entire belt of agrarian lands stretching from the Mediterranean basin to China. It was by virtue of this vision, which in fact accords with the worldwide demographic distribution of Muslims (as seen in the table), that Hodgson could appreciate Islam's truly global character and its capacity to integrate far-flung civilizations. And third, Hodgson broke with most earlier Islamic historiography by not treating the post-Abbasid history of Islam as one of protracted decline. It was of course true that the Abbasids had developed a high, cosmopolitan culture that touched on and communicated with all the older world civilizations, and that with the destruction of Baghdad and the caliphate in 1258, Muslims had lost their central political focus. But Hodgson more than most historians emphasized the coincidence of, and relationship between, political fragmentation and cultural florescence in Islamic history. Above all, he understood that it was only in the centuries after 1258 that the

[11] Factors internal to Islam may also be relevant here, as Muslims themselves have always accorded special prestige to the place of Arab culture in Islam. The Qur'an, revealed in Arabic, repeatedly refers to itself as 'an Arabic Qur'an' (12:2, 42:7, 43:3), and therefore Muslims consider that it cannot properly be translated into any other language. Islamic liturgy remains exclusively Arabic. The five daily prayers are directed towards Mecca, and Islam's central ritual, the pilgrimage to the Ka'ba in Mecca, continuously reinforces the religion's Arab roots. This aspect of Islamic identity would therefore tend to reinforce European associations of Islam with the Arab world.

Islamic religion, as a belief system *and* as a world civilization, grew among the peoples of Asia and Africa.

If Marshall Hodgson's work broke new ground conceptually, it has been followed by a good deal of empirical research on Islamic history—the spadework on which historical generalists depend—that has vastly expanded our understanding of Islam as a global phenomenon. One of the most pervasive concerns of this new research has been the historical formation and growth of new Muslim communities, or Islamization, in Asia and Africa. No single book has pulled together all of the complex elements of this process, but a volume edited by N. Levtzion, *Conversion to Islam* (1979), remains perhaps the best summary. The dominant trend among scholars studying the Islamization process appears to be the effort to see it not as an expansion, which implies imposition, and which in turn implies the use of force, an old European stereotype; but rather to view it as an assimilation. Thus, instead of adopting the perspective of one standing in Mecca, looking out upon an ever-widening, ever-expanding religious tide that is uniform and monolithic, one adopts the perspective of someone standing in a remote and dusty village, incorporating into his existing religious system elements considered useful or meaningful that drift in from beyond the ocean, from over the mountains, or simply from the neighbouring village. This shift in perspective has dramatically changed the way in which scholars think not only about Islam, but about the dynamics of religious change. With this in mind, let us look more closely at the growth of Islam beyond the Middle East, and at the state of historical scholarship concerning that growth.

Where India is concerned, two lines of historical enquiry are discernible, one of them intellectual, the other social. The former consists of efforts to unravel the complex and fascinating ways that Muslims hailing from points to the west came to grips intellectually with India's highly developed Hindu–Buddhist systems of religion and thought. Arab rule in eighth century Sind having weakened and died, it was left to Persianized Turks to establish a permanent Muslim presence in India from the thirteenth century. But what would the new ruling class, itself only recently converted to Islam in Central Asia, make of the land of the Buddha, Śiva, and the marvelous incarnations of Vishnu? And to what extent would Islam adapt or change in order to find for itself a niche in India's rich cultural universe? Lurking behind these apparently innocent questions were fundamental issues, both for modern historians looking back over the past seven centuries and for Indian Muslims living in any one of them. In its manifold accommodation with India's culture, was Islam becoming diluted? Or was it simply growing with the times, adapting to new circumstances, building on what was already there? These were urgent questions, because in coming to terms with India's formidable cultural legacy, Muslims were also compelled to come to terms with their own. As recent research suggests, Indian Muslims felt a deep-seated ambivalence toward Indian culture, with responses ranging from an enthusiastic embrace of Hindu philosophy (for example, by Dara Shikoh, d. 1659) to an outright rejection of Hindus as 'worshippers of idols and cow-dung' (Zia al-Din Barani, d. 1357).[12]

Whatever urban intellectuals may have felt about Indian culture, however, at the folk level millions of Indians were converting to Islam, or more precisely, assimilating Islamic rituals, cosmologies, and literatures into their local religious systems. Beginning in the fourteenth century and continuing through the Mughal period (1526–1858), converted Indian Muslims became the majority community in the eastern and western wings of the subcontinent. Regarding these regions, as elsewhere in the Muslim world, scholars are developing understandings of the conversion process far more refined than earlier, cruder stereotypes of Islam as a warrior religion. Recent research suggests that the growth of sedentary agriculture in lightly Hinduized regions of India will tell us more about conversion than will the movement of medieval armies. For in both wings of India that became Muslim-majority regions— Bengal in the east, Punjab and Sind in the west—the growth of Muslim societies correlated with the adoption of sedentary agriculture. And both regions were still frontier societies where Hindu religious values and the hierarchic social ideals of Brahmin priests had not yet deeply penetrated.

Thus in Punjab and Sind, shrines of great Sufis attracted and integrated pre-agrarian and non-Muslim pastoral clans into their ritual, socio-economic, and political orbits. Descendants of such Sufis then established marriage alliances with the leaders of the pastoralist clans, while the Delhi sultans and Mughal emperors granted huge tracts of rich land for the support of the ritual ceremonies performed at the shrines. The shrines thus served as important mediating agencies—both with the state and with Islamic cosmology—at the very moment that these communities were passing from a life of pastoral nomadism to one of settled wheat agriculture. Also involved here was the expansion of irrigation technology which, as noted earlier, typically accompanied Islamic civilization and in this case permitted a rapid growth in wheat

---

[12] Mohammad Habib, *The Political Theory of the Delhi Sultanate* (Allahabad: Kitab Mahal, n.d.), 47.

production. A similar thing happened at the other end of India, in Bengal, where Muslim pioneers acquired grants from the Mughals to clear virgin forests for expanding the empire's area of rice cultivation. These pioneers also constructed mosques that functioned as magnets integrating non-Muslim forest peoples both into an agrarian way of life focused on the mosques and into a locally structured style of Islam heavily inflected with the culture of saints and saint veneration. As a result of such processes, by the eighteenth century large communities of Muslim peasants had appeared in both Punjab and Bengal. In contrast, in India's heartland, where both agriculture and a sedentary Hindu society were well established, conversion to Islam was far less significant.

India's southwestern coastal region, Malabar, also saw a dramatic growth of local Muslim communities. Unlike Punjab or Bengal, Malabar lay beyond the orbit of Mughal imperial influence and the Persianized culture associated with it. Rich in pepper, cardamom, and ginger, and strategically located at the midpoint of Indian Ocean trade routes, Malabar did, however, fall within the orbit of Arab maritime commercial influence. From at least the ninth century, when the oldest surviving mosque appeared, Arab merchants had established a fixed residence in port cities along the spice-rich coastline. By the fourteenth and fifteenth centuries, when the pace of this trade quickened and the entire Indian Ocean came alive with Arab dhows loaded with spices and textiles, a substantial resident community of Arab traders appeared in Malabar, living under the protection of Hindu kings (who profited handsomely from the trade). Eventually, a sizeable Muslim community emerged through Arab intermarriage with the local population. In the sixteenth century, the appearance of the Portuguese, aggressively hostile rivals for the pepper trade, dramatically solidified the Malabar Muslims, transforming a loosely-knit body of merchants and their local affiliates into an armed community with fixed social boundaries. Of great significance for Indian history, the confrontation also illustrates an important theme of global history: a clash of two expanding and ideologically hostile trade diasporas, each adhering to a universal religion.

In many respects Islamization in Southeast Asia resembled that of Malabar: As a spice-exporting region it was integrated into a maritime trade network under Islamic hegemony; it had hinterlands of rice-cultivating peasants informed by Hindu religious culture; and at a crucial phase in its cultural evolution it was challenged by aggressive European commercial powers hostile to Muslim traders. But the source materials for reconstructing the growth of Islam in Southeast Asia—fragments of Sufi poetry, barely decipherable gravestones, highly stylized court chronicles—are not only sparse but are so elusive that the line dividing mythology from history (a line whose presence is perhaps problematic in any historical writing) appears to vanish completely. Nevertheless, it is certain that by the end of the thirteenth century a Muslim city-state appeared at Pasai, in the northern tip of Sumatra. This was followed in the fourteenth and early fifteenth centuries by other predominantly Muslim city–states along the coasts of Sumatra and North Java, and most important, at Malacca in the Straits of Malacca. When Malacca was captured by Portuguese captains in 1511, Muslim trade shifted to Aceh on Sumatra's northern coast, and when Dutch power arrived a century later, Muslim merchants again shifted, this time to Macassar on the southwest coast of Celebes (Sulawesi).

Modern historians have focused on two main lines of argument in explaining the penetration of Islam in Malay-speaking Southeast Asia. One centres on the extraordinary expansion of regional and international maritime trade in the Indian Ocean during the fourteenth and fifteenth centuries. This activity resulted in turn from the diminished use of land-based trade routes following the Mongol invasions of Central and West Asia, together with increased demand in Europe for Southeast Asian spices. Thus there emerged in the Straits of Mallaca and the Java Sea an exceptionally cosmopolitan atmosphere that was multi-ethnic—with traders from South China, Gujarat, Tamil Nadu, Bengal, Malabar, and the Arabian Peninsula—but ideologically unified around Islam, with the proliferation everywhere of Persian and Arabic literature. A century of heated scholarly controversy aimed at identifying from where Islam came and who brought it—South India and south China are currently leading contenders—probably missed the point. The whole Indian Ocean had become so culturally fused, and its port cities so imbued with an overriding Islamic ethos, that the ethnic identity of particular merchants mattered little. Although historians agree on a clear correlation between Islamization and expanding trade networks in the Malay world, the precise links between the two still seem to elude their grasp.

A second line of argument focuses not on the quickened pace of commerce as such, but on the intellectual and spiritual networks that emerged as a consequence of, or along with, the commercial diaspora. In 1512–15, the Portuguese traveller Tome Pires noted that foreign merchants in Southeast Asian port towns were accompanied by 'chiefly Arab *mullâs*', a category that could have included scholars and Sufis as well as preachers. Seizing on this clue, and building on the fragmentary writings that Sufis and scholars themselves have left, historians such as Anthony Johns have attempted to reconstruct the intellectual and spiritual milieu of the commercial port towns in the sixteenth and seventeenth centuries and the nature of their contacts both with their Sumatran or Javanese hinterlands, and with scholars in India or Arabia. By painstakingly identifying who studied with whom, where, when, and under whose (if anybody's) patronage, the hope is that we may one day be able to make more meaningful statements about the process of Islamization in the Malay world.

Coinciding with the developments described above, from the late fifteenth century, Muslim city-states of Java's north coast—notably Demak—began expanding into the interior of Java, Southeast Asia's richest and most densely populated island. Here Muslims confronted, not European merchant captains, but ancient Hindu–Buddhist civilizations possessing hierarchically organized social structures, refined literati, elaborate court rituals, revenue-collecting aristocracies, and dense populations of rice-cultivating peasants. In the early sixteenth century, a coalition of Muslim kingdoms defeated the Hindu–Buddhist kingdom of Madjapahit, which was replaced by several new Muslim states, the most important being the Sultanate of Mataram in central Java. The history of this state, which reached its height of power under Sultan Agung (1613–46), was marked by the appearance of enormously influential Javanese Sufis (*kiyayi*)—shadowy figures about whom fantastic legends have been embroidered—who seem occasionally to have assisted sultans to power and occasionally to have used their considerable influence with the rural masses to undermine the sultans' power. Despite state persecution and their own tenuous historicity, however, the kiyayi have survived in the collective memory of the Javanese peasantry as vivid culture heroes. Cut off from regular exposure to the wider Islamic world of the port cities, the kiyayi cultivated forms of Islamic mysticism that were heavily tinged with Hindu–Buddhist and native Javanese conceptions. Hence, if the Islamization of the outer islands was linked to the rise of international trade and its spiritual and intellectual offshoots, the patterns of Islamization in the more densely populated interior of Java are associated with the activities of countless roaming saints whose luminous quasi-mythological lives have served, for subsequent generations, to connect Hindu Java with Muslim Java.

In Sub-Saharan Africa, as in Southeast Asia, Muslim communities rose most typically with the growth of trade. Unlike the Romans or Byzantines, who had drawn fortified lines between themselves and the native Berber pastoralists of North Africa whom they considered 'barbarian' (hence Berber), the Arabs endeavoured to incorporate these peoples into the Muslim community after their conquest of the region in the early eighth century. In fact, the Arab expedition across Gibraltar to Spain was in reality a joint Arab–Berber endeavour. To the south, one branch of Berbers, the Sanhajah, had already expanded across the Sahara Desert and established commercial contact with the black peoples of the broad east–west Sudanic belt. Their camel caravans carried salt down from North Africa in exchange for gold brought up from West Africa, which ultimately wound up in Europe. Sometime in the tenth century, the Sanhajah Berbers nominally converted to Islam, and towards the end of that century, the kingdom of Ghana expanded far enough north to meet them, thereby inaugurating a process that has continued for the past thousand years: the gradual Islamization of West Africa.

Although the commitment of the Sanhajahs to Islam was initially tentative, this changed when one of their chiefs, Yahya ibn Ibrahim, made the pilgrimage to Mecca in 1035. As is typical for pilgrims coming from the edges of the Muslim world, the experience of joining in ritual solidarity with Arabs, Turks, Indians, Persians, and Egyptians conveyed to this chief the truly global scope of Islam, in contrast to the more particularistic cults familiar to him in his native land. Inspired to impart such a religious vision to his own people, Yahya ibn Ibrahim brought back with him an educated Arab teacher, Abdullah ibn Yasin, for instructing the Sanhajah on the finer points of the faith. More than that, this teacher, on the model of the Prophet Muhammad's original movement in Western Arabia, revitalized the Berbers in the name of Islam and sparked a military expansionist movement, the Almoravid, that swept over all Morocco and Spain in the eleventh and twelfth centuries.[13]

To the south, meanwhile, Arab and Berber merchants continued to open up trade routes that criss-crossed the Sahara and Sudanic belts of Africa and linked Cairo, Tripoli, Tunis, and Fez in the north with Lake Chad, Mali, and Ghana in the south. Consequently, the earliest Muslims to appear in places like eleventh-century Ghana were foreign traders from the North who lived in separate town quarters under pagan kings. Islamization began only after agricultural peoples became drawn into expanding commercial networks of such traders, as happened to the Soninke, a former agricultural group that took up trading between the Ghanaian goldfields and Muslim merchants from the North. As African communities such as the Soninke became detached from their peasant way of life, their attachment to local deities diminished; and as their association with foreign merchants increased, they gradually incorporated Muslim rituals. So tight was the fit between trade and Islam, in fact, that when this process was reversed, as is documented

---

[13] Marilyn R. Waldman, 'The Islamic World', *The New Encyclopaedia Britannica*, 15th ed. (Chicago: University of Chicago Press, 1991), 22:122–3.

in several cases of converted merchant groups that returned to a peasant life, they reverted to their former pagan cults.

As long as West African rulers remained pagan, however, mass conversion among the peasantry did not occur. And despite the presence of influential Muslim merchant classes in their midst, the rulers tended to remain at least nominally pagan, since their political legitimacy rested on rituals and beliefs associated with local cults popular among the peasantry on whose loyalty they depended. In these circumstances, the physical expansion of kingdoms and the consequent conversion of their kings often led to Islamization. For example, as thirteenth-century Mali expanded from a small chiefdom to a vast empire, in the process incorporating peoples of varying ethnic backgrounds attached to various cults, the religious orientation of its rulers aligned with Muslim merchants, the only community whose territorial reach spanned the whole empire. Hence, by the fourteenth century, Mali was internationally recognized as a Muslim state. But in the fifteenth century when it shrank back to its nuclear polity and was abandoned by many of its Muslim merchants, Mali's rulers reverted to the kingdom's former cults.

If merchants first introduced the religion of Allah and kings patronized it when politically expedient, it was left to scholars to stabilize it. For unlike the indigenous cults whose authority was based on mortal priests, Islamic authority was based on written scripture, giving Islam a status among West African cults that was by comparison immortal and unchallengeable. Moreover, in West Africa as in India, Muslims first introduced paper and papermaking technology. And with paper came the knowledge of writing and a class of scholars expert in applying the Sacred Law. In this way networks of teachers and students, together with the corps of literate jurists and judges they produced, came to provide the sturdy scaffolding that would hold together a permanent Muslim community. In the thirteenth and fourteenth centuries, centres of learning sprang up all over West Africa, by far the most illustrious being Timbuktu. Strategically located on the bend of the Niger River and at the juncture of the desert and the savanna, Timbuktu had emerged around 1100 as an important commercial centre, but by 1400 its mercantile wealth was visibly converted into scholarship. Indeed, Timbuktu is West Africa's finest example of the mutual interdependence of mercantile activity and the maintenance of Islamic educational institutions. So in West Africa it was not Sufis who played the initial roles in Islamization—they appeared in the eighteenth century with reformist movements—but mercantile and scholar classes. Nonetheless, in West Africa as in Bengal and much of Southeast Asia, the Islamic religion was accepted and assimilated as part and parcel of the broader world civilization into which Islam had evolved by the thirteenth century.

DÂR al-ISLÂM AS A WORLD SYSTEM

In recent years there has been much talk in historical circles of *world systems theory* as an approach to global history. This theory is concerned with the expansion of economic networks, especially capitalist networks, that historically have cut across political boundaries in efforts to incorporate peoples into uniform structures. Whatever may be the validity of such an approach for students of global history, historians of Islam are beginning to realize that in the post-thirteenth-century period, Muslims also constructed a world system, but one radically different from that modelled on *Homo oeconomicus*. It was, rather, a world system linking men and women through informal networks of scholars and saints, built on shared understandings of how to see the world and structure one's relationship to it. Above all, it was a world system constructed around a book, the Qur'an, and of humanity's attempt to respond to its message by fulfilling both its external project of building a righteous social order and its internal project of drawing humans nearer their Maker.

Nowhere is this Islamic world system more vividly captured than in the genre of 'travel literature' that emerged in the post-thirteenth-century period. The Qur'an itself enjoins its community to 'journey in the land, then behold how He originated creation' (29:20). From the earliest days of Islam, pious Muslims followed this injunction; indeed the tradition of peripatetic scholars and saints is traceable in part to this verse. In the fourteenth and fifteenth centuries yet another purpose for 'journeying in the land' appeared when increased European demand for spices and Mongol disruptions of overland routes triggered trade diasporas throughout the Indian Ocean and Sahara Desert. For both pious and commercial reasons, Muslims during these two centuries began moving through the known world in unprecedented numbers, also recording their experiences. The most famous of the travel genre is doubtless the *Rihla* of Ibn Battuta (d. 1368–69), the fourteenth-century cosmopolitan Moroccan and man for all seasons: pilgrim, judge, scholar, devotee of Sufism, ambassador at large, connoisseur of fine foods and elegant architecture, and honoured guest of Muslim princes and merchants everywhere.

It has been Ibn Battuta's fate to be repeatedly referred to in Western literature as the Marco Polo of the Muslim world. But the comparison is badly misleading. First, having for thirty years criss-crossed North and West Africa, West Asia, the steppes of Central Asia, India, Southeast Asia and China, for an estimated total of 73,000 miles, Ibn Battuta travelled much further and visited many more places than did Marco Polo. Second, unlike the hard-nosed Venetian, Ibn Battuta emerges as a far more engaging fellow who shares with us just about everything he sees, learns, or feels—e.g., his severe culture shock on first disembarking in China, the altercations between rival Sufi brotherhoods in Anatolia over which one would have the honor of hosting him, the sexual customs of the Maldive Islanders, the techniques of coconut harvesting in Arabia, and the ritual ceremonies of the kings of Mali.

The two travellers differed most profoundly in their relationship to the societies they visited. Marco Polo, who died in 1324, the year before Ibn Battuta embarked from Morocco, had been a stranger everywhere he went, and he knew it. Indeed, his fame derives from his having introduced Europe, which in the thirteenth century was just emerging from being a global backwater, to a fabulous but utterly alien world of which it had only the haziest impressions. In contrast, Ibn Battuta, in his intercontinental wanderings, moved through a single cultural universe in which he felt utterly at home. Most of his travels were within what Muslims have always called *Dâr al-Islâm*, the 'abode of Islam'; that is, the inhabited earth where Muslims predominated, or failing that, where Muslim authorities were in power and could uphold the Sharî'a. Everywhere he went he found the civilized company of merchants, scholars, Sufis, or princes; and with them he would converse, in Arabic, on topics ranging from mysticism to jurisprudence, and especially on events taking place elsewhere in *Dâr al-Islâm*. Overall, his book conveys a self-assured tone in which the cultural unity of *Dâr al-Islâm*, from Spain to China, was not even an issue. It was simply taken for granted. This was a world in which a judge learned in the Sacred Law could expect to find employment serving the Muslim community wherever he went. Indeed, the Moroccan traveller spent many of his thirty years away from home doing just that.

If Ibn Battuta intuitively understood that the Muslim world of his day constituted a truly global civilization, even a 'world system' (though he would have taken offense at such vulgar social science jargon), it has taken Western historians some considerable time to understand it as such. To be sure, in just the past generation historians have sharply refined both their conceptual and geographical understandings of Islamic history. Conceptually, Europe's nineteenth century mystification of Islam, and more broadly, of Orientalism, though still alive in a few dusty corners, has for the most part given way to newer approaches. Social scientists, for their part, have been collecting data on the history of Muslim societies, while historians of religion have been exploring systems of meaning embedded in the indigenous conceptions and the discourses of Muslims themselves. Thus far, both approaches have yielded rich harvests.

Geographically, too, the field has expanded. Although the study of Islam in China and the former Soviet Union remains the most serious deficiency in historical scholarship today—even estimates of the current population of Chinese Muslims are only guesses, ranging from 15 million to 50 million—major regions such as West Africa, South Asia, and Southeast Asia are beginning to be integrated into larger surveys of Islamic history. At the same time, the study of Islam is gradually extricating itself from the grip of Near Eastern studies and the easy equation of Islam with Arab culture. We have also witnessed a burst of research monographs covering almost every corner of the Muslim world. But just adding discussion of more Muslim nations to our courses and our textbooks—a lecture here or a chapter there—is not enough. The key is to understand the global nature of the umma, and above all that the nation-state, Muslim or otherwise, is itself a very recent European political category having no roots in Islamic history. Indeed, as the political expression of an ethnic community, the nation-state concept is fundamentally hostile to the Islamic vision of the umma, the community of believers, the 'abode of Islam'.

If this fact seems less obvious to us today than it would have to Ibn Battuta, it is because in recent times the Islamic umma has been split asunder into modern nation-states—the long-term legacy of the French Revolution. Nationalist sentiments have even infected Muslims themselves, as recent conflicts between Islamic states repeatedly demonstrate. Hence the challenge facing historians is to transcend perspectives rooted in recent times and to appreciate the centrality of Islamic history in world history. Chronologically, Islamic history is the link between the ancient and modern worlds. Spatially, having originated in the heart of the Afro-Eurasian land mass, Islamic civilization grew to become history's first bridge connecting the agrarian belt stretching from Gibraltar to China. Historians have come far in appreciating this much, but we have far to go in grasping its full implications.

2

Comparative History as World History:
Religious Conversion in Modern India*†

This essay argues for the comparative method as a promising approach
to the larger project of writing world history. Comparative historians
typically apply hypotheses derived from one set of data to data drawn
from altogether different contexts, or analyse and compare case studies
taken from any time or place in order to scrutinize a given historical
problem. Consequently such scholars are especially well positioned to
help free the profession from conventions that have bedeviled so much
history-writing in the past, in particular, the convention of tying history
to nation-states or civilizations. To the comparativist, the topic, the
problem, or the process is the focus of attention, not the place. By
concentrating on one such topic—religious conversion—this article illustrates how the comparative approach can be used to explore the
mechanics of a worldwide process. Specifically, I raise the question of
why, in modern-day cross-cultural encounters where Europeans directly
administered non-European colonies, some communities in colonies
converted to Christianity and others did not. This seemingly straightforward question raises some thorny methodological and theoretical
issues. What, for example, is conversion? What is religion?

One may readily admit that societies continuously construct,
reconstruct, and reconstitute themselves both socially and culturally,
as a result of which no religion can be said to possess a fixed and

* I wish to thank Philip D. Curtin and members of his seminar on comparative
world history at Johns Hopkins University, especially David Gutelius, for useful
input on an earlier draft of this paper, presented 7 November 1995. I also thank
Christopher R. King and Robert E. Frykenberg for initiating my interest in the
Nagas.

† Reprinted from *Journal of World History* 8, no. 2 (Fall, 1997), 243–71.

unchanging essence. For the student of religious conversion movements, this proposition suggests that we can no longer conceptualize the phenomenon of conversion, as early generations did, in terms of the 'spread' of an essentialized tradition from point A to point B—typically, from metropolis to periphery—as though it were a substance, like molasses or lava, flowing outward from some central point, engulfing and incorporating all that it passes over while itself remaining unchanged. Rather, we should adopt the perspective of the society actually undergoing change and see conversion not as passive acceptance of a monolithic, outside essence, but as 'creative adaptation' of the unfamiliar to what is already familiar, a process in which the former may change to suit the latter.[1] This formulation in effect inverts the modern Western lay understanding of religious conversion, informed by generations of institutionalized Protestant effort, which tends to look at the process from the standpoint of the agent—i.e., the 'missionary' who goes out and 'converts' the 'native' to his or her religion—rather than from that of the society undergoing change. All of this raises the interesting question of who, in the meeting of two cultures, is actually changing whom. And what, in the end, is actually changing?

If we accept the definition of religion proposed by anthropologist Melford Spiro—'an institution consisting of culturally patterned interaction with culturally postulated superhuman beings'[2]—it follows that a society-wide conversion movement would involve a change in the identities of both the humans involved and the superhuman beings with whom they interact. If this is so, changes in the naming patterns of both humans and superhumans, in addition to self-ascription as reflected in census data, would appear to be our most reliable indices of religious change. With these considerations in mind, I propose to examine one of the best documented conversion movements to occur during the modern colonial encounter: the Christianization of Naga communities inhabiting the high, rugged mountains of northeastern

---

[1] I am borrowing the notion of 'creative adaptation' from John Smail, who some years ago wrote, in a different context, that "remembering that the essence of acculturation is the acceptance of change by the acculturating group—and hence that there can be no question, in the last analysis, of forced culture change—we can bring the problem of culture change in late colonial Indonesia under the more suggestive heading of creative adaptation" (John R. W. Smail, 'On the Possibility of an Autonomous History of Modern Southeast Asia,' *Journal of Southeast Asian History* 2, no. 2 [July 1961]: 91).

[2] Melford E. Spiro, 'Religion: Problems of Definition and Explanation,' in *Anthropological Approaches to the Study of Religion*, edited by Michael Banton (London: Tavistock, 1969), 96.

India. In addition to a substantial body of missionary data in the form of informal correspondence, official reports, published Scriptures, and the like, we also have decennial census data for the entire period of conversion and several important ethnographies—some of them classics in anthropological literature—that were written by district officers and anthropologists who had no vested interest in the conversion movement, and that cover the period both before and after the movement had got under way.[3] One must carefully sift through all these data to locate the Nagas' own voice as they gradually changed their religious identities between 1881 and the present.

In terms of percentage of Christians to the total population, the Nagas experienced the most massive movement to Christianity in all of Asia, second only to that of the Philippines. By 1990, fully 90 per cent of the Naga population of about 1 million was formally Christian,[4] a culmination of a century-long movement (see Table 2.1). Yet, as Tables 2.2 and 2.3 show, the responses of the larger Naga groups were far from uniform, especially in light of the strenuous efforts foreign missionaries had made to convert them. The Ao Nagas, who were heavily proselytized between the 1880s and the 1950s, led all other Naga groups in converting to Christianity, as is indicated in both Census and baptismal data. On the other hand the Angami Nagas, who were also heavily proselytized in the same period, responded at a far slower rate. Conversely, the Sema Nagas, who were virtually ignored by missionaries in this period, like the Aos readily took on a Christian identity. The challenge to the student of comparative history, then, is to account for these very different outcomes. Moreover, Nagas as a whole converted most dramatically

---

[3] Official missionary records relating to the movement are found at the American Baptist Historical Society, Rochester, New York. Unofficial private records of the missionaries—letters, papers, translated scriptures, and memoirs—were deposited in the Bethel Theological Seminary Library, St. Paul, Minnesota. British ethnographies began with E. G. Gait's report in the 1891 census, followed by a series of important ethnographies by Naga Hills District officers: John H. Hutton's studies of the Angami and Sema Nagas appeared in 1921, and J. P. Mills' study of the Ao Nagas appeared in 1926. About the same time sociologist William C. Smith also studied the Ao Nagas. In 1931 Mills followed up his earlier studies with a monograph, 'The Effect on the Tribes of the Naga Hills District of Contacts with Civilisation'. Similarly, Hutton later reflected on the movement in his 'Mixed Culture of the Naga Tribes,' published in 1965. These studies were supplemented by those of noted anthropologists Christoph von Fürer-Haimendorf, who published several important monographs between 1939 and 1976, and Verrier Elwin, whose studies of the Nagas appeared in the 1960s.

[4] Julian Jacobs, *The Naga Hill Peoples of Northeast India: Society, Culture, and the Colonial Encounter* (London: Thames and Hudson, 1990), 174.

only *after* the dismantling of the colonial state and the expulsion of foreign missionaries by the newly independent Government of India (see Table 2.1). Therefore, blanket explanations focusing on monolithic abstractions like 'colonialism' or on activities of the missionaries alone—as though these were independent, explanatory variables—clearly will not do.[5]

Table 2.1. Christian Population of Nagaland, by
Census Data, 1881–1981

Year	Total Population	Christian Population	Christians as Percentage of Total
1881	94,380	3	0.003
1891	122,867	231	0.18
1901	102,402	601	0.58
1911	149,623	3,308	2.2
1921	160,960	8,734	5.4
1931	178,844	22,908	12.8
1941	189,641	34,000	17.9
1951	205,950	93,423	45.7
1961	369,200	195,588	52.9
1971	516,449	344,798	66.7
1981	774,930	621,571	80.2
1990			90.0

Source: *Census of India*, 1881, Assam, 22, 38; 1891, Assam, 16; 1901, 4/2:1, 9; 1911, 3/2:2, 14; 1921, 3/1:26, 61; 1931, 3/1:200; 1941, 9:2, 23, 10:8, 1951, 12/2A:2, 107; 1961, 23/2A:154; *Statistical Handbook of Nagaland*, 1973, 44–6; *Census of India*, 1981, national volume, 151–6. The percentage for 1990 is an approximate figure and not an official census figure. See Jacobs, *Nagas*, 174.

Each of the case studies considered here represents a movement from an ethnic to a world religion in the context of a society's incorporation into wider social and economic relations through colonialism. In this respect they resemble conversion movements to Islam or Christianity in colonial Africa, the study of which has produced considerable discussion about religious change generally. Noteworthy has been Robin

[5] For a differing perspective, focusing more on the agency of missionaries and factors like 'discourses of the imperial imagination' than on the changing cosmologies of the people actually undergoing conversion, see Jean Comaroff and John Comaroff, *Of Revelation and Revolution: Christianity, Colonialism, and Consciousness in South Africa*, vol. 1 (Chicago: University of Chicago Press, 1991), and *Ethnography and the Historical Imagination* (Boulder: Westview Press, 1992).

Horton's 'intellectualist theory,' which seeks to explain religious change in terms of changed experience of social relations.[6] The theory argues that cosmologies of indigenous African religions typically have two tiers: an upper tier consisting of a high god who rules the macrocosm, or the world beyond the local community; and a lower tier consisting of numerous lesser superhuman beings who watch over and participate in a community's immediate natural and social worlds. While communities have more frequent and intense interactions with lesser beings of the lower tier, the high god tends to be vaguely elaborated and seldom approached. With increasing contact with a world beyond their immediate microcosm, however, people tend to give greater attention to their high god, who is understood to control that larger world. This

Table 2.2. Christian Share of Major Naga Groups, 1971

	Christian Percentage (Baptismal records)	Christian Percentage (Census data)
Ao	44.0	98.1
Sema	43.4	77.4
Angami	12.0	40

Source: Puthavail T. Philip, *The Growth of Baptist Churches in Nagaland*, 2nd ed. (Guwahati: Christian Literature Centre, 1983), 78, 92, 110.

Table 2.3. Foreign Missionary Service among Ao, Sema, and Angami Nagas

	Number of Missionaries	Total Missionary Years	Inclusive Dates
Ao	17	170	1876–1954
Sema	2	7	1948–1955
Angami	7	117	1880–1955

Source: Najekhu Y. Sema, 'A Study of the Growth and Expansion of Baptist Churches in Nagaland with Special Reference to the Major Tribes,' master of theology thesis, Bethel Theological Seminary, 1972, 31.

[6] See Robin Horton, 'African Conversion,' *Africa* 41, no. 2 (April 1971): 85–108; and Horton, 'On the Rationality of Conversion,' *Africa* 45 (1975): 219–35, 373–99. For a discussion of the theory's relevance for other cases of conversion in Africa, see J. D. Y. Peel, 'Conversion and Tradition in Two African Societies: Ijebu and Buganda', *Past and Present* 77 (November 1977): 108–42. For a recapitulation of Horton's ideas, see his *Patterns of Thought in Africa and the West: Essays on Magic, Religion, and Science* (Cambridge: Cambridge University Press, 1993), 359–69, 374–5.

can occur, and often has occurred, within the framework of indigenous religions, quite unaffected by the influence of outside religions. But, as Horton argues, if Islamic or Christian influences happen to be 'in the air' when a community is widening its social contacts, their natural shift of attention to a high god can take the form of conversion to one of those world religions, both of which have their own highly articulated conceptions of the macrocosm and its high god. Such an outcome is especially likely when the Christian or Islamic high god is accommodated within the indigenous cosmology—for example, when that god is identified with the indigenous high god.

In short, the intellectualist theory removes from centre stage the role of religious proselytizers, focusing instead on the social and cosmological dynamics experienced by the host populations themselves. 'There is now a very general agreement,' wrote Horton in 1993, 'that the phenomenon of "conversion" can only be understood if we put the initial emphasis, not on the incoming religious messages, but rather on the indigenous religious frameworks and on the challenges they face from massive flows of novel experience'.[7]

RELIGION AND CULTURE AMONG THE NAGAS OF INDIA

By the mid-nineteenth century, most of the peoples of South Asia had been assimilated into one or another of the region's great text-based religious traditions, whether Jain, Buddhist, Hindu, Sikh, or Islamic. Over the preceding centuries, as they penetrated societies living in India's great alluvial plains, these religious traditions carried with them, or associated themselves with, the characteristic traits of plains culture, such as urban life, social stratification, irrigated rice cultivation, a cash economy, centralized political authority, a stable priesthood, and a literary tradition. By the time India came under British colonial rule in the nineteenth century, however, many peoples inhabiting the outlying, forested hill tracts of the subcontinent still remained untouched, or lightly touched, by such text-based religious traditions and the cultural traits associated with them.

Among these peoples were the natives of the Naga Hills—today, Nagaland.[8] Occupying an area roughly the size of Connecticut, this

---

[7] Horton, *Patterns of Thought*, 315.

[8] In an earlier article I explored aspects of this subject as it related to Nagas as a whole. See Richard M. Eaton, 'Conversion to Christianity among the Nagas, 1876–1971,' *Indian Economic and Social History Review* 11, no. 1 (1984): 1–43. While drawing on much of the material that appeared in that article, the present

region is separated from Burma (Myanmar) to the east and the Indian state of Assam to the west by massive mountain ridges. In the mid-nineteenth century, its inhabitants, the Nagas, were divided into some fourteen major linguistic groups, most of which traditionally practiced shifting, or 'slash-and-burn' (*jhum*) agriculture. Economically self-sufficient, these people never developed sustained trade relations with the plains peoples, nor were they familiar with Assamese, the language of the closest literate culture. Even within the hills the various Naga languages, though all belonging to the Tibeto-Burman family, were mutually unintelligible, so that communication between communities of villages had to be carried out by the use of sign language.[9] Their mountain-top villages, moreover, were fortified by defensive stockades. Institutionalized inter-village warfare and the cultural values on which such warfare rested, which included head-hunting,[10] had the effect of narrowing very considerably the Nagas' vision of the world.[11]

Hemmed in both by huge mountain ranges and by their own village stockades, the Nagas developed religious systems that were very locality-specific—that is, highly elaborated with respect to the immediate, localized microcosm in which villagers lived. In 1891, some fifteen years after British armies gained a secure foothold in the Naga Hills, we get the first outside reports of Naga religion. In the census of India for that year, E. A. Gait wrote, 'There is a vague but very general belief in some one omnipotent being, who is well disposed towards men, and whom therefore there is no necessity for propitiating. Then come a number of evil spirits, who are ill disposed towards human beings, and to

---

study incorporates more recent literature and addresses comparative and theoretical issues that did not arise in the earlier piece.

[9] John H. Hutton, *The Angami Nagas* (1921; reprint, London: Oxford University Press, 1969), 291.

[10] As Fürer-Haimendorf remarked, 'a Naga village could not even ideally remain at peace as long as there prevailed the belief that the occasional capture of a human head was essential for maintaining the fertility of the crops and the well-being of the community' (Christoph von Fürer-Haimendorf, 'Morality and Prestige among the Nagas,' in *Anthropology and Archaeology: Essays in Commemoration of Verrier Elwin, 1907–64*, edited by M. C. Pradhan [London: Oxford University Press, 1969], 156).

[11] 'To the Naga,' wrote Fürer-Haimendorf, 'mankind appears as sharply divided between the small circle of his co-villagers and clansmen, from whom he expects assistance and to whom he is bound by a number of obligations, and the entire outward world consisting of the people of his own tribe living in other villages as well as the people of neighbouring tribes, who are his potential enemies and also potential victims of headhunting' (Fürer-Haimendorf, 'Morality and Prestige,' 156).

whose malevolent interference are ascribed all the woes which afflict mankind. To these, therefore, sacrifices must be offered. These malevolent spirits are sylvan deities, spirits of the trees, the rocks and streams, and sometimes also of the tribal ancestors.'[12]

This religious cosmology compares remarkably with the sort of indigenous religious systems Robin Horton found among preliterate societies in nineteenth century West Africa. Again one finds a high god who rules the universe and who, though benevolent, is but vaguely understood and seldom approached because of his perceived remoteness from society's everyday concerns. Below him are a host of minor spirits who are more sharply perceived and are given far greater attention because they control such concrete phenomena as disease, crops, rain, or human fertility. The Nagas regarded these spirits as generally malevolent, or at least whimsical, and so appeased them in the form of sacrifices of pigs, fowl or other living things, to keep them from bringing havoc upon individuals or whole villages. This required the services of village specialists, some interacting with those spirits who could affect the village as a whole, and others with spirits affecting individuals.

IMPERIALISM AND CONVERSION AMONG THE NAGAS

In broad outline, then, this was the society that for more than a century encountered and interacted with both British imperialists and American missionaries. Seeking to protect its infant tea industry, the English East India Company had been drawn into the Naga Hills following its annexation of Assam in 1842. By the 1870s the British had persuaded the Nagas to accept in their midst an English officer who would arbitrate disputes not only between the Nagas and the British, but also among the Nagas themselves. In 1878 the British established a political officer in their headquarters at Kohima, in the Angami country; by 1889 the Ao country to the north had been brought under British administration; and in the early 1900s colonial rule was extended to include the Sema country (Map 1).

Christian proselytization in the Naga Hills grew apace with, and under the umbrella of, the British Raj. The area's first district officer, Captain Johnstone, later recalled that in 1875, 'I pointed out that the Nagas had no religion; that they were highly intelligent and capable of receiving civilization; that with it they would want a religion, and that we might just as well give them our own, and make them in that way a source of strength, by thus mutually attaching them to us. . . . It

---

[12] *Census of India,* 1891 (Calcutta: Bengal Secretariat Press, 1891), Assam, 1:93.

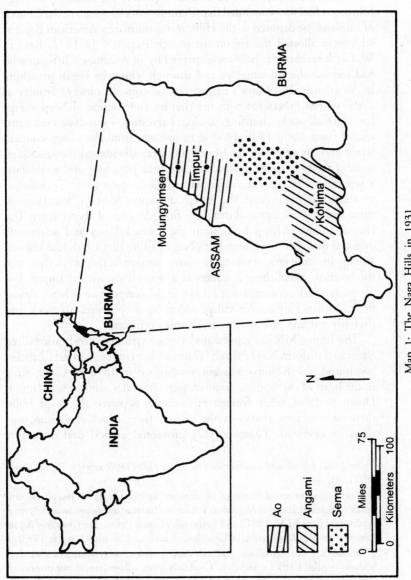

Map 1: The Naga Hills in 1931

cannot be doubted, that a large population of Christian hill-men between Assam and Burmah, would be a valuable prop to the State.'[13] Although Johnstone had recommended that a 'competent clergyman of the Church of England' be deputed to the Hills, it was ultimately American Baptists who were allotted the region for proselytization.[14] In 1872, Rev. E. W. Clark reached the hills accompanied by an Assamese Christian who had learned the Ao language and through whom he began preaching in Ao villages. But Clark's insistence that converts observe Sunday as a 'day of rest' interfered with the rhythm and routine of Naga village life, since all work—hunting, sowing, harvesting—was done on a communal basis. So in 1876, bowing to pressure from the village council, Clark and his tiny band of fifteen followers abandoned the stockaded walls of the first village in which he had been preaching and established a separate, all-Christian village named Molungyimsen.[15] Encouraged by Clark's initial success, the American Baptist Mission Board sent in three more missionaries during the final decades of the century. But two of them, arriving fresh from the United States and adamantly opposed to the compromises with Naga culture that Clark had allowed among his converts, resolved to move mission activities further into the interior, establishing a station at a new village named Impur. For his part, Clark remained until 1911 in Molungyimsen where, almost in the manner of an Ao village elder, he shepherded his flock and tirelessly worked at his many translation projects.

The Impur Mission represented a more systematic and rationalized effort to transform Naga culture. The same was true of a second Christian beachhead, the Kohima Mission, established in 1878 by C. D. King in the heart of the Angami country, some 85 miles southwest of Impur. Down to 1954, when foreign missionaries departed the Naga Hills, these two stations remained the centres from which American missionaries operated. Together, they promoted a good deal of culture

---

[13] Sir James Johnstone, *Manipur and the Naga Hills* (1896; reprint, Delhi: Vivek, 1971), 43, 44.

[14] The best accounts of Christian missions in the Naga Hills are Joseph Puthenpurakal, *Baptist Missions in Nagaland: A Study in Historical and Ecumenical Perspective* (Calcutta: Firma KLM, 1984); and Puthuvail Thomas Philip, *The Growth of Baptist Churches in Nagaland*, 2nd ed. (Guwahati: Christian Literature Centre, 1983).

[15] 'Families from other villages gradually came in and we soon numbered a hundred houses,' recalled Clark's wife Mary. 'Gradually other villages, seeing our prosperity, began asking for teachers, and the Nagas not being sufficiently advanced, a few Assamese Christians were called for evangelistic and educational work' (Mary M. Clark, *A Corner in India* [Philadelphia: American Baptist Publications Society, 1907], 91).

change, only part of which was religious. For example, linguists at the two stations, eager to place vernacular translations of the New Testament in circulation as quickly as possible, reduced the various Naga languages to written forms and built up the first written literature Naga peoples possessed. This in turn simplified the linguistic landscape, for by selecting from among many dialects of a language just one for reduction to Roman script, the missionaries doomed most other dialects to oblivion. As literacy became the key to education, which in turn, in the newly established colonial context, became the key to social mobility, Ao Nagas realized the advantage of learning the dialect selected by Clark and his successors as the 'standard' dialect. The same would occur among the Angami, the Sema, and other Naga peoples.

The principal institution facilitating both education and conversion was the village school. In 1905 the Chief Commissioner of Assam summoned the second missionary posted in Kohima, Sidney Rivenburg, to discuss the establishment of village schools in the Naga Hills.[16] Like the missionaries, government officials also wished to promote literacy, prohibit inter-village warfare, and break down barriers that isolated Nagas from fellow Naga groups. Their further motive, of course, was to create a cadre of clerks to run the revenue and judicial administration in the newly-formed Naga Hills District. But unlike the missionaries, district officers, interested in maintaining peace and security, wished to avoid interfering with Naga culture, especially religion. After all, Englishmen in India had bitter memories of the 1857 uprising, which had followed a period of aggressive British interference in Indian culture in the name of 'reform'.

But as to the desirability of educating the Nagas, Mission and Government were of one mind. The result was a three-way cooperative effort: villages desiring a school provided the building and the rice for a teacher, the Government paid the teacher's salary and financed the printing of textbooks, while the missionaries wrote the texts and trained the teachers at Kohima or Impur. Pupils completing three years in village schools could then leave their native villages and enroll as secondary school pupils in either the Kohima or Impur Mission Training Schools.[17] There, students learned carpentry, blacksmithing, typewriting, or rice terrace cultivation, in addition to pursuing regular academic courses.

---

[16] Sidney W. Rivenburg, *The Star of the Naga Hills* (Philadelphia: Judson, 1941), 96–7. By this time Rivenburg had already translated a primer and books on arithmetic and hygiene, as well as parts of the New Testament, into Angami.

[17] American Baptist Foreign Mission Society, *96th Annual Report* (Boston: American Baptist Foreign Mission Society, 1910), 78.

From there they typically joined government service or returned to villages to become primary school teachers themselves.[18] By this time, however, they had been exposed to considerable Christian influence, such that in 1923 the Baptist Foreign Mission Society could note with satisfaction that 'the government can secure the service of practically none but Christians as teachers.'[19] Moreover, missionaries circumvented the teacher training schools' secular façade (necessitated by the fact of partial government support) by counting Sundays as one of the required school days, so that students had to attend church services to get credit for regular school attendance.[20] Too, the vast majority of the staff at the training schools were themselves Naga converts.[21] Consequently, when villages requested teachers for what was typically their first local school, they were usually sent a Christian youth whom the Mission paid, in addition to their government salary, a sum of about $4 a month to preach in addition to doing his school work.[22] In his field report for 1937, the senior missionary at Kohima summed it up nicely: 'With a mission school there immediately follows a Sunday School and out of that grows a church. The history of many a church in Assam can be traced back to an investment of say, forty dollars per year and the placement of a Christian teacher in an otherwise unevangelized village.'[23]

But what did these missionaries mean by conversion? In theory, they might have been content with Nagas accepting Christian baptism and simply abandoning, as one of them put it, 'the miserable worship patterns handed down to them by their ancestors.'[24] But in practice they called for a total cultural transformation. As Mary Clark wrote, 'the Nagas, once civilized and Christianized, will make a manly, worthy

[18] Papers of J. E. Tanquist, Bethel Theological Seminary Library, St. Paul, Minnesota, MS, 1935, 223b (hereafter cited as Tanquist Papers). By 1923 the mission ran 208 schools, chiefly primary, serving 5,438 pupils. American Baptist Foreign Mission Society, *109th Annual Report* (Valley Forge, Pa.: American Baptist Foreign Mission Society, 1923), 113.

[19] American Baptist Foreign Mission Society, *109th Annual Report*, 115.

[20] 'There may be some complaint,' J. E. Tanquist admitted, 'because directly religious work is carried out in a Government-supported religious-community school. But what then? Would it not be better to lose that support than to be in any way hindered from carrying out our God-given task of winning souls for Christ?' (Tanquist Papers, MS, 1923, pp. 117–18).

[21] Tanquist Papers, MS, 1942, 300.

[22] Tanquist Papers, MS, 1934, 204.

[23] Tanquist Papers, MS, 1937, 249.

[24] Tanquist Papers, MS, 1922, 126.

people.'[25] Accordingly, early converts had to wear the Assamese jacket and body cloth,[26] while later converts wore European dress—long shirts, mauve coats, khaki shorts, or white blouses imported from the plains.[27] Missionaries also forbade male converts to live in the *morung*, the village guard-house and lodge where young men of the same exogamous clan slept before they married and moved into separate lodgings. Located near the village gates, a morung was also the focal point for the elaborate sequence of feasts that marked the Nagas' ritual year and which served as a channel of social mobility, since such feasts raised a sponsor's position in the eyes of his peers.[28] Finally, the Baptists strictly prohibited converts from drinking rice beer, which was central to traditional feasts.[29] In fact, the missionaries developed such an obsession with the issue that non-drinking, noted a district officer in 1931, 'is often regarded as the outstanding mark of a Christian.'[30]

Most foreign missionaries in the Naga Hills were Prohibitionist American Baptists who understood religion in strongly moral terms and consequently saw conversion as a conscious moral turn-about, of which markers like Western dress or abstinence from alcohol were outward signs. To be sure, some missionaries seem to have realized that Naga religion could not simply be isolated and excised out of the matrix of Naga culture in which it was embedded.[31] But most seem not to have been bothered. 'These people are very interesting,' wrote one of them in 1913, 'but that is not the main purpose of our being

[25] Clark, *Corner in India*. 33.

[26] Ibid., 54.

[27] But on this latter point the government—always desiring not to rock the cultural boat—intervened and in 1925 refused to allow the mission to start work in a new area until it agreed not to impose Western clothing on converts. Tanquist Papers, MS, 1925, 135.

[28] Christoph von Fürer-Haimendorf, *Return to the Naked Nagas* (New York: Vikas, 1976), 47–50.

[29] Christoph von Fürer-Haimendorf wrote that 'to the Ao a feast without rice beer is unthinkable' (*Return to the Naked Nagas*, 48) and that without rice beer the life of the Angami is little more than a bad dream (*The Naked Nagas*, 2nd rev. Indian ed. [Calcutta: Thacker, Spink, 1962], 7).

[30] J. P. Mills, 'The Effect on the Tribes of the Naga Hills District of Contacts with Civilisation,' in *Census of India, 1931*, vol. 3, part 1, report, appendix A (Calcutta, 1932), iv.

[31] Tanquist once cited the 'cleavages and animosities incident to the spread of Christianity among people who are closely knit together in village life and whose very village customs constitute their old religion' (Tanquist Papers, MS, 1936, 239).

here, simply to study these interesting people; but we are here to strive to help them to something better.'[32] Not surprisingly, then, missionaries and Nagas held rather different notions of what constituted conversion—a difference that is reflected in discrepancies in the data on the size of the Christian population. Owing to their strict criteria of what constituted a convert, the missionaries' baptismal tabulations always lagged behind the much larger Christian 'community', which comprised those who, regardless of what the missionaries thought, considered themselves Christian and told the Census officials so (see Table 2.2).

Given the stringent demands of the missionaries on the one hand, and the extent to which Naga religion was integrated with the rest of Naga life on the other—and given, too, the colonial regime's growing dismay with the missionaries' meddling in Naga culture—how did the conversion movement take place? Why did it occur at all? Certainly, considering the negative correlation between the incidence of conversion and the presence of missionaries in either time or space (see tables 2.1–3), the distribution of foreign missionaries can hardly tell the whole story. Nor can one make a convincing case that Nagas were 'rice Christians'—that is, that they converted in order to acquire some non-religious benefit.[33] Further, one finds no correlation between conversion and the sort of severe decline in economic standards that might have placed the hill people in a state of 'relative deprivation', such that religious change would have ridden the back of a movement for socio-economic reform.

Here we may turn to Horton's 'intellectualist theory,' which considers how indigenous cosmologies interacted with widening social relations. The Nagas clearly represent a previously insulated society that, during the first half of the twentieth century, became dramatically drawn into a wider world, making many Nagas aware of a macrocosm lying beyond their local communities. Some were physically uprooted from the Hills and placed in drastically alien environments. For example, some 4,000 Nagas were formed into a Labour Corps during World War I and sent to France, where they saw 'how the great civilised nations fought

---

[32] William C. Smith in *Standaret*, 31 December 1913, cited in Tanquist Papers, MS, 1913, 75.

[33] One British official theorized that exemption from payment of village taxes, granted to converts by the government in 1905, promoted the movement to Christianity. But potential converts would have had to weigh the benefits of nonpayment of several baskets of rice against the severe disapprobation of the other villagers on whom they depended for economic, political, and social support. Moreover, the truly large conversion movement did not begin until four decades after that exemption was put in place. Hutton, *Angami Nagas*, 373–4.

for their ends and interests while Nagas were condemned as barbarous for their head-hunting ways.'[34] Back in the Naga Hills, meanwhile, kerosene lanterns replaced reed torches, buttons replaced shells, safety matches replaced friction devices, steel needles replaced bamboo needles, and firearms replaced spears.[35] Signaling the region's first economic integration with a plains civilization, metal currency in the form of the silver rupee replaced unhulled rice as the medium of commercial exchange. At the same time, new scourges such as tuberculosis and venereal disease were introduced from the plains.[36]

Without question, colonial rule destabilized venerable Naga institutions. As a result of imperial criminalization of headhunting and inter-village warfare, noted one observer, the Nagas' ethos of a rigid discipline weakened, 'and the village chiefs, who were the leaders of the community organized on a war footing, starting losing their hold over their younger warriors'.[37] Indeed, it was these same 'younger warriors' who were responding most readily to Christian teachings as presented to them in village schools,[38] leaving village women as the ones most devoted to local crop deities.[39] Moreover, the face-to-face, fluid nature of pre-colonial village authority—whether vested in chiefs as in the more autocratic Sema villages, or in village councils as in the more representative Angami villages—was gradually undermined and replaced by a fixed, written authority in the form of codified laws. Now, should aggrieved villagers be dissatisfied with the decisions of their local chiefs or councils, they could seek redress with a higher authority, the District Magistrate.

Yet it would be wrong to see Naga conversions simply as a function of social change or of 'colonialism', for while all Nagas experienced the sort of disruptions mentioned above, their responses to Christianity varied considerably from group to group. To explain these different

---

[34] Asoso Yonuo, *The Rising Nagas* (Delhi: Vivek Publishing House, n.d.), 125; cited in Kevikyiekielie Linyii, *The Angami Church Since 1950* (Bangalore: United Theological College, 1983), 23.

[35] William C. Smith, *The Ao Naga Tribe of Assam* (London: Oxford University Press, 1925), 180–1.

[36] Mills, 'Effect on the Tribes,' 11. The last point recalls George Orwell's characterization of the British Raj as 'Pox Britannica.'

[37] V. K. Anand, *Nagaland in Transition* (New Delhi: Associated Publishing House, 1967), 93.

[38] 'On the Mission Field,' noted Tanquist, 'the spiritual reform movements nearly always originate with the young people' (Tanquist Papers, MS, 1934, 203).

[39] Mary Clark to J. W. Murdock, 5 August 1880, American Baptist Foreign Mission Society, Rochester, N.Y., correspondence, reel FM–59.

outcomes, we need to examine the groups individually, paying especially close attention to differences in their pre-contact cosmologies, to the different ways those cosmologies interacted with their changing social and political worlds, and to the different ways Christian doctrines interacted with Naga cosmologies. In short, we must practice comparative history. Three of the largest communities, about whom we have the richest data, are here considered in turn: the Ao, the Sema, and the Angami Nagas.

THE AO CASE

The supreme deity among the Ao Nagas, Lungkijingba, was believed to live high in the sky and to be concerned with the ultimate destiny of all humans. But, as the missionary-sociologist William Smith noted in 1925, this god was considered to be so remote that his effective contact was limited to other deities and did not extend to humans.[40] Ao villagers did not even make offerings to this high god. As Smith remarked, 'He is represented as sitting upon the dome of his stone house as on a throne, where he pulls to pieces certain leaves, pronouncing on each piece a fate or destiny. The spirits of men come and each one picks up a piece of leaf, and the fate pronounced upon it becomes his lot in life. But since there is no mark on the piece of leaf, telling that particular destiny it portends, *the great god does not know what is to be the lot of each man*; it resolves itself into a mere blind game of chance.'[41] Less remote in Ao cosmology was Lizaba, considered the creator of the earth and the deity in control of the rains, and consequently of the food supply for the dry rice-growing Aos. He also commanded sickness and disease. Living in closer relation to human society, Lizaba seems to have been more clearly defined than Lungkijingba, and accordingly most village offerings and sacrifices were made to him. Such rituals were directed by village priests called *putirs*, who were chosen 'by public opinion' from among the eldest males of each clan in an Ao village. They were compensated for their services on the occasion of village feasts. While putirs dealt with the village as a whole, another class of specialists, *arasentsurs*, communicated with the spirit world on behalf of individuals, especially for the purpose of exorcising malevolent spirits.[42]

[40] Smith, *Ao Naga Tribe*, 78.
[41] Ibid. (emphasis added). Smith is here summarizing observations made in Edward W. Clark, *Ao-Naga Dictionary* (Calcutta: Baptist Mission Press, 1911), 360–2.
[42] J. P. Mills, *The Ao Nagas* (London: Macmillan, 1926), 244.

Lungkijingba and Lizaba were both *tsungrems*, 'spirits,' who, when given a proper name or identified with a place, were endowed with power and personality. Thus, Ao cosmology also contained sky spirits *(anung tsungrem)*; house-site spirits (*kimung tsungrem*), who were fixed beings that haunted the same house-site no matter who occupied it; house-spirits (*ki-tsung tsungrem*), who were attached to individuals and moved with them wherever they went; and jungle ghosts (*arem tsungrem*), understood as malevolent dwarf creatures.[43] As the swarms of spirits that inhabited the everyday world of the Aos were often harmful, elaborate ceremonies were required to keep them at bay.[44] Moreover, these spirits were closely identified with the topography of the Ao country. As E. W. Clark noted in 1911, 'Lizaba was accredited to have been the world maker. But the *Aos* never travelled much beyond their own country and their horizon was supposed to embrace all there was of the world, so though *Lizaba* has the credit of being world maker, all he did (by tradition) was to level the surface of the plain of the Assam Valley.'[45] Similarly, the Aos' ancestors were thought to have come out of the earth at six stones located at a particular spur on the right bank of the Dikhu River,[46] while the path to paradise was identified with a particular long ridge that sloped west to east.[47] In sum, the precontact Ao cosmology was characterized by a vaguely-conceived, seldom-approached, and generally otiose high god (Lungkijingba), below whom were a large number of well-defined, frequently-approached, and territorially-identified spirits that watched over and participated in the Aos' immediate microcosm.

How, then, did the missionaries deal with Naga religion? For all their condemnation of Naga ritual and social life, the missionaries were extraordinarily accommodating toward Naga doctrine and cosmology, in which they and their Naga converts systematically sought points of

[43] Mills, *Ao Nagas*, 222–3; Smith, *Ao Naga Tribe*, 77–8.

[44] Wrote the ethnographer J. P. Mills, 'On their goodwill largely depend a man's health and happiness. They are everywhere—in the village, in the field, in the jungle, by streams, in trees, and, most favourite haunt of all, in the huge boulders which were so numerous in the Ao country' (Mills, *Ao Nagas*, 216).

[45] Clark, *Ao-Naga Dictionary*, 350.

[46] Mills, *Ao Nagas*, 6.

[47] Hutton, *Angami Nagas*, 186. Moreover, Mills observed that Ao spirits, or *tsungrem*, 'are regarded as resembling the people of the locality in which they live. For instance, should a sick man be told by the "medicine man" whom he consults that it is a *tsungrem* of the Pham country [another Naga group, to the east] which is holding his soul to ransom, he will offer a little thread of the kind which the Pham buy keenly from the Aos' (Mills, *Ao Nagas*, 216).

entry for Christian terms and ideas.[48] In fact, the terminological strategies adopted by foreign missionaries and their native assistants in the very earliest translations of scripture proved crucial for the success or failure of accommodating Christianity to indigenous religions. It was these native assistants who worked to assimilate Christian ideas, names, and terms into the Nagas' own linguistic, and hence religious, universe.[49] One missionary who had supervised several translation projects recalled that the Nagas 'rather resent the idea of introducing an outside word, as they are proud of their own language and think it is deep enough and that they can find the expressions necessary, when you get to working with these pundits.'[50]

Let us examine what the missionaries and 'these pundits' did. In translating God into Ao scripture, E. W. Clark and his native assistants did not use the term for any single Ao deity—neither the high god Lungkijingba, nor the important creator and crop deity Lizaba. Nor were foreign terms like Jehovah used. Rather, Clark's Ao New Testament translated both *kyrios*, 'Lord, master', and *theos*, 'god, God', by the Ao word tsungrem, which as we have seen denotes 'a spirit' not endowed with specific attributes. J. P. Mills, who had lived among the Aos as a district official from 1917 to 1937, considered this a risky translation because 'tsungrem means a spirit attached to a specific place, of a

[48] 'The old religion of these people furnishes a splendid basis for Christianity,' wrote E. W. Clark in 1881. 'The fundamental ideas are there, perverted it is true, but there. And most of the needful terms are there' (E. W. Clark to J. W. Murdock, 10 March 1881, American Baptist Foreign Mission Society, Rochester, N.Y., correspondence, reel FM–59). For her part, Mary Clark was certain that the Aos believed in an individual soul and an after-life, that they had a notion of sin and a need for salvation, and that they had an apocalyptic vision that approximated Judgment Day (Clark, *Corner in India*, 57–63).

[49] Reverend Clark, who compiled an Ao-English dictionary, was himself pivotal in the process, bringing out an Ao translation of Matthew in 1883. A complete Ao New Testament appeared in 1929, translated by Rev. R. B. Longwell and Rev. William Smith, 'with the help of Ao Christians.' Similarly, the first Angami New Testament appeared in 1927, translated by Reverend Tanquist, assisted by several Angami converts. In 1928 Tanquist also directed translation of Mark into the Sema language, assisted by another Naga convert; the complete Sema New Testament, published in 1950, was revised by three other converts. Similarly, the first Gospels to appear in the Lotha language, in the 1930s, were prepared by three Lotha converts. J. S. M. Hooper, *Bible Translation in India, Pakistan and Ceylon*, 2nd ed. (London: Oxford University Press, 1963), 166–7.

[50] Reverend Tanquist, interviewed by Christopher R. King in St. Paul, Minnesota, 11 May 1968.

character which at best is neutral and is always liable to be hostile.'[51] But a tsungrem was attached to a place only when a word designating that place was attached to the word; otherwise, it was a generic term, a neutral concept with no specific attributes. By using this term for God, then, the missionaries effectively pulled together what the entire Ao pantheon shared in common—its 'spiritness,' or 'tsungrem-ness'— and endowed that notion with the power and universality of the Biblical supreme deity. Moreover, as in English or other vernaculars, God was always capitalized as Tsungrem in Roman script, while the generic term *god* (as in Acts 14:11) was left in the lower case, tsungrem.

At the topmost level of the Ao cosmology, then, the missionaries and their native assistants effectively replaced Lungkijingba, the high god who was only vaguely perceived, with a far more sharply defined universalization of a generic term. And they simply liquidated the entire lower tier of lesser spirits. These developments correspond precisely to Max Weber's notion of religious rationalization—that is, the process of elaborating and clarifying the supreme power of a single, universal deity at the expense of all others.[52] Additionally, by using Tsungrem instead of foreign terms like Jehovah in early editions of Christian scripture, Clark utilized, and in fact enlarged upon, an indigenous conceptual category, rather than imposing an alien one.[53] Although later, more conservative, missionaries opposed this accommodationist strategy and even tried to reverse it, the tradition established by Clark and his native assistants has persisted to the present day.[54]

[51] Mills, *Ao Nagas*, 367.

[52] 'The decisive consideration,' wrote Weber, 'was and remains: who is deemed to exert the stronger influence on the individual in his everyday life, the theoretically supreme god or the lower spirits and demons? . . . The process of rationalization (*ratio*) favoured the primacy of universal gods; and every consistent crystallization of a pantheon followed systematic rational principles to some degree, since it was always influenced by professional sacerdotal rationalism or by the rational striving for order on the part of secular individuals' (Max Weber, *The Sociology of Religion*, translated by Ephraim Fischoff [Boston: Beacon Press, 1964], 20, 22).

[53] This, of course, is precisely what the Apostle Paul did when preaching before the elite of Athens in the first century. 'Men of Athens,' he declared, 'I have seen for myself how extremely scrupulous you are in all religious matters, because I noted, as I strolled around admiring your sacred monuments, that you had an altar inscribed: to an Unknown God. Well, the God whom I proclaim is in fact the one whom you already worship without knowing it' (Acts 17:22–23).

[54] In 1945 Tanquist supervised a revised Ao New Testament that replaced *Tsungrem* with *Jihova*. But, as the veteran missionary later admitted, 'the people were not enthusiastic about the change, to say the least,' and they continued to use the Ao term *Tsungrem* (Tanquist to A. F. Merrill, administrative secretary, Public Relations

This translation strategy was not by itself a cause of conversion. Yet it is significant that Clark and his assistants were elaborating the nature and power of an indigenous conception of a high god at the very time—the early decades of the twentieth century—when Ao Nagas had begun paying more attention to the upper tier of their religious cosmology. This new focus of attention was one of the intellectual consequences of the dramatic integration of Ao society with the outside world that had come with colonial rule. 'You should hear their exclamation of wonder as they turn the pages of "Harper's Weekly",' wrote Mary Clark in 1907 from the midst of the Ao country.

They are in a world of which they never dreamed. When our missionary map from Boston was hung up before them, 'Wah! wah! wah! father, what does it speak?' uttered in reverent exclamation gave opportunity for such a lesson as led old Deacon Scubungallumba to drop his head and mutter almost under his breath, 'Ish! Ish! how great we have thought ourselves, as though we were the big part of all creation.'[55]

This passage speaks to the cognitive disruption that accompanied the intrusion of colonial rule among a once isolated community. Clearly, the confines of the Aos' experienced world became suddenly and drastically enlarged with this intrusion, such that what yesterday had comprised the entire universe, bounded by a distant mountain range, was now but a speck on a vast globe.

This enlargement of the experienced world created a space for an enlargement of a conception of a high god understood as underpinning and controlling that world. Meanwhile, Aos began paying less attention to the many lesser tsungrems who occupied their former cosmology. These spirits, whose authority had been limited to the much smaller domain of everyday village life, now became otiose, or simply irrelevant. Even intermediate gods seemed to have lost their grip on the world. Before the British annexation of the Ao country in 1889, Lizaba, the god of the rains and of sickness, was regularly importuned in village-wide celebrations. In those days, Lizaba was believed to manifest himself several times a year, visiting certain villages where he would bring portents of coming events such as smallpox, good harvests, war, etc. But since

Department, American Baptist Convention, New York City, 8 March 1960, copy in author's possession). In Tanquist's personal copy of an Ao hymnal in which *God* was consistently rendered as *Tsungrem*, the latter term was crossed out in pencil and replaced by *Jihova* (*Otzütajung Ken* [Ao Naga Hymnal] [Calcutta: B. I. Anderson, n.d.], in Bethel Theological Seminary Library, St. Paul, Minn.).
[55] Clark, *Corner in India*, 108.

the advent of British rule, it was noted in 1925, 'Lizaba has not appeared. They say he has gone on a journey to the ends of the world.'[56]

Further favouring the rise of Tsungrem to supremacy over the entire Ao cosmology was his association with the new and potent power of the written word: the Aos' very first written literature was Biblical scripture. In 1883, E. W. Clark managed to procure a second-hand American printing press which, he noted, took 'all the men of the village about a week' to haul up to his mission village of Molungyimsen. There, he at once began printing a catechism, a biography of Joseph, and the Gospel of Matthew, which he had translated into the Ao language and prepared for printing in Roman script.[57] Clark seems to have understood that the susceptibility of preliterate groups to Christian scripture—and the corresponding imperviousness of Hindus, Muslims, and others already exposed to scriptural authority—was related to the power of written authority per se.[58] As J. D. Y. Peel noted in his study of conversion among the Yoruba of modern Nigeria:

In non-literate societies . . . the past is perceived as entirely servant of the needs of the present, things are forgotten and myth is constructed to justify contemporary arrangements; there are no dictionary definitions of words. . . . In religion there is no sense of impersonal or universal orthodoxy of doctrine; legitimate belief is as a particular priest or elder expounds it. But where the essence of religion is the Word of God, where all arguments are resolved by an appeal to an unchangeable written authority . . . religion acquires a rigid basis. . . . [Religion] comes to be thought of as a system of rules, emanating from an absolute and universal God, which are quite external to the thinker, and to which he must conform and bend himself, if he would be saved.[59]

Lizaba may disappear beyond the mountains; forest spirits may rise or fall in their capacity to do harm depending on a people's ad hoc experiences with them; potent tsungrems of one generation may be ignored by the next. But Tsungrem, the one deity preached by the Christians, was seen as possessing a fixed and unalterable status in the cosmos.

---

[56] Smith, *Ao Naga Tribe*, 79.

[57] Puthenpurakal, *Baptist Missions in Nagaland*, 81.

[58] As early as 1876 Clark wrote that 'it is a well-recognized fact in India that aboriginal tribes like the Nagas who are not Hindu, Mussalman or Buddhists constitute by far the most promising field of missionary labor in India' (E. W. Clark to J. W. Murdock, 17 May 1876, American Baptist Foreign Mission Society, Rochester, N.Y., correspondence, reel FM-59).

[59] J. D. Y. Peel, 'Syncretism and Religious Change,' *Comparative Studies in Society and History* 10 (1967–68):139–40.

His commands and promises, frozen in time by the power and the technology of the written word, could not easily be ignored or forgotten.

In short, we see here a fusion of literacy and religion. Literate, young men who in an earlier generation would have been head-hunting warriors, were now becoming primary school teachers in villages distant from their own, where they would read to other villagers the unchangeable Word of God and display the life of Christ with color slides illuminated by lanterns.[60] As one missionary-translator reported, 'The few who can read will recite all the words to the many who are illiterate.'[61] In this way the incorporation of the Naga Hills into a larger political and economic universe—a function of colonialism—was paralleled by the region's incorporation into a literate universe, and by the Aos' own incorporation of a more powerful and permanent conception of a high god into their cosmology. For Tsungrem was not an alien deity imposed upon the Aos from the outside; it was their own generic term made universal by the Bible's message, and made permanent by the medium of print technology.

THE SEMA CASE

We may contrast the Ao experience with Christianity with that of their neighbours to the south, the Semas. Although they occupied an area remote from the mission stations at Kohima or Impur (see Map 1) and experienced virtually no direct missionary influence, the Sema Nagas converted to Christianity at an astónishingly rapid rate. J. H. Hutton, who compiled an important monograph on them, recalled that in the period 1915–20 there was only one small Christian village and a few scattered Christian households in villages along the roads leading into the Sema country.[62] In the mid-1920s, however, a missionary from Impur, J. R. Bailey, toured the region and found many Christian groups with their own meeting houses, holding regular services without visible leadership. This appeared so strange to him that he refrained from baptizing the converts or organizing them in a more regular way for fear that he might interfere with this seemingly spontaneous movement. In 1936 the senior missionary on the other side of the Sema country,

---

[60] Bengt I. Anderson, 'On Tour in the Naga Hills,' MS, 1931, 3, in Papers of B. I. Anderson, Bethel Theological Seminary Library, St. Paul, Minn. (Hereafter cited as Anderson Papers).

[61] Tanquist Papers, MS, 1944, 328–9.

[62] John H. Hutton, *The Sema Nagas* (1921; reprint, London: Oxford University Press, 1968), preface to 2nd ed.

J. E. Tanquist of Kohima, toured the same territory and reported seeing 'marvels of spiritual transformation the likes of which I have never seen before': villages where around sixty households were Christian, who had been worshiping for three or four years without leadership and without ever having seen communion conducted.[63] From about this time Sema-speaking boys educated in either the Impur or the Kohima training schools were sent as teacher-pastors back into the Sema country where they organized Christian communities into churches. By 1938 every Sema village to which such teachers had been sent was entirely Christian.[64] How did this happen?

A political explanation appears readily at hand. Unlike the Aos' system of village councils composed of elders representing various clans, Sema villages were generally ruled by a single autocratic chief who belonged to a ruling lineage that extended throughout the Sema country. These powerful chiefs directed the villages in war, decided all matters of relations with other villages, and determined what lands the village would cultivate.[65] In return for land, wives, and food when necessary, a chief's subject-dependents—whom Hutton called 'serfs'—gave him obeisance, regular labour in his personal fields, the leg of any sacrificed animal, and help in war.[66] Owing in part to the dynamics of their political system, the Semas were perhaps the most migratory of all Naga groups. For, although they followed a general principle of primogeniture, sons and brothers of a former chief also had claims on the latter's lands and labour. To prevent such men from pressing their claims, a Sema chief had constantly to transfer retainers to his kin, who would then move away and colonize new villages or conquer old ones, themselves becoming chiefs in the process. As Hutton noted, 'The authority of a Sema chief is quickly sapped when he can no longer shed off his brothers and sons to found new villages with retainers of their own. In such circumstances he ceases in a generation to be socially distinct from others of his family, and a decline in his political authority follows as a matter of course.'[67]

The advent of colonial ideology in the Naga Hills, and in particular the British prohibition of warfare in lands they administered, naturally

[63] Tanquist Papers, MS, 1936, 240–1.

[64] Bengt I. Anderson, 'Annual Report for the Year 1938, Impur', MS, Anderson Papers.

[65] Hutton, *Sema Nagas*, 150.

[66] John H. Hutton, 'The Mixed Culture of the Naga Tribes,' *Journal of the Royal Anthropological Institute of Great Britain and Ireland* 95 (1965): 33.

[67] Hutton, 'The Mixed Culture of the Naga Tribes,' 23.

hampered the Sema chiefs' ability to expand as they had formerly done.[68] By the 1930s, colonial officials were suggesting that the rapid conversion movement of that time was at bottom political, since dependent clients seeking to break away from allegiance to their weakened chiefs did so by breaking with their chiefs' religious ideology.[69] This may be true, for we do hear of village chiefs in some cases driving Christians out of their villages and into the forest where they formed small groups living on roots and leaves.[70] But it is also true that many Sema chiefs, unable to shed their kin from the village, and becoming increasingly isolated politically, opted to convert to Christianity and even take the lead in conversion movements among their clients.[71] Thus the Semas' political system—stressed by the advent of British rule—drove both chiefs and their villager-dependents to conversion, though for different reasons.

Yet there was also a religious dimension to Sema conversions. Because of their migratory habits, the Semas had for long incorporated into their own religious cosmology the deities of those they conquered.[72]

---

[68] The 1891 census reported the Semas' occupation of the large Tizu Valley within the previous thirty or forty years and noted the severe pressure they had recently put on the southern Ao country. *Census of India, 1891*, Assam, 1:246. As Hutton observed, 'the process of expelling Ao villages went on right down to the annexation of the country by government [in 1906 and 1921], which alone saved the Aos from being driven north and west of Mokokchung' (Hutton, *Sema Nagas*, 17).

[69] Tanquist Papers, MS, 1936, 240.

[70] American Baptist Foreign Mission Society, *116th Annual Report* (Boston: American Baptist Foreign Mission Society, 1930), 120.

[71] In 1931 the American missionary Bengt Anderson visited a large Sema village of 300 houses whose powerful chief was a well-known opponent of Christian teachings. Anderson describes meeting the old chief, who reminisced about the old days when his village had been strong and his people headhunters. He complained that the government and mission had broken up their old customs and that converted villagers refused to drink, participate in the old war dances, or pay proper respect to their chief. But to Anderson's surprise, the interview ended with the old man requesting a Christian teacher for his village. It seems that the chief's younger brother had been baptized a year earlier and was now the leader of a large section of the village's retainer population. Unable to shed his brother from the village and thereby monopolize the village's dependent families for his own service, the old chief was forced to give in (Anderson, 'On Tour in the Naga Hills,' 1931, 3). In 1939 Anderson recalled that while ten years earlier Sema chiefs had shown extreme hostility to the mission, 'they have now become converted and most of them are very loyal and a good many of them spiritual leaders as well' (Anderson, 'On Tour in the Naga Hills,' 1939, 2).

[72] Hutton, *Sema Nagas*, preface to 2nd ed.

More importantly, the Semas, more clearly and with greater elaboration than other Naga communities, affirmed the existence of a single over-arching supreme god, Alhou. This conforms to Horton's intellectualist theory, which predicts that a community's wider social experience—which in the Semas' case was a function of a more migratory life—would dispose that community to paying greater attention to their high god. 'Omniscience and omnipotence are vaguely ascribed to Him [i.e., Alhou],' noted Hutton in 1921, 'and though He is remote and inaccessible, He seems to be all-good as well as almighty and all-knowing. . . . Alhou is the supreme dispenser of good and evil, and it is He who makes men rich or poor.'[73] Elsewhere Hutton wrote that the Semas did not locate Alhou in any particular quarter of the cosmos—an anthropomorphic conception characteristic of most Naga deities—but rather in all space between heaven and earth. 'And,' he continued, 'I have heard a Sema attribute to Him the quality of omnipresence, even if not of absolute infinity, though the Sema in question was not educated or even semi-christianized.'[74] In Sema folklore, men's fortune was even understood as lying within the 'will of Alhou'.[75] This sharply defined understanding of a high god thus contrasts dramatically with the experience of other, less-migratory, Naga communities.

Here again, the translators' strategies proved crucial. The Gospel of Mark was first translated into Sema by Tanquist and his native assistants in 1928, followed in the next decade by the rest of scripture and a steady stream of hymn books. In all of this the Christian God was not, as in the Ao case, translated by the generic word for 'spirit', but simply identified with Alhou.[76] This translation strategy seems greatly to have facilitated the cognitive transfer from the old to the new; or perhaps more accurately, it involved no real transfer at all, but only a refinement and elaboration of a thoroughly indigenous conception. Especially significant is that even before the arrival of Christian missionaries, the Semas had already been paying increasing attention to Alhou, their high god. In this way Christianity, by identifying its God with Alhou, rode the coattails of an indigenous movement that, well

---

[73] Ibid., 194.

[74] Ibid., 191n.

[75] Ibid., 194.

[76] As in Matthew 5:34 ('Do not swear at all, either by heaven, since that is God's throne . . . ' or 22:21 ('Give back to Caesar what belongs to Caesar—and to God what belongs to God'). *Sümi Bible Kaku Akitheu: The New Testament (Sema Naga)* (Calcutta: Bible Society of India and Ceylon, 1950). See also *Alhou Kishe Le: Gospel Songs in Sema-Naga* (Impur: American Baptist Mission, 1941).

before the advent of colonial rule, had acquired its own logic and its own momentum.

THE ANGAMI CASE

Like the Aos, Angami Nagas were heavily exposed to both colonial rule and missionary proselytization from the dawn of Western influence in the region. In 1878 the Baptists planted their first mission headquarters in the very heart of Angami country, at Kohima, which was also the political headquarters of the Naga Hills District. Like both the Aos and Semas, the Angamis were swiftly integrated into the wider world of British India, while their language was reduced to script by foreign missionaries, who produced their first written literature. Yet the rate of Angami conversions, whether traced by census or baptismal data, was markedly slower than that of the Aos or Semas. As late as 1971, after nearly a century of intense missionary proselytization, only 12 per cent of the Angami population appeared in baptismal records, and only 40 per cent identified themselves as Christians in census returns. Why this different outcome?

First, the Angamis, alone among the Nagas, did not practice shifting (slash-and-burn) agriculture, but rather built elaborate systems of ter-racing and irrigation by which steep hills were transformed into flooded rice-fields. Tied thus to the land, the Angamis were the least migratory of all Nagas,[77] a fact that carried several religious implications. For one, the chief Angami deities relating to agriculture—Ukepenopfu, the supreme being, and Maweno, the deity of fruitfulness—were both female, as is typical among the more sedentary, agrarian societies of South Asia. For another, Angami religion, more than the religious systems of less sedentary Nagas, was characterized by a close fit between their land and their fertility cult. Since agrarian societies with such religious systems are notoriously slow in assimilating neighboring deities,[78] the Angamis' ecological orientation may well have hindered their reception, or assisimilation, of a Christian identity.

Second, the missionaries' translation strategy seems to have retarded the assimilation of Christian terminology, and hence Christian ideas,

---

[77] It also endeared them to British administrators who, arriving with their experience in the Indian plains, had come to admire what they saw as the virtues of a fixed—and hence docile and taxable—peasantry.

[78] In early Christian history, for example, the word *pagan* (one who did not adopt the new religion) originally meant 'agrarian society' or 'country-dweller,' pointing to the tendency of sedentary, agrarian societies to resist religious innovation, at least relative to more mobile communities or classes.

among the Angamis, just as it hastened such assimilation among Aos and Semas. Whereas Tsungrem represented an inflation of the Aos' generic term for 'spirit' into an all-embracing supreme god, and whereas Alhou represented an existing supreme god whose power became enhanced through identification with the Biblical deity, the translation of scriptural names into Angami proved far less successful. In his 1890 translation of Matthew, followed soon by John and Acts, Stanley Rivenburg used the foreign term Jehovah not only for the New Testament's supreme deity, but also for the generic term *god*.[79] Two years later, having spent five years in Kohima without having made a single Angami convert, Rivenburg returned to the United States, broken in health and utterly discouraged. As late as 1906, after twenty-six years of proselytization by several American missionaries, only 35 baptized Angami converts appeared in Mission records.[80]

In 1918 the fourth missionary sent to Kohima, J. E. Tanquist, supervised an entire retranslation of scripture, this time replacing Jehovah with the name of the Angami supreme goddess and ancestress of the human race, Ukepenopfu.[81] At the time Tanquist did not realize that 'pfu' was a grammatically feminine ending; nor was he aware that in Angami folklore Ukepenopfu's husband had wandered off to the Indian plains, which explains why a 'father-figure' was absent from the Angami cosmology. Tanquist later recalled that in 1922 both he and Rivenburg had come to realize that Ukepenopfu, 'which could have the meaning "the female who gave us birth," or "She who is near us," signified a goddess at the least, and however manipulated and explained (e.g., they would in the course of time come to regard the name as masculine) all sorts of linguistic and theological difficulties would be encountered both in the New Testament and the Old.'[82] Accordingly, even though Hutton had noticed in 1921 that Ukepenopfu in the Angami mind was 'apparently at present undergoing a process of change from female to male,'[83] the Americans now decided to abandon Ukepenopfu and reinstate Jehovah as the proper translation of the Christian supreme

---

[79] Acts 14:11, then, instead of reading, 'These people are gods who have come down to us disguised as men,' would have read 'These people are Jehovahs who have come down . . .' Tanquist to Merrill, 8 March 1960. See also S. W. Rivenburg, *Hymns in Angami Naga* (Kohima: Baptist Mission Press, 1892).

[80] Philip, *Growth of the Baptist Churches*, 84.

[81] Joseph E. Tanquist, ed., *A New Selection of Hymns in Angami Naga* (Kohima: Baptist Mission Press, 1918).

[82] Tanquist to Merrill, 8 March 1960.

[83] Hutton, *Angami Nagas*, 181 n.

being.[84] But the strategy of identifying the Christian high god first with a foreign term, then with a fertility goddess, and finally with a foreign term again, appears to have worked against the easy assimilation of Christian ideas into the Angami religious system. To make matters worse, the generic term for 'spirit' (*terhoma*), whose equivalent in the Ao language had been capitalized and elevated to stand for God, in the Angami was demoted to stand for 'Satan'. As Hutton observed, the missionaries 'teach the Angami convert to regard all terhoma as evil.'[85] Nonetheless, Angami religious categories, like Ao and Sema categories, ultimately prevailed. In 1983 Christian Angamis, still a minority among the Angami population, persisted in identifying the Christian high god with their own, traditional supreme goddess.[86]

CONCLUSION

Table 2.4 summarizes the comparative data presented here with reference to significant correlates of religious change, highlighting similarities and differences between the three Naga communities. Several uniformities emerge among the three groups: all were conquered by an outside power that (indirectly) patronized the new, Christian religion (no. 1); all were integrated into a broader economic and political order as a result of colonial rule (no. 2); and all had been preliterate prior to contact with British imperialists or American missionaries (no. 3).

From this point on, we encounter significant differences between the three Naga groups, including different rates of conversion, which can be accounted for by Robin Horton's intellectualist theory. So long as the social experience of the Aos and the Angamis—but not the Semas—remained confined to their immediate locale (no. 4), the lesser beings of their cosmology, identified as they were with that locale, retained their capacity to explain, predict and control the Nagas' experience of reality. At the same time, these two communities largely ignored their cosmology's upper tier, the domain of the high god (no. 5). This meant that before colonial institutions had broken down the social isolation of these groups and exposed them to a larger social

---

[84] See *The Gospels, Acts, Romans, and Corinthians in Angami*, 3rd ed. (Kohima: American Baptist Foreign Mission Society, 1923).

[85] Hutton, *Angami Nagas*, 180.

[86] 'Once thought to be far away,' noted an Angami Christian, 'Ukepenuopfii is brought nearer through the gospel, [and] man is allowed to talk and have fellowship with God personally' (Linyii, *The Angami Church since 1950*, 75).

world—a process that did not really get under way until World War I, accelerating with and beyond World War II—the early missionaries had been elaborating precisely that part of the Ao and Angami religious cosmologies, the upper tier, with which villagers had been least concerned. This would explain the Christian movement's slow start among those groups. As the twentieth century progressed, however, increasing integration of the hill region with British India confronted all Nagas with a far larger reality than their local spirits could be seen as controlling. Accordingly, they began paying greater attention to the high god who, as sovereign of the entire universe, was seen as more clearly in charge of things. It was at this point that the missionaries' earlier labours, concerned as they were with elaborating indigenous notions of the high god, finally bore fruit in the form of what appeared as conversions to Christianity.

Table 2.4. Correlates of Conversion among the Nagas

		Ao	Sema	Angami
1.	Conquest by an outside power patronizing a new cult	+	+	+
2.	Integration into a broader economic or political order	+	+	+
3.	Extent of literacy in the pre-contact society	–	–	–
4.	Degree of sedentarism in the pre-contact society	+	–	+
5.	Degree of attention paid to the pre-contact high god	–	+	–
6.	Degree of perceived break with the pre-contact cosmology	–	–	+
7.	Degree of proselytization on behalf of the new cult	+	–	+

Because the Sema Nagas were more migratory than the other two groups (no. 4) and hence had a greater experience of a larger social universe, they had a more highly developed conception of their indigenous high god than did the other groups (no. 5). Therefore, the decision to identify the Christian god with the Semas' high god helps explain the rapid conversion of this community despite a lack of extensive Christian proselytization among them. Neither the Aos nor the Semas, then, experienced much difficulty domesticating the Christian high god into their own cosmologies (no. 6). In the case of the Aos, the Christian god was identified with the generic term for 'spirit' in a system whose own high god was already otiose and largely ignored. In the case of the Semas, the Christian god was identified with an already important high god. The Angamis, however, owing to the contradictory and dubious translation strategies adopted by missionaries in the field, could not as readily assimilate the Christian high god into their religious system.

Finally, there is no positive correlation between the degree of proselytization and the rate of conversion among the various Naga groups (no. 7). Since the Semas converted to Christianity with little or no direct missionary activity, we can virtually eliminate the degree of exposure to missionary preaching as a significant variable in the conversion process. What mattered, in the last analysis, was the nature of Naga cosmologies and the things that were happening within those cosmologies at the time of contact with outsiders, together with the Nagas' experience of a wider world. If we are to explain religious change in colonial encounters, this, I believe, is where we must focus our attention, and not on some notion of a monolithic 'colonial discourse'.

It must be added that since the Nagas' Christian identity clearly marks them apart from Hindus, Muslims, or other peoples of the Indian plains, that identity has been of great use in their ongoing resistance to political assimilation with the republic of India. This highly-charged political context has doubtless helped consolidate a Christian identity among the Nagas since 1947.[87] But it would be wrong to see that identity as simply a foil for political resistance. The degree to which Christianity has been assimilated into the Nagas' ethnic identity, and even transformed into a genuinely Naga religion, is suggested in the following reflection by an anonymous informant: 'Europeans do not have a monopoly on Christianity. When Europeans became Christians they made it a European indigenous religion. Now I, like many Nagas, am a Christian, but I am not a European. Now my God can speak to me through my dreams, just as happened to my Angami ancestors. . . . What I am talking about is Naga Christianity—an indigenous Naga Christianity.'[88]

This statement not only reveals the individual's determination to dissociate his own religious identity from that of a former colonial ruler. It also shows his historical consciousness. He is aware that Christianity

[87] For a thoughtful review of this issue, see J. J. Ray Burman, 'Impact of Christianity among the Tribes of North-East India,' in *Tribal Situation in North-East India*, edited by Sarthak Sengupta (New Delhi: Inter-India Publications, 1994), 165–83.

[88] *The Naga Nation and Its Struggle against Genocide* (Copenhagen: International Work Group for Indigenous Affairs, 1986), 107.

was at one time as alien to Europeans as it was to his own ancestors and that—through a process that we may call 'creative adaptation'—he and his recent ancestors had self-assertively made it an indigenous Naga religion, just as Europeans had earlier 'made it a European indigenous religion.'

3

Multiple Lenses:
Differing Perspectives of Fifteenth-Century Calicut[*]

In the wake of the quincentennial of Christopher Columbus's voyage
to America, it is sometimes difficult to recall that, in 1492, India not
America was the centre of all the fuss in Europe. After all, Columbus's
famous voyage sought not to discover any unfamiliar 'new world' but
to reestablish direct contact with the old. In the very year of Columbus's
voyage, a book entitled *India Recognita* appeared, based on the Asian
travels of the Venetian merchant Nicolo Conti.[1] The book's title, 'India
Reacquainted,' evokes Europe's hazy memory of the lands beyond the
Muslim Middle East, described by the ancient Greeks, and well known
to the Roman empire, but cut off from direct commercial contact with
Europe since the fall of Rome. Its publication points to Europe's desire
to reestablish such links.

INDIA, THE 'HONEY JAR'

The reasons Europeans were so eager to find a direct, all-sea route to
India are not hard to find. Brimming with agricultural and manufactured
riches, India had for centuries been the world's 'honey jar,' the land
peoples all over Eurasia had clamoured to reach. Arab maritime contact
with western India in the early eighth century had thrown open West
Asia, Africa, and Europe to India's agricultural treasures, effectively
incorporating all these regions for the first time into a single agricultural
universe. Between the eighth and tenth centuries Arabs had brought

[1] Donald F. Lach, *Asia in the Making of Europe*, vol. 1: *The Century of Discovery*
(Chicago: University of Chicago Press, 1965), 59–63.

[*] Reprinted from Laurie J. Sears, ed., *Autonomous Histories, Particular Truths: Essays
in Honor of Professor John R. W. Smail*, (Madison: University of Wisconsin Southeast
Asia Monographs, 1993), 71–86

back from India, and successfully begun cultivating, staples such as hard wheat, rice, sugar-cane, and new varieties of sorghum; fruits such as banana, sour orange, lemon, lime, mango, watermelon, and the coconut palm; vegetables such as spinach, artichoke, and eggplant; and the key industrial crop, cotton. From Iraq most of these crops diffused westward all the way to Spain, which was transformed into a veritable garden under Muslim rule, while other Indian crops passed by ship from southern Arabia as far south as Madagascar. Still others, especially cotton, moved by caravan from northwest Africa across the Sahara to tropical West Africa. Finally, from the thirteenth century onward, most of these crops were introduced into Europe via Spain, Sicily, and Cyprus.[2]

On the other hand, a few valuable crops—among them pepper, clove, and cinnamon—were not so easily grown in Europe, and merchants had to travel to India to purchase them. Moreover, for centuries India's master weavers had turned out the world's finest cotton textiles, the legacy of which survives in the names of many of our own articles of clothing: pajama, shawl, bandana, dungarees, chintz, calico, seersucker, khaki, and others. For these items, too, foreigners had to come to India. But Europe possessed nothing that India wanted in exchange for her textiles and spices—nothing, that is, except gold and silver, for which Europeans were more than ready to plunder western Africa and the 'New World'. In fact, Europe, with its smaller population base, its less sophisticated administrative structure, and its more primitive manufacturing and agricultural technology, would have to be considered an underdeveloped region compared to China, India, and the Islamic world. Stuck on Eurasia's far northwestern edge, only in the fourteenth and fifteenth centuries were Europeans breaking out of their relative backwardness and isolation. For them, the discovery of a direct route to the larger, older, and richer civilizations to the east was a very significant event.

Six years after Columbus's voyage, in 1498, the Portuguese captain Vasco da Gama managed to reach India by an all-sea route around the southern tip of Africa, thereby accomplishing what Columbus had tried but failed to do. Upon his return to Portugal the following year, the people of Lisbon triumphantly acclaimed da Gama a hero, and so he has been regarded ever since by patriotic Portuguese as well as by Europeans and American generally. From a European perspective, da Gama's success in reestablishing Europe's direct ties with India, broken

[2] Andrew Watson, *Agricultural Innovation in the Early Islamic World: The Diffusion of Crops and Farming Techniques, 700–1100* (Cambridge: Cambridge University Press, 1983).

since the seventh century when rising Muslim states intruded between India and Europe, was truly sensational. However, for most Indians, located in the heart of the Indian Ocean and occupying the centre of a busy maritime trading world, the arrival of the Europeans was hardly a significant event. Indeed, India's larger states hardly noticed the coming of the mariners from the west. Both the empire of Vijayanagara and the Delhi sultanate, the largest states in those days, were based on land not sea power. For them, with their capital cities located deep in India's interior, the arrival of Europeans on the coasts was simply irrelevant. Not surprisingly, there are no contemporary accounts answering the question of how Indians responded to the arrival of Vasco da Gama.

CALICUT AND THE 'CLASH OF VISIONS'

But there is a more interesting question that is quite answerable. Would Columbus, had he succeeded in reaching Asia, have made his way to the city of Calicut, which was also da Gama's goal? Of all India's cities, Calicut occupied the most prominent place in the European consciousness around the turn of the sixteenth century. It is the only real non-European city mentioned by Thomas More in his book *Utopia*, published in 1517. And, significantly, when the book's protagonist, Raphael Nonsenso, returns to Europe from Utopia ('no place'), it is from Calicut that he embarks aboard a Portuguese vessel. For More and many other Europeans, it was Calicut that linked 'this place'—the actual Europe at the turn of the fifteenth century—with an imaginary, idealized realm situated somewhere 'out there'.

Lying on the southwestern (or Malabar) coast, this city was in the fifteenth century India's busiest port. As was noted by contemporary Portuguese themselves, it was even larger than Lisbon.[3] Foreigners gathered there from every part of the world to trade, from China, Central Asia, and Russia, as well as from western Europe. In cosmopolitan Calicut—on its bustling waterfront, in its crowded bazaars, and in the king's palace—peoples of different cultural backgrounds met and formed their opinions of one another. Like one of Italo Calvino's 'invisible cities', the form and texture of fifteenth-century Calicut resolved into ever-changing images depending upon who was doing the observing, and through what cultural lenses they did so. The Chinese saw the city through Chinese lenses, Arabs through Arab lenses, and so forth.

[3] E. G. Ravenstein, trans. and ed., *A Journal of the First Voyage of Vasco da Gama, 1497–1499*, rpt. (New York: Burt Franklin, n.d., 125, originally published by the Hakluyt Society, first series, vol. 99).

It is the classic Indian fable of the 'Elephant and the Five Blind Men,' in which each man, having stumbled into an elephant and taking hold of a different part of the animal, imagines the beast to be something other than what it really is. What, then, were the different images of Calicut in the fifteenth century?

Calicut owed its prominence to two circumstances. The first was its export of pepper, which, produced in the rolling fields of its immediate hinterland, was judged the finest in the world. For centuries it dominated markets from Europe to China. In Vasco da Gama's day a hundredweight of pepper sold in Calicut for only three ducats but cost eighty in Venice, a staggering markup of more than 2,500 per cent.[4] At the other end of Asia, the Chinese metropolis of Hangchow also imported most of its pepper from the Calicut area, consuming it at a rate of nearly a thousand pounds a day in the thirteenth century.[5] Second, Calicut served as the principal port for the transshipment of goods between the two great segments of the Indian Ocean: the western half, extending from Africa to India; and the eastern half, extending from India to the Malay Peninsula. Since East Asia and West Asia were too distant for ships to transport goods from one end of the ocean to the other in a single monsoon season, Calicut, lying more or less in the middle, served as a convenient point at which goods were unloaded, stored in warehouses, and loaded again the following season for the second half of the trip.

In the fifteenth century Calicut was an independent city-state under the control of a Hindu king known as the Samudri Raja, a wealthy and business-minded prince who welcomed merchants and shippers from all over the world. The city derived fabulous profits from the sale of locally produced pepper, as well as from warehouse and docking fees charged to international shippers. Since merchants and shippers often had to wait many months for the monsoon winds to shift before resuming their sailing, foreign merchants tended to settle in semipermanent communities. Ethnically these enclaves were quite diverse, consisting of Gujaratis, Bengalis, Malays, Chinese, Persians, and Arabs, though most tended to share a common religious identity as Muslims. With Mecca located only a few weeks' voyage across the western Indian Ocean, many were pilgrims even while they were merchants, peddling goods around the ocean en route to Islam's holiest shrine. The Islamic

---

[4] Lach, *Asia in the Making of Europe*, 1:98, 99.
[5] Tapan Raychauduri and Irfan Habib, eds, *The Cambridge Economic History of India*, vol. 1: c. 1200–c. 1750 (Cambridge: Cambridge University Press, 1982), 142.

religion lent to the Indian Ocean in the fifteenth century a certain cultural coherence. The practical-minded raja, though himself a Hindu, seems to have recognized as much, for he arranged that the Muslims would have large mosques in which to worship, and that holidays be celebrated according to proper Islamic law.[6]

THE CHINESE IN CALICUT, 1406–33

Let us look more closely at some of the people who reached Calicut in Columbus's century, and try to discern from their writings what they saw there. Although individual Chinese had been trading in Calicut for centuries, written accounts of their reactions to India have survived only from the time of the famous expeditions of the early Ming period. In fact, reaching Calicut was the principal objective of Cheng Ho's first voyage into the Indian Ocean. For four months, between December 1406 and April 1407, his enormous fleet, consisting of 317 ships and 27,870 men, was anchored in Calicut harbour while the chief officer went ashore to proclaim the emperor's will, to bestow 'honours' on the Samudri Raja and his chiefs, and, of course, to receive the latter's formal submission.[7] With such a show of force, we may assume that the Chinese envoy succeeded. Two years later Cheng Ho made a second expedition to India to officiate at the installation of Calicut's new raja, a political necessity now that the Chinese regarded him as one of their 'tributaries'.[8] On this occasion the Chinese captain erected on shore a commemorative plaque, which read,

> Though the journey from this country to the Central Country [China] is more than a hundred thousand *li*, yet the people are very similar, happy and prosperous, with identical customs. We have here engraved a stone, a perpetual declaration for ten thousand ages.[9]

Cheng Ho could hardly have believed that the customs of the Indians were 'identical' to those of the Chinese. From the imperial Chinese perspective, however, since the people of Calicut were tributary vassals of the Ming empire, it seems to have been ideologically necessary that

[6] R. H. Major, ed., *India in the Fifteenth Century, Being a Collection of Narratives of Voyages to India in the Century Preceding the Portuguese Discovery of the Cape of Good Hope; from Latin, Persian, Russian, and Italian Sources*, rpt. (New York: Burt Franklin, n.d.), 1:14–15.

[7] J. V. G. Mills, trans., *Ma Huan, Ying-yai Sheng-lan, 'The Overall Survey of the Ocean's Shores' (1433)* (Cambridge: Cambridge University Press, 1970), 10.

[8] Ibid., 11.

[9] Ibid., 138.

they be understood as happy and prosperous, and 'civilized', which to the Chinese meant that they must in some measure *be* Chinese. We do not know what the Samudri Raja and his advisors thought of Cheng Ho's imposing presence in Calicut. Pepper and spices continued to be exported to China as before, though now under the rhetorical guise of 'tribute'.

Our best Chinese account of Calicut was written by Ma Huan, a Chinese Muslim employed as an interpreter on the expeditions of 1413, 1421, and 1431. He recognized that Indian society was divided into different social strata consisting of Brahman priests, Chetty and Kling merchants, and Mukavas, or untouchables. He also noted that 'the great chiefs of the country are Muslims,' the wealthy merchants who formed the pillars of the city's economy. In fact, he observed that most of Calicut's population was Muslim and that the city had between twenty and thirty mosques.[10] A Muslim himself, Ma Huan identified his coreligionists and correctly described their customs.

On the other hand Ma Huan was mistaken when he identified the king as 'a firm believer in the Buddhist religion,' adding that he had a brass image of the Buddha and had built a 'temple of Buddha'. 'Every day at dawn,' he continued,

the king goes to (the well), draws water, and washes (the image of) Buddha; after worshiping, he orders men to collect the pure dung of yellow oxen; this is stirred with water in a brass basin (until it is) like paste; (then) it is smeared all over the surface of the ground and walls inside the temple.[11]

This is a nearly perfect description of the purification ceremony performed for a state deity by a traditional Hindu king. Never having seen Hindus or Hindu society before, Ma Huan had no intellectual category for them. But, aware of Buddhist institutions in China, Ma Huan would have been at least somewhat familiar with Buddhist practices, and doubtless knew that Buddhism originally had come from India. In short, as the idea of a Buddhist prince would have been familiar to the Chinese, that is what they saw in Calicut.

Ma Huan was impressed especially by the impeccable business ethic he saw in Calicut, a city founded on business and trade, after all. In particular, he mentioned 'two great chiefs,' both of them Muslims, who administered the affairs of the country and represented the state in all commercial transactions. These chiefs negotiated with their Chinese

[10] Ibid., 140.
[11] Ibid., 138–9.

counterparts through Hindu brokers, and once they had settled on a price for their merchandise,

the broker then says "In such a such a moon on such and such a day, we have all joined hands and sealed our agreement with a hand-clasp; whether (the price) be dear or cheap, we will never repudiate it or change it." . . . Goods are given in exchange according to (the price fixed by) the original hand-clasp—there is not the slightest deviation.[12]

Ma Huan was also astonished at the speed with which the merchants of Calicut performed calculations with the twenty digits of their hands and feet, without using an abacus. In other words, although the Chinese came to India imagining themselves to be the rulers of client subjects, in practice they behaved like Calicut's other resident communities, demonstrating an unerring respect for the city's customs and local business practices.

A MUSLIM IN CALICUT, 1442

We may contrast these Chinese impressions with the observations of Abdul Razzaq, a Muslim Turk from Herat, in what is now Afghanistan, who reached Calicut ten years after Ma Huan returned to China. Razzaq had been sent to represent his own prince, the khan of Herat, as ambassador to the powerful Vijayanagara empire in the interior of the Indian peninsula. His picture of Calicut, like those of earlier Muslims, and unlike those of the Chinese who seem to have confined themselves to their huge junks in the harbour, gives us something of a dockside view of the city. As a Muslim, Abdul Razzaq fraternized with the many Muslim merchants who lived and worked near the warehouses and on the wharf where the sea lapped up against the Arab *dhows* and Chinese junks anchored in the harbor. Arriving by sea from the Persian Gulf in 1442, he wrote that,

Calicut is a perfectly secure harbour, which, like that of Ormuz, brings together merchants from every city and from every country; in it are to be found abundance of precious articles brought thither from maritime countries, and especially from Abyssinia, Zirbad, and Zanguebar [Zanzibar]; from time to time ships arrive there from the shores of the House of God [Mecca] and other parts of the Hedjaz, and abide at will, for a greater or longer space, in this harbour; the town is inhabited by Infidels, and situated on a hostile shore.[13]

---

[12] Ibid., 141.
[13] Major, *India in the Fifteenth Century*, 1:13.

Although he was from Central Asia, Abdul Razzaq's vantage point was clearly that of the northwestern Arabian Sea; he viewed Calicut as though he were standing in Mecca or Hormuz. His notion of Calicut as situated on a 'hostile shore' and inhabited by unbelievers reinforces this perspective while reflecting the binary ideology of classical Islam (and, for that matter, of medieval Christianity), which divided the world sharply between believers and unbelievers.

In fact, though, Razzaq knew that the Samudri Raja was a tolerant prince, and he noted that with only one exception Hindu law was not given the weight of state sanction. The only things absolutely forbidden in Calicut, he wrote, were cow slaughter and beef eating, both of which was punishable by death. Like many modern western travellers in India, Abdul Razzaq was amazed at the degree to which the cow was venerated.[14] Yet he also understood that the city was dominated by a Muslim merchant community, and he remarked on the 'considerable number' of Muslims who lived there permanently. He noted the presence of congregational mosques, a Muslim judge, and a Muslim holy man.[15] And, like Ma Huan, he remarked upon the city's strict mercantile code. Whereas in other ports merchant vessels might be seized and plundered by the local inhabitants, in Calicut, he wrote, 'every ship, whatever place it may come from, or wherever it may be bound, when it puts into this port is treated like other vessels, and has no trouble of any kind to put up with.'[16]

Befitting his rank as a diplomat, Abdul Razzaq was given comfortable lodgings in the city and granted a formal audience with the Samudri Raja. The two men failed, however, to impress one another. The raja showed Razzaq little consideration during the audience, apparently because the gifts the ambassador presented in court—a horse, a fur-lined cloak, a gilded garment, and a cap for the celebration of the Persian New Year—were insufficient, or inappropriate, or both.[17] Nor did the raja impress the ambassador. The king's audience hall was filled with two or three thousand Hindus, bare from the waist up and armed with daggers and shields, and around the raja stood the city's most important Muslim leaders. In Razzaq's opinion the raja was simply 'a man with his body naked, like the rest of the Hindus'.[18] Coming from the highlands of Afghanistan, the Muslim ambassador was accustomed

[14] Ibid., 19–20.
[15] Ibid., 14.
[16] Ibid.
[17] Ibid., 18.
[18] Ibid., 17–18.

to seeing much more clothing than he found in sweltering, tropical Calicut. He would also have expected the king to appear in greater finery than his subjects, as did his own prince in Herat. Instead he saw a king who was as scantily clad as everyone else. Finally, like Ma Huan, Razzaq remarked upon the raja's matrilineal succession.[19] This apparently struck both men as odd, for in the Islamic World, as in China, royal descent was invariably patrilineal.

As a Muslim, Abdul Razzaq could fraternize with his fellow Muslims, who enjoyed socioeconomic predominance not only in Calicut but throughout the Indian Ocean. That Razzaq understood this may be seen in his general tone of self-confidence and self-assuredness, and also in his irritation with having to live among infidels in a city he called 'this disagreeable place'.[20] Here one notes a clear contrast between Razzaq and Ma Huan. Even though envoys of the Ming empire considered themselves to be legally in control of Calicut, their behaviour was marked by a decorum and deference that indicated otherwise, betraying their status as a newcomers to the Indian Ocean.

A RUSSIAN IN CALICUT, C. 1470

The next foreign traveller to reach Calicut who left a surviving account of his voyage was Afanasy Nikitin, a petty merchant from Tver, an early principality in medieval Russia. In 1466, Nikitin obtained permission to leave his native country, heard prayers at his local church, and embarked upon a lonely and dangerous trip down the Volga River and into the land of the dreaded Turks. Having passed Kazan unmolested, Nikitin, together with a party of several dozen Russians, ran into trouble at Astrakhan, where the Volga empties into the Caspian Sea. Sailing past the city by moonlight, they were apprehended by Turkish brigands who plundered the boat upon which all of Nikitin's goods were stored. Throwing themselves at the feet of the local Turkish ruler, the party begged for the means to return to their native land, weeping bitterly when they were told that such means would not be forthcoming. 'Those of us who owned something in Russia left for Russia,' he recalled, 'and those who had debts there went wherever they could.'[21]

Nikitin apparently found himself in the second category, for he continued south, moving first to Baku and then to Bukhara, staying

[19] Ibid., 17.

[20] Ibid., 18.

[21] Serge A. Zenkovsky, trans. and ed., *Medieval Russia's Epics, Chronicles, and Tales* (New York: E. P. Dutton, 1974), 337.

in the latter city for six months before wandering into Iran—through Mazandaran, Rey, Kashan, Yazd, and Bandar Abbas—apparently supporting himself through itinerant peddling. Finally he reached the port of Hormuz on the Persian Gulf, and there he loaded his horses on a vessel bound for India. Upon reaching Gujarat, he slowly made his way into the interior where he wandered for more than a year. In the meantime his horsepeddling trade seems to have fallen on hard times, and his money dwindled. Ultimately he had to sell his last stallion.[22] Alone and far from home, Nikitin began worrying about day-to-day survival. 'I have spent the whole of my money,' he complained, 'and being alone I spend daily for my food one-sixth of an altyn [unit of exchange]; nor do I drink wine.'[23]

In this somewhat desperate state the Russian peddler reached Calicut, probably in 1470. He was hardly received with open arms by the city's Muslims, as was Abdul Razzaq, or with the royal pomp accorded to Cheng Ho and the Chinese navy. Nikitin was a vagabond in Calicut, living on a hand-to-mouth basis. Like his predecessors he recognized the city as 'a big harbour on the Indian Sea' and he listed its principal exports, namely, pepper, nutmeg, cloves, cinnamon, and ginger.[24] But, unlike his more illustrious predecessors, who were given royal audiences, Nikitin does not mention a meeting with the Samudri Raja or even an awareness of his existence. Rather, he moved in Calicut's marginalized circles, socially far removed from the king.

What is most fascinating about Nikitin's narrative is its psychological dimension. Here we see an apparently integrated personality gradually disintegrating, as Nikitin, doubtless the sole Russian in India at the time, strayed further and further from his Russian Orthodox environment. 'When I go out,' he wrote, 'many people follow me, and stare at the white man.'[25] The deeper he penetrated into India, the more culturally disoriented he became and the more frequently he succumbed to outbursts that betray not just homesickness but a nearly pathological sense of anomie.

I have nothing with me; no books whatever; those that I had taken from Russia were lost when I was robbed. And I forgot the Christian faith and the Christian festivals, and know not Easter nor Christmas, nor can I tell Wednesday from Friday, and I am between the two faiths.[26]

[22] Ibid., 343.
[23] Major, *India in the Fifteenth Century*, 3:25.
[24] Zenkovsky, *Medieval Russia's Epics*, 346.
[25] Major, *India in the Fifteenth Century*, 3:9.
[26] Ibid., 18.

Then he remarked, significantly,

And so, my Christian brothers of Russia, those of you who want to go to the land of India must leave their faith in Russia and invoke Mohammed and only then go to the land of Hindustan.[27]

Nikitin did not convert to Islam, as he appears to be recommending here, though he did adopt a Muslim name, Khwaja Yusuf Khurasani, under which he apparently attempted to pass as a Muslim.[28] Moreover, although in his lonely isolation he fervently desired to observe the Christian holidays, he clearly found this impossible and began adopting Muslim ritual practices. During the month of Ramazan, for example, he joined Muslims in observing the fast.[29] His statement that he couldn't 'tell Wednesday from Friday' also reveals his sense of cultural dis-orientation. And throughout his narrative we hear him crying out and using a mix of names for God drawn from his Russian Orthodox heritage, from various Turkic tribes he had met in Central Asia, and above all from the Islamic tradition.

Allah, abr Allah, Allah kerim, Allah rahim![30]
Allah, Khuda, O God, Tangri!
In thee I trust, O God!
I know not my way!
Whither shall I go from Hindustan?[31]
Save me, O Lord!

Such outbursts suggest a man who, uprooted from his familiar and comfortable culture, was in the process of reorienting himself according to whatever was at hand.

Above all, the pronounced Islamic element in his speech, seen in the Arabic or Persian names for God, suggests that Islam was the dominant cultural system in the places he visited and among the groups he came to know. In this sense Nikitin's narrative confirms that of Abdul Razzaq, for both reflect the dominant position enjoyed by Muslims around the shores of the Indian Ocean in the fifteenth century.

THE PORTUGUESE IN CALICUT, 1498–1500

The last known foreign visitor to reach Calicut in Columbus's century was the Portuguese captain, Vasco da Gama, whose three ships dropped

---

[27] Zenkovsky, *Medieval Russia's Epics*, 341.
[28] Ibid., 343.
[29] Ibid., 345.
[30] Ibid., 340.
[31] Ibid., 351.

anchor in May 1498. To their dismay, the first people the Portuguese saw in Calicut were Muslims. Here they had travelled thousands of arduous miles as part of a grand plan to circumvent the Muslim and Venetian grip on the European spice trade, reaching India only to find Muslims firmly entrenched all along the coast and dominating the export trade. Moreover, unlike the Atlantic Ocean, which in Columbus's day was an uncharted sea empty of traffic, the Indian Ocean of da Gama's day was a busy thoroughfare well known to generations of Arab, Persian, Indian, Malay, and Chinese navigators—a fifteenth-century equivalent of America's East Coast corridor from Boston to Washington.

By contrast, Portuguese navigators had no idea of how to reach India once they rounded the Cape. In fact, they had hired an Arab master pilot to guide them from the East African port of Milindi to the Indian port of Calicut. According to one tradition, the pilot who guided da Gama to India, Ahmad bin Majid, was not only among the most skillful Arab pilots of the age but a scholar who had written many learned treatises on the art of navigating the Indian Ocean.[32] According to another, on da Gama's first day ashore in India (21 May 1498), he was greeted, in Spanish, by two North African Muslims with the words 'May the Devil take you! What brought you here?' To this da Gama gave his famous reply that he had come in search of Christians and spices.[33]

Illustrating the old adage that one sees only what one wishes to see, the anonymous sailor who recorded da Gama's response continued with the comment that 'the city of Calecut is inhabited by Christians'.[34] Convinced that they had found what they had long sought, da Gama's party looked at Calicut and saw nothing but Christianity, although in fact it had not a trace of Christian influence. The drama that followed the Portuguese arrival makes sense only in light of this remarkable misunderstanding.

On 28 May, a week after reaching India, Vasco da Gama donned his finest clothes and was rowed ashore from his flagship. There, ac-

---

[32] G. R. Tibbetts, trans., *Arab Navigation in the Indian Ocean before the Coming of the Portuguese, Being a Translation of 'Kitab al-Fawa'id fi usul al-bahr wa'l-qawa'id' of Ahmad b. Majid al-Najdi* (London: Luzac, 1971). See also 'Les *Muallim* Ibn Majid et Sulayman al-Mahri,' in Gabriel Ferrand, *Instructions Nautiques et Routiers Arabes et Portugais des XVe et XVIe Siecles* (Paris: Librarie Orientalists Paul Geuthner, 1928), 3:177–237.

[33] Ravenstein, *Journal of Vasco da Gama*, 48.

[34] Ibid., 49.

companied by trumpets and flags, the Captain was carried in a palanquin through the city's crowded streets on his way to an official audience with the Samudri Raja. It was a magnificent procession, and da Gama cut a most dashing figure, adorned with a long cloak of tawny satin lined with smooth brocade and covered by a short tunic of blue satin. His white, laced boots reached almost to his knees, while on his head he wore a cap with lappets of blue velvet and a white feather fastened under a splendid medal. An enamel collar hung from his shoulders, and at his side he wore a rich sash with a handsome dagger. Accompanying him was a page dressed in red satin, and preceding him his men marched in single file.[35] No Arab merchant, this, and no disoriented Russian pedlar.

Excited women and children fell in line behind the magnificent parade. Winding through Calicut's thronged streets, the procession passed an enormous hewn-stone Hindu temple, probably the great Shiva temple in Thali in the heart of the city. Mistaking the temple for a Christian church, da Gama ordered his troupe to halt while he got out of his palanquin. Ascending the temple's stone steps, he and his chief attendants entered through a bronze door and approached the image of a Hindu goddess, probably Kali or Lakshmi. Supposing it to be a statue of the Virgin Mary, they offered prayers. Seeing Brahman priests in the temple's precincts, the Portuguese took these to be church servants and compared the Brahman's sacred threads with the stoles of their own deacons. Along the walls were painted images of Hindu deities, some with teeth protruding an inch from their mouths, and having four or five arms. These da Gama and his fellows mistook for Christian saints.[36] Thus, in one of the most significant moments in India's encounter with the western world, we discover a colossal confusion of categories. The spectre of Vasco da Gama offering prayers in a Hindu temple, supposing it to be a church, is every bit as dramatic as Columbus's much better known error. For both, hope triumphed over reality, as one explorer mistook native Americans for Indians and the other mistook Indians for Christians.

Actually, the Portuguese were as thoroughly mistaken about the city's Hindu population as the Chinese had been, and probably for the same reason. To the Chinese eunuchs who staffed Cheng Ho's expedition, the non-Confucian world was divided into two principal

---

[35] Henry E. J. Stanley, trans., *The Three Voyages of Vasco de Gama, and his Viceroyalty, from the 'Lendas da India' of Gaspar Correa*, rpt. (New York: Burt Franklin, n.d., 192), originally published by the Hakluyt Society, first series, vol. 42.

[36] Ravenstein, *Journal of Vasco da Gama*, 52–5.

groups, Buddhists and Muslims. Hence when they reached Calicut, they saw Buddhists and Muslims. The Portuguese who sailed under da Gama's command also conceived the world as divided into two principal groups, Christians and Muslims, and when they reached Calicut that is what they saw. To make the circle nearly complete, even the Chinese, who had reached Calicut only eighty years before da Gama, and whose memory was still very much alive there, were considered by da Gama's men to have been Christians. Of their nationality, however, the Portuguese were less certain. 'If they were Germans,' a member of the crew reported, 'it seems to me that we should have had some notice about them; possibly they may be Russians if they have a port there.'[37] Here, as elsewhere, the Portuguese were projecting onto Calicut the very limited conceptual categories available to them at the time: Hindus were understood to be Christians, as were the Chinese, who might also have been Germans, or maybe Russians.

Resuming his magnificent procession, da Gama and his party reached the Samudri Raja's palace an hour before sunset, but only after forcing their way through the throngs around the palace, 'giving many blows to the people'. Passing through four doorways, da Gama was ushered before the king. The raja was seated beneath a gilded canopy, 'reclining upon a couch covered with a cloth of green velvet'. He was chewing betel nut and pitching the husks into a golden spittoon measuring sixteen inches at its mouth.[38] Given da Gama's ignorance of India, not to mention the raja's ignorance of the Portuguese, and with neither knowing the other's language, this historic interview was bound to be a fiasco. It certainly got off to an awkward start. By way of salute, da Gama clasped his hands, 'as is done by Christians when addressing God,' and then began quickly opening and closing his fists. The raja beckoned him to approach but the latter did not do so, supposing that only the betel servant was permitted that privilege. Finally da Gama ordered his thirteen compatriots to be seated while the king served everybody bananas. This was itself a novelty to the Europeans, and it provoked a royal smile.

Next the raja gestured for da Gama to address his Muslim courtiers who, as had been the case with the Chinese under Cheng Ho, stood in court in the king's attendance. When da Gama indicated that he wished to convey his message only to the king, the latter had him conducted to a smaller chamber. There, through one of his Arabic-speaking interpreters, da Gama told the raja that for sixty years his

---

[37] Ibid., 131.
[38] Ibid., 56.

people had been making discoveries in the direction of India, as they knew that there were Christian kings there, like the raja himself. As da Gama explained it, 'This was the reason which induced [the kings of Portugal] to order this country to be discovered.'[39] He went on to add that his own king 'had ordered him not to return to Portugal until he should have discovered this King of the Christians, on pain of having his head cut off.' Apparently pleased to learn that his 'discovery' had spared da Gama his head, the raja replied that the Portuguese were most welcome in Calicut. As it was by then 10:00 p.m., and raining outside, the king ordered that suitable lodgings be prepared for his guest, and the audience came to an end.[40]

Next morning, da Gama went to a second audience with the raja intending this time to present gifts, as was the custom in Indian courts. The gifts he selected were at least as inappropriate as those Abdul Razzaq had presented to the raja's predecessor. They included striped cloth, four red hoods, six hats, four strings of coral, sugar, honey, oil, and six washbasins. This motley collection provoked laughter from the court's Muslim officials, who advised the captain that such gifts were unworthy of the poorest merchant from Mecca. At this da Gama truculently resolved to visit the king the next day without bringing any gifts at all. His sour attitude doubtless played a part in the classic encounter between Asia and Europe that followed. So, too, did the fact that when he reached the palace the Portuguese captain was kept waiting in an antechamber for four hours. When he was admitted at last, the audience got off to a poor start from which it never really recovered.

Raja: I expected you yesterday.

Da Gama: The road was long, and I became tired.

Raja: You told me you came from a very rich kingdom, yet you have brought me nothing.

Da Gama: I have brought nothing because the purpose of my voyage was merely to make discoveries. However, when other ships come, I will see what they have brought for you.

Raja: What is it you have come to discover, stones or men? If you came to discover men, as you say, then why have you brought nothing? Moreover, I have been told that you carried with you the golden image of a Santa Maria.

Da Gama: The Santa Maria is not of gold—and even if it were, I would not part with her, since she has guided me across the ocean and shall guide me back to my home.

Raja: What sort of merchandise is found in your country?

[39] Ibid., 58.
[40] Ibid., 58–60.

Da Gama: We have much grain, cloth, iron, bronze, and many other things.
Raja: Do you have any such merchandise with you?
Da Gama: I have a little of each, as samples. If permitted to return to my ships I shall order them to be landed. In the meantime, four or five of my men shall remain at the assigned lodgings.
Raja: No! You should take all your men with you, securely moor your ships, land your merchandise, and then sell it at the best price.[41]

The audience, which ended on this unhappy note, revealed the cultural divide separating the prince of Calicut and the Portuguese captain. For one thing, the custom of gift giving in Indian courts was fundamental to any sort of fruitful interaction since gifts reflected a petitioner's respect for a patron as well as his seriousness of purpose. Thus, da Gama's arrival at the raja's court empty-handed hardly could have led to a productive meeting. One can only speculate how much worse things might have gone had he carried out his original plan of presenting the raja with six washbasins.

Lurking behind the conversation one also senses the raja's suspicions as to da Gama's real design. His insistence that the Portuguese not spend their nights ashore but return to their ship, and that they simply sell their goods at the best local price, suggests the king's intent to keep the European association with Calicut on a strictly commercial basis. In fact, there was good reason for the king's suspicions, for the city's Muslims had already advised him that the Portuguese were thieves. Once the newcomers were admitted to his country, they warned, no more ships would visit from Mecca or anywhere else. They added that the raja would derive no profit from the Portuguese, since they had nothing to give. Rather, they would take from him, so that his country would be ruined.[42]

In fact, this is what happened. It is true that the Portuguese did not intend to trade for India's goods in peaceful competition with rival merchants. That they sought to gain a monopoly on that trade by armed force may be seen in the events surrounding the second Portuguese mission sent to Calicut two years later, in 1500, under the command of Pedro Cabral. Cabral was instructed to demand that Indian hostages be placed on board his ships before he went ashore, and he was to inform the king that he was not 'a merchant like the others who come to his country' but the captain of a Portuguese fleet.[43] Second, he was

---

[41] Ibid., 62–3.

[42] Ibid., 71–2.

[43] William Brooks Greenlee, trans., *The Voyage of Pedro Cabral to Brazil and India, from Contemporary Documents and Narratives*, Hakluyt Society, second series,

told to refuse to pay the high port duties normally demanded by the raja.[44] Finally, he was instructed to seize, plunder, and destroy any Arab ships encountered at sea, and to ask the raja, whom the Portuguese still considered a fellow Christian, to expel all Muslim ships from his harbour.[45] In the spirit of these instructions, while the Portuguese fleet of seven vessels was moored at Calicut, Cabral captured a loaded Arab ship as it was putting out to sea. This led to a riot on shore that resulted in bloodshed among both Muslims and Portuguese. At this, Cabral ordered that ten Arab ships be seized and plundered, and their crews, numbering more than five hundred men, massacred. He burned the unloaded ships and the next day subjected the entire city to a withering bombardment of cannon fire, which, according to a Portuguese eyewitness, killed 'an endless number of people'.[46]

This early Portuguese experience at Calicut set the tone for their subsequent dealings in India. From then on huge forts bristling with cannon, such as the one still standing at Diu further up the coast, came to symbolize their relationship to the subcontinent. Diu's massive walls and fortified towers reflect the Portuguese intention of achieving and enforcing a monopoly on the maritime export of Indian merchandise.

SUMMARY

To conclude, the argument of this essay has been that the behaviour of Calicut's fifteenth-century visitors was shaped by their impressions of the city and its inhabitants, as well as by the visitors' individual cultural backgrounds. What is more, it is by comparing and contrasting the different foreigners' experiences with each other—placing each one in relief, profiled against the others—that we can best explain the behaviour of any one of them.

For Abdul Razzaq, Calicut was simply one among many port cities linked through an informal commercial network dominated by fellow Muslims. For him, visiting the Samudri Raja, whom he dismissed as an infidel, was a necessary chore undertaken to keep the goods flowing. For Nikitin, the uprooted and impoverished Russian pedlar, Calicut, with its large Muslim population, added to his sense of disorientation and contributed to his gradual assimilation of Islamic modes of piety and prayer. Finally, the impressions of and responses to Calicut on

---

vol. 81 (London: Hakluyt Society, 1938), 171, 175.

[44] Ibid., 173.

[45] Ibid., 180–1.

[46] Ibid., 183–5.

the part of the two larger missions, the Chinese and the Portuguese, were diametrically opposed. Although the Chinese under Cheng Ho had come to Calicut in order to secure the city's political submission to the Ming emperor, they eventually submitted to the city's business ethic and behaved in a decorous way with both Muslims and Hindus, the latter of whom they conveniently mistook for Buddhists. Although they came as rulers, they ultimately behaved like merchants. The reverse was the case with the Portuguese, who came as merchants but in the end behaved like rulers. Certainly, the Portuguese binary vision of the world as an arena of Muslim-Christian conflict not only caused them to misread the Hindu raja as a Christian prince. It also hastened their adoption of an aggressive policy of achieving a commercial monopoly by means of armed force.

In retrospect, we know that neither Vasco da Gama nor Ma Huan 'discovered' India, any more than Columbus discovered America.[47] What Columbus did do, of course, was to actualize Europe's ambition to *colonize* the earth's western hemisphere, or at least to place in motion the process by which Europeans would reproduce themselves and their cultures on American soil (this is why Americans continue to commemorate 1492, regardless of their differing responses to the events of that year). In the same way, whereas da Gama's 1498 trip did not represent a discovery of India, it blazed new maritime routes thither. Moreover, with da Gama, and even more clearly with his successor Cabral, one finds a systematic policy of substituting armed force for free trade as the basis for Europe's commercial interaction with India. Although the Portuguese had no means of colonizing India—or even of launching sustained offensives against its Muslim sultanates, Vijayanagara, or later the Mughal empire—by blasting their way into commercial harbours, establishing armed enclaves along the western shore, and making grandiose claims of sovereignty, they established the mental framework that would lead other Europeans to dominion. This, in the last analysis, is the most important difference between the Portuguese and representatives of the other cultures who visited Calicut in the fifteenth century.

[47] It is now generally understood that the Italian navigator was not the first European to sail west to reach America. This much certainly was accomplished by Norse explorers in the early eleventh century and possibly, too, by Irish monks in the sixth. In fact, it was on account of those earlier voyages of discovery that news of Columbus's voyage provoked so little stir in western and northern Europe after his return to Spain. See John L. Allen, 'From Cabot to Cartier: the Early Exploration of Eastern North America, 1497–1543,' *Annals of the Association of American Geographers* 82, no. 3 (September 1992): 501–3.

4

Temple Desecration and Indo-Muslim States[*]

FRAMING THE ISSUE

In recent years, especially in the wake of the destruction of the Baburi Mosque in 1992, much public discussion has arisen over the political status of South Asian temples and mosques, and in particular the issue of temples desecrated or replaced by mosques in the pre-British period. While Hindu nationalists like Sita Ram Goel have endeavored to document a pattern of wholesale temple destruction by Muslims in this period,[1] few professional historians have engaged the issue, even though it is a properly historical one. This essay aims to examine the available evidence of temple desecration with a view to asking: what temples were in fact desecrated in India's pre-modern history? When, and by whom? How, and for what purpose? And above all, what might any of this say about the relationship between religion and politics in pre-modern India? This is a timely topic, since many in India today are looking to the past to justify or condemn public policy with respect to religious monuments.

Much of the contemporary evidence on temple desecration cited by Hindu nationalists is found in Persian materials translated and published during the rise of British hegemony in India. Especially influential has been the eight-volume *History of India as Told by its Own Historians*,

---

[1] See Sita Ram Goel, *Hindu Temples: What Happened to Them*, vol. 1: *A Preliminary Survey* (New Delhi: Voice of India, 1990); vol. 2, *The Islamic Evidence* (New Delhi: Voice of India, 1991).

[*] Reprinted from David Gilmartin and Bruce B. Lawrence, eds, *Beyond Turk and Hindu: Shaping Indo-Muslim Identity in Premodern India* (Gainesville: University Press of Florida, 2000).

first published in 1849 and edited by Sir Henry M. Elliot, who oversaw
the bulk of the translations, with the help of John Dowson. But Elliot,
keen to contrast what he understood as the justice and efficiency of
British rule with the cruelty and despotism of the Muslim rulers who
had preceded that rule, was anything but sympathetic to the
'Muhammadan' period of Indian history. As he wrote in the book's
original preface,

> The common people must have been plunged into the lowest depths of wretched-
> ness and despondency. The few glimpses we have, even among the short
> Extracts in this single volume, of Hindus slain for disputing with Muhammadans,
> of general prohibitions against processions, worship, and ablutions, and of
> other intolerant measures, of idols mutilated, of temples razed, of forcible
> conversions and marriages, of proscriptions and confiscations, of murders and
> massacres, and of the sensuality and drunkenness of the tyrants who enjoined
> them, show us that this picture is not overcharged....[2]

With the advent of British power, on the other hand, 'a more stirring
and eventful era of India's History commences . . . when the full light
of European truth and discernment begins to shed its beams upon the
obscurity of the past.'[3] Noting the far greater benefits that Englishmen
had brought to Indians in a mere half century than Muslims had
brought in five centuries, Elliot expressed the hope that his published
translations 'will make our native subjects more sensible of the immense
advantages accruing to them under the mildness and the equity of our
rule.'[4]

Elliot's motives for delegitimizing the Indo-Muslim rulers who had
preceded English rule are thus quite clear. Writing on the pernicious
influence that this understanding of pre-modern Indian history had
on subsequent generations, the eminent historian Mohammad Habib
once remarked, 'The peaceful Indian Mussalman, descended beyond
doubt from Hindu ancestors, was dressed up in the garb of a foreign
barbarian, as a breaker of temples, and an eater of beef, and declared
to be a military colonist in the land where he had lived for about
thirty or forty centuries.... The result of it is seen in the communalistic
atmosphere of India today.'[5] Although penned many years ago, these

[2] H. M. Elliot and John Dowson, trans. and eds, *The History of India as Told by
its Own Historians*, 8 vols. (Allahabad: Kitab Mahal, n. d.), 1:xxi.

[3] Elliot and Dowson, *History of India*, 1:xvi.

[4] Elliot and Dowson, *History of India*, 1:xxii, xxvii.

[5] K. A. Nizami, ed., *Politics and Society during the Early Medieval Period: Collected
Works of Professor Mohammad Habib* (New Delhi: People's Publishing House,
1974), 1:12.

words are relevant in the context of current controversies over the history of temple desecration in India. For it has been through selective translations of pre-modern Persian chronicles, together with a selective use of epigraphic data, that Hindu nationalists have sought to find the sort of irrefutable evidence—one of Goel's chapters is titled 'From the Horse's Mouth'—that would demonstrate a persistent pattern of villainy and fanaticism on the part of pre-modern Indo-Muslim conquerors and rulers.

In reality, though, each scrap of evidence in the matter requires scrutiny. Consider an inscription dated 1455, found over the doorway of a tomb-shrine in Dhar, Madhya Pradesh, formerly the capital of Malwa. The inscription, a 42-verse Persian *ghazal*, mentions the destruction of a Hindu temple by one 'Abdullah Shah Changal during the reign of Raja Bhoja, a renowned Paramara king who had ruled over the region from 1010 to 1053. In his book *Hindu Temples: What Happened to Them*, Sita Ram Goel accepts the inscription's reference to temple destruction more or less at face value, as though it were a contemporary newspaper account reporting an objective fact.[6] Unlike Goel, however, the text is concerned not with documenting an instance of temple destruction, but with narrating and celebrating the fabulous career of 'Abdullah Shah Changal, the saint who lies buried at the site of the tomb. A reading of a larger body of the text reveals, in fact, a complex historiographical process at work:

> This centre became Muhammadan first by him [i.e., 'Abdullah Shah Changal], (and) all the banners of religion were spread. (I have heard) that a few persons had arrived before him at this desolate and ruined place. When the muazzin raised the morning cry like the trumpet-call for the intoxicated *sufis*, the infidels (made an attack from) every wall (?) and each of them rushed with the sword and knife. At last they (the infidels) wounded those men of religion, and after killing them concealed (them) in a well. Now this (burial place and) grave of martyrs remained a trace of those holy and pious people.
>
> When the time came that the sun of Reality should shine in this dark and gloomy night, this lion-man ['Abdullah Shah Changal] came from the centre of religion to this old temple with a large force. He broke the images of the false deities, and turned the idol-temple into a mosque. When Rai Bhoj saw this, through wisdom he embraced Islam with the family of all brave warriors. This quarter became illuminated by the light of the Muhammadan law, and the customs of the infidels became obsolete and abolished.
>
> Now this tomb since those old days has been the famous pilgrimage-place

---

[6] Goel, *Hindu Temples*, 2: 115–16. Goel does, however, consider it more likely that the event took place during the reign of Raja Bhoja II in the late thirteenth century than during that of Raja Bhoja I in the eleventh century.

of a world. Graves from their oldness became leveled (to the ground), (and) there remained no mount on any grave. There was also (no place) for retirement, wherein the distressed *darvish* could take rest. Thereupon the king of the world gave the order that this top of Tur [Mount Sinai] be built anew. The king of happy countenance, the Sultan of horizons (i.e., the world), the visitors of whose courts are Khaqan (the emperor of Turkistan) and Faghfur (the emperor of China), 'Alau-d-din Wad-dunya Abu'l-Muzaffar, who is triumphant over his enemies by the grace of God, the Khilji king Mahmud Shah, who is such that by his justice the world has become adorned like paradise, he built afresh this old structure, and this house with its enclosure again became new.[7]

The narrative divides a remembered past into three distinct moments. The first is the period before the arrival of the Hero, 'Abdullah Shah Changal. At this time a small community of Muslims in Malwa, with but a tenuous foothold in the region, were martyred by local non-Muslims, their bodies thrown into a well. The narrative's second moment is the period of the Hero, who comes from the 'centre of religion' (Mecca?), smashes images, transforms the temple into a mosque, and converts to Islam the most famous king of the Paramara dynasty—deeds that collectively avenged the martyred Sufis and, most importantly, served to (re)establish Islam in the region. The narrative's third moment is the period after the Hero's lifetime when his grave-site, although a renowned place of pilgrimage, had suffered from neglect. Now enters the narrative's other hero, Sultan Mahmud Khalaji—the 'king of the world' and 'of happy countenance,' to whose court the emperors of China and Central Asia pay respect, and by whose justice the world has become adorned like paradise. His great act was to patronize the cult of 'Abdullah Shah by (re)building his shrine which, we are told at the end of the text, included a strong vault, a mosque, and a caravan-sarai. The inscription closes by offering a prayer that the soul of the benevolent sultan may last until Judgment Day and that his empire may last in perpetuity.

Although Indo-Muslim epigraphs are typically recorded near in time to the events they describe, the present one is hardly contemporary, as it was composed some four hundred years after the events to which it refers. Far from being a factual account of a contemporary incident, then, the text presents a richly textured legend elaborated over many generations of oral transmission until 1455, when the story of 'Abdullah Shah Changal and his deeds in Malwa became frozen in the written

---

[7] G. Yazdani, ed. and trans., 'The Inscription of the Tomb of 'Abdullah Shah Changal at Dhar,' *Epigraphia Indo-Moslemica* (1909), 1–5.

word that we have before us. As such, the narrative reveals a process by which a particular community at a particular time and place—Muslims in mid-fifteenth century Malwa—constructed their origins. Central to the story are themes of conversion, martyrdom, redemption, and the patronage of sacred sites by Indo-Muslim royalty, as well as, of course, the destruction of a temple. Whether or not any temple was actually destroyed four hundred years before this narrative was committed to writing, we cannot know with certainty. However, it would seem no more likely that such a desecration had actually occurred than that the renowned Raja Bhoja had been converted to Islam, which the text also claims.

In any event, it is clear that by the mid-fifteenth century the memory of the destruction of a temple, projected into a distant past, had become one among several elements integral to how Muslims in Malwa—or at least those who patronized the composition of this *ghazal*—had come to understand their origins. The case thus suggests that caution is necessary in interpreting claims made in Indo-Muslim literary sources to instances of temple desecration. It also illustrates the central role that temple desecration played in the remembered past of an Indo-Muslim state or community.

EARLY INSTANCES OF TEMPLE DESECRATION

It is well known that, during the two centuries before 1192, which was when an indigenous Indo-Muslim state and community first appeared in north India, Persianized Turks systematically raided and looted major urban centers of South Asia, sacking temples and hauling immense loads of movable property to power bases in eastern Afghanistan.[8] The pattern commenced in 986, when the Ghaznavid Sultan Sabuktigin (r. 977–97) attacked and defeated the Hindu Shahi raja who controlled the region between Kabul and northwest Punjab. According to Abu Nasr 'Utbi, the personal secretary to the sultan's son, Sabuktigin

marched out towards Lamghan [located to the immediate east of Kabul], which is a city celebrated for its great strength and abounding in wealth. He conquered it and set fire to the places in its vicinity which were inhabited by infidels, and demolishing the idol-temples, he established Islam in them.[9]

[8] A good summary of the political history of this period is found in André Wink, *al-Hind: The Making of the Indo-Islamic World*, vol. 2: *The Slave Kings and the Islamic Conquest, 11th–13th Centuries* (Leiden: Brill, 1997), 111–49.

[9] 'Utbi, *Tarikh-i Yamini*, in Elliot and Dowson, *History of India*, 2:22. For a thirteenth century Persian translation of 'Utbi's original Arabic, made in 1206,

Linking religious conversion with conquest—with conquest serving to facilitate conversion, and conversion serving to legitimize conquest—'Utbi's brief notice established a rhetorical trope that many subsequent Indo-Muslim chroniclers would repeat, as for example in the case of the 1455 inscription at Dhar, just discussed.

Notwithstanding 'Utbi's religious rhetoric, however, subsequent invasions by Sabuktigin and his more famous son Mahmud of Ghazni (r. 998–1030) appear to have been undertaken for material reasons. Based in Afghanistan and never seeking permanent dominion in India, the earlier Ghaznavid rulers raided and looted Indian cities, including their richly endowed temples loaded with movable wealth, with a view to financing their larger political objectives far to the west, in Khurasan.[10] The predatory nature of these raids was also structurally integral to the Ghaznavid political economy: their army was a permanent, professional one built around an elite corps of mounted archers who, as slaves, were purchased, equipped, and paid with cash derived from regular infusions of war booty taken alike from Indian and Iranian cities.[11] From the mid-eleventh century, however, Mahmud's successors, cut off from their sources of military manpower in Central Asia first by the Seljuqs and then by the Ghurids, became progressively more provincial, their kingdom focused around their capital of Ghazni in eastern Afghanistan with extensions into the Punjab. And, while the later Ghaznavids continued the predatory policies of raiding the Indian interior for booty, these appear to have been less destructive and more sporadic than those of Sabuktigin and Mahmud.[12]

see Abu Sharaf Nasih al-Jurradqani, Tarjuma-yi tarikh-i Yamini (Teheran: Bangah-i Tarjomeh va Nashr-i Kitab, 1345 A.H.), 31.

[10] C. E. Bosworth, *The Later Ghaznavids, Splendour and Decay: The Dynasty in Afghanistan and Northern India, 1040–1186* (1977; repr. New Delhi: Munshiram Manoharlal, 1992), 32, 68.

[11] Mahmud did not hesitate to sack Muslim cities. His plunder of the Iranian city of Ray, in 1029, brought him 500,000 dinars' worth of jewels, 260,000 dinars in coined money, and over 30,000 dinars' worth of gold and silver vessels. India, however, possessed far more wealth than the more sparsely populated Iranian plateau. Somnath alone brought in twenty million dinars' worth of spoil. C. E. Bosworth, *The Ghaznavids: Their Empire in Afghanistan and Eastern Iran, 994–1040* (Edinburgh: Edinburgh University Press, 1963), 78.

[12] The contemporary historian Baihaqi recorded the first attack on Benares conducted by a Turkish army, carried out in 1033 by the Ghaznavid governor of Lahore. 'He marched out with his warriors and the army of Lahore,' wrote Baihaqi, 'and exacted ample tribute from the Thakurs. He crossed the river Ganges and went down the left bank. Unexpectedly (*nā-gāh*) he arrived at a city which is called Banāras, and which belonged to the territory of Gang. Never had a Muslim

The dynamics of north Indian politics changed dramatically, however, when the Ghurids, a dynasty of Tajik (eastern Iranian) origins, arrived from central Afghanistan toward the end of the twelfth century. Sweeping aside the Ghaznavids, Ghurid conquerors and their Turkish slave generals ushered in a new sort of state quite unlike that of the foreign-based Ghaznavids. Aspiring to imperial dominion over the whole of north India from a base in the middle of the Indo-Gangetic plain, the new Delhi Sultanate (1206–1526) signalled the first attempt to build an indigenous Muslim state and society in north India. With respect to religious policy, we can identify two principal components to this project: (a) state patronage of an India-based Sufi order, and (b) a policy of selective temple desecration that aimed not, as earlier, to finance distant military operations on the Iranian Plateau, but to delegitimize and extirpate defeated Indian ruling houses. Let us consider these in turn.

SUFISM AND STATE-BUILDING

'The world is bound up closely with that of the men of faith,' wrote the Bahmani court-poet 'Abd al-Malik 'Isami in 1350.

In every country, there is a man of piety who keeps it going and well. Although there might be a monarch in every country, yet it is actually under the protection of a fakir [Sufi shaikh].[13]

Here we find a concise statement of one of the leading medieval Perso-Islamic conceptions of how religion and politics interrelate. In 'Isami's view, what had saved the Delhi Sultanate from Mongol conquest was the respect showed by Sultan Muhammad bin Tughluq (r. 1325–51) for the memory of the founder of the Chishti order of Sufis in India, Shaikh Mu'in al-Din Chishti (d. 1236), to whose tomb in Ajmer the sultan had made a pilgrimage just after engaging with a Mongol army.[14]

---

army reached this place. . . . The markets of the drapers, perfumers, and jewellers, were plundered, but it was impossible to do more. The people of the army became rich, for they all carried off gold, silver, perfumes, and jewels, and got back in safety.' Baihaqi, *Tarikh-i Baihaqi.* In Elliot and Dowson, *History of India,* 2:123–4. Text: 'Ali Akbar Fayyaz, ed., *Tarikh-i Baihaqi* (Mashshad: University of Mashshad, 1971), 517.

[13] 'Jahān-rā ki asās-i matīn basta-and, bi iqdām-i mardān-i dīn basta-and. Bi har kishwarī hast ṣāḥib-dilī, bi har 'arṣat hast bā ḥāṣilī. Bi har mulk garchi amīrī būd, wali dar panāh-i faqīrī būd.' 'Abd al-Malik 'Isami, *Futuhus-salatin by Isami,* ed. A. S. Usha (Madras: University of Madras, 1948), 455; Agha Mahdi Husain, ed. and trans., *Futuhu's-salatin, or Shah Namah-i Hind of 'Isami* (London: Asia Publishing House, 1967), 3:687.

[14] Ibid., text, 466; trans. 3:702.

'Isami also felt, however, that the decline of Delhi, and of the Tughluq empire generally, had resulted in a large part from the demise in 1325 of Shaikh Nizam al-Din Auliya, Delhi's most renowned Sufi shaikh. Conversely, he considered that the arrival in the Deccan of one of Nizam al-Din Auliya's leading spiritual successors, Burhan al-Din Gharib (d. 1337), was the cause of that region's flourishing state at mid-century.[15]

Among all South Asian Sufi orders, the Chishtis were the most closely identified with the political fortunes of Indo-Muslim states, and especially with the planting of such states in parts of South Asia never previously touched by Islamic rule. The pattern began in the first several decades of the fourteenth century, when the order's rise to prominence among Delhi's urban populace coincided with that of the imperial Tughluqs. The two principal Persian poets in India of that time, Amir Hasan and Amir Khusrau, and the leading historian, Zia al-Din Barani, were all disciples of Delhi's principal Chishti shaikh, Nizam al-Din Auliya. As writers whose works were widely-read, these men were in effect publicists for Nizam al-Din and his order. And since the three were also patronized by the Tughluq court, the public and the ruling classes alike gradually came to associate dynastic fortune with that of the Chishti order.[16] Moreover, as the spiritual power of a charismatic Sufi was believed to adhere after his lifetime to his tomb-site, shrines at such tombs were patronized by Indo-Muslim rulers just as they were frequented by Muslim devotees. And since the tomb-shrines of the greatest shaikhs of this order were located within South Asia, and not in distant Central Asia or West Asia as was the case with those of other orders, a ruling dynasty's patronage of Chishti shrines could bolster its claims to being both legitimately Islamic and authentically Indian.

Thus Chishti shaikhs repeatedly participated in the launching of new Indo-Muslim states. At the core of 'Isami's narrative of the Bahmani Revolution, which in 1347 threw off Tughluq overlordship and launched an independent Indo-Muslim state in the Deccan, is a narrative of the passing of the Prophet Muhammad's own mantle (*khirqa*) from Abu Bakr, the first caliph, down to Burhan al-Din Gharib's leading disciple, Zain al-Din Shirazi (d. 1369). It was from that very mantle—'by whose scent one could master both worlds'—that the founder of the Bahmani

---

[15] Ibid., text, 456, 458; trans., 3:689, 690–2. 'As soon as that holy man of virtue [Nizam al-Din Auliya] departed from Dehli to the other world,' he wrote, 'the country, in general, and the city, in particular, fell into a turmoil and were subjected to ruin and destruction.'

[16] See Simon Digby, 'The Sufi Shaikh as a Source of Authority in Mediaeval India,' in Marc Gaborieau, ed., *Islam and Society in South Asia,* in *Purusartha* 9 (Paris: Ecole des Hautes Etudes en Sciences Sociales, 1986), 69–70.

Sultanate, Sultan Hasan Bahman Shah (r. 1347–58), was said to have received his own power and inspiration.[17] We see the same pattern in Bengal, another former Tughluq province that asserted its independence from Delhi in the mid-fourteenth century. The earliest-known monument built by the founder of Bengal's Ilyas Shahi dynasty (1342–1486) was a mosque dedicated in 1342 to Shaikh 'Ala al-Haq (d. 1398), a Sufi shaikh whose own spiritual master was—like Zain al-Din's spiritual master—a disciple of the great shaikh of imperial Delhi, Nizam al-Din Auliya (d.1325). What is more, the political ascendancy of the Ilyas Shahi dynasty coincided exactly with the spiritual ascendancy of Shaikh 'Ala al-Haq and his own family. Down to the year 1532, fully fourteen successive sultans of Bengal enlisted themselves as disciples of the descendants of this shaikh, while the tomb-shrine of 'Ala al-Haq's own son and successor, Nur Qutb-i 'Alam, became in effect a state shrine to which subsequent sultans made annual pilgrimages.[18]

In short, within the space of just five years, between 1342 and 1347, founders of independent Indo-Muslim dynasties in both Bengal and the Deccan patronized local Chishti shaikhs whose own spiritual masters had migrated from Delhi where they had studied with the imperial capital's preeminent Sufi shaikh, Nizam al-Din Auliya. The pattern was repeated elsewhere, as the Tughluq empire continued to crumble, giving rise to more provincial successor-states. In 1396, the Tughluq governor of Gujarat, Muzaffar Khan, proclaimed his independence from Delhi immediately after marching to Ajmer, where he paid his respects to the tomb of Mu'in al-Din Chishti, the 'mother-shrine' of the Chishti order in India.[19] In 1404, soon after proclaiming his own independence from Delhi, the former Tughluq governor of Malwa, Dilawar Khan, described himself as 'the disciple of the head of the holy order of Nasir Din Mahmud.'[20] The reference here was to Nizam al-Din Auliya's most eminent disciple to have remained in Delhi—Shaikh Nasir al-Din Mahmud (d. 1356), over whose grave Sultan Firuz Shah Tughluq (r. 1351–88) had raised a magnificent tomb several decades earlier.[21]

---

[17] 'Isami, *Futuhus-salatin*, text, 7–8; trans., 1:11–13.

[18] Richard M. Eaton, *The Rise of Islam and the Bengal Frontier, 1204–1760* (Berkeley: University of California, 1993), 86, 91.

[19] Muhammad Qasim Firishta, *Tarikh-i Firishta*, trans. John Briggs, *History of the Rise of the Mahomedan Power in India* (1829; repr. 4 vols, Calcutta: Editions Indian, 1966), 4:4.

[20] Zafar Hasan, 'The Inscriptions of Dhar and Mandu,' *Epigraphia Indo-Moslemica* (1909), 12. (*muṅd-i shaikh-i ṭaṅqat-i Naṣir-i Dīn Maḥmūd, ki būd maljā'-i autād wa marja'-i abdāl*).

[21] Iqtidar Husain Siddiqui, 'The Early Chishti Dargahs,' in Christian W. Troll,

Nor did the pattern cease with the launching of Tughluq successor states. On entering Delhi in 1526, Babur prayed at the shrine of India's second great Chishti shaikh, Bakhtiyar Kaki (d. 1235), while the new emperor's brother-in-law rebuilt the tomb of Nizam al-Din Auliya. In 1571 Akbar built a tomb for his father Humayun near Nizam al-Din's shrine, and in the same year he began building his new capital of Fatehpur Sikri at the hospice-site of Salim Chishti, the shaikh who had predicted the birth of the emperor's son. Towards the end of his life this same shaikh tied his turban on the head of that son, the future Jahangir, and pronounced him his spiritual successor. As emperor himself, Jahangir built gates and other buildings at or near the foundational Chishti shrine at Ajmer, as did Shah Jahan as part of his victory celebrations after defeating the raja of Mewar. That emperor's daughter, Jahan Ara, even wrote a biography of Mu'in al-Din Chishti. Shah Jahan's son and successor Aurangzeb, who sought to build another pan-Indian empire on the Tughluq model, visited and made sizeable contributions to Chishti tomb-sites in former Tughluq provinces such as at Gulbarga or Khuldabad in the Deccan, in addition to sites in Ajmer and Delhi. Even the later Mughals patronized those Chishti shrines to which they still had access in their dwindling domains, as when 'Alamgir II repaired and made additions to the tomb of Nizam al-Din Auliya. Bringing the pattern to a full circle, the last Mughal emperor, Bahadur Shah II (deposed 1858), built his own mansion adjacent to the shrine of Bakhtiyar Kaki, the very site where Babur had prayed more than three centuries earlier.[22]

In sum, the entire Mughal dynasty, believing that the blessings of Chishti shaikhs underpinned their worldly success, vigorously patronized the order. Two of Akbar's fourteen pilgrimages to the shrine of Mu'in al-Din Chishti at Ajmer, those of 1568 and 1574, were made immediately after conquering Chitor and Bengal respectively.[23] Discussing his military successes with the historian 'Abd al-Qadir Badauni, Akbar remarked, 'All this (success) has been brought through the Pir [Mu'in al-Din].'[24] Vividly dramatized by Akbar's pilgrimages from Agra to Ajmer, several

ed., *Muslim Shrines in India: Their Character, History and Significance* (Delhi: Oxford University Press, 1989), 21.

[22] Catherine B. Asher, *Architecture of Mughal India*, vol. I:4 of *The New Cambridge History of India* (Cambridge: Cambridge University Press, 1992), 293, 34–5, 51, 100, 134, 174, 215, 260, 307, 310.

[23] P.M. Currie, *The Shrine and Cult of Mu'in al-Din Chishti of Ajmer* (Delhi: Oxford University Press, 1992), 100.

[24] 'Abd al-Qadir Badauni, *Muntakhab al-tawarikh*, trans. W. H. Lowe (1899; repr. Delhi: Idarah-i Adabiyat-i Delli, 1973), 2:243.

of them made by foot, the Mughal-Chishti partnership even survived the collapse of the Mughal state. In a sense it persists to this day. The ceremonies, the terminology, and the protocol still found at Chishti shrines generally, and at the Ajmer shrine particularly, all reflect the extraordinary intrusion of the Mughals' courtly culture into that of the Chishti order.[25]

TEMPLE DESECRATION AND STATE BUILDING

By effectively injecting a legitimizing 'substance' into a new body politic at the moment of its birth, the royal patronage of Chishti shaikhs contributed positively to the process of Indo-Muslim state-building. Equally important to this process was its negative counterpart: the sweeping away of all prior political authority in newly-conquered and annexed territories. When such authority was vested in a ruler whose own legitimacy was associated with a royal temple—typically one that housed an image of a ruling dynasty's state-deity, or *raṣṭra-devatā* (usually Vishnu or Śiva)—that temple was normally looted, redefined, or destroyed, any of which would have had the effect of detaching a defeated raja from the most prominent manifestation of his former legitimacy. Temples that were not so identified, or temples formerly so identified but abandoned by their royal patrons and thereby rendered politically irrelevant, were normally left unharmed. Such was the case, for example, with the famous temples at Khajuraho south of the Middle Gangetic Plain, which appear to have been abandoned by their Candella

---

[25] It has been noted recently that the *qauwāli* protocols observed during the annual 'urs ceremonies at Ajmer, which commemorate the deathdate of Mu'in al-Din Chishti, 'betray the impact of Mughal court etiquette. The diwan, dressed Mughal fashion, represents in fact the Mughal king rather than a religious dignitary, and comes escorted by the torch-bearers and mace-bearers wearing Mughal costumes. He takes his seat on the cushion (*gadela*) under a special tent (*dalbadal*) erected for the occasion. . . . On his arrival in the shrine the diwan kisses the tomb and offers flowers, and then one of the *khadims*, who happens to be his *wakil*, like the other pilgrims, ties a *dastar* (turban) over his head, spreads the cloth sheet over his bowed head, prays for him, and then gives him *tabarruk*, consisting of flowers, sandal and sweets. . . . Then he [the diwan] sits down and the *fatiha khwans*, who are permanently and hereditarily employed, recite the fatiha, as well as prayers for the sovereign (*badshah-i Islam*), the diwan, the mutawalli and other officials, and for the general public.' Syed Liyaqat Hussain Moini, 'Rituals and Customary Practices at the Dargah of Ajmer,' in Christian Troll, ed., *Muslim Shrines in India: their Character, History and Significance* (Delhi: Oxford University Press, 1989), 72, 74.

royal patrons before Turkish armies reached the area in the early thirteenth century.[26]

It would be wrong to explain this phenomenon by appealing to an essentialized 'theology of iconoclasm' felt to be intrinsic to the Islamic religion. For, while it is true that contemporary Persian sources routinely condemned idolatry (*but-parasti*) on religious grounds, it is also true that attacks on images patronized by enemy kings had been, from about the sixth century AD on, thoroughly integrated into Indian political behavior. With their lushly sculpted imagery vividly displaying the mutual interdependence of kings and gods and the commingling of divine and human kingship, royal temple complexes of the early medieval period were thoroughly and pre-eminently political institutions. It was here that, after the sixth century, human kingship was established, contested, and revitalized.[27] Above all, the central icon housed in a royal temple's 'womb-chamber' and inhabited by the state-deity of the temple's royal patron, expressed the shared sovereignty of king and deity. Moreover, notwithstanding that temple priests endowed a royal temple's deity with attributes of transcendent and universal power, that same deity was also understood as having a very special relationship, indeed a sovereign relationship, with the particular geographical site in which its temple complex was located.[28] As revealed in temple narratives, even the physical removal of an image from its original site could not break the link between deity and geography.[29] The bonding

[26] Wink, *al-Hind*, 2:324.

[27] 'The need to link one's royal origins to religious and divine forces,' writes B. D. Chattopadhyaya referring to the period 700–1200, 'led to the extraordinary temple building of this period.' B. D. Chattopadhyaya, 'Historiography, History, and Religious Centers: Early Medieval North India, circa AD 700–1200,' in Vishakha N. Desai and Darielle Mason, eds., *Gods, Guardians, and Lovers: Temple Sculptures from North India, AD 700–1200* (New York: Asia Society Galleries, 1993), 40.

[28] Michael Willis suggests that one of the reasons the imperial Pratiharas did *not* build great monumental temple complexes was precisely their determination to avoid the localization of sovereign power that temples necessarily projected. According to this reasoning, the most active patrons of temple construction in this period were subordinate kings who did not have such vast imperial pretensions as did the Pratiharas. Willis, 'Religion and Royal Patronage in north India,' in Desai and Mason, eds., *Gods, Guardians, and Lovers*, 58–9.

[29] Richard H. Davis, *Lives of Indian Images* (Princeton: Princeton University Press, 1997), 122, 137–8. Davis here cites David Shulman: 'A divine power is felt to be present *naturally* on the spot. The texts are therefore concerned with the manner in which this presence is revealed and with the definition of its specific attributes.' David D. Shulman, *Tamil Temple Myths: Sacrifice and Divine Marriage in the South Indian Saiva Tradition* (Princeton: Princeton University Press, 1980), 48. Emphasis mine.

between king, god, temple, and land in early medieval India is well illustrated in a passage from the *Bṛhatsaṃhitā*, a sixth century text: 'If a Śiva linga, image, or temple breaks apart, moves, sweats, cries, speaks, or otherwise acts with no apparent cause, this warns of the destruction of the king and his territory.'[30] In short, from about the sixth century on, images and temples associated with dynastic authority were considered politically vulnerable.

Given these perceived connections between temples, images, and their royal patrons, it is hardly surprising that early medieval Indian history abounds in instances of temple desecration that occurred amidst inter-dynastic conflicts. In AD 642, according to local tradition, the Pallava king Narasimhavarman I looted the image of Ganesha from the Chalukyan capital of Vatapi. Fifty years later armies of those same Chalukyas invaded north India and brought back to the Deccan what appear to be images of Ganga and Yamuna, looted from defeated powers there. In the eighth century, Bengali troops sought revenge on king Lalitaditya by destroying what they thought was the image of Vishnu Vaikuntha, the state deity of Lalitaditya's kingdom in Kashmir. In the early ninth century the Rashtrakuta king Govinda III invaded and occupied Kanchipuram, which so intimidated the king of Sri Lanka that he sent Govinda several (probably Buddhist) images that had represented the Sinhala state, and which the Rashtrakuta king then installed in a Śaiva temple in his capital. About the same time the Pandyan king Srimara Srivallabha also invaded Sri Lanka and took back to his capital a golden Buddha image—'a synecdoche for the integrity of the Sinhalese polity itself'—that had been installed in the kingdom's Jewel Palace. In the early tenth century the Pratihara king Herambapala seized a solid gold image of Vishnu Vaikuntha when he defeated the Sahi king of Kangra. By the mid-tenth century the same image was seized from the Pratiharas by the Candella king Yasovarman and installed in the Lakshmana temple of Khajuraho. In the early eleventh century the Chola king Rajendra I furnished his capital with images he had seized from several prominent neighbouring kings: Durga and Ganesha images from the Chalukyas; Bhairava, Bhairavi, and Kali images from the Kalingas of Orissa; a Nandi image from the Eastern Chalukyas; and a bronze Śiva image from the Palas of Bengal. In the mid-eleventh century the Chola king Rajadhiraja defeated the Chalukyas and plundered Kalyani, taking a large black stone door guardian to his capital in Thanjavur, where it was displayed to his subjects as a trophy of war.[31]

---

[30] Cited in Davis, *Lives*, 53.

[31] Davis, *Lives*, 51–83, *passim.* The same pattern continued after the Turkish

While the dominant pattern here was one of looting royal temples and carrying off images of state deities,[32] we also hear of Hindu kings engaging in the destruction of the royal temples of their political adversaries. In the early tenth century, the Rashtrakuta monarch Indra III not only destroyed the temple of Kalapriya (at Kalpa near the Jamuna River), patronized by the Rashtrakutas' deadly enemies the Pratiharas, but they took special delight in recording the fact.[33]

In short, it is clear that temples had been the natural sites for the contestation of kingly authority well before the coming of Muslim Turks to India. Not surprisingly, Turkish invaders, when attempting to plant their own rule in early medieval India, followed and continued established patterns. The table and the corresponding maps in this essay by no means give the complete picture of temple desecration after the establishment of Turkish power in upper India. Undoubtedly some temples were desecrated but the facts in the matter were never recorded, or the facts were recorded but the records themselves no longer survive. Conversely, later Indo-Muslim chroniclers, seeking to glorify the religious zeal of earlier Muslim rulers, sometimes attributed acts of temple desecration to such rulers even when no contemporary evidence supports the claims.[34] As a result, we shall never know the precise

---

conquest of India. In the 1460s, Kapilendra, the founder of the Suryavamshi Gajapati dynasty in Orissa, sacked both Saiva and Vaishnava temples in the Kaveri delta in the course of wars of conquest in the Tamil country. See Phillip B. Wagoner, *Tidings of the King: A Translation and Ethnohistorical Analysis of the Rāyavācakamu* (Honolulu: University of Hawaii Press, 1993), 146. Somewhat later, in 1514, Krishna Deva Raya looted an image of Bala Krishna from Udayagiri, which he had defeated and annexed to his growing Vijayanagara state. Six years later he acquired control over Pandharpur, where he seems to have looted the Vittala image and carried it back to Vijayanagara, with the apparent purpose of ritually incorporating this area into his kingdom. Davis, *Lives*, 65, 67.

[32] In the late eleventh century, the Kashmiri king Harsha even raised the plundering of temples to an institutionalized activity; and in the late twelfth and early thirteenth century, while Turkish rulers were establishing themselves in north India, kings of the Paramara dynasty attacked and plundered Jain temples in Gujarat. See Romila Thapar, Harbans Mukhia, and Bipan Chandra, *Communalism and the Writing of Indian History* (Delhi: People's Publishing House, 1969), 14, 31.

[33] Willis, 'Religion and Royal Patronage,' 59.

[34] In 1788, for example, the author of the *Riyaz al-salatin* claimed that Muhammad Bakhtiyar demolished local temples after he conquered Bengal in 1204, though no contemporary evidence suggests that he did so. Ghulam Hussain Salim, *Riyazu-s-Salatin: A History of Bengal*, trans. Abdus Salam (1903; repr. Delhi: Idarah-i Adabiyat-i Delli, 1975), 64. Even contemporary sources could make false claims. An inscription on a mosque in Bidar, dated 1670, claims that the Mughal governor

number of temples desecrated in Indian history. Nonetheless, by relying strictly on evidence found in contemporary or near-contemporary epigraphic and literary evidence spanning a period of more than five centuries (1192–1729), one may identify eighty instances of temple desecration whose historicity appears reasonably certain. Although this figure falls well short of the 60,000 claimed by some Hindu nationalists,[35] a review of these data suggests several broad patterns.

First, acts of temple desecration were nearly invariably carried out by military officers or ruling authorities; that is, such acts that we know about were undertaken by the state. Second, the chronology and geography of the data indicate that acts of temple desecration typically occurred on the cutting edge of a moving military frontier. From Ajmer in Rajasthan, the former capital of the defeated Cahamana Rajputs—also, significantly, the wellspring of Chishti piety—the post-1192 pattern of temple desecration moved swiftly down the Gangetic Plain as Turkish military forces sought to extirpate local ruling houses in the late twelfth and early thirteenth century (see Table and Map 2a: nos. 1–9). In Bihar, this included the targeting of Buddhist monastic establishments at Odantapuri, Vikramasila, and Nalanda. Detached from a Buddhist laity, these establishments had by this time become dependent on the patronage of local royal authorities, with whom they were identified. In the 1230s Iltutmish carried the Delhi Sultanate's authority into Malwa (nos. 10–11), and by the onset of the fourteenth century the Khalaji sultans had opened up a corridor through eastern Rajasthan into Gujarat (nos. 12–14, 16–17).

Delhi's initial raids on peninsular India, on which the Khalajis embarked between 1295 and the early decades of the fourteenth century (nos. 15, 18–19), appear to have been driven not by a goal of annexation but by the Sultanate's need for wealth with which to defend north India from Mongol attacks.[36] For a short time, then, peninsular India

---

Mukhtar Khan had destroyed a temple and built the mosque on its site. 'But as a matter of fact,' noted the epigraphist who published the inscription, 'the mosque is a new construction, and the rock does not seem to have been disturbed, for it still survives.' *Epigraphia Indo-Moslemica, 1927–28* (Calcutta: Government of India, 1931), 32.

[35] Entry for the date 1688 in 'Hindu Timeline,' *Hinduism Today* (December, 1994), cited in Cynthia Talbot, 'Inscribing the Other, Inscribing the Self: Hindu-Muslim Identities in Pre-Colonial India,' *Comparative Studies in Society and History* 37, no.4 (Oct., 1995), 692.

[36] In 1247 Balban, the future sultan of Delhi, had recommended raiding Indian states for precisely this purpose. See Minhaj Siraj Juzjani, *Tabakat-i-Nasiri*, trans. H. G. Raverty (1881; repr. New Delhi: Oriental Books Reprint Corp., 1970), 2:816.

stood in the same relation to the north—namely, as a source of plunder for financing distant military operations—as north India had stood in relation to Afghanistan three centuries earlier, in the days of Mahmud of Ghazni. After 1323, however, a new north Indian dynasty, the Tughluqs, sought permanent dominion in the Deccan, which the future Sultan Muhammad bin Tughluq established by uprooting royally patronized temples in western Andhra (nos. 20–22). Somewhat later, Sultan Firuz Tughluq did the same in Orissa (no. 23).

From the late fourteenth century, after the tide of Tughluq imperialism had receded from Gujarat and the Deccan, newly emerging successor states sought to expand their own political frontiers in those areas. This, too, is reflected in instances of temple desecration, as the ex-Tughluq governor of Gujarat and his successors consolidated their authority there (see Table and Map 2b: nos. 25–26, 31–32, 34–35, 38–39, 42), or as the Delhi empire's successors in the south, the Bahmani sultans, challenged Vijayanagara's claims to dominate the Raichur doab and the Tamil coast (nos. 33, 41). The pattern was repeated in Kashmir by Sultan Sikandar (nos. 27–30), and in the mid-fifteenth century when the independent sultanate of Malwa contested renewed Rajput power in eastern Rajasthan after Delhi's authority there had waned (nos. 36–37). In the early sixteenth century, when the Lodi dynasty of Afghans sought to reassert Delhi's sovereignty over neighbouring Rajput houses, we again find instances of temple desecration (nos. 43–45). So do we in the late sixteenth and early seventeenth centuries, when the Bahmani Kingdom's principal successor states, Bijapur and Golconda, challenged the territorial sovereignty of Orissan kings (nos. 55, 59; Maps 2b and 2c), of Vijayanagara (no. 47), and of the latter's successor states—especially in the southern Andhra country (nos. 50–51, 53–54, 60–61; Maps 2b and 2c).

Unlike the Deccan, where Indo-Muslim states had been expanding at the expense of non-Muslim states, in north India the Mughals under Babur, Humayun, and Akbar—that is, between 1526 and 1605—grew mainly at the expense of defeated Afghans. As non-Hindus, the latter had never shared sovereignty with deities patronized in royal temples, which probably explains the absence of firm evidence of temple desecration by any of the early Mughals, in Ayodhya or elsewhere.[37] However,

---

[37] The notion that Babur's officer Mir Baqi destroyed a temple dedicated to Rama's birthplace at Ayodhya and then got the emperor's sanction to build a mosque on the site—the notorious Baburi Masjid—was elaborated in 1936 by S. K. Banerji. However, the author offered no evidence that there had ever been a temple at this site, much less that it had been destroyed by Mir Baqi. The mosque's

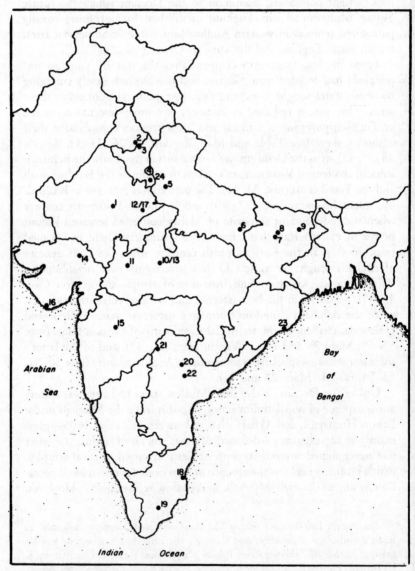

Map 2a: Temple desecrations, 1192–1394, imperialism of the Delhi Sultanate
(See table at the end of the chapter)

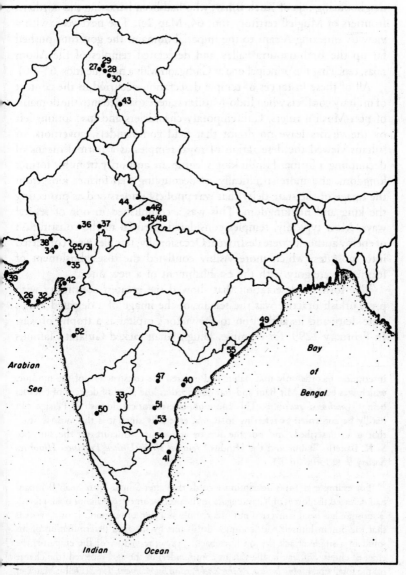

Map 2b: Temple desecrations, 1394–1600, the growth of regional sultanates
(See table at the end of the chapter)

whenever Mughal armies pushed beyond the frontiers of territories formerly ruled by the Delhi sultans and sought to annex the domains of Hindu rulers, we again find instances of temple desecration. In 1661, the governor of Bengal, Mir Jumla, sacked the temples of the neighbouring raja of Kuch Bihar, who had been harassing the northern frontiers of Mughal territory (no. 64; Map 2c). The next year, with a view to annexing Assam to the imperial domain, the governor pushed far up the Brahmaputra valley and desecrated temples of the Ahom rajas, replacing the principal one at Garhgaon with a mosque (nos. 65–66).

All of these instances of temple desecration occurred in the context of military conflicts when Indo-Muslim states expanded into the domains of non-Muslim rulers. Contemporary chroniclers and inscriptions left by the victors leave no doubt that field commanders, governors, or sultans viewed the desecration of royal temples as a normal means of decoupling a former Hindu king's legitimate authority from his former kingdom, and more specifically, of decoupling that former king from the image of the state-deity that was publicly understood as protecting the king and his kingdom. This was accomplished in one of several ways. Most typically, temples considered essential to the constitution of enemy authority were destroyed. Occasionally, temples were converted into mosques, which more visibly conflated the disestablishment of former sovereignty with the establishment of a new one.[38]

The form of desecration that showed the greatest continuity with pre-Turkish practice was the seizure of the image of a defeated king's state-deity and its abduction to the victor's capital as a trophy of war. In February 1299, for example, Ulugh Khan sacked Gujarat's famous

---

inscription records only that Babur had ordered the construction of the mosque, which was built by Mir Baqi and was described as 'the place of descent of celestial beings' (*mahbū-i qudsiyān*). This commonplace rhetorical flourish in Persian can hardly be construed as referring to Rama, especially since it is the mosque itself that is so described, and not the site or any earlier structure on the site. See S. K. Banerji, 'Babur and the Hindus,' *Journal of the United Provinces Historical Society* 9 (1936), 76–83.

[38] For example, a 1406 inscription records that after Sultan Firuz Shah Bahmani had defeated the forces of Vijayanagara in the much-contested Raichur doab region, 'a mosque has been converted out of a temple as a sign of religion'. It then records that the Sultan himself had 'conquered this fort by the firm determination of his mind in a single attack (lit. on horseback). After the victory of the emperor, the chief of chiefs, Safdar (lit. the valiant commander) of the age, received (the charge of) the fort.' *Epigraphia Indica, Arabic and Persian Supplement, 1962* (Delhi: Manager of Publications, 1964), 57–8.

temple of Somnath and sent its largest image to Sultan 'Ala al-Din Khalaji's court in Delhi (no. 16; Map 2a). When Firuz Tughluq invaded Orissa in 1359 and learned that the region's most important temple was that of Jagannath located inside the raja's fortress in Puri, he carried off the stone image of the god and installed it in Delhi 'in an ignominious position' (no. 23). In 1518, when the court in Delhi came to suspect the loyalty of a tributary Rajput chieftain in Gwalior, Sultan Ibrahim Lodi marched to the famous fortress, stormed it, and seized a brass image of Nandi evidently situated adjacent to the chieftain's Śiva temple. The sultan brought it back to Delhi and installed it in the city's Baghdad Gate (no. 46; Map 2b). Similarly, in 1579, when Golconda's army led by Murahari Rao was campaigning south of the Krishna River, Rao annexed the entire region to Qutb Shahi domains and sacked the popular Ahobilam temple, whose ruby-studded image he brought back to Golconda and presented to his sultan as a war trophy (no. 51). Although the Ahobilam temple had only local appeal, it had close associations with prior sovereign authority since it had been patronized and even visited by the powerful and most famous king of Vijayanagara, Krishna Deva Raya.[39]

In each of these instances, the deity's image, taken as war trophy to the capital city of the victorious sultan, became radically detached from its former context and in the process was transformed from a living to a dead image. However, sacked images were not invariably abducted to the victor's capital. In 1556, the Gajapati raja of Orissa had entered into a pact with the Mughal emperor Akbar, the distant adversary of the sultan of Bengal, Sulaiman Karrani. The raja had also given refuge to Sulaiman's more proximate adversary, Ibrahim Sur, and offered to assist the latter in his ambitions to conquer Bengal and overthrow the Karrani dynasty. As Sulaiman could hardly have tolerated such threats to his stability, he sent an army into Orissa which went straight to the Gajapati kingdom's state temple of Jagannath and looted its images. But here the goal was not annexation but only punishment, which might explain why the Gajapati state images were not carried back to the Bengali capital as trophies of war.[40]

Whatever form they took, acts of temple desecration were never

[39] Briggs, *Rise of Mahomedan Power*, 3:267. The temple's political significance, and hence the necessity of desecrating it, would have been well understood by Murahari Rao, himself a Marathi Brahman.

[40] Khwajah Ni'mat Allah, *Tarikh-i Khan Jahani wa Makhzan-i-Afhani*, ed. S.M. Imam al-Din (Dacca: Asiatic Society of Pakistan, 1960), 1:413–15; Abu'l-fazl, *Akbar-nama*, trans. Henry Beveridge (repr. New Delhi: Ess Ess Publications, 1979), 2:381–2, 480.

directed at the people, but at the enemy king and the image that incarnated and displayed his state-deity. A contemporary description of a 1661 Mughal campaign in Kuch Bihar, which resulted in the annexation of the region, makes it clear that Mughal authorities were guided by two principal concerns. The first was to destroy the image of the state-deity of the defeated raja, Bhim Narayan. And the second was to prevent Mughal troops from looting or in any way harming the general population of Kuch Bihar. To this end, we are informed, the chief judge of Mughal Bengal, Saiyid Muhammad Sadiq,

> was directed to issue prohibitory orders that nobody was to touch the cash and property of the people, and he should go personally and establish order everywhere. He was asked to confiscate the treasure of Bhim Narayan, break the idols and introduce the laws of Islam. Sayyid Sadiq issued strict prohibitory orders so that nobody had the courage to break the laws or to plunder the property of the inhabitants. The punishment for disobeying the order was that the hands, ears or noses of the plunderers were cut. Sayyid Sadiq busied himself in giving protection to the life and property of the subjects and the destitutes.[41]

In newly annexed areas formerly ruled by non-Muslims, as in the case of Kuch Bihar, Mughal officers took appropriate measures to secure the support of the common people, who after all created the material wealth upon which the entire imperial edifice rested.

TEMPLE PROTECTION AND STATE MAINTENANCE

If the idea of conquest became manifest in the desecration of temples associated with former enemies, what happened once the land and the subjects of those enemies were integrated into an Indo-Muslim state? On this point, the data are quite clear: pragmatism as well as time-honoured traditions of both Islamic and Indian statecraft dictated that temples lying within such states be left unmolested. We learn from a Sanskrit inscription, for example, that in 1326, thirteen years after he annexed the northern Deccan to the Tughluq empire, Sultan Muhammad bin Tughluq appointed Muslim officials to repair a Śiva temple in Kalyana (in Bidar District), thereby facilitating the resumption of normal worship that had been disrupted by local disturbances.[42] According to that sultan's interpretation of Islamic Law, anybody who

---

[41] S. Moinul Haq, trans., *Khafi Khan's History of 'Alamgir* (Karachi: Pakistan Historical Society, 1975), 142–3.

[42] P. B. Desai, 'Kalyana Inscription of Sultan Muhammad, Saka 1248,' *Epigraphia Indica* 32 (1957–58), 165–8.

paid the poll-tax (*jizya*) could build temples in territories ruled by Muslims.[43]

Such views continued to hold sway until modern times. Within several decades of Muhammad bin Tughluq's death, Sultan Shihab al-Din (1355–73) of Kashmir rebuked his Brahman minister for having suggested melting down Hindu and Buddhist images in his kingdom as a means of obtaining quick cash. In elaborating his ideas on royal patronage of religion, the sultan referred to the deeds of figures drawn from classical Hindu mythology. 'Some [kings],' he said,

have obtained renown by setting up images of gods, others by worshiping them, some by duly maintaining them. And some, by demolishing them! How great is the enormity of such a deed! Sagara became famous by creating the sea and the rivers.... Bhagiratha obtained fame by bringing down the Ganges. Jealous of Indra's fame, Dushyanata acquired renown by conquering the world; and Rama by killing Ravana when the latter had purloined Sita. King Shahvadina [Shihab al-Din], it will be said, plundered the image of a god; and this fact, dreadful as Yama [death], will make the men in future tremble.[44]

About a century later, Muslim jurists advised the future Sikandar Lodi of Delhi (r. 1489–1517) that 'it is not lawful to lay waste ancient idol temples, and it does not rest with you to prohibit ablution in a reservoir which has been customary from ancient times.'[45]

The pattern of post-conquest temple protection, and even patronage, is especially clear when we come to the imperial Mughals, whose views on the subject are captured in official pronouncements on Sultan Mahmud of Ghazni, one of the most controversial figures in Indian history. It is well known that in the early eleventh century, before the establishment of Indo-Muslim rule in north India, the Ghaznavid sultan had made numerous, and very destructive, attacks on the region. Starting with the writings of his own contemporary and court poet, Firdausi (d. 1020), Mahmud's career soon became legend, as generations of Persian poets lionized Mahmud as a paragon of Islamic kingly virtue, celebrating his infamous attacks on Indian temples as models for what other pious sultans should do.[46] But the Ghaznavid sultan never un-

[43] Ibn Battuta, *Travels in Asia and Africa, 1324–1354*, trans. H. A. R. Gibb (1929; repr. New Delhi: Oriental Books Reprint Corporation, 1986), 214.

[44] S. L. Sadhu, ed., *Medieval Kashmir, Being a Reprint of the Rajataranginis of Jonaraja, Shrivara and Shuka*, trans. J. C. Dutt (1898; repr. New Delhi: Atlantic Publishers & Distributors, 1993), 44–5.

[45] Nizamuddin Ahmad, *Tabaqat-i-Akbari*, trans. B. De, 3 vols (Calcutta: Bibliotheca Indica, 1927–39), 1:386.

[46] A useful discussion of Mahmud, his legend, and the question of iconoclasm

dertook the responsibility of actually governing any part of the subcontinent whose temples he wantonly plundered. Herein lies the principal difference between the careers of Mahmud and Abu'l-fazl, Akbar's chief minister and the principal architect of Mughal imperial ideology. Reflecting the sober values that normally accompany the practice of governing large, multi-ethnic states, Abu'l-fazl attributed Mahmud's excesses to fanatical bigots who, having incorrectly represented India as 'a country of unbelievers at war with Islam,' incited the sultan's unsuspecting nature, which led to 'the wreck of honour and the shedding of blood and the plunder of the virtuous'.[47]

Indeed, from Akbar's time (r. 1556–1605) onward, Mughal rulers treated temples lying within their sovereign domain as state property; accordingly, they undertook to protect both the physical structures and their Brahman functionaries. At the same time, by appropriating Hindu religious institutions to serve imperial ends—a process involving complex overlappings of political and religious codes of power—the Mughals became deeply implicated in institutionalized Indian religions, in dramatic contrast to their British successors, who professed a hands-off policy in this respect. Thus we find Akbar allowing high-ranking Rajput officers in his service to build their own monumental temples in the provinces to which they were posted.[48] His successors went further. Between 1590 and 1735, Mughal officials repeatedly oversaw, and on occasion even initiated, the renewal of Orissa's state cult, that of Jagannath in Puri. By sitting on a canopied chariot while accompanying the cult's annual car festival, Shah Jahan's officials ritually demonstrated that it was the Mughal emperor, operating through his appointed officers (*manṣabdār*), who was the temple's—and hence the god's—ultimate lord and protector.[49] Such actions in effect projected a hierarchy of hybridized political and religious power that descended downward from the Mughal emperor to his manṣabdār, from the manṣabdār to the god Jagannath and his temple, from Jagannath to the sub-imperial king who patronized the god, and from the king to his subjects. For

prior to the establishment of Islamic states in India is found in Davis, *Lives*, chs. 3 and 6.

[47] Abu'l-fazl 'Allami, *A'in-i Akbari*, vol. 3, trans. H. S. Jarrett, ed., Jadunath Sarkar (2nd edn. Calcutta: Asiatic Society of Bengal, 1927; repr. New Delhi: Oriental Books Reprint Corp., 1977–78), 377.

[48] Catherine B. Asher, 'The Architecture of Raja Man Singh: A Study of Sub-Imperial Patronage,' in Barbara Stoler Miller, ed., *The Powers of Art: Patronage in Indian Culture* (Delhi: Oxford University Press, 1992), 183–201.

[49] P. Acharya, 'Bruton's Account of Cuttack and Puri,' *Orissa Historical Research Journal* 10, no. 3 (1961), 46.

the Mughals, politics within their sovereign domains never meant an-
nihilating prior authority, but appropriating it within a hierarchy of
power that flowed from the Peacock Throne to the mass of commoners
below.

Such ideas continued in force into the reign of Aurangzeb (1658-
1707), whose orders to local officials in Benares in 1659 clearly indicate
that Brahman temple functionaries there, together with the temples at
which they officiated, merited state protection:

In these days information has reached our court that several people have, out
of spite and rancour, harassed the Hindu residents of Benares and nearby
places, including a group of Brahmans who are in charge of ancient temples
there. These people want to remove those Brahmans from their charge of
temple-keeping, which has caused them considerable distress. Therefore, upon
receiving this order, you must see that nobody unlawfully disturbs the Brahmans
or other Hindus of that region, so that they might remain in their traditional
place and pray for the continuance of the Empire.[50]

By way of justifying this order, the emperor noted that, 'According to
the Holy Law (*sharī'at*) and the exalted creed, it has been established
that ancient temples should not be torn down.' On this point, Aurangzeb
aligned himself with the theory and the practice of Indo-Muslim ruling
precedent. But then he added, 'nor should new temples be built'—a
view that broke decisively from Akbar's policy of permitting his Rajput
officers to build their own temple complexes in Mughal territory.[51]
Although this order appears to have applied only to Benares—many
new temples were built elsewhere in India during Aurangzeb's reign[52]—
one might wonder what prompted the emperor's anxiety in this matter.

TEMPLE DESECRATION AND STATE MAINTENANCE

It seems certain that Indo-Muslim rulers were well aware of the highly
charged political and religious relationship between a royal Hindu patron
and his client-temple. Hence, even when former rulers or their descendants had been comfortably assimilated into an Indo-Muslim state's

[50] *Journal of the Asiatic Society of Bengal* (1911), 689–90. Order to Abu'l-Hasan
in Benares, dated 28 Feb., 1659. My translation. The 'continuance of the empire,'
of course, was always forefront on the minds of the Mughals, regardless of what
religious functionary was praying to which deity.
[51] 'Az rū-yi shar'-i sharīf wa millat-i munif muqartar chunīn ast, ki dair-hāyi dīrīn
bar andākht nashavad, wa but-kada-hā tāza banā nayābad.' Ibid., my translation.
[52] See Eaton, *Rise of Islam*, 184–5, 263.

ruling class, there always remained the possibility, and hence the occasional suspicion, that a temple's latent political significance might be activated and serve as a power-base to further its patron's political aspirations. Such considerations might explain why it was that, when a subordinate non-Muslim officer in an Indo-Muslim state showed signs of disloyalty—and especially if he engaged in open rebellion—the state often desecrated the temple(s) most clearly identified with that officer. After all, if temples lying within its domain were understood as state property, and if a government officer who was also a temple's patron demonstrated disloyalty to the state, from a juridical standpoint ruling authorities felt justified in treating that temple as an extension of the officer, and hence liable for punishment.

Thus in 1478, when a Bahmani garrison on the Andhra coast mutinied, murdered its governor, and entrusted the fort to Bhimraj Oriyya, who until that point had been a Bahmani client, the sultan personally marched to the site and, after a six-month siege, stormed the fort, destroyed its temple, and built a mosque on the site (no. 40). A similar thing occurred in 1659, when Shivaji Bhonsle, the son of a loyal and distinguished officer serving the 'Adil Shahi sultans of Bijapur, seized a government port on the northern Konkan coast, thereby disrupting the flow of external trade to and from the capital. Responding to what it considered an act of treason, the government deputed a high-ranking officer, Afzal Khan, to punish the Maratha rebel. Before marching to confront Shivaji himself, however, the Bijapur general first proceeded to Tuljapur and desecrated a temple dedicated to the goddess Bhavani, to which Shivaji and his family had been personally devoted (no. 63; Map 2c).

We find the same pattern with the Mughals. In 1613 while at Pushkar, near Ajmer, Jahangir ordered the desecration of an image of Varaha that had been housed in a temple belonging to an uncle of Rana Amar of Mewar, the emperor's arch enemy (See Table and Map 2c: no. 56). In 1635, his son and successor, Shah Jahan, destroyed the great temple at Orchha, which had been patronized by the father of Raja Jajhar Singh, a high-ranking Mughal officer who was at that time in open rebellion against the emperor (no. 58). In 1669, there arose a rebellion in Benares among landholders, some of whom were suspected of having helped Shivaji, who was Aurangzeb's arch enemy, escape from imperial detention. It was also believed that Shivaji's escape had been initially facilitated by Jai Singh, the great grandson of Raja Man Singh, who almost certainly built Benares's great Vishvanath temple. It was against this background that the emperor ordered the destruction

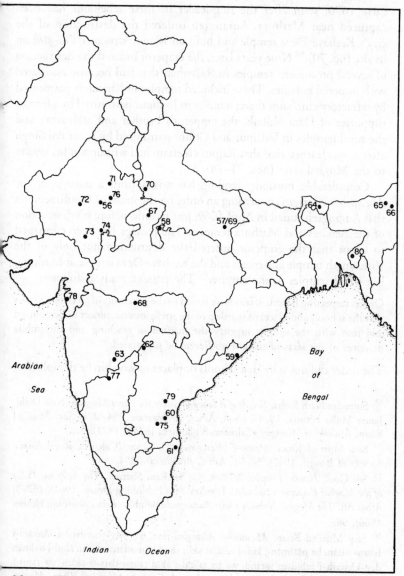

Map 2c: Temple desecrations, 1600–1760, expansion and reassertions of Mughal authority
(See table at the end of the chapter)

of that temple in September, 1669 (no. 69).[53] About the same time, serious Jat rebellions broke out in the area around Mathura, in which the patron of that city's congregational mosque had been killed. So in early 1670, soon after the ring-leader of these rebellions had been captured near Mathura, Aurangzeb ordered the destruction of the city's Keshava Deva temple and built an Islamic structure ('*id-gāh*) on its site (no. 70).[54] Nine years later, the emperor ordered the destruction of several prominent temples in Rajasthan that had become associated with imperial enemies. These included temples in Khandela patronized by refractory chieftains there; temples in Jodhpur patronized by a former supporter of Dara Shikoh, the emperor's brother and arch-rival; and the royal temples in Udaipur and Chitor patronized by Rana Raj Singh after it was learned that that Rajput chieftain had withdrawn his loyalty to the Mughal state (nos. 71–74).

Considerable misunderstanding has arisen from a passage in the *Ma'athir-i 'Alamgiri* concerning an order on the status of Hindu temples that Aurangzeb issued in April 1669, just months before his destruction of the Benares and Mathura temples. The passage has been construed to mean that the emperor ordered the destruction not only of the Vishvanath temple at Benares and the Keshava Deva temple at Mathura, but of all temples in the empire.[55] The passage reads as follows:

Orders respecting Islamic affairs were issued to the governors of all the provinces that the schools and places of worship of the irreligious be subject to demolition and that with the utmost urgency the manner of teaching and the public practices of the sects of these misbelievers be suppressed.[56]

The order did not state that schools or places of worship be demolished,

---

[53] Surendra Nath Sinha, *Subah of Allahabad under the Great Mughals* (New Delhi: Jamia Millia Islamia, 1974). 65–8; Asher, *Architecture*, 254, 278; Saqi Must'ad Khan, *Ma'athir-i 'Alamgiri* (Calcutta: Bibliotheca Indica, 1871), 88.

[54] Saqi Must'ad Khan, *Maasir-i 'Alamgiri*, tr. J. Sarkar (Calcutta: Royal Asiatic Society of Bengal, 1947), 57–61; Asher, *Architecture*, 254.

[55] See Goel, *Hindu Temples*, 2:78–9, 83; Sri Ram Sharma, *The Religious Policy of the Mughal Emperors* (2nd edn.: London: Asia Publishing House, 1962), 132–3; Athar Ali, *The Mughal Nobility under Aurangzeb* (Bombay: Asia Publishing House, 1966), 98n.

[56] Saqi Must'ad Khan, *Ma'athir-i 'Alamgiri*, text, 81. My translation. Aḥkām-i Islām- niẓām ba nāẓimān-i kull-i ṣūbajāt ṣādir shud ki mudāris wa mu'ābid-i bidīnān dast-khwash-i inhidām sāzand, wa ba ta'kīd-i akīd ṭaur-i dars-o-tadrīs wa rasm-i shayū'-i madhāhib-i kufr-āyīnān bar andāzand. Cf. Saqi Must 'ad Khan, *Maasir-i-'Alamgiri: A History of the Emperor Aurangzeb-'Alamgir*, trans. Jadunath Sarkar (Lahore: Suhail Academy, 1981), 51–2.

but rather that they be *subject* to demolition, implying that local authorities were required to make investigations before taking action.

More importantly, the sentence immediately preceding this passage provides the context in which we may find the order's overall intent. On 8 April 1669, Aurangzeb's court received reports that in Thatta, Multan, and especially in Benares, Brahmans in 'established schools' (*mudāris-i muqarrar*) had been engaged in teaching false books (*kutub-i bāṭila*) and that both Hindu and Muslim 'admirers and students' had been travelling over great distances to study the 'ominous sciences' taught by this 'deviant group'.[57] We do not know what sort of teaching or 'false books' were involved here, or why both Muslims and Hindus were attracted to them, though these are intriguing questions. What is clear is that the court was primarily concerned, indeed exclusively concerned, with curbing the influence of a certain 'mode' or 'manner' of teaching (*ṭaur-i dars-o-tadrīs*) within the imperial domain. Far from being, then, a general order for the destruction of all temples in the empire, the order was responding to specific reports of an educational nature and was targeted at investigating those institutions where a certain kind of teaching had been taking place.

In sum, apart from his prohibition on building new temples in Benares, Aurangzeb's policies respecting temples within imperial domains generally followed those of his predecessors. Viewing temples within their domains as state property, Aurangzeb and Indo-Muslim rulers in general punished disloyal Hindu officers in their service by desecrating temples with which they were associated. How, one might then ask, did they punish disloyal Muslim officers? Since officers in all Indo-Muslim states belonged to hierarchically ranked service cadres, infractions short of rebellion normally resulted in demotions in rank, while serious crimes like treason were generally punished by execution, regardless of the perpetrator's religious affiliation.[58]

---

[57] *Ma'athir-i 'Alamgiri*, text, 81. Ba 'arẓ-i khudāvand-i dīn-parvar rasīd ki dar ṣūba-yi Thatta wa Multān khuṣūṣ Banāras brahminān-i-baṭṭalar-nishān dar mudāris-i muqarrar ba tadrīs-i kutub-i bāṭila ishtighāl dārand, wa rāghibān wa ṭālibān az hunūd wa musulmān musāfat-hāyi ba'īda ṭaiy numūda, jihat-i-taḥṣīl-i 'ulūm-i-shūm nazd-i ān jamā'at-i gumrāh miāyand. Cf. Jadunath Sarkar, trans., *Maasir-i-'Alamgiri* (Lahore: Suhail Academy, 1981), 51.

[58] Consider the swift and brutal punishment of Baha al-Din Gurshasp, a high-ranking officer in Tughluq imperial service and a governor in the Deccan. In 1327, Gurshasp joined forces with the raja of Kampila in an unsuccessful rebellion against Sultan Muhammad bin Tughluq. When captured, the raja, who had never sworn allegiance to Tughluq authority, got the relatively light punishment of a beheading. But the rebel governor, who was not only a former Tughluq officer

No evidence, however, suggests that ruling authorities attacked public monuments like mosques or Sufi shrines that had been patronized by disloyal or rebellious officers. Nor were such monuments desecrated when one Indo-Muslim kingdom conquered another and annexed its territories. To the contrary, new rulers were quick to honour and support the shrines of those Chishti shaikhs that had been patronized by those they had defeated. As we have seen, Babur, upon seizing Delhi from the last of the city's ruling sultans in 1526, lost no time in patronizing the city's principal Chishti tomb-shrines. The pattern was repeated as the Mughals expanded into provinces formerly ruled by Indo-Muslim dynasties. Upon conquering Bengal in 1574, the Mughals showered their most lavish patronage on the two Chishti shrines in Pandua—those of Shaikh 'Ala al-Haq (d. 1398) and Shaikh Nur Qutb-i 'Alam (d. 1459)—that had been the principal objects of state patronage by the previous dynasty of Bengal sultans.[59] And when he extended Mughal dominion over defeated Muslim states of the Deccan, the dour Aurangzeb, notwithstanding his reputation for eschewing the culture of saint-cults, made sizable contributions to those Chishti shrines in Khuldabad and Gulbarga that had helped legitimize earlier Muslim dynasties there.

TEMPLES AND MOSQUES CONTRASTED

Data presented in the foregoing discussion suggest that mosques or shrines carried very different political meanings than did royal temples in independent Hindu states, or temples patronized by Hindu officers serving in Indo-Muslim states. For Indo-Muslim rulers, building mosques was considered an act of royal piety, even a duty. But all actors, rulers and ruled alike, seem to have recognized that the deity worshipped in mosques or shrines had no personal connection with a Muslim monarch. Nor were such monuments thought of as underpinning, far less actually constituting, the authority of an Indo-Muslim king. This point is well illustrated in a reported dispute between the Emperor

---

but the emperor's first cousin, was spat upon by his female relatives and flayed alive; then his skin was stuffed with straw and paraded throughout the imperial provinces as a cautionary tale to the public, while his body was mixed with rice and fed to elephants. See 'Isami, *Futuhu's-salatin,* trans., 3:658–89; Mahdi Husain, trans., *The Rehla of Ibn Battuta (India, Maldive Islands and Ceylon)* (Baroda: Oriental Institute, 1953), 96. As a final indignity to Gurshasp, we are told by Ibn Battuta that the elephants refused to eat the meal that had been mixed with the rebel's body.

[59] Eaton, *Rise of Islam,* 176–7.

Aurangzeb and a Sufi named Shaikh Muhammadi (d. 1696). As a consequence of this dispute, in which the shaikh refused to renounce views that the emperor considered theologically deviant, Shaikh Muhammadi was ordered to leave the imperial domain. When the Sufi instead took refuge in a local mosque, Aurangzeb claimed that this would not do, since the mosque was also within imperial territory. But the shaikh only remarked on the emperor's arrogance, noting that a mosque was the house of God and therefore only His property. The standoff ended with the shaikh's imprisonment in Aurangabad fort—property that was unambiguously imperial.[60]

This incident suggests that mosques in Mughal India, though religiously potent, were considered detached from both sovereign terrain and dynastic authority, and hence politically inactive. As such, their desecration could have had no relevance to the business of disestablishing a regime that had patronized them. Not surprisingly, then, when Hindu rulers established their authority over territories of defeated Muslim rulers, they did not as a rule desecrate mosques or shrines, as, for example, when Shivaji established a Maratha kingdom on the ashes of Bijapur's former dominions in Maharashtra, or when Vijayanagara annexed the former territories of the Bahmanis or their successors.[61] In fact, the rajas of Vijayanagara, as is well known, built their own mosques, evidently to accommodate the sizable number of Muslims employed in their armed forces.

By contrast, monumental royal temple complexes of the early medieval period were considered politically active, inasmuch as the state-deities they housed were understood as expressing the shared sovereignty of

[60] Muzaffar Alam, 'Assimilation from a Distance: Confrontation and Sufi Accommodation in Awadh Society,' in R. Champakalakshmi and S. Gopal, eds, *Tradition, Dissent, and Ideology: Essays in Honour of Romila Thapar* (Delhi: Oxford University Press, 1996), 177n.

[61] Examples of mosque desecrations are strikingly few in number. In 1697–8 in Sambhar, in Rajasthan's Jaipur District, Shah Sabz 'Ali built a mosque on the site of a temple. In the reign of Shah 'Alam (1707–12), however, non-Muslims came to dominate the region and demolished the mosque, which was subsequently rebuilt in the reign of Farrukh Siyar. (See Z. A. Desai, *Published Muslim Inscriptions of Rajasthan* [Jaipur: Government of Rajasthan, 1971], 157). Similarly, there is evidence that in 1680, during Aurangzeb's invasion of Rajasthan, the Rajput chief Bhim Singh, seeking to avenge the emperor's recent destruction of temples in Udaipur and elsewhere, raided Gujarat and plundered Vadnagar, Vishalnagar, and Ahmedabad, in the latter place destroying thirty smaller mosques and one large one. (*Rāja-samudra-prasasti*, XXII, v. 29, an inscription composed ca. 1683, which appears in Kaviraj Shyamaldas, *Vir Vinod* [Udaipur: Rajayantralaya, 1886]; cited in R. C. Majumdar, ed., *The Mughal Empire* [Bombay, Bharatiya Vidya Bhavan, 1974], 351).

king and deity over a *particular* dynastic realm.[62] Therefore, when Indo-Muslim commanders or rulers looted the consecrated images of defeated opponents and carried them off to their own capitals as war trophies, they were in a sense conforming to customary rules of Indian politics. Similarly, when they destroyed a royal temple or converted it into a mosque, ruling authorities were building on a political logic that, they knew, placed supreme political significance on such temples. That same significance, in turn, rendered temples just as deserving of peace-time protection as it rendered them vulnerable in times of conflict.

TEMPLE DESECRATION AND THE RHETORIC OF STATE BUILDING

Much misunderstanding over the place of temple desecration in Indian history results from a failure to distinguish the rhetoric from the practice of Indo-Muslim state-formation. Whereas the former tends to be normative, conservative, and rigidly ideological, the latter tends to be pragmatic, eclectic, and non-ideological. Rhetorically, we know, temple desecration figured very prominently in Indo-Muslim chronicles as a necessary and even meritorious constituent of state-formation.[63] In 1350, for example, the poet-chronicler 'Isami gave the following advice to his royal patron, 'Ala al-Din Hasan Bahman Shah, the founder of the Bahmani kingdom in the Deccan:

If you and I, O man of intellect, have a holding in this country and are in a position to replace the idol-houses by mosques and sometimes forcibly to break the Brahmanic thread and enslave woman and children—all this is due to the glory of Mahmud [of Ghazni].... The achievements that you make to-day will also become a story to-morrow.[64]

---

[62] One can hardly imagine the central focus of a mosque's ritual activity, the prayer niche (*miḥrāb*), being taken out of the structure and paraded around a Muslim capital by way of displaying Allah's co-sovereignty over an Indo-Muslim ruler's kingdom, in the manner that the ritual focus of a royal temple, the image of the state-deity, was paraded around many pre-modern Hindu capitals in elaborate 'car' festivals.

[63] Aiming to cast earlier invaders or rulers in the role of zealous and puritanical heroes, later chroniclers occasionally attributed to such figures the desecration of staggering numbers of temples. Mahmud of Ghazni, for example, is said to have destroyed 10,000 temples in Kanauj and 1,000 in Mathura, his grandson Ibrahim 1,000 in the Delhi Doab and another 1,000 in Malwa, Aibek 1,000 in Delhi, and Muhammad Ghuri another 1,000 in Benares—figures that Hindu nationalists like Sita Ram Goel have accepted at face value. Goel, *Hindu Temples*, 269.

[64] 'Isami, *Futuhu's-salatin*, trans, 1:66–7.

But the new sultan appears to have been more concerned with political stability than with the glorious legacy his court-poet would wish him to pursue. There is no evidence that the new sultan converted any temples to mosques. After all, by carving out territory from lands formerly lying within the Delhi Sultanate, the founder of the Bahmani state had inherited a domain void of independent Hindu kings and hence void, too, of temples that might have posed a political threat to his fledgling kingdom.

Unlike temple desecration or the patronage of Chishti shaikhs, both of which figured prominently in the contemporary rhetoric on Indo-Muslim state-building, a third activity, the use of explicitly Indian political rituals, found no place whatsoever in that rhetoric. Here we may consider the way Indo-Muslim rulers used the rich political symbolism of the Ganges River, whose mythic associations with imperial kingship had been well established since Mauryan times (321–181 BC). Each in its own way, the mightiest imperial formations of the early medieval peninsula—the Chalukyas, the Rashtrakutas, and the Cholas—claimed to have 'brought' the Ganges River down to their southern capitals, seeking thereby to legitimize their claims to imperial sovereignty. Although the Chalukyas and the Rashtrakutas did this symbolically, probably through their insignia, the Cholas literally transported pots of Ganges water to their southern capital.[65] And, we are told, so did Muhammad bin Tughluq in the years after 1327, when that sultan established Daulatabad, in Maharashtra, as the new co-capital of the Delhi Sultanate's vast, all-India empire.[66] In having Ganges water carried a distance of forty days' journey from north India 'for his own personal use,' the sultan was conforming to an authentically Indian imperial ritual. Several centuries later, the Muslim sultans of Bengal, on the occasion of their own coronation ceremonies, would wash themselves with holy water that had been brought to their capital from the ancient holy site of Ganga Sagar, located where the Ganges River emptied into the Bay of Bengal.[67]

No Indo-Muslim chronicle or contemporary inscription associates the use of Ganges water with the establishment or maintenance of Indo-Muslim states. We hear this only from foreign visitors: an Arab traveller in the case of Muhammad bin Tughluq, a Portuguese friar in the case of the sultans of Bengal. Similarly, the image of a Mughal

---

[65] Davis, *Lives*, 71–6.

[66] Husain, *Rehla of Ibn Battuta*, 4.

[67] Sebastião Manrique, *Travels of Fray Sebastien Manrique, 1629–1643*, trans. E. Luard and H. Hosten (Oxford: Hakluyt Society, 1927), 1:77.

official seated in a canopied chariot and presiding over the Jagannath car festival comes to us not from Mughal chronicles but from an English traveller who happened to be in Puri in 1633.[68] Such disjunctures between the rhetoric and the practice of royal sovereignty also appear, of course, with respect to the founding of non-Muslim states. We know, for example, that Brahman ideologues, writing in chaste Sanskrit, spun elaborate tales of how warriors and sages founded the Vijayanagara state by combining forces for a common defense of *dharma* from assaults by barbaric (*mleccha*) Turkic outsiders. This is the Vijayanagara of rhetoric, a familiar story. But the Vijayanagara of practical politics rested on very different foundations, which included the adoption of the titles, the dress, the military organization, the ruling ideology, the architecture, the urban design, and the political economy of the contemporary Islamic world.[69] As with Indo-Muslim states, we hear of such practices mainly from outsiders—merchants, diplomats, travellers—and not from Brahman chroniclers and ideologues.

CONCLUSION

One often hears that between the thirteenth and eighteenth centuries, Indo-Muslim states, driven by a Judeo-Islamic 'theology of iconoclasm,' by fanaticism, or by sheer lust for plunder, wantonly and indiscriminately indulged in the desecration of Hindu temples. Such a picture cannot, however, be sustained by evidence from original sources for the period after 1192. Had instances of temple desecration been driven by a 'theology of iconoclasm,' as some have claimed,[70] such a theology would have committed Muslims in India to destroying all temples everywhere, including ordinary village temples, as opposed to the highly selective operation that seems actually to have taken place. Rather, the original data associate instances of temple desecration with the annexation of newly conquered territories held by enemy kings whose domains lay on the path of moving military frontiers. Temple desecrations also occurred when Hindu patrons of prominent temples committed acts of treason or disloyalty to the Indo-Muslim states they served. Otherwise,

---

[68] P. Acharya, 'Bruton's Account of Cuttack and Puri,' in *Orissa Historical Research Journal* 10, no. 3 (1961), 46.

[69] See Phillip B. Wagoner, '"Sultan among Hindu Kings": Dress, Titles, and the Islamicization of Hindu Culture at Vijayanagara,' *Journal of Asian Studies* 55, no. 4 (Nov. 1996), 851–80; *idem.*, 'Harihara, Bukka, and the Sultan: the Delhi Sultanate in the Political Imagination of Vijayanagara,' in the Political Imagination of Vijayanagara,' in David Gilmartin and Bruce B. Lawrence, eds., *Beyond Turk and Hindu: Rethinking Religious Identities in Islamicate South Asia* (Gainesville: University Press of Florida, 2000), 300–26.

[70] See Wink, *al-Hind*, 2:294–333.

temples lying within Indo-Muslim sovereign domains, viewed normally as protected state property, were left unmolested.

Finally, it is important to identify the different meanings that Indians invested in religious monuments, and the different ways these monuments were understood to relate to political authority. In the reign of Aurangzeb, Shaikh Muhammadi took refuge in a mosque believing that that structure—being fundamentally apolitical, indeed above politics—lay beyond the Mughal emperor's reach. Contemporary royal temples, on the other hand, were understood to be highly charged political monuments, a circumstance that rendered them fatally vulnerable to outside attack. Therefore, by targeting for desecration those temples that were associated with defeated kings, conquering Turks, when they made their own bid for sovereign domain in India, were subscribing to, even while they were exploiting, indigenous notions of royal legitimacy. It is significant that contemporary inscriptions never identified Indo-Muslim invaders in terms of their religion, as Muslims, but most generally in terms of their linguistic affiliation (most typically as Turk, 'turushka'). That is, they were construed as but one ethnic community in India amidst many others.[71] In the same way, B. D. Chattopadhyaya locates within early medieval Brahmanical discourse an 'essential urge to legitimize' any ruling authority so long as it was effective and responsible. This urge was manifested, for example, in the perception of the Tughluqs as legitimate successors to the Tomaras and Cahamanas; of a Muslim ruler of Kashmir as having a lunar, Pandava lineage; or of the Mughal emperors as supporters of *Rāmarājya* (the 'kingship of Lord Rama').[72] It is likely that Indo-Muslim policies of protecting temples within their sovereign domains contributed positively to such perceptions.

In sum, by placing known instances of temple desecration in the larger contexts of Indo-Muslim state-building and state-maintenance, one can find patterns suggesting a rational basis for something commonly dismissed as irrational or worse. These patterns also suggest points of continuity with Indian practices that had become customary well before the thirteenth century. Such points of continuity in turn call into serious question the sort of civilizational divide between India's 'Hindu' and 'Muslim' periods first postulated in British colonial historiography and subsequently replicated in both Pakistani and Hindu nationalist schools. Finally, this essay has sought to identify the different meanings that

---

[71] See Talbot, 'Inscribing the Other,' 701.

[72] Brajadulal Chattopadhyaya, *Representing the Other? Sanskrit Sources and the Muslims (8th–14th century)* (New Delhi: Manohar, 1998), 49–50, 53, 60, 84.

contemporary actors invested in the public monuments they patronized or desecrated, and to reconstruct those meanings on the basis of the practice, and not just the rhetoric, of those actors. Hopefully, the approaches and hypotheses suggested here might facilitate the kind of responsible and constructive discussion that this controversial topic so badly needs.

INSTANCES OF TEMPLE DESECRATION, 1192–1760

(e) = emperor (s) = sultan (g) = governor (c) = commander
(p) = crown prince

No.	Date	Site	District	State	Agent	Source
For nos. 1–24, see Map 2a: Imperialism of the Delhi Sultanate, 1192–1394						
1	1193	Ajmer	Ajmer	Rajast.	Md. Ghuri (s)	23:215
2	1193	Samana	Patiala	Punjab	Aibek	23:216–17
3	1193	Kuhram	Karnal	Haryana	Aibek (g)	23:216–17
4	1193	Delhi		U.P.	Md. Ghuri (s)	1(1911):13 23:217,222
5	1194	Kol	Aligarh	U.P.	Ghurid army	23:224
6	1194	Benares	Benares	U.P.	Ghurid army	23:223
7	c.1202	Nalanda	Patna	Bihar	Bakhtiyar Khalaji (c)	20:90
8	c.1202	Odantapuri	Patna	Bihar	Bakhtiyar Khalaji	22:319; 21:551–2
9	c.1202	Vikramasila	Saharsa	Bihar	Bakhtiyar Khalaji	22:319
10	1234	Bhilsa	Vidisha	M.P.	Iltutmish (s)	21:621–2
11	1234	Ujjain	Ujjain	M.P.	Iltutmish	21:622–3
12	1290	Jhain	Sawai Madh.	Rajast.	Jalal al-Din Khalaji (s)	27:146
13	1292	Bhilsa	Vidisha	M.P.	'Ala al-Din Khalaji (g)	27:148
14	1298– 1310	Vijapur	Mehsana	Gujarat	Khalaji invaders	2(1974): 10–12
15	1295	Devagiri	Aurang- abad	Mahara.	'Ala al-Din Khalaji (g)	24:543
16	1299	Somnath	Junagadh	Gujarat	Ulugh Khan (c)	25:75
17	1301	Jhain	Sawai Madh.	Rajast.	'Ala al-Din Khalaji (s)	25:75–6
18	1311	Chidamb- aram	South Arcot	Tamil Nadu	Malik Kafur (c)	25:90–1

19	1311	Madurai	Madurai	Tamil Nadu	Malik Kafur	25:91
20	c.1323	Warangal	Warangal	A.P.	Ulugh Khan (p)	33:1–2
21	c.1323	Bodhan	Nizama-bad	A.P.	Ulugh Khan	1(1919–20): 16
22	c.1323	Pillalamarri	Nalgonda	A.P.	Ulugh Khan	17:114
23	1359	Puri	Puri	Orissa	Firuz Tughluq (s)	26:314
24	1392–93	Sainthali	Gurgaon	Haryana	Bahadur K. Nahar (c)	3(1963–64): 146

For nos. 25–55, see Map 2b: Growth of Regional Sultanates, 1394–1600

25	1394	Idar	Sabar-K.	Gujarat	Muzaffar Khan (g)	14–3:177
26	1395	Somnath	Junagadh	Gujarat	Muzaffar Khan	6–4:3
27	c.1400	Paraspur	Srinagar	Kashmir	Sikandar (s)	14–3:648
28	c.1400	Bijbehara	Srinagar	Kashmir	Sikandar	34:54
29	c.1400	Tripuresvara	Srinagar	Kashmir	Sikandar	34:54
30	c.1400	Martand	Anantnag	Kashmir	Sikandar	34:54
31	1400–1	Idar	Sabar-K.	Gujarat	Muzaffar Shah (s)	14–3:181
32	1400–1	Diu	Amreli	Gujarat	Muzaffar Shah	6–4:5
33	1406	Manvi	Raichur	Karn.	Firuz Bahmani (s)	2(1962): 57–8
34	1415	Sidhpur	Mehsana	Gujarat	Ahmad Shah (s)	29:98–9
35	1433	Delwara	Sabar-K.	Gujarat	Ahmad Shah	14–3: 220–1
36	1442	Kumbhalmir	Udaipur	Rajast.	Mahmud Khalaji (s)	14–3:513
37	1457	Mandalgarh	Bhilwara	Rajast.	Mahmud Khalaji	6–4:135
38	1462	Malan	Banaska-ntha	Gujarat	'Ala al-Din Suhrab (c)	2(1963): 28–9
39	1473	Dwarka	Jamnagar	Gujarat	Mahmud Begdha (s)	14–3: 259–61
40	1478	Kondapalle	Krishna	A.P.	Md. II Bahmani (s)	6–2:306
41	c.1478	Kanchi	Chingle-put	Tamil Nadu	Md. II Bahmani	6–2:308

42	1505	Amod	Broach	Gujarat	Khalil Shah (g)	1(1933): 36
43	1489–1517	Nagarkot	Kangra	Him. P.	Khawwas Khan (g)	35:81
44	1507	Utgir	Sawai Madh.	Rajast.	Sikandar Lodi (s)	14–1:375
45	1507	Narwar	Shivpuri	M.P.	Sikandar Lodi	14–1:378
46	1518	Gwalior	Gwalior	M.P.	Ibrahim Lodi (s)	14–1:402
47	1530–31	Devarkonda	Nalgonda	A.P.	Quli Qutb Shah (s)	6–3:212
48	1552	Narwar	Shivpuri	M.P.	Dilawar Kh. (g)	4(Jun 1927): 101–4
49	1556	Puri	Puri	Orissa	Sulaiman Karrani (s)	28:413–15
50	1575–76	Bankapur	Dharwar	Karn.	'Ali 'Adil Shah (s)	6–3:82–4
51	1579	Ahobilam	Kurnool	A.P.	Murahari Rao (c)	6–3:267
52	1586	Ghoda	Poona	Mahara.	Mir Md. Zaman (?)	1:(1933–34): 24
53	1593	Cuddapah	Cuddapah	A.P.	Murtaza Khan (c)	6–3:274
54	1593	Kalihasti	Chittoor	A.P.	I'tibar Khan (c)	6–3:277
55	1599	Srikurman	Visakh.	A.P.	Qutb Shahi general	32–5:1312

For nos. 56–80, see Map 2c: Expansion and Reassertions of Mughal Authority, 1600–1760

56	1613	Pushkar	Ajmer	Rajast.	Jahangir (e)	5:254
57	1632	Benares	Benares	U.P.	Shah Jahan (e)	31:36
58	1635	Orchha	Tikam-garh	M.P.	Shah Jahan	7:102–3
59	1641	Srikakulam	Srikaku-lam	A.P.	Sher Md. Kh. (c)	3(1953–54): 68–9
60	1642	Udayagiri	Nellore	A.P.	Ghazi 'Ali (c)	8:1385–86
61	1653	Poonamalle	Chingle-put	Tamil Nadu	Rustam b. Zulfiqar (c)	1(1937–38):53n2

62	1655	Bodhan	Nizama-bad	A.P.	Aurangzeb (p, g)	1(1919–20): 16
63	1659	Tuljapur	Osmana-bad	Mahara.	Afzal Khan (g)	16:9–10
64	1661	Kuch Bihar	Kuch Bihar	W. Beng.	Mir Jumla (g)	9:142–3
65	1662	Devalgaon	Sibsagar	Assam	Mir Jumla	9:154, 156–57
66	1662	Garhgaon	Sibsagar	Assam	Mir Jumla	36:249
67	1664	Gwalior	Gwalior	M.P.	Mu'tamad Khan (g)	10:335
68	1667	Akot	Akola	Mahara.	Md. Ashraf (c)	2(1963): 53–54
69	1669	Benares	Benares	U.P.	Aurangzeb (e)	11:65–8; 13:88
70	1670	Mathura	Mathura	U.P.	Aurangzeb	12:57–61
71	1679	Khandela	Sikar	Rajast.	Darab Khan (g)	12:107; 18:449
72	1679	Jodhpur	Jodhpur	Rajast.	Khan Jahan (c)	18:786; 12:108
73	1680	Udaipur	Udaipur	Rajast.	Ruhullah Khan (c)	15:129–30; 12:114–15
74	1680	Chitor	Chitor-garh	Rajast.	Aurangzeb	12:117
75	1692	Cuddapah	Cuddapah	A.P.	Aurangzeb	1(1937–38): 55
76	1697–98	Sambhar	Jaipur	Rajast.	Shah Sabz 'Ali (?)	19:157
77	1698	Bijapur	Bijapur	Karn.	Hamid al-Din Khan (c)	12:241
78	1718	Surat	Surat	Gujarat	Haidar Quli Khan (g)	1(1933):42
79	1729	Cumbum	Kurnool	A.P.	Muhammad Salih (g)	2(1959–60): 65
80	1729	Udaipur	West	Tripura	Murshid Quli Khan	30:7

SOURCES

1: *Epigraphia Indo-Moslemica*
2: *Epigraphia Indica, Arabic & Persian Supplement*
3: *Annual Report of Indian Epigraphy*
4: *Indian Antiquary*
5: Jahangir, *Tuzuk-i-Jahangiri*, tr. A. Rogers, (Delhi, 1968), v. 1
6: Firishta, *Tarikh-i Firishta* tr. J. Briggs, *History of the Rise of the Mahomedan Power in India* (Calcutta, 1971), 4 vols.

7: Kanbo, '*Amal-i Salih* (text: Lahore, 1967), v. 2

8: A. Butterworth and V.V. Chetty. *A Collection of the Inscriptions on Copper-Plates & Stones in the Nellore District* (Madras, 1905), v. 3

9: Khafi Khan, *Khafi Khan's History of 'Alamgir*, tr. S.M. Haq (Karachi, 1975)

10: A. Cunningham, *Four Reports Made during 1862-65* (Varanasi, 1972)

11: S.N. Sinha, *Subah of Allahabad under the Great Mughals* (New Delhi, 1974)

12: Saqi Must'ad Khan, *Maasir-i 'Alamgiri*, tr. J. Sarkar (Calcutta, 1947)

13: Saqi Must'ad Khan, *Maasir-i 'Alamgiri* (text: Calcutta, 1871)

14: Nizamuddin Ahmad, *Tabaqat-i Akbari*, tr. B. De (Calcutta, 1973), 3 vols.

15: Ishwardas Nagar, *Futuhat-i 'Alamgiri*, tr. T. Ahmad (Delhi, 1978)

16: Surendranath Sen, ed. & tr., *Siva Chhatrapati* (Calcutta, 1920), v. 1

17: P. Sreenivasachar, ed., *Corpus of Inscriptions in the Telingana Districts of H.E.M. the Nizam's Dominions*, pt. 2 (Hyderabad, 1940)

18: Shah Nawaz Khan, *Maathir-ul-Umara*, tr. H. Beveridge (Patna, 1979), v. 1

19: Z.A. Desai, *Published Muslim Inscriptions of Rajasthan* (Jaipur, 1971)

20: G. Roerich, tr., *Biography of Dharmaswamin* (Patna, 1959)

21: Minhaj-i Siraj, *Tabakat-i Nasiri*, tr. H. Raverty (New Delhi, 1970), v. 1

22: Chattopadhyaya, D., ed., *Taranatha's History of Buddhism in India* (Calcutta, 1980)

23: Hasan Nizami, *Taj al-ma'athir*, in Elliot & Dowson, History, v. 2

24: Amir Khusrau, *Miftah al-futuh*, in Elliot & Dowson, *History*, v. 3

25: Amir Khusrau, *Khaza'in al-futuh*, in Elliot & Dowson, *History*, v. 3

26: Shams-i Siraj, *Tarikh-i Firuz Shahi*, in Elliot & Dowson, *History*, v. 3

27: Zia al-Din Barani, *Tarikh-i Firuz Shahi*, in Elliot & Dowson, *History*, v. 3

28: Khwajah Ni'mat Allah, *Tarikh-i Khan-Jahani wa makhzan-i-Afghani* (text: Dacca, 1960), v. 1

29: Sikandar bin Muhammad, *Mirat-i Sikandari*, in E.C. Bayley, *Local Muhammadan Dynasties: Gujarat*, ed. N Singh (repr. New Delhi, 1970)

30: Azad al-Husaini, *Nau-Bahar-i Murshid Quli Khani*, tr., Jadu Nath Sarkar, *Bengal Nawabs* (1952, repr. Calcutta, 1985)

31: 'Abd al-Hamid Lahori, *Badshah-nama*, in Elliot & Dowson, *History*, v. 7

32: *South Indian Inscriptions* (New Delhi: Archaeological Survey of India)

33: George Michell, 'City as Cosmogram,' *South Asian Studies* 8 (1992)

34: Jonaraja, *Rajatarangini*, ed. S.L. Sadhu, trans. J.C. Dutt (repr. New Delhi, 1993)

35: Iqtidar Husain Siddiqui, tr., *Waqi'at-e-Mushtaqui of Shaikh Rizq Ullah Mushtaqui* (New Delhi, 1993)

36: Jagadish Narayan Sarkar, *Life of Mir Jumla* (Calcutta, 1952)

5

(Re)imag(in)ing Other²ness:
A Postmortem for the Postmodern in India[*]

East is East and West is West, and never the twain shall meet.
—R. Kipling, 1889

Colonialism seems to have created much of what is accepted as
Indian "tradition".
—N. Dirks, 1989

I

This essay raises a number of questions on recent trends in the writing of Indian history. First, how can one account for the appearance of post-modernist thought and postcolonial criticism in Indian historiography? Second, what has been the history of this encounter? And third, how has our understanding of Indian history in the 'postcolonial,' the 'colonial', or the 'precolonial' periods been influenced by these perspectives and critiques?

The appearance of post-modernist influences in the writing of Indian history is related to the evolution of the highly influential Subaltern Studies movement, launched in Calcutta in 1982. Scholars contributing to early issues of the movement's publication, *Subaltern Studies*, were collectively concerned with restoring voice and agency to those classes of India's non-elite 'subalterns'—peasants, industrial workers, women, and tribals, among others—that had been excluded from previous historiographical traditions. The first three issues of *Subaltern Studies* presented a number of meticulously researched case studies of peasants, workers, and other such groups acting assertively, even if unsuccessfully, on behalf of liberating Indians from the social, political,

* Reprinted from *Journal of World History* 11, no. 1 (Spring, 2000), 57–78.

and ideological snares of colonialism. Sustained by an extraordinary sense of commitment, members of the Subaltern Studies Collective revitalized the writing of Indian history as perhaps no such movement had done before. Moreover, since most of their case studies unearthed new historical materials, early contributors made enormous contributions to our knowledge of nineteenth and twentieth century Indian history even while radically challenging earlier models of that history.

Post-modernism, of course, had very different origins. The growth of an intellectual tradition of experiential and epistemological decenteredness is at least indirectly associated with the explosion of global capitalism and transnational corporations that occurred in the 1980s. At that time, as a result of economic measures taken by European and American governments that radically loosened national controls on the export of capital, together with the collapse of the Soviet economic system and the opening of previously closed economies in China, Latin America, and India itself, capitalism became divorced from its historic origins in Europe.[1] These developments had momentous socio-cultural consequences everywhere. For the 'Western world,' two familiar cosmological anchors were at once swept away. The first was the paradigm of a single planet divided into three territorially fixed and mutually exclusive components according to ideological or economic criteria: the First, the Second, and the Third World. With capital now radically transnationalized, and the Second World having disappeared altogether, the geopolitical cosmology with which several generations of Americans grew up lost its explanatory power; while instead, elements of all three 'worlds' were found everywhere.[2] Second, the linear story of capitalism, formerly a Euro-American narrative linked intellectually to bourgeois liberal and classical Marxist thought, and tied educationally to the growth of Western Civilization courses taught in American colleges and universities from World War I onward, was seriously discredited. Yet no alternative grand narrative emerged to replace the linked doctrines of the Three Worlds, the promise of an emerging Marxist utopia, or the story of Western Civilization with its happy ending in the Euro-American Age of Modernity.

More generally, as Anne McClintock has argued, what collapsed in the mid-1980s was the notion of 'progress' as a linear teleology that

[1] Arif Dirlik, 'The Postcolonial Aura: Third World Criticism in the Age of Global Capitalism,' *Critical Inquiry* 20, no. 2 (Winter, 1994), 348–56. See also Simon During, 'Postmodernism or Postcolonialism?' *Landfall* 39/3 (Sept. 1985), 368.

[2] Aijaz Ahmad, *In Theory: Classes, Nations, Literatures* (London: Verso, 1992), 95–105, and ch. 8.

underlay both the capitalist and the socialist worldviews.[3] This collapse carried with it the long-venerated tripartite periodization of European history in terms of Ancient-Medieval-Modern, such that for the first time in centuries it became conceptually impossible to theorize present or future time—except, that is, in reference to the unhinged chronological space coming *after* the last of these three eras. Hence, the term 'post-modern'. It was such an origin that endowed the term with notions of decenteredness, which is but the spatial equivalent to temporal nowhereness. Filling as it did an empty conceptual niche, just as the idea of the 'Third World' did at the onset of the Cold War,[4] post-modernism from the mid-1980s on swiftly became what McClintock has called 'a dazzling marketing success'.[5] Having evolved its own jargon and distinctive patterns of word-play (not to mention a baffling and often impenetrable prose style), the new movement spread like wildfire within the towers of academe, especially within English departments, but also in the softer and more interpretive of social sciences such as anthropology and history. By the 1990s it began spilling outside academe; the title of the lead article in a recent issue of *Harper's Magazine*, for example, speaks of 'post-modern sex'—whatever that might be.[6]

In point of theoretical orientations, the Subalternist and post-moder-nist intellectual traditions differed profoundly. While the former centered agency and voice on a very specific group—the marginalized, subaltern classes—the other diffused and decentered agency and relativized knowle-dge in such a way as to question the possibility of any stable voice or collective consciousness among any social class. And while early Sub-alternist historians viewed history in terms of the liberation and self-realization of subaltern classes, postmodernists challenged the linear and teleological structures that underlay all the metanarratives of modern Indian history. The Colonial narrative, from their perspective, was self-evidently teleological and Eurocentric, while the Nationalist narrative, though assigning important roles to some Indian elites, had used European tropes of Reason and Progress to explain the transition from British to Indian rule and hence could not be embraced as authentically

---

[3] Anne McClintock, 'The Angel of Progress: Pitfalls of the Term "Postcolonial",' *Social Text* 31/32 (1992), 96.

[4] Carl Pletsch, 'The Three Worlds, or the Division of Social Scientific Labor, circa 1950–75,' *Comparative Studies in Society and History* 23/4 (Oct. 1981), 565–90.

[5] McClintock, 'Angel of Progress,' 93.

[6] Edwin Dobb, 'A Kiss is Still a Kiss (Even if the Sex is Postmodern and the Romance Problematic),' *Harper's Magazine* 292, No. 1749 (Feb. 1996), 35.

Indian. And Marxism deployed a universalist mode-of-production narrative that was dismissed as both teleological and Europe-derived.[7]

. In view of these profound differences in intellectual orientation, one might never have predicted that post-modernist perspectives would have made inroads in the Subaltern Studies Collective. By the mid-1980s, however, members of that group had begun re-reading already-known materials with a view to capturing their discursive modes and structures. This strategy had the effect of shifting the group from a positivist and empiricist orientation to one grounded more squarely in a literary criticism which draped itself in the banner of an amorphous, obscurantist phrasing: cultural studies. Disdaining the old tasks of literary criticism (which were after all honest and straightforward and never claimed to be speaking for global cultures or transnational discourse), self-styled 'cultural critics' became the trendy mint-masters of ambiguity and diversity. Bernard Cohn's essay in the 1985 volume of *Subaltern Studies*, 'The Command of Language and the Language of Command,' was, as the author acknowledged, 'obviously influenced by the work of Michel Foucault'.[8] And in the same volume Gayatri Spivak criticized Subalternist historians for having adopted positivist methodologies and for treating the objects of their research—the subaltern classes—as enduring, essentialized categories, suggesting that the quest for a subaltern consciousness by these scholars had been misplaced and perhaps even futile. Nonetheless, Prof. Spivak, herself a literary critic, urged historians to continue their efforts to recover subaltern consciousness even while knowing this was impossible, and to do so by deploying 'a *strategic* use of positivist essentialism in a scrupulously visible political interest'.[9] Articles in subsequent volumes of *Subaltern Studies* reflected the new discursive approaches pioneered in the 1985 volume, while an increasing number of historians of India—both in Indian and Euro-American circles, and both inside and outside the Subalternist Collective—began

[7] Gyan Prakash, 'Postcolonial Criticism and Indian Historiography,' *Social Text* 31–2 (1992), 8.

[8] Bernard S. Cohn, 'The Command of Language and the Language of Command,' in Ranajit Guha, ed., *Subaltern Studies IV: Writings on South Asian History and Society* (Delhi: Oxford University Press, 1985), 284.

[9] Gayatri Chakravorty Spivak, 'Subaltern Studies: Deconstructing Historiography,' in Ranajit Guha, ed., *Subaltern Studies: Writings on South Asian History and Society*, IV (Delhi: Oxford University Press, 1985), 342. Emphasis in the original. 'I read *Subaltern Studies* against the grain,' wrote Spivak, 'and suggest that its own subalternity in claiming a *positive* subject-position for the subaltern might be reinscribed as a strategy for our times.' Ibid., 345.

incorporating post-modernist perspectives into their scholarship.[10] Typically, the method was to read historical records 'against the grain,' with a view to turning up new interpretations of elite projects, new evidence of smothered subaltern voices, or of counter-identities elaborated by marginalized intellectuals.[11]

II

How can one explain the reception of post-modernist methodologies by the most vital school of modern South Asian history at the very moment that the Subaltern School was at its height of influence in rewriting Indian history? A clue, I think, is found in the movement's original agenda as proclaimed by its founder, Ranajit Guha, in a manifesto that appeared in the first issue of *Subaltern Studies*:

It is the study of this historic failure of the nation to come into its own, a failure due to the inadequacy of the bourgeoisie as well as the working class to lead it into a decisive victory over colonialism...—it is the study of this failure which constitutes the central problematic of the historiography of colonial India.[12]

By focusing the movement's agenda on the study of a failure, that is to say, a non-event, Guha in effect led the Subaltern Studies project into a well-known historical fallacy—that of explaining a counter-factual proposition. At the same time, in addition to noting heroic but failed instances of resistance to colonial domination, the stress on studying failures led inevitably to the need to account for them. And post-modernism, to the extent that it cast the subalterns' failures in terms of the ability of discursive regimes of power to coopt Indian social classes, seems to have met that need. One can see, moreover, how an emphasis on discourse analysis could have appealed to marginalized leftist intellectuals at a time when the political Left everywhere felt

[10] Prominent among these were Arjan Appadurai, Carol Breckenridge, Dipesh Chakrabarti, Partha Chatterjee, Bernard Cohn, Nicholas Dirks, Ronald Inden, Lata Mani, Gyan Prakash, Peter van der Veer, and Gauri Viswanathan. See footnotes for references.

[11] Florencia Mallon, 'The Promise and Dilemmas of Subaltern Studies,' *American Historical Review* 99, No. 5 (Dec. 1994), 1506. A good example of this sort of scholarship is found in the volume of essays edited by Partha Chatterjee, *Texts of Power: Emerging Disciplines in Colonial Bengal* (Minneapolis: University of Minnesota Press, 1995).

[12] Ranajit Guha, in *Subaltern Studies: Writings on South Asian History and Society*, 1 (Delhi: Oxford University Press, 1982), 7.

beleaguered and in retreat.[13] 'The interpretive turn,' notes Meera Nanda, 'allows the left to create in discourse what it is unable to realize in the rough and tumble of real politics: a world where all ideologies have been deconstructed, revealed, and readied for overthrow; a world where all can live by their own lights.'[14] The turn to discourse studies also served an implicit Indian nationalist purpose inasmuch as it shifted blame for the subalterns' persistent failures from Indians onto the British, who were the ultimate authors of the discourse of colonial power.[15]

But the effort to harmonize post-modernist methods of textual and literary analysis with the radical politics that had informed the early Subalternist movement nonetheless proved difficult, to say the least. At the second meeting of the Subalternist Collective, held in Calcutta in January 1986, the split erupted in the open. On the one hand was the desire to discover and celebrate the radical politics of non-elites understood as autonomous actors in their own right; on the other, the desire to expose the discursive formulations— 'colonial discourse,' as it came to be known—through which British rule actually operated. Concretely, things boiled down to whether 'the subaltern' possessed his or her own voice, or whether such voice was inevitably smothered or coopted by powerful domains of imperial discourse.[16] In 1992 Rosalind O'Hanlon and David Washbrook drew attention to this tension, remarking metaphorically that one could not simultaneously ride two horses—one, a belief in fundamental rights embracing the possibility of human emancipation, and the other a post-modernist relativism that rejected any 'foundational' ground on which such rights could rest.

[13] Sumit Sarkar has suggested that 'an obsessive focus on the totalizing nature of power relations' may be traced to the dousing of radical hopes in the aftermath of Vietnam and May 1968, and more recently, in today's context of a unipolar world. See Sumit Sarkar, 'Orientalism Revisited: Saidian Frameworks in the Writing of Modern Indian History,' *Oxford Literary Review* 16 (1994), 208.

[14] 'The inverse relationship between an explosion of high theory and a decline in political efficacy,' Nanda added, 'appears to be as true today as it was when Perry Anderson first observed it nearly two decades ago in his *Considerations of Western Marxism.*' Meera Nanda, 'The Science Wars in India,' *Dissent* (Winter, 1997), 78.

[15] As C. A. Bayly noted, 'in a paragraph from the much-quoted CID report on the Kisan Sabha which does not find its way into the analysis in *Subaltern Studies* the writer remarks that it is "only a very foolish landlord who cannot build up a party to support him in his own villages."' C. A. Bayly, 'Rallying Around the Subaltern,' *Journal of Peasant Studies* 16 (Oct., 1988), 119.

[16] This issue is explored in detail in Rosalind O'Hanlon, 'Recovering the Subject: *Subaltern Studies* and Histories of Resistance in Colonial South Asia,' *Modern Asian Studies* 22/1 (1998), 189–224.

But Gyan Prakash responded to this challenge by insisting that for his own part, he would 'hang on to two horses, inconstantly'.[17] But was it really possible to straddle two opposing intellectual positions?

This tension never disappeared; indeed, it surfaced repeatedly, such as at a conference held at Ann Arbor on 'Colonialism and Culture'. Recalled Nicholas Dirks, the conference organizer, 'We kept trying to find new ways to rescue subaltern voices among the colonized, only to find that colonialism was about the history by which categories such as the colonizer as well as the colonized, elite as well as subaltern, became established and deployed.'[18] In marked contrast to the efforts of the early Subalternist Collective, Dirks then added, 'And while not wishing to align our scholarship with power itself, many of us feared that the glorification of resistance trivialized the all-pervasive character of power, particularly in colonial regimes.'[19] For many conference participants, in other words, an all-pervasive colonial power had smothered the very subaltern classes whose voices and agency the founders of the Subaltern Collective had so earnestly sought to recover. In both America and India, the study of such marginalized classes as constituted the original 'subalterns' was thus gradually replaced by the study of the discourses of the elite groups who dominated them, as in Gauri Viswanathan's argument that British colonial hegemony in India rested ultimately on the teaching of English literature, and not on the exercise of direct force.[20] As Ramachandra Guha sardonically observed, subaltern studies had become 'bhadralok studies,' that is, the study of elites.[21]

Although some scholars today continue to write Indian history from within a post-modernist framework, from the early 1990s the movement

---

[17] Rosalind O'Hanlon and David Washbrook, 'After Orientalism: Culture, Criticism and Politics in the Third World,' *Comparative Studies in Society and History* 34 (1992), 141–67; Gyan Prakash, 'Can the 'Subaltern' Ride? A Reply to O'Hanlon and Washbrook,' in ibid., 168–84. Elsewhere Prakash argues that while it is tempting to see the discovery of discourses and texts as an abandonment of the search for subaltern groups, 'subalterns and subalternity do not disappear into discourse but appear in its interstices, subordinated by structures over which they exert pressure.' Gyan Prakash, 'Subaltern Studies as Postcolonial Criticism,' *American Historical Review* 99, no. 5 (Dec., 1994), 1482.

[18] Nicholas Dirks, ed., *Colonialism and Culture* (Ann Arbor: University of Michigan Press, 1992), p. 14.

[19] Ibid.

[20] Gauri Viswanathan, *Masks of Conquest: Literary Study and British Rule in India* (New York: Columbia University Press, 1989).

[21] Ramachandra Guha, 'Subaltern and Bhadralok Studies,' *Economic and Political Weekly* (August 19, 1995), 2056–8.

seems to have lost its vitality, at least within India. A key date here is 6 December 1992, when a frenzied mob of Hindu fundamentalists tore down the Baburi Masjid, a sixteenth century mosque in eastern Uttar Pradesh, believing that the Mughal emperor Babur had built the mosque on the site of the birthplace of the god Rama. Concerned Indian intellectuals realized that behind this act of vandalism lay the ominous threat of religious fascism, given Hindu fundamentalists' links with prominent political parties in India. And for some historians, the events of December 1992 made particularly urgent the need to understand the recent deterioration of Hindu-Muslim relations, and especially to historicize the Baburi Masjid incident and the widespread violence it touched off.[22] Put concretely, they asked the sort of questions that characteristically distinguish historians from other kinds of social scientists: they wanted to know 'Why here, and not there? Why now, and not then?'

Efforts to find answers to such questions, however, were logically doomed to failure when both time and space had been collapsed and annihilated by an all-pervasive, ahistorical discursive formulation.[23] In their 1993 book *Khaki Shorts and Saffron Flags*, Tapan Basu, Pradip Datta, Sumit Sarkar, Tanika Sarkar, and Sambuddha Sen sought to explain the historical origins the Hindu Right, noting:

Currently fashionable theories of overwhelmingly dominant 'colonial discourse' have furbished the [line of argument explaining Hindu-Muslim tensions in terms of British divide-and-rule strategies], replacing the conspiratorial by the structural. Western categories and modes of analysis (imposed via census operations, for instance) are held responsible for the cutting up of Indian society into distinct, often mutually opposed, blocs of religion, tribe, or caste.[24]

---

[22] 'Communalism,' write Ania Loomba and Suvir Kaul, 'is clearly one of the most urgent concerns for Indian activists and intellectuals today, and the need to understand and combat its vicious attributes has led, apart from much else, to a radical challenge to any simple dichotomy between nationalism and colonialism....' 'In the wake of the destruction of the Babri Masjid,' they add, 'more and more academics are making the connections between intellectual and activist work.' Editors' Introduction to Ania Loomba and Suvir Kaul, eds., 'On India: Writing History, Culture, Post-Coloniality,' *Oxford Literary Review* 16 (1994), 7 and note.

[23] This problem was noted as early as 1987, when Benita Parry observed that because colonial discourse analysis 'does not produce its own account of change, discontinuity, differential periods and particular social conflicts, there is a danger of distinctive moments being homogenized.' Benita Parry, 'Problems of Current Theories of Colonial Discourse,' *Oxford Literary Review* 9/1–2 (1987), 33–4.

[24] Tapan Basu, et al., *Khaki Shorts and Saffron Flags: A Critique of the Hindu Right* (New Delhi: Orient Longman, 1993), 5.

But, they asked, why did class tensions get distorted? Why did political manipulations succeed? And to what extent did a 'colonial discourse' really dominate the subcontinental mind? 'It may be observed,' they added, 'that a notion of an all-powerful colonial discourse tends to cast Indians in the role of simple victims and exempt them from their own initiative or agency.'[25]

Victims? Agency? But the original aim of the Subalternist Collective, one recalls, had been precisely to restore agency to India's non-elite classes and to promote an historiography that ceased making victims of such classes. What had happened? What had gone wrong? One way of approaching this problem is to examine what Sumit Sarkar, one of the Collective's original founders and later one of its most trenchant critics, has called 'the decline of the Subaltern in *Subaltern Studies*'.[26] Paralleling and contributing to that decline was the ascent of post-modernist perspectives in the study of Indian history, until the point where that 'intervention,' too, had reached a dead end. It reached this end, moreover, well before Alan Sokol's infamous 1996 hoax that exposed the inability of the Western academic post-modernist establishment to distinguish gibberish parody from serious argument.[27] What ultimately sealed the movement's fate was its manifest inability to make sense of recent events of monumental significance, in particular the rise of Hindu fundamentalism and of communal violence so appallingly concretized in the events of December 1992 and their aftermath.[28]

This, then, might be an appropriate time for a postmortem, for an assessment of the difficulties encountered in the effort to write Indian history using postmodernist methods. A modest list of such difficulties would include, in addition to an inability to account for specific events or movements, issues of agency, of essentialism, of Eurocentrism, the decline of field research, and the disappearance of pre-British history.

---

[25] Ibid.

[26] Sumit Sarkar, 'The Decline of the Subaltern in *Subaltern Studies*,' Ch. 3 of Sumit Sarkar, *Writing Social History* (Delhi: Oxford University Press, 1997), 82–108.

[27] Alan D. Sokal, 'Transgressing the Boundaries: Toward a Transformative Hermeneutics of Quantum Gravity,' *Social Text* 46–7 (1996), 217–52. See also 'Postmodern Gravity Deconstructed, Slyly,' *New York Times* (18 May, 1996), and 'Mystery Science Theater,' *Lingua Franca* (July–August, 1996), 54–64.

[28] '*Subaltern* historiography in general,' writes Sumit Sarkar, 'has faced considerable difficulties in tackling this phenomenon of a communal violence that is both popular and impossible to endorse. There is the further problem that the Hindu Right often attacks the secular, liberal nation-state as a Western importation, precisely the burden of much late-*Subaltern* argument....' Sarkar, 'Decline,' 107.

III

It seems clear that the first victim of post-modernism's advent in Indian historiography was the Indians' own agency, as the quote from Basu et al indicates. In the original Subalternist view, it was their possession of an active, autonomous agency that had enabled subaltern classes to resist imperial domination, and in resistance, to attain at least the possibility of liberation. This line of thinking is of course traceable to Marx, who had argued that it was only when proletarians become conscious of their objective class relations that they could or would do something about them. This in turn was why, for Marx, class consciousness provided the motor of historical change. Within the Subaltern Studies Collective, however, once the intellectual shift from Marx to Gramsci to Foucault had become more or less complete, agency itself had migrated from Indian subjects to monolithic fields of discursive power. Thus 'colonialism,' or rather an all-pervasive 'colonial discourse,' became not only an actor in its own right, but ultimately the only true actor in modern Indian history.[29] Studies appearing in the 1980s and 1990s seemed to suggest that the various social classes of British India were so enmeshed in webs of power and discourses of power, even to the extent of collaborating with the colonial state, that resistance to the colonial system was rendered ineffective or futile.[30] In retrospect, it seems ironic that historians, of all people, should have identified as the engine of history a discursive framework that, being itself ahistorical and structuralist, could not logically be used to explain anything that occurred in any specific time and place,[31] or indeed, to explain any

[29] Discussing the work of historians writing within what he calls a 'Saidian framework,' Sumit Sarkar notes that 'in such analyses all agency is now confined to colonialists, due to a highly simplified and homogenized conception of domination.' Sarkar, 'Orientalism,' 215.

[30] This problem, too, was first noted by Benita Parry, who wrote in 1987 that analytical strategies focusing on the deconstruction of the colonialist text 'either erase the voice of the native or limit native resistance to devices circumventing and interrogating colonial authority.' Parry, 'Problems,' 34. See also Sarkar, 'Decline,' 91.

[31] The tension between efforts to establish specific connections in order to explain historical particularities, and a reliance on totalizing discourses that purport to explain everything—and hence explain nothing—is discussed by John M. Mac-Kenzie. 'Above all,' writes MacKenzie of Edward Said's enormously influential literary output, and especially his book *Orientalism*, 'it is difficult for historians to find in all this work a single instance in which cultural artifacts are directly influenced by specific events or themselves have bearing on individual decision-making or developments in the European imperial relationship with particular

change whatsoever.[32] That is to say, 'colonial discourse' analysis proved quite useless to historians, and, as we have seen, was ultimately discarded by Indian scholars concerned with explaining quite specific events, such as the destruction of the Baburi Masjid and that incident's historical antecedents.

A second difficulty created by post-modernism's appearance in Indian historiography was its tendency to essentialize categories of analysis. Many observers noted the irony that scholars who decried the essentialism Europeans imputed to the 'Orient,' or to colonial India, failed to see the same sort of essentialism that they themselves were imputing to 'Europe,' or to European thought, as in one of Edward Said's formulations of Orientalism as a monolithic ideology, coherent and all-pervasive, extending from Homer to Henry Kissinger.[33] Some, to be sure, recognized the problem of essentializing Europe. Dipesh Chakrabarty, for one, observed in a 1992 essay that liberal-minded scholars would protest that 'any idea of a homogeneous, uncontested "Europe" dissolves under analysis'. But in the very next sentence, he asserted that 'just as the phenomenon of orientalism does not disappear simply because some of us have now attained a critical awareness of it, similarly, a certain version of 'Europe,' reified and celebrated in the phenomenal world of everyday relationships of power as the scene of the birth of the modern, continues to dominate the discourse of history. Analysis does not make it go away.'[34] Like Prakash, straddling his two horses, Chakrabarty moves uncertainly between two contradictory positions: at one moment analysis dissolves Europe, and at another it does not

---

territories, although such connections abound.' John M. MacKenzie, 'Edward Said and the Historians,' *Nineteenth-Century Contexts* 18/1 (1994), 20.

[32] Surveying the impact of post-modernism on the study of nineteenth century England, Richard Price writes, 'If meaning is understood as a never-ending series of discursive codes, texts behind texts (raising the question of infinite regress), and if relationships are essentially chaotic rather than structured, then the notion of change as a historical process as opposed to a matter of continual, shifting indeterminacy is both moot and unimportant.' Richard Price, 'Historiography, Narrative, and the Nineteenth Century,' *Journal of British Studies* 35/2 (April 1996), 238.

[33] See James Clifford's review of Edward Said's *Orientalism* in *History and Theory* 19 (1980), and Aijaz Ahmad, 'Between Orientalism and Historicism: Anthropological Knowledge of India,' *Studies in History* 7/1 (1991), 135–63. For an elaboration of this point, see John M. MacKenzie, *Orientalism: History, Theory and the Arts* (Manchester: Manchester University Press, 1995), Ch. 1.

[34] Dipesh Chakrabarty, 'Postcoloniality and the Artifice of History: Who speaks for "Indian" Pasts?', *Representations* 37 (1992), 1–2.

dissolve Europe. In short, even though trained historians seemed aware—at least more so than 'cultural critics'—of the dangers of essentializing Europe, the reliance on discursive strategies of writing history seems to have led ineluctably to the reification, and essentialization, of 'a certain version of "Europe"'.

In the late 1980s and early 1990s post-modernist concerns and perspectives gradually evolved into, and in many cases were replaced by, concerns of 'postcolonialism' and the so-called 'condition of post-coloniality'. Although the term 'postcolonial' actually dates to the early 1970s, when it appeared in the context of political theory,[35] its more recent deployment seems to have been related to changing configurations in the sociology of Western academe in the 1980s, and in particular, to the arrival in Euro-American universities of non-Western scholars of culture and cultural history.[36] In their uprooted and culturally alienated state,[37] many such 'diasporic' intellectuals repudiated post-modernism's tradition of decentredness and vigorously reaffirmed notions of centredness, difference, and cultural authenticity. Some saw themselves as 'incommensurable others' vis-à-vis Euro-America, or subscribed to the idea of an *a priori* and enduring Indian community, a *Gemeinschaft*, that had been suppressed by British colonialism and which had now to be recovered and celebrated—a sentiment traceable to nineteenth century European romanticism.[38] 'As the Western Other,'

---

[35] Aijaz Ahmad, 'Postcolonialism: What's in a Name?', in Roman de la Campa, E. Ann Kaplan, and M. Sprinker, eds, *Late Imperial Culture* (New York: Verso, 1995), 11–32.

[36] Dirlik, 'The Postcolonial Aura', 329. 'Postcoloniality,' wrote Kwame Anthony Appiah, 'is the condition of what we might ungenerously call a comprador intelligentsia: of a relatively small, Western-style, Western-trained, group of writers and thinkers who mediate the trade in cultural commodities of world capitalism at the periphery.' Kwame Anthony Appiah, *In My Father's House: Africa in the Philosophy of Culture* (New York: Oxford University Press, 1992), 149.

[37] Speaking on behalf of what Appiah calls the 'comprador intelligentsia,' Anouar Majid recently opined, 'Cultural imperialism is real, and the presence of the Third World [sic] intellectual in the West—despite the proverbial exceptions and other conscious complicities—is a stark manifestation of this reality. Yet no leftist or radical Western scholar seems to measure accurately the degree of our alienation, to read the exotic presence of the Other in the Academy as a reminder of our vulnerabilities and organic uprootedness....' Anouar Majid, 'Can the Postcolonial Critic Speak? Orientalism and the Rushdie Affair,' *Cultural Critique* 32 (Winter, 1995–96), 26–7.

[38] Thomas Blom Hansen, 'Inside the Romanticist Episteme,' *Thesis Eleven* 48 (February, 1997), 21–31, 35–6. Hansen finds this sentiment reflected most clearly in the work of Partha Chatterjee, who sees a suppressed narrative of community

writes Thomas Hansen, 'articulated through the colonial and post-colonial state is posited as alien, non-authentic and outside, the inside, that is the popular and subordinated, becomes, by implication, both authentic and original.'[39] Such politically conservative notions found an especially warm reception in an American intellectual climate suffused with identity politics, quests for ethnic authenticity, and the celebration of diversity and multiculturalism.[40]

The shift from the post-modern to the postcolonial thus represented a sharp return to the sort of all-embracing dichotomy between Europe and India that had characterized so much earlier history-writing on South Asia, including that written from within the early Subalternist paradigm.[41] Ultimately, of course, such a conceptual dichotomy is what had facilitated and justified European imperialism in India in the first place. It was in 1889, at the height of the British Raj, that Rudyard Kipling penned his infamous observation that 'East is East and West is West, and never the twain shall meet'. A century later, well after the dismantling of the Raj, the intellectual offspring of Edward Said gave new life to Kipling's sentiments by declaring and celebrating the same totalizing opposition, as in Nicholas Dirks's 1989 formulation that 'colonialism seems to have created much of what is accepted as Indian "tradition"'.[42] The difference was that while both Kipling and

---

in Hegel's notion of the nuclear family as the site of 'natural' solidarity and love (in the sense of the free surrender of individual wills). Whereas in Europe this narrative of community had been suppressed by the narrative of capital, Chatterjee argues, in India it was suppressed by British colonialism. See Partha Chatterjee, *The Nation and its Fragments: Colonial and Postcolonial Histories* (Princeton, N.J.: Princeton University Press, 1993), 230–9.

[39] Hansen, 'Inside,' 27. 'Postcolonialism,' writes Simon During, 'is the name for products of the ex-colonies' need for an identity granted not in terms of the colonial power, but in terms of themselves.... The postcolonial self knows itself in universal terms, that is, in terms of international centres, of a colonial past.' During, 'Postmodernism,' 369.

[40] Hansen suggests that the collapse of the Soviet Union as Euro-America's Other also facilitated a new and ironic form of Otherness. 'Post-coloniality,' he writes, 'seeks in part to fill this vacant position of the Other and to install the post-colonial world as the true Other of the West.' Hansen, 'Inside,' 35.

[41] As David Ludden notes, 'The many historians of modern South Asia who focus today on the cultural politics of colonialism, elitism, subordination, and resistance seem deeply committed to an all embracing dichotomy between India and Europe, and seven volumes of *Subaltern Studies* offer perspectives—"from below"—on Indian civilisation as it is defined inside this opposition.' David Ludden, 'History Outside Civilisation and the Mobility of South Asia,' *South Asia* 17/1 (1994), 2.

[42] Nicholas Dirks, 'The Invention of Caste: Civil Society in Colonial India,' *Social*

Dirks saw 'East' and 'West' as absolutely opposed, the 'East' in the postcolonialist view is understood as the creation of the 'West,' and more particularly, as the product of a European 'colonial discourse'.[43]

All of this injected into the intellectual climate winds that were distinctly conservative, Eurocentric, and ultimately neo-colonial.[44] One sees this in the postcolonialists' vigorous reaffirmation not only of a totalizing dichotomy between India and Europe, but also of linear time, which post-modernists, with their notions of decentered time and space, had earlier rejected.[45] Indeed, the postcolonialists' understanding of Indian time envisioned a linear periodization that, surpassing the crudest Orientalist schemes, privileged the European imperial Self. Even the Orientalists' triadic formulation of 'Hindu-Islamic-British,' while blatantly essentialist and statist in nature, had never gone so far as to privilege any one of these 'periods' such that the other two were seen in reference to it. But the notion of 'postcoloniality' situated *all* Indian time in reference to the British imperial period: time was either precolonial, colonial, or postcolonial. Indeed, even the dismantling of the Raj could not release India from colonial Britain's discursive grip.[46] Just as the early Subalternist and before them Nationalist historians had thought they had removed British actors from the limelight of Indian history, postcolonialist writers effectively brought those same actors back on stage, front and centre. Moreover, the terms they deployed for India's historical periodization have thoroughly taken hold of ordinary usage. Today, when one speaks of the 'colonial' period of Indian history, we all 'know' that it is the British colonial empire that is intended, as

---

Analysis 5 (Sept. 1989), 43.

[43] See note 51.

[44] It has been observed that the use of the term 'postcolonial' in the late twentieth century has served to obfuscate or disguise the continuing imperial presence of the United States or its clients in places like Cuba, Chile, Panama, Kuwait, Arabia, Afghanistan, or the West Bank. McClintock, 'Angel of Progress,' 89–91.

[45] 'The "post-colonial",' writes Ella Shohat, 'implies a narrative of progression in which colonialism remains the central point of reference in a march of time neatly arranged from the pre to the "post," but which leaves ambiguous its relations to new forms of colonialism, i.e. neo-colonialism.' Ella Shohat, 'Notes on the "Post-Colonial",' *Social Text* 31/32 (1992), 107.

[46] One of the postcolonial 'predicaments,' write Carol Breckenridge and Peter van der Veer, is that 'decolonization does not entail immediate escape from colonial discourse.' Carol A. Breckenridge and Peter van der Veer, eds, *Orientalism and the Postcolonial Predicament: Perspectives on South Asia* (Philadelphia: University of Pennsylvania Press, 1993), 2.

if there had never been any empire in India before Britain's.[47] Yet, because 'colonialism' has become synonymous with but one historical imperial formation, it became terminologically impossible to bring other such formations into the picture.

The distortions this created for theorizing Indian time were severe indeed and appear to have been rooted in the post-modernist belief that discourse not only precedes essence, but underpins, shapes, and determines it. Moreover, in view of the tight fit between discourse and power that lay at the heart of this line of thinking, inasmuch as the advent of the British colonial discourse coincided historically with the advent of its carriers, it followed that the history of India began epistemologically, and hence conceptually, with the British themselves. Before the advent of European colonial rule, India's past, to the extent that it was epistemologically accessible at all, presented a merely flat, two-dimensional screen, a period in which things might well have happened, but nothing could or did change in any meaningful way. 'History and colonialism,' writes Prakash, 'arose together in India. As India was introduced to history, it was also stripped of a meaningful past; it became a historyless society brought into the age of History.'[48]

The logic of post-modernism and postcolonialism thus ended up restating the old Orientalist position that for millennia India slumbered, awaiting its tryst with destiny when the English East India Company would arrive and give definition to this sleeping civilization. For example, if Orientalist scholars had interpreted the intellectual history of early nineteenth century Bengal positively in terms of an awakening to the fruits of Western knowledge, a colonial discourse analysis would interpret that same topic negatively in terms of an awakening to enslavement; yet both versions, as Sumit Sarkar has argued, assumed a one-way flow of inspiration or power and viewed the modern history of India in terms 'of total rupture or tabula rasa, with colonialism completely

---

[47] It is perhaps impossible at this late date to salvage the critical distinction between colonialism (from *colonus*, 'farmer') and imperialism (from *imperium*, 'the right to rule over'), which was clear enough to the ancient Romans, who, after all, practiced both forms of political control. That is, they sent out colonies of Roman farmers to colonize untilled territory, and they also sent out imperial armies to rule over existing non-Roman farming communities. Yet the continued use of 'colonial' in the sense of 'imperial' in the context of British India only impoverishes our vocabulary and deprives us of the sort of analytic tools essential for understanding the nature of this political formation, or for comparing it with other political formations in the history of India.

[48] Prakash, 'Postcolonial Criticism and Indian Historiography,' *Social Text* 31/32 (1992), 17.

remoulding such indigenous structures [as caste, gender, or class], making them dependent or derivative.'[49] Such a rupture is seen, for example, in a recent volume of essays edited by Nicholas Dirks, who observed that 'much of what we now recognize as culture was produced by the colonial encounter;' 'culture,' he notes, 'is a colonial formation.'[50]

Indeed, by such reasoning, ancient Indian institutions that had experienced enormous transformations during the many centuries preceding the advent of British rule either got washed out as timeless 'tradition' or interpreted as inventions of the Raj. Dirks concluded that the caste system, shaped and refashioned by colonial British rulers as an instrument of domination, was 'more a product of rule than a predecessor of it',[51] In this way, by extending the logic of 'imagined communities' and 'the invention of tradition' to its ultimate conclusion, post-modernist and postcolonialist critiques effectively annihilated all history and all historical process that preceded the advent of those who did the imagining and inventing, or anyway, of those whose imaginings or inventions were politically significant—the British and their native collaborators.[52] In effect, these critiques resolved into a simple model of Indian history strikingly reminiscent of the 1950s and 1960s, the heyday of modernization theory. A binary temporal division that in Walt Rostow's era had opposed 'tradition' and 'modernity' was now replaced by, and effectively identified with, a binary division opposing the 'precolonial' and the 'colonial'.

There was irony here. The Subaltern Studies Collective, a movement originally launched in an attempt to recover India's history from Colonial, Nationalist, and Marxist metanarratives, was ultimately taken over by an intellectual movement which, referring to the ways that power and discourse were mutually implicated, ended up *reaffirming* the overwhelming centrality of the British intrusion in India.[53] Still more ironic

49 Sarkar, 'Orientalism,' 208, 217.

50 Dirks, *Colonialism and Culture*, 3.

51 Ibid., 8. In an article provocatively entitled 'The Invention of Caste: Civil Society in Colonial India,' Dirks asserts that 'colonialism seems to have created much of what is now accepted as Indian "tradition", including an autonomous caste structure with the Brahman clearly and unambiguously at the head....' 'In order to rule an immensely complex society,' he continued, caste 'was appropriated, and reconstructed by the British.' Dirks, 'Invention of Caste,' 43.

52 'The "imagined communities" of Hindu and Muslim nationalism,' write Carol Breckenridge and Peter van der Veer, summarizing Arjun Appadurai, 'were produced in the colonial *imaginaire* as "enumerated communities".' Breckenridge and van der Veer, eds, *Orientalism*, 9.

53 This centrality is reinforced by the persistent tendency of literary studies of

was that, in academe's current spirit of political correctness and anti-imperialist rhetoric, people who seem to have thought they were exposing the wicked ends and means of British domination were instead placing the entire explanatory weight of India's long history and complex socio-cultural institutions on a European discursive formulation that deprived Indians themselves of agency or the ability to make their own history. Indeed, the notion of an enduring European imperial world became so pervasive that 'postcolonial' scholars, Indians and Westerners alike, even referred to academic institutions in present-day Europe and America as comprising 'the metropolitan academy,'[54] in contrast to the 'provincial' universities of Asia or Africa.[55]

Yet another victim of post-modernist historiography in India was empirical field work, an outcome that more or less followed from post-modernist epistemological assumptions. As Florencia Mallon recently observed, 'It is hard to return to the archive or the field after engaging in a post-modern critique of the transparency of the enterprise. If we are no longer looking for "truth" as irrefutable, clearly knowable information, what are we looking for?'[56] Indeed, the 1980s and 1990s saw a sharp drop from levels of earlier decades in the number of historians who applied for support or for permission to conduct research out in the *mufaṣṣal*—that is, in district archives, local libraries, private collections, zamindari records, etc. Most ended up in London, and a few in national or state archives in India, studying colonial records that were then subjected to discourse analysis.[57]

---

colonial encounters to privilege the European canon over non-European voices. This is why Dane Kennedy questions whether figures like Yeats or Fanon could be entirely representative of colonized peoples' reactions to colonial rule, as Edward Said has argued they are. Kennedy goes on to note the deeply Eurocentric character of recent studies of travel literature in European colonies. Dane Kennedy, 'Imperial History and Post-Colonial Theory,' *Journal of Imperial and Commonwealth History* 24/3 (September 1996), 355–6.

[54] Prakash, 'Postcolonial Criticism,' 10.

[55] Dirks, *Colonialism and Culture*, 12. As Arjun Appadurai and Carol Breckenridge write, 'the postcolonial pathologies of various colonial sites are again being globalized and retrojected into the politics of the metropolis.' Cited in Breckenridge and van der Veer, eds, *Orientalism*, 14.

[56] Mallon, 'Promises and Dilemmas,' 1506.

[57] Nor is it coincidental that scholarship on the pre-British history of South Asia has eroded in recent years. Of the 118 proposals submitted in the fall of 1996 to the American Institute of Indian Studies, the principal U.S. institution supporting American scholarly research in India, all but a handful were crowded into the nineteenth or twentieth century.

Ultimately, however, to do Indian history one has to visit the Indian hinterland, which means doing what good historians have always done: developing a 'nose' for new materials and imaginatively reconstructing the past through critical engagement with those materials. What the turn to discourse analysis did, on the other hand, was to enable scholars to cast new interpretive spins on data that not only were already published (and which were, conveniently, in English), but were relatively accessible. For Americans, this then made it feasible *not* to go to India or to undertake original field research, while providing unlimited opportunities for armchair theorizing.[58] In fact, it is this armchair quality that explains the sense of *déjà vu* one experiences on reading so many of the writings on India influenced by post-modernism. It is worth recalling, after all, that a telling feature of classical Orientalist scholarship on India had been precisely its detached, armchair quality. Never having been to India themselves, and greatly dependent on normative textual materials published in Europe, Orientalist scholars like James Mill, Karl Marx, or Max Weber—to name just a few—were innocent of the kind of ground-level data that might better have informed their views of the peoples whom they so grandly theorized.

IV

Although postcolonial scholarship trained its attention on British India, there remains plenty of space for a reinterpretation of pre-British history, or of what postcolonialists would call 'precolonial' history. Specifically, a careful reading of pre-British historical data can turn up historical continuities where post-modernist and postcolonial scholarship, inclined as it is to privilege European discursive traditions and the epistemological disruptions they brought, perceives only discontinuities.[59] It can also contribute to building up a less Eurocentric understanding of Indian history by revealing the antecedents to what has thus far passed for

---

[58] 'If discourse is indeed the new interpretive key,' wrote Bryan Palmer, 'all of that mucking around in original sources is hardly necessary. A few key "texts" will suffice, and their creative "reading" will offer up a history untainted by costly, often uncomfortable, research trips, years in front of the microfilm reader, or months of breathing the dust off of old archival documents.' Bryan D. Palmer, *Descent into Discourse: the Reification of Language and the Writing of Social History* (Philadelphia: Temple University Press, 1990), 205.

[59] Writes Sumit Sarkar, following arguments advanced by Aijaz Ahmad, 'Colonial rule is assumed to have brought about an absolute rupture: the colonized subject is taken to have been literally constituted by colonialism alone.' Sarkar, 'Decline,' 92.

the British 'colonial discourse'. I wish to illustrate these points by considering two texts composed near the close of the sixteenth century.

The first is an extract from the *Akbar-nama* by Abu'l-fazl, the chief advisor, promoter and imperial theorist for the Mughal Emperor Akbar. The portion of the text examined here was composed in 1579, just four years after Mughal armies had marched down the Gangetic plain and swept away the last dynasty of independent sultans in Bengal. At that time the Mughals, a north Indian ruling house that was utterly alien to Bengal and to Bengali culture, were much occupied absorbing this newly won province into their growing Indian empire. Imperial officers were busy setting up a new administrative apparatus, subduing local landholders, coopting the former ruling class, dispatching their own revenue agents into the countryside, and collecting local knowledge about military and revenue affairs. The timing of the text's composition, therefore, should at once alert us to the nexus between power and knowledge so crucial for the analysis of Michel Foucault, Edward Said, and their intellectual offspring. 'The country of Bengal,' wrote Abu'l-fazl,

is a land where, owing to the climate's favouring the base, the dust of dissension is always rising. From the wickedness of men families have decayed, and dominions [have been] ruined. Hence in old writings it was called Bulghākkhāna [i.e., 'house of turbulence'].[60]

Here we find a remarkable theory of political devolution and decay: an enervating climate corrupts men, and corrupted men ruin sovereign domains, thereby implicitly preparing the way for conquest by stronger, uncorrupted outsiders.

In linking Bengal's climate with the debased behaviour of people exposed to it, Abu'l-fazl's theory of sociopolitical decay may be compared with the following statement, also about Bengal, written in 1763 by Robert Orme. We can again note the political context. Just as the extract from Abu'l-fazl was written four years after the Mughal conquest of Bengal, Orme's was written three years after the English East India Company's conquest of the same region.

The abundance of advantages peculiar to this country, through a long course of generations, have concurred with the languor peculiar to the unelastic atmosphere of the climate, to debase all the essential qualities of the human race, and notwithstanding the general effeminacy of character which is visible in

---

[60] Abu'l-fazl 'Allami, *Akbar-nāma*, ed. Abdur Rahim (3 vols., Calcutta: Asiatic Society of Bengal, 1873–87), 3:290; trans. Henry Beveridge (3 vols, Calcutta: Asiatic Society of Bengal, 1897–1921. Repr. New Delhi: Ess Ess Publications, 1979), 3:427.

all the Indians throughout the [Mughal] empire, the natives of Bengal are still of weaker frame and more enervated disposition than those of any other province.[61]

good point

Whether located in the modern imposition of European rule over the peoples of Asia, or whether traced to the writings of Dante or Homer, Orientalism, or the 'colonial discourse,' is persistently identified as uniquely European in origin and character.[62] But when we compare Abu'l-fazl's remarks written in 1579 with those of Orme, written nearly two centuries later, it would seem that elements of such a discourse were rooted not in Europe but in India itself, and specifically in Mughal culture as articulated in or with reference to the imperial province of Bengal. Rather than bringing to Bengal ideas that were 'inherently' European, then, men like Orme appear to have appropriated and assimilated values and attitudes that were already present in India, and more specifically, values and attitudes that were associated with Bengal's former ruling class. If, then, we are talking about any sort of colonial discourse, it is a Mughal and not a European discourse that we have here. More accurately, perhaps, what we have is a generic discourse of imperialism, quite independent of this or that ethnic identity or imperial tradition.

My second example takes us from Bengal to the Deccan, and the text I wish to consider was written around 1595, approximately the time Abu'l-fazl was writing about Bengal. The text, the *Rāyavācakamu*, is a Telugu narrative that situates itself in the reign of the Vijayanagara emperor Krishna Deva Raya (r. 1509–1529). In the year 1565—chronologically midway between the reign of the emperor and the composition of the text—the imperial capital of Vijayanagara had been physically destroyed by a coalition of sultanates occupying the northern Deccan: Bijapur, Ahmadnagar, and Golconda. Although Vijayanagara's imperial mystique would persist for centuries and serve to legitimate several successor kingdoms in the extreme south, the fate of the empire was so tightly intertwined with that of the city that the imperial polity never overcame the city's destruction. Indeed, the *Rāyavācakamu*, composed in the court of one of Vijayanagara's successor states in the South, constantly invoked the memory of that city.

Of special interest is how the author of this text depicted and char-

---

[61] Robert Orme, *History of the Military Transactions of the British Nation in Indostan* (repr., Madras: Pharoah, 1861), 2:4–5.

[62] The reference here is to the seminal work of Edward Said, *Orientalism* (New York: Pantheon, 1978). For a discussion of the author's contradictory uses of the term 'Orientalism,' see Aijaz Ahmad, *In Theory*, 160–70.

acterized the three northern sultanates responsible for Vijayanagara's physical destruction. Significantly, he never refers to the rulers of these states as Muslims, which they were, but as 'Turks'. At one point in the narrative, through the words of an envoy from Vijayanagara who had been secretly sent to spy on the court of one of the northern sultanates, the author details court life, including the manner in which justice was meted out. The Turks, he wrote, would punish people in front of their audience hall by slicing them in two at the waist, by cutting them apart with saws, by tying them up in gunny sacks and beating them with iron maces, by flogging them with strings with sharp horn tips, by tying them in bundles and letting them die in the hot sun, by dismembering their feet, hands, ears, or noses, or by crushing them to death under the feet of elephants. In short the text suggests a code that, to say the least, clearly distinguished civilized from barbaric systems of justice, with the 'Turkish' rulers obviously identified with the latter. And the cause of these rulers' dissolution and barbarism is said to have been their love of wine and opium. In this respect the 'Turks' are contrasted with Brahmans, who, thanks to their diet of rice, which they take with salt and *sambar,* did not suffer from such pride or malice.[63]

Several points are worth noting here. First, the stereotypes that emerge in both texts were not of religious communities, but of regional or linguistic groups. Abu'l-fazl never wrote of 'Hindus' in Bengal; nor did the *Rāyavācakamu* speak of the 'Muslims' of the Deccan. Clearly, codes of cultural marking prevalent in the late sixteenth century differed greatly from what would appear during British imperial rule. Secondly, the corrupted behavior of each group was taken not as an inherent or unalterable quality, but simply as a function of their geography or diet. For Abu'l-fazl, it was Bengal's torpid climate that corrupted the Bengalis; and for the *Rāyavācakamu* it was a diet of wine and opium that debased the Deccan's 'Turkish' rulers.

Finally, though appearing long before the rise of European power in India, both texts exhibit cultural stereotypes that are today commonly associated with Orientalism, or with a European 'colonial discourse'. Yet most 'colonial discourse' studies, because they see power and knowledge in terms of a one-way flow from colonizer to colonized, contend that 'Orientalist' intellectual categories had been evolved first by Europeans.[64] Partha Chatterjee, for example, argues that late

---

[63] Phillip B. Wagoner, *Tidings of the King: A Translation and Ethnohistorical Analysis of the Rāyavācakamu* (Honolulu: University of Hawaii Press, 1993), 113, 115.

[64] See, for example, Ronald Inden, *Imagining India* (Oxford: Basil Blackwell, 1990),

nineteenth century nationalist histories of India stereotyping Muslims as 'fanatical, bigoted, warlike, dissolute, and cruel,' grew out of European scholarship on India that had emerged in the context of British colonial rule.[65] The sixteenth century texts quoted above, however, suggest a need for a more flexible conception of discourse than is provided by 'colonial discourse' or 'invention of tradition' models, both of which share a hopelessly shallow sense of temporal depth.[66] Clearly, British rulers borrowed and built upon the ideas, stereotypes, and values of pre-British Indian rulers, just as the latter had borrowed and built upon those of their own political predecessors.[67] In short, we need to acknowledge that time, discourse, culture, and history were not simply inventions of the Raj, but to the contrary, that Indian communities have been continuously defining and redefining both themselves and 'others' for as long as—nay, longer than—we can ever know.

What, then, does post-modernism's balance-sheet look like so far as concerns the study of Indian history? On one side of the ledger, nobody could object to the usefulness of sensitizing new generations of scholars to the complex webs of power relations in which texts are always enmeshed, or to considering the possibilities of different readings of texts, even of the same texts, according to factors of class, gender, and race, as well as political power. Careful historians have always done these things.[68] But this modest reminder seems vastly outweighed by

---

36–48. Carol Breckenridge and Peter van der Veer even advise persistent vigilance against the 'danger' of studying Orientalism 'outside its colonial framework'. See Breckenridge and van der Veer, eds, *Orientalism*, 18.

[65] Partha Chatterjee, 'History and the Nationalization of Hinduism,' *Social Research* 59/1 (Spring, 1992), 140–1.

[66] For reflections on some of the difficulties and excesses of the extremely influential notion of 'the invention of tradition', according to one of its own 'inventors,' see Terence Ranger, 'The Invention of Tradition Revisited: The Case of Colonial Africa,' in Terence Ranger and Olufemi Vaughan, eds, *Legitimacy and the State in Twentieth-Century Africa* (London: Macmillan Press, 1993), 62–111.

[67] Yet it would be wrong to conclude that a common imperial discourse effaced any and all qualitative differences between the British Raj and earlier Indian empires, such as the Mughals or Vijayanagara. Enormous differences distinguished the Raj from its predecessors, most importantly its association with capitalism, which triggered profound social, economic, and political transformations that were quite without precedent in Indian history. See, for example, Ranajit Guha, *Rule of Property for Bengal: An Essay on the Idea of Permanent Settlement* (Paris: Mouton, 1963).

[68] Regrettably, the American academy today is widely misperceived as polarized between, on the one hand, scholars whose work has been enriched by the insights of literary theory and cultural studies, and on the other, scholars ranging from neoconservatives like Gertrude Himmelfarb to Marxists like Bryan Palmer who,

the other side of the ledger, a reinsertion of the British Raj to the centre stage of Indian history, a neo-colonial vision of an essentialized India and Europe locked in implacable binary opposition, an ahistorical and structuralist methodology incapable of explaining historical particularity, and an understanding of discourse and culture that renders independent South Asia ensnared in Orientalist discursive residues and the region's pre-British history befogged in timeless 'tradition'—opaque, distant, and inaccessible.

---

dwelling in 'Historyland,' are stigmatized as objectivists, empiricists, or positivists and are chided for fetishizing archives or for naively confusing archival evidence for Reality. See Bernard Cohn, 'History and Anthropology: The State of Play,' in *An Anthropologist among Historians* (Delhi: Oxford University Press, 1987), 18–49; Peter Novick, *That Noble Dream: The Objectivity Question and the American Historical Profession* (New York: Cambridge University Press, 1988); Martha L. Hildreth, 'Lamentations on Reality: A Response to John M. Mackenzie's "Edward Said and the Historians",' *Nineteenth-Century Contexts* 19/1 (1995), 65–73.

SECTION 2
THE DECCAN

6

The Articulation of Islamic Space in the Medieval Deccan[*]

THE 'MAGINOT LINE' OF DECCAN HISTORIOGRAPHY

Despite the current popularity of notions like 'invented traditions' or 'imagined communities,' constructions of sacred space in Indian history and historiography are hardly new. Nor can they be explained entirely or even mainly in terms of a nineteenth century 'colonial discourse,' of 'Orientalism,' or of backward projections of twentieth century nationalist movements or present-day geopolitical conflicts. Rather, the cultural construction of sacred space extends deep in time. Events such as the destruction of one sort of edifice or the construction of another, or warfare between medieval Indian states, provided screens onto which subsequent generations of hagiographers or chroniclers, themselves writing well before the eighteenth century, projected their own vision of how history happened, or at least, ought to have happened. Inasmuch as these visions were then used by nineteenth or twentieth century imperialists, nationalists, or religious revivalists for their own purposes, it would seem that the project for historians today has as much to do with unravelling complicated historiographies as it does with writing histories. Perhaps one cannot even separate the two.

These themes are vividly seen in the history of India's Deccan plateau. For people like Samuel Huntington the Dardanelles forms a deep, dangerous, and impermeable civilizational frontier demarcating 'Western Civilization' from the world of Islam.[1] For most modern historians of

[1] Samuel P. Huntington, 'The Clash of Civilizations?', *Foreign Affairs* (June, 1993), 22–49.

[*] Reprinted from Irene A. Bierman, ed., *Islam on the Margins* (Los Angles: Center for Near Eastern Studies, UCLA, 2000)..

India the Krishna River, running through the middle of the Deccan plateau, has formed a similar such civilizational frontier. In effect, the river is the Deccan's historiographical 'Maginot Line'. To the north, from the fourteenth through the late seventeenth centuries, lay the Bahmani Kingdom and its successor sultanates—all of them ruled by Muslims—and to the south lay the Vijayanagara Kingdom, often characterized as a 'Hindu bulwark' against Muslim encroachments from the north. The question I would pose is this: To what extent is this 'Maginot Line' of the Deccan a product of modern-day tensions, reinforced perhaps by an academic division of labour according to which people who study Persian and Urdu work north of the Krishna, and those who study Sanskrit or the Dravidian languages work south of that river? Conversely, to what extent did such a line actually exist in the period to which it is supposed to refer, the fourteenth through seventeenth centuries? In short, how was Islamic space articulated in the medieval Deccan? What, for that matter, was Islamic about the Deccan plateau?

STRUCTURAL SIMILARITIES BETWEEN BAHMANI AND VIJAYANAGARA STATES

As early as the 1960s, Marshall Hodgson (d. 1968) wrote that 'by the sixteenth century, most of the East Christian, Hindu, and Theravada Buddhist peoples found themselves more or less enclaved in an Islamicate world where Muslim standards of taste commonly made their way even into independent kingdoms, like Hindu Vijayanagara or Norman Sicily.'[2] That is, beyond those areas having predominantly Muslim populations—in places like Sicily or the southern Deccan—there lay a transregional, cosmopolitan cultural zone that, even if not populated by large numbers of Muslims, was defined and inspired by the political, material, literary, and aesthetic vision of Islam. That this zone could and did include non-Muslims is fundamental to Hodgson's notion of 'Islamicate,' as opposed to 'Islamic,' a term properly restricted to the specifically religious dimensions of the Muslim community's collective culture.[3] Indeed, Hodgson's notion of 'an Islamicate world' holds the

[2] Marshall Hodgson, 'The Role of Islam in World History,' *International Journal of Middle East Studies* 1/2 (April 1970), 118.

[3] Thus, in applying the ideas of Immanuel Wallerstein to pre-modern Islamic history, John Voll has formulated the notion of an 'Islamic world-system,' which, he argues, was based on a 'mutually intelligible discourse among all who identify themselves as Muslims within the Dar al-Islam.' See John Obert Voll, 'Islam as a Special World-System,' *Journal of World History* 5, no. 2 (1994), 219.

key, I believe, to understanding the complex range of exchanges that occurred between Turko-Persian and Indic cultures in medieval South Asia. Otherwise, what would one make, for example, of Hindu landholders (*zamīndārs*) who built temples architecturally indistinguishable from mosques sponsored by their Muslim overlords? Or of Hindu monarchs who adopted Persian personal names, Arabic titles, Turko-Arab garments, and Iranian notions of statecraft?

The remarkable similarities between the states that emerged on either side of the Krishna River between the fourteenth and seventeenth century would appear to refute the idea that that river had ever formed a cultural 'Maginot Line'. The moral economy of the Vijayanagara state, for example, compares remarkably with that of the Bahmani kingdom and its successor states, and indeed, with that of states all over the medieval Perso-Islamic world. Such states typically espoused ideals found in the 'Mirror for Kings' literature well-known to students of medieval Persian history. Here are the words of the early thirteenth century political theorist of Herat, Fakhr al-Din Razi (d. 1209):

Wealth is gathered from the subjects;
The *subjects* are made servants by justice;
Justice is the axis of the prosperity of the world.[4]

And here is a verse quoted from the Telugu work *Badde-nīti*, a popular work on royal conduct and statecraft composed in the Andhra country in the twelfth or thirteenth century, that is, before the appearance of Turkish Muslims there in the early fourteenth century:

To acquire *wealth*: make the *people* prosper.
To make the *people* prosper: justice is the means.
O Kirti Narayana!
They say that *justice* is the treasury of kings.[5]

Both extracts postulate a conceptual linkage between wealth, subjects, and justice, forming thereby a unified, coherent political ideology. Since no comparable statement can be found in classical Sanskrit texts on governance, it would appear that such a conception of a state's proper moral economy became current in the subcontinent only after the rise of Indo-Turkish rule in north India. Moreover, as the maxim cited

---

[4] Fakhr al-Din Razi, *Jāmi' al-'ulūm*, ed. Muhammad Khan Malik al-Kuttab (Bombay, A.H. 1323 [A.D. 1905],), 207. Emphasis mine.
[5] Quoted in Phillip B. Wagoner, *Tidings of the King: A Translation and Ethnohistorical Analysis of the Rāyavācakamu* (Honolulu: University of Hawaii Press, 1993), 95. Emphasis mine.

above was later quoted by sixteenth century writers in Vijayanagara,[6] one may assume that the ideology continued to inform the practice of statecraft south of the Krishna throughout the fifteenth and sixteenth centuries, just as it did the sultanates to the north.

Shared conceptions of moral economy comprise but one aspect of the 'Islamicate world-system' that straddled both sides of the Krishna River. Another is material culture, and in particular the shared wearing apparel that served to articulate a common courtly etiquette throughout the Deccan. Phillip Wagoner has shown how certain kinds of garments, adopted and distributed by the court of Vijayanagara, served to define political legitimacy in that kingdom, just as they did in the northern sultanates, and for that matter, the entire Islamicate world-system. These garments include, in particular, the high, conical cap of brocaded fabric, known in Telugu as *kullāyi*, a term derived from the Persian *kulāh*; and a long tunic known in Telugu as *kabāyi*, derived from the Arabic *qabā*.[7] Worn and distributed by non-Muslim monarchs in the Deccan, these garments may be compared with the ornamentations in a royal chapel, the coronation robes, or the bird-shaped containers patronized by Christian princes in twelfth century Sicily as discussed by Oleg Grabar,[8] or with the Mamluk-styled bronze trays used in the thirteenth century Byzantine court as discussed by Robert Nelson.[9] All these illustrate and document the vibrant material culture of an Islamicate world-system that flourished beyond the world of predominantly Muslim believers.

By the fourteenth century, states in both the northern and southern Deccan had also evolved similar institutions respecting their political economies. Together with the 'Mirror for Kings' ideology mentioned above, it seems that the *iqtā'* was introduced to northern India in the

---

[6] Ibid.

[7] Royal gifts circulating in the Vijayanagara court included cap, ornamental shirt, necklace, pearl earrings, yellow shawl, musk, and betel. Those circulating in the northern sultanates included sash, tunic, turban, and turban band. The Orissa kingdom's gifts included turban, gold necklace, pearl earring, shirt, sash, musk, and betel. See Wagoner, *Tidings*, 106, 116, 149. See also idem., ' "Sultan among Hindu Kings:" Dress, Titles, and the Islamicization of Hindu Culture at Vijayanagara,' *Journal of Asian Studies* 55/4 (Nov. 1996), 851–80.

[8] Oleg Grabar, 'A Ceiling, a Mantle, a Bird,' paper read at the Fifteenth Giorgio Levi della Vida Award and Conference, 'The Experience of Islamic Art,' UCLA, Los Angeles, 10–13 May, 1996.

[9] Robert S. Nelson, 'Letters and Language: Ornament and Identity in Byzantium and Islam,' paper read at the Fifteenth Giorgio Levi della Vida Award and Conference, 'The Experience of Islamic Art,' UCLA, Los Angeles 10–13 May, 1996.

eleventh century by Persianized Turks under the later Ghaznavids and that by the late thirteenth century the principles of this institution had seeped southward into the eastern Deccan, where kings of the Kakatiya dynasty employed an analogous institution called *nāyaṃkara*.[10] Both terms referred to a distinctive mode of land tenure that linked a state's revenue system to its armed forces. Specifically, nobles were given land assignments commensurate in area and productive capacity with the size of cavalry or other military units that they were expected to maintain. In the mid-fourteenth century, the iqṭā was introduced to the northern Deccan by the earliest Bahmani sultans,[11] and from about the same time kings in Vijayanagara began issuing nāyaṃkara grants, with an especially large number of them appearing in the sixteenth century.[12] Phillip Wagoner has described these tenures as 'an Indic adaptation of the iqṭā' system';[13] one may also see them as yet more evidence of the Deccan plateau's integration into the medieval Islamicate world-system.

On both sides of the Krishna, too, one finds a shared terminology for the head of state. There is inscriptional evidence that in 1347, the very year that the Bahmani sultanate was established in the northern Deccan, Marappa, one of the five brothers who launched the Vijayanagara state, was styled *hindu-raya-suratrana*, or 'Sultan of/among the Indian rajas'.[14] Several years later, in 1354, his brothers Harihara I

---

[10] For epigraphic evidence of *nāyaṃkara* tenures in the Andhra country in the late twelfth century, see Cynthia Talbot, 'Political Intermediaries in Kakatiya Andhra, 1175–1325,' *Indian Economic and Social History Review* 31/3 (1994), 261–89.

[11] Saiyid 'Ali Tabataba, who completed his *Burhān-i ma'āthir* in 1595–6, recorded that in 1347, immediately after chasing the last Tughluq troops out of the Deccan, the first Bahmani sultan began naming his closest confederates to the highest posts of state. The historian continued: 'Each of the kingdom's *amīrs*, *vazīrs*, and nameworthy cavalrymen, having been distinguished with a *jāgīr* and *muqāṣṣā* according to his own rank, received an *iqṭā'* in towns and parganas, and he maintained troops, attendants, and equipage that were proportionate to those [lands].' Saiyid 'Ali Tabataba, *Burhān-i ma'āthir* (Delhi: Jam'i Press, 1936), 16. My translation.

[12] Cynthia Talbot, 'Local Lordship in Sixteenth-Century Andhra: The Epigraphic Perspective on *Amara-Nayankara*,' a paper read at the Twenty-fifth Annual Conference on South Asia, Madison, Wisconsin, 18–20 October, 1996. See also Wagoner, *Tidings*, 198–9.

[13] Phillip Wagoner, '*Iqṭā'* and *Nāyaṃkara*: Military Service Tenures and Political Theory from Saljuq Iran to Vijayanagara South India', paper read at the Twenty-fifth Annual Conference on South Asia, Madison, Wisconsin, 18–20 October, 1996.

[14] *Mysore Archaeological Reports*, 1929, no. 90, p. 159–73. Line 39. Cited in Hermann Kulke, 'Maharajas, Mahants and Historians: Reflections on the Historiography of Early Vijayanagara and Sringeri,' in A. L. Dallapiccola, ed., *Vijayanagar, City*

and Bukka were praised with the same title.[15] Thereafter, the kings of Vijayanagara were regularly styled *sulṭān*, or with some variation of the formula 'Sultan of/among the Indian rajas'. Notable among these were Devaraya II (1425–46)[16] and the most famous and powerful of all Vijayanagara kings, Krishna Deva Raya (1509–29).[17] None of this should be astonishing. Devaraya II more than any other monarch was responsible for the assimilation of Muslim cavalry and troops, together with Turko-Persian modes of warfare, into Vijayanagara's military system, while Krishna Deva Raya reigned during the period of Vijayanagara's most extensive cultural exchanges with the sultanates of the northern Deccan.

The use of the Arabic title sulṭān by these kings well illustrates Hodgson's distinction between 'Islamicate' and 'Islamic'. Whereas religious leadership of Sunni Muslims was invested formally in the caliph, and informally in local Sufi shaikhs, political leadership of both Muslims and non-Muslims resided in the head of state, or sulṭān, who was understood as the de facto sovereign over the *entire* population of his sultanate. Because early Indo-Muslim political culture thus sharply separated 'Church' and 'State,' it was not uncommon for both Muslim and Hindu rulers aspiring to political grandeur—and more particularly, when claiming suzerainty over mere kings (whether *māliks* or *rājās*)—to style themselves 'sulṭān'. This was, after all, the most powerful and prestigious term available in the political vocabulary of the medieval Islamicate world. Thus, in 1367 Kapaya Nayak, a Telugu chieftain who had successfully rebelled against the Delhi Sultanate's authority in the eastern Deccan, styled himself 'Andhra *suratrāṇa*,' or 'Sultan of Andhra'.[18] Kapaya Nayak's use of this title seems to have derived from

---

and Empire: New Currents of Research, vol. 1 (Wiesbaden: Franz Steiner Verlag, 1985), 120–43. Vasundhara Filliozat, however, has doubts about the authenticity of this inscription on the grounds that it lacks a royal seal and that the minister mentioned in it, who is also mentioned in a 1391 inscription, would not likely have served for so long. See Vasundhara Filliozat, *l'Épigraphie de Vijayanagar du début à 1377* (Paris: Publications de l'École Française d'Extrême-Orient, vol. 91, 1973), xv.

[15] Filliozat, *l'Épigraphie de Vijayanagar*, nos. 35 and 36, pp. 23–4. See also Wagoner, 'Sultan among Hindu Kings'. It is worth noting that these are the earliest known instances in which Indians referred to themselves as 'Hindu'. At this time, the term seems to have had a geographical and ethnic meaning—that is, 'a native of India'—and not the religious meaning that it would acquire later.

[16] H. K. Sherwani and P. M. Joshi, eds., *History of Medieval Deccan (1295–1724)*, 2 vols. (Hyderabad: Government of Andhra Pradesh, 1973), 166.

[17] *Epigraphia India*, XIV: No. 12, p. 173, cited in Wagoner, 'Sultan among Hindu Kings'.

[18] Sherwani and Joshi, eds, *History of Medieval Deccan*, 1:81.

his close contacts with the founders of the Bahmani Kingdom, whom he had recently assisted in their own struggle for independence from Tughluq rule.

In large part, common historical origins can explain these structural similarities among the great states that crystallized on either side of the Krishna River. The usual interpretation of Vijayanagara's origins, heavily inflected by modern communalist biases, is that the state emerged as an expression of Hindu resistance to the Islamic religion as carried south by the sultans of Delhi and as institutionalized there by the Bahmani sultans. This view, which effectively maps a 'Maginot Line' along Vijayanagara's northern frontier formed by the Krishna River, misses the important point that the Vijayanagara and Bahmani states did not arise out of opposition to each other, but rather emerged about the same time—the former in 1346 and the latter the next year—for essentially the same reasons.[19] Both states began as revolutionary regimes that had evolved out of armed resistance to a common, northern, imperial power—the Delhi Sultanate—whose ruler, Muhammad bin Tughluq (r. 1325–51), openly displayed disdain for the Deccan and its distinctive culture.[20] It was from a common desire to throw off northern rule that Telugu chieftains, who had already succeeded in overthrowing the Tughluqs in the eastern and southern Deccan, assisted Hasan Bahman Shah in founding the Bahmani state in the west.[21] What is more, prior service in the Delhi Sultanate helped confer political authority and

[19] On the origins of Vijayanagara, a topic that has excited much debate, see Kulke, 'Maharajas, Mahants and Historians'. Kulke concludes that 'the emergence of Vijayanagara's statehood was a gradual and protracted process. But there can be no doubt that the 'festival of victory' in the year 1346 and the existence of a new capital and new imperial titles in the year 1368 formed, according to our present knowledge, major steps towards this development.' Ibid., 126.

[20] Around 1333, it was noted that whenever Muhammad bin Tughluq was in Daulatabad, then co-capital of the Tughluq empire (along with Delhi), the sultan refused to use local Deccani water and insisted instead on using water hand-carried to Daulatabad from the Ganges River, a forty days' journey to the north. Without arguing that the sultan actually believed in the sanctity of Ganges water, one can certainly detect in his behavior a north Indian chauvinism vis-à-vis the south, not unlike the sort of chauvinism that some thirty years earlier his Khalaji predecessors, themselves comfortably accommodated to north Indian culture, had displayed vis-à-vis Bengal. Religion was not an issue here; but regional chauvinism certainly was. See Mahdi Husain (tr.), *The Rehla of Ibn Battuta (India, Maldive Islands and Ceylon)* (Baroda: Oriental Institute, 1953), 4. See also Richard M. Eaton, *The Rise of Islam and the Bengal Frontier, 1204–1760* (Berkeley: University of California Press, 1993), 40.

[21] Sherwani and Joshi, *History of Medieval Deccan*, 1:81.

legitimacy on the founders of *both* the Bahmani and the Vijayanagara states.[22] In this respect, both polities may properly be understood as Tughluq successor states in the Deccan. Indeed, the rulers of the two kingdoms seemed to have considered their states as such, as witnessed by their bold claims to being sultān, a powerful title to which the Tughluq emperor had staked sole claim in India. Small wonder, then, that Marshall Hodgson included Vijayanagara within the Islamicate world.

SACRED SPACE AND THE BAHMANI SULTANATE

Despite these striking similarities between the Vijayanagara and Bahmani kingdoms, there were important differences, too, and these sprang mainly from the contrasting notions of sacred space that were constructed by contemporary ideologues representing propertied classes on the two sides of the Krishna.

First, it is essential to understand the world-historical context in which the Bahmani Kingdom appeared in 1347. Perso-Islamic civilization had taken root on the Deccan plateau during the high-tide of the Mongol Age in western Asia. Genghis Khan himself had reached the Indus River in 1221; thereafter, subsequent armies of Mongols would threaten Delhi in 1297, 1299, 1303 and 1327. Responsible for maintaining the peace in North India during this period, the Indo-Turkish rulers of the Delhi Sultanate were keenly aware of the firestorm of destruction that Mongol armies had already unleashed on the heart of the Islamic world. Viewing the Mongols as savage and violent unbelievers, officials of the Delhi Sultanate were prepared to take any measures necessary to preserve stability and security in their own quarter of that world. And they well understood that resources were necessary in order to defend north India from Mongol invasions. Indeed, in the mid-thirteenth century Balban, the future Sultan of Delhi, advocated raiding

---

[22] The earliest Sanskrit sources concerning the founding of Vijayanagara—the *Rājakālanimaya* and the *Vidyāraṇyakālajñāna*—mention that the kingdom's founders, the brothers Harihara and Bukka, had rebelled against Tughluq imperial authority in the Deccan and were captured and taken to Delhi as prisoners of war. There they impressed the Delhi sultan, who gave them land in Karnataka and sent them back south to govern in Tughluq imperial service. But they again rebelled, this time successfully, and went on to establish the Vijayanagara state. Contrary to later, communalist, interpretations of these events, the original sources make no claim that the brothers had converted to Islam while in Delhi or were 'reconverted' to Hinduism upon their return to the Deccan. See Wagoner, 'Sultan among Hindu Kings', 874.

Indian states for precisely this purpose.[23] Strategically, then, one can see the Delhi Sultanate's invasions of the Deccan, which began in the late thirteenth century when the Mongol threat to north India intensified, as a continuation of an earlier policy of looting Indian cities beyond the Sultanate's frontiers in order to defend itself from Central Asian attackers.[24]

But there was more to the Deccan invasions than strategy and security. Or rather, there was a deeper sort of security that was at stake here than simply political security. In 1258, Mongol armies under Hülegü Khan had sacked Baghdad, executed the Abbasid caliph, and abolished the office of the caliphate—events that collectively represented perhaps the deepest crisis in Islamic history up to that point. In 1260, soon after these momentous events had taken place, India's most prominent historian of the age, Minhaj Siraj Juzjani, somberly observed,

Notwithstanding that, by the will of the Almighty, and the decrees of Destiny, the turn of sovereignty passed unto Chingiz Khan, the Accursed, and his descendants, after the kings of Iran and Turan, that the whole of the land of Turan and the East fell under the sway of the Mughals [i.e., Mongols], and that *the authority of the Muhammadan religion departed from those regions*, which became the seat of paganism, the kingdom of Hindustan [i.e., North India], by the grace of Almighty God, and the favour of fortune ... *became the focus of the people of Islam, and orbit of the possessors of religion.*[25]

In short, thoughtful Muslims of the later thirteenth century had come to see India as destined to play a very special role for Islam in the post-Mongol world. In their view, only India, now deemed the 'focus' of the world-wide Muslim community, could save the Islamic enterprise from certain calamity. The Delhi Sultanate's need for security and its

[23] 'It is advisable,' he said in 1247, 'that, during this year, the sublime standards should be put in motion for the purpose of ravaging and carrying on holy war in the extreme parts of the territory of Hindustan, in order that the independent (Hindu) tribes, and Raes and Ranahs, who, during the last few years, have not been punished, may receive a thorough chastisement, that booty may fall into the hands of the troops of Islam, and means to repel the infidel Mughals [Mongols], in the shape of wealth, may be amassed.' Minhaj Siraj Juzjani, *Tabaqāt-i Nāṣiri* (Tehran: Dunya-yi Kitab, 1363 A.H.), 2:57. Trans., H.G. Raverty, *Tabakat-i-Nasiri*, (1881; repr. New Delhi: Oriental Books Reprint Corp, 1970), 2:816.

[24] This idea was first suggested by Carl Ernst, *Eternal Garden: Mysticism, History, and Politics at a South Asian Sufi Center* (Albany: State University of New York, 1992), 107.

[25] Minhaj, *Tabaqāt-i Nāṣiri* (Tehran edn.), 2:90. Trans., H.G. Raverty, *Tabakat-i-Nasiri*, 2:869–900. Emphasis mine.

Deccan invasions of the late thirteenth and early fourteenth centuries must be seen in this larger, geo-religious context.

On the other hand, by the early fourteenth century, when the Deccan was annexed outright to the Delhi Sultanate, the rulers of Delhi had become so Indianized that they saw themselves as the protectors not just of Islam and Muslims, but of north Indian civilization generally. One glimpses this attitude in Muhammad bin Tughluq's refusal to drink the water of the Deccan, insisting instead on having his water hand-carried from the Ganges River to Daulatabad. More importantly, by the early fourteenth century, with the caliphate in Baghdad abolished and north India now deemed the 'focus of the peoples of Islam,' Sufi shaikhs belonging to the Chishti order had emerged as the preeminent patrons of Indo-Muslim kingship. Unlike other Sufi orders of the day, the tomb sites of whose major shaikhs were located in distant Central Asia or West Asia, the tombs and shrines of the major Chishti shaikhs were located *within* the subcontinent. This focus on India gave shaikhs of the Chishti order, among all members of India's formal or informal Muslim establishment, the best claims to being both legitimately Islamic *and* authentically Indian. This explains why, as first the Khalaji and then the Tughluq sultans of Delhi expanded militarily over the sub-continent, it was Chishti shaikhs who accompanied imperial governors and future rulers to India's far-flung corners, there to indigenize and legitimate new, satellite Indo-Muslim polities.

The critical role that early Chishti shaikhs played in state-formation in medieval India is seen in the recorded sayings of Nizam al-Din Auliya (d. 1325), the greatest Chishti shaikh of fourteenth century Delhi. Having just met with Sultan Muhammad bin Tughluq at his hospice, and while the future Sultan Hasan Bahman Shah (r. 1347–58), founder of the Bahmani Sultanate, was waiting outside, Nizam al-Din is said to have remarked, 'One sultan has left my door; another is waiting there'.[26] This illustrates the theme, common in thirteenth and fourteenth century Indo-Persian literature, of a Sufi shaikh predicting future kingship for some civilian, with such 'prediction' actually serving as a rhetorical form of royal appointment. That is, in the Perso-Islamic literary and cultural universe of the day, it was implicitly assumed that spiritually powerful Sufi shaikhs were the only genuinely valid sovereigns over this world; but, so that they might concentrate on purely spiritual concerns from which they derived their own legitimacy and credibility, these same shaikhs were thought to have leased out political sovereignty

---

[26] Saiyid 'Ali Tabataba, *Burhān-i ma'āthir* (Delhi: Jam'i Press, 1936), 12; Muhammad Qasim Firishta, *Tārīkh-i Firishta* (Lucknow: Nawal Kishor, 1864–5), 1:274.

(*ḥukūmat*) to kings, who were thus charged with the messy and very worldly business of administration, taxation, warfare, and so forth. This amounted to a variation on the sort of dual sovereignty that had earlier emerged in the Iranian Plateau in the eleventh and twelfth centuries, where Turkish strongmen held de facto political power as 'sultans' while the caliph in Baghdad held juridical and religious authority. By the fourteenth century, however, it was now Sufi shaikhs who lent juridical and religious legitimacy to Indo-Muslim states, since no functioning caliph had existed since 1258.

'Abd al-Malik 'Isami, the earliest panegyrist at the Bahmani court, clearly stated the view that spiritually powerful Sufi shaikhs could 'entrust' royal sovereignty, or *ḥukūmat*, to future kings, whose rule was understood as dependent on such shaikhs. Indeed, in 'Isami's view, history itself was but the working out of divine will as mediated by spiritually powerful shaikhs, especially those of the Chishti order. 'It is well known,' he wrote, 'that the existence of the world is bound up closely with that of the men of faith.' Then he added,

In every country there is a man of piety who keeps it going and well. Although there might be a monarch in every country, yet it is actually under the protection of a fakir [i.e., a Sufi shaikh]. The monarchs are, to all appearance, the head of the State, but it is the fakirs who avert the impending calamities.[27]

Accordingly, the poet noted that with the death in 1325 of Delhi's greatest Chishti master, Shaikh Nizam al-Din Auliya, the city and empire of Delhi sank to an irredeemable state of desolation, tyranny, and turmoil. But the Deccan, wrote 'Isami, suffered no such fate. To the contrary, in 1329, just four years after Nizam al-Din's death, one of that shaikh's leading disciples, Burhan al-Din Gharib, moved from Delhi to the Tughluqs' Deccan capital of Daulatabad, which prospered mightily as a result of the immigrant's presence. When Burhan al-Din died in 1337, the spiritual protection of Daulatabad, and by implication all Deccan territories under the city's jurisdiction, passed on to his own leading disciple, Shaikh Zain al-Din Shirazi (d. 1369). As the Deccan's principal Chishti shaikh at the time of the Bahmani revolution of 1347, Zain al-Din played a pivotal role in transforming a rebel state to a legitimate Islamic kingdom. Indeed, according to 'Isami, the very robe worn by the Prophet Muhammad on the night he ascended to Paradise—a robe subsequently passed on through twenty-three generations of holymen until it was finally received by Zain al-Din—was

[27] 'Abd al-Malik 'Isami, *Futuhu's Salatin*, tr. Agha Mahdi Husain (London: As Publishing House, 1967), 3:687.

bestowed upon the poet's own royal patron and founder of the Bahmani state, Sultan Hasan Bahman Shah.[28]

Once in power in the new Deccani capital of Gulbarga, Sultan Hasan Bahman Shah wasted no time expressing his gratitude to his various Chishti supporters. On the occasion of his coronation, he ordered a gift of five *man* (200 lbs.) of gold and ten *man* (400 lbs.) of silver to be given to the shrine of Burhan al-Din Gharib, located in Khuldabad in the northern Deccan.[29] The new sultan's substantial gift to the Khuldabad shrine was politically astute, since it acknowledged not only Burhan al-Din Gharib, but that shaikh's own master, Nizam al-Din Auliya, the former spiritual sovereign of North India's Tughluq Empire who had predicted the new sultan's temporal sovereignty and had granted Burhan al-Din spiritual sovereignty (*wilāyat*) over the Deccan plateau.[30]

To understand the attraction of charismatic Sufis to state builders like Sultan Hasan Bahman Shah, one must contrast the terms wilāyat and ḥukūmat, not only as differing types of Islamic authority, but also as differing conceptions of Islamic space. Whereas ḥukūmat, royal authority, was always limited in reach, and never coincided with the entire Muslim world—far less with the entire planet—the spiritual sovereignty of Sufis, wilāyat, was theoretically unlimited in territorial extent, and hence far greater than the worldly sovereignty of sultans. These differing conceptions of Islamic space are vividly seen in an encounter that took place in the late fourteenth century between Shah Ni'mat Allah Kirmani, Iran's most eminent shaikh of the day, and Timur, or Tamerlane, the world's most successful conqueror of the day. 'My state is a world without end,' said the shaikh to the emperor, 'while yours extends from Khaṭāy [i.e. Cathay] to Shiraz.'[31] That is, whereas Timur's domain was restricted to the 'limited' space between northern China and southern Iran—an area in fact comprising over half the known world!—that of the shaikh was without limit.

In practice, however, the domain of a Sufi's jurisdiction, or wilāyat, was just as limited as the territorial reach of his royal patron's worldly

---

28 'Isami, *Futuhu's Salatin*, English tr., 3:691–2, 696.

29 Firishta, *Tārīkh-i Firishta* (Lucknow edn), 1:277.

30 Majd al-Din Kashani, *Gharā'ib al-karāmāt*, 11. Cited in Carl Ernst, *Eternal Garden*, 119. Kashani, the author of this unpublished narrative, was a disciple of Shaikh Burhan al-Din and compiled the work in 1340, just several years after his master's death.

31 'Mulk-i man 'ālamīst bī pāyān; va ān-i tū khaṭāst tā Shīrāz.' Mufid Mustawfi Yazdi, *Jāmi'-yi mufīd*, in Jean Aubin, ed., *Matériaux pour la Biographie de Shah Ni'matullah Wali Kermani* (Teheran: Département d'Iranologie de l'Institut Franco-Iranien, 1956), 167.

domain (ḥukūmat), if not more so. Nonetheless, the inclusion of any territory within the wilāyat of a powerful Sufi shaikh was always charged with political significance, since it meant that such territory could not be viewed—as the Deccan formerly had been—as land ready for plunder, like a ripe plum. The latter view, after all, had justified Indo-Turkish raids in the Deccan for the purpose of protecting north India from Mongol attack.[32] But whereas Khalaji and Tughluq conquests in the Deccan lacked a moral basis and were undertaken for plunder pure and simple, the extension of the Sufis' notion of wilāyat into the region lent moral legitimacy to the planting of subsequent Indo-Muslim states there. To borrow from the rhetoric of classical Islam, Sufi shaikhs—first in Delhi, then in the Deccan—could transform yesterday's Abode of War, *Dār al-Ḥarb*, into today's Abode of Peace, or *Dār al-Islām*, thereby bringing about an internally coherent basis for the legitimate transplanting of Indo-Muslim rule and civilization from region to region within South Asia.

SACRED SPACE AND THE VIJAYANAGARA KINGDOM

The claims to legitimate sovereignty made by the Bahmani kings, or by their supporters, contrast dramatically with those made by kings to the south of the Krishna River, in Vijayanagara. Although that state's political origins were tied to the same anti-Tughluq revolutions that produced the Bahmani state, its religious origins had very different roots. Recent research has traced these origins to the growth of a river goddess cult that had emerged on the southern banks of the Tungabhadra River as early as the seventh century.[33] At that time the site was known simply as Pampā's *tīrtha*—or the 'crossing' of the river goddess Pampā— where passing chieftains would halt and make votive offerings during military campaigns. By the ninth century the first temple had appeared at the site, dedicated evidently to this goddess. By the early eleventh century, donations began to be made to the male deity Mahakala Deva, the violent aspect of Śiva, associated with destruction and death.

By the twelfth century, however, a temple complex dedicated to Virupaksa, who represented Śiva's more universal and benign aspect,

---

[32] It was also the view later adopted by servants of the eighteenth century East India Company, when Englishmen plundered the wealth of Bengal for no nobler an ideal than that of 'shaking the pagoda tree'.

[33] See Phillip B. Wagoner, 'From " Pampa's Crossing" to "The Place of Lord Virupaksa": Architecture, Cult, and Patronage at Hampi before the Founding of Vijayanagara,' in D. Devaraj and C.S. Patil, eds, *Vijayanagara: Progress of Research, 1988–1991* (Mysore: Directorate of Archaeology and Museums, 1996), 141–74.

had emerged at the site. Unlike the earlier phase, when she was merely protected by Mahakala Deva to whom she was in no way subordinate, the river goddess Pampā was now reduced to a subordinate status as Śiva's 'consort'. By this time, too, South Indian texts had begun describing Pampa's marriage to Virupaksa in terms that paralleled the all-Indian myth of Śiva's marriage to Parvati. In short, between the seventh and twelfth century, this regional shrine had gradually become 'Sanskritized,' as a local river goddess was pulled up into, and in the process transformed by, the big world of pan-Indic Śaivism.

Throughout this long period of religious evolution, the site became an ever more important pilgrimage centre, as we know from inscriptions that enumerate the many hundreds of households then located there. Most important, from the thirteenth century politically ambitious or already-dominant rulers in the area began cultivating closer ties with the shrine and its deities, in contrast to the earlier phase, when the shrine was patronized by none but passing chieftains. By the late thirteenth century members of the Kampila dynasty, who had managed to carve out a small state that resisted assimilation into larger Hindu kingdoms both to the north and the south, had emerged as the shrine's principal patrons. For a while in the early fourteenth century, the rajas of this fledgling dynasty even repelled Turkish armies sent down by the Delhi Sultanate. In 1327, however, Muhammad bin Tughluq overpowered the Kampilas' stronghold at Kummata, where both the raja and his son died in the struggle.[34] Although the short-lived Kampila state ultimately failed to survive the onslaught of Tughluq power, its attempt to build a state on the site of a goddess-cum-Śiva shrine, thereby to reap the ritual and political benefits of an expanding religious cult, established an important precedent for the kings who subsequently ruled from the site. For, very soon after the Kampilas' defeat by Delhi, a new capital began to emerge on the old site of 'Pampā's crossing,' with a new family of chieftains, the Sangamas, established as its 'protectors'. The place would ultimately be called Vijayanagara, or City of Victory.

By the sixteenth century, the rulers of Vijayanagara had adopted brazenly imperial titles and patronized the great Vaishnava temple at Tirupati with its pan-South Indian connections, while the state itself had evolved into a large and powerful empire that sprawled all over southern India. Nonetheless, it never shed its rootedness to a fixed

---

[34] Channabasappa S. Patil, 'Mummadi Singa, Kampila and Kumara Rama,' in D. V. Devaraj and Channabasappa S. Patil, eds, *Vijayanagara: Progress of Research, 1987–88* (Mysore: Directorate of Archaeology and Museums, 1991), 179–198; and idem., 'Kummata,' in ibid., 199–216.

and ancient shrine dedicated to a river goddess. Indeed, the major royal and religious monuments even of Vijayanagara's later days were architecturally aligned to this goddess shrine.[35]

COMPARISONS AND CONTRASTS

In important respects, the so-called 'Islamic' Bahmani kingdom and the 'Hindu' Vijayanagara kingdom were a good deal alike. Sharing similar historical origins, and comparable in terms of military organization, political economy, moral economy, aesthetic tastes, royal dress, titles, and public comportment, both states were firmly integrated into the medieval Islamicate 'world-system'.

The two kingdoms differed most fundamentally, however, in their contrasting conceptions of sacred space, as reflected in the different ways they constructed themselves ideologically. The Bahmani sultans, for their part, made universalist claims to legitimacy in a post-1258 world that no longer possessed a centralized caliphate. In fact, for the first century after the Mongols' destruction of Baghdad, the Delhi Sultanate had become a major refuge of Islam, and for Turks and Persians in the eastern Islamic world, *the* refuge of Islam. This meant that a revolution against that sultanate could be justified only by making extravagant appeals to much higher authority than anything found within India. And, like French or American revolutionaries, who justified their inherently illegal acts by appealing to territorially unlimited claims like the Universal Rights of Man or the Pursuit of Liberty, Bahmani revolutionaries made universalist claims in order to justify their seditious acts. One way they did this was to patronize Sufi shaikhs whose territorial sovereignty was theoretically unlimited; another was to receive, quite literally, the mantle of the Prophet of Islam.

It must also be remarked that Sufi shaikhs, like robes or mantles, were highly mobile, which is another reason they played such critical roles in launching new states in the Deccan, as they did elsewhere in medieval India. Both charismatic and peripatetic, these luminous figures exemplified an Islamicate world very much 'on the move' in the thirteenth and fourteenth centuries. This was, as André Wink has argued, a world of long-distance trade, of mobile wealth, of extensive monetization, and of easily recruitable and purchasable military slaves.[36] In such a

---

[35] See George Michell, *Where Kings and Gods Meet* (Tucson: University of Arizona Press, 1984), 153.

[36] André Wink, *al-Hind: The Making of the Indo-Islamic World*. Volume II: *The Slave Kings and the Islamic Conquest of India, 11th-13th Centuries* (Leiden: Brill, 1997). See Ch. 6, 'A World on the Move'.

fluid context, Turko-Persian states could emerge virtually anywhere, since military leadership depended upon outside recruits and not upon territorially-rooted warrior lineages like the Rajputs. Hence the problem for would-be´ dynastic figures like Hasan Bahman Shah always came to this: how to sink down permanent roots and rule with security and credibility in a land that only a generation earlier had been plundered with impunity? This was where immigrant Sufi shaikhs, as portable vessels of spiritual sovereignty, played their crucial role. By contrast, the Vijayanagara state was built upon a religious cult whose geographical focus, a river, was territorially fixed. Royal patrons gravitated toward a shrine to a river goddess that was already endowed with sanctity, and whose sanctity increased with increasing royal patronage. State-building at Vijayanagara, then, was not a matter of recruiting and patronizing mobile holymen brought in from some sacred centre elsewhere, but of appropriating and then exploiting the sacred power of a fixed religious site through public acts of patronage.

There is no evidence, however, that these contrasting strategies of state legitimization led to polarized notions of 'Islamic' and 'Hindu' civilizations in the medieval Deccan. Such polarization appears rather to have resulted from fierce interstate competition over control of one of the wealthiest strips of land in the entire peninsula, the Raichur Doab, which lay directly between Vijayanagara and Bahmani domains.[37] The numerous wars fought over this fertile tract between the late fourteenth and mid-sixteenth centuries in time generated a rhetoric of mutual demonization by states on either side of the Doab. In Vijayanagara, the Brahmans who controlled fixed wealth were frequent losers in these conflicts since temples were often targeted for attack and looting by northern armies. Inscriptions or chronicles patronized by Brahmans, or by men with a Brahmanic perspective, tended therefore to stigmatize state enemies as *adharmic*, or opposed to 'order' in the sense of both social stability and cosmic harmony.[38]

North of the Krishna River, meanwhile, the medieval Persian chroniclers who wrote the histories of the Bahmani Kingdom and its successors—Saiyid 'Ali Tabataba, Rafi' al-Din Shirazi, or Muhammad Qasim Firishta—were all high-born Iranian immigrants who tended

---

[37] See P. M. Joshi, 'The Raichur Doab in Deccan History—a Reinterpretation of a Struggle,' *Journal of Indian History* 36 (1958), 379–96.

[38] See Wagoner, *Tidings*, 109–24. Cynthia Talbot, 'Inscribing the Other, Inscribing the Self: Hindu-Muslim Identities in Pre-Colonial India,' *Comparative Studies in Society and History* 37/4 (October 1995), 695–704.

to adopt a colonialist view towards non-Muslim Indian society.[39] Transplanted from their native homelands in Iran, such immigrant writers routinely stigmatized the people of Vijayanagara as 'infidels'. Since these men were hired to chronicle their patrons' grand deeds, many of which focused on struggles with Vijayanagara over control of the Raichur Doab, these struggles became the principal context in which subsequent readers would see this period of history. Replete with mutually demonizing tropes, the rhetoric of warfare generated by literate ideologues on both sides of the Krishna ultimately took on a life of its own and hardened into the Maginot Line that today continues to divide Deccani historiography into a 'Hindu' south and a 'Muslim' north.

Such rhetoric, however, has prevented more recent generations from appreciating the degree to which both Vijayanagara and its northern neighbours were integrated into a multi-ethnic, transregional universe knit together by shared political norms, cultural values and aesthetic tastes—the Islamicate 'world-system'. Vijayanagara's rulers did not patronize Islamicate culture as a deliberate strategy for controlling their Muslim subjects, in the way that, for example, French colonial rulers did in North Africa.[40] Rather, as in the case of Sicilian and Byzantine courts of the twelfth and thirteenth centuries, rulers of fourteenth and fifteenth century Vijayanagara chose to participate in a territorially decentred Islamicate world-system that was compelling precisely because it was *not* identified with political domination from any hegemonic centre. Although the territorial reach of a Sufi's wilāyat was theoretically unlimited, in practice it was always identified with well-defined, specific localities, just as the river goddess Pampā was unalterably identified with the Tungabhadra River. By contrast association with the courtly and cosmopolitan Islamicate world-system, being detached from any particular religious or ethnic community and lacking any clearly locatable centre or periphery, proved eminently useful for aspiring kings or states of all kinds in the medieval Deccan.

[39] Tabataba's *Burhān-i maʾāthir* was completed in 1595–6 under the patronage of the Nizam Shahi kings of Ahmadnagar. Shirazi's *Tazkirat al-mulūk* was composed in 1608 under the patronage of the 'Adil Shahi kings of Bijapur, who also patronized Firishta's *Tārīkh-i Firishta*, completed in 1623.

[40] Zeynep Celik, ' "Islamic" Architecture in French Colonial Discourse,' paper read at the Fifteenth Giorgio Levi della Vida Award and Conference, 'The Experience of Islamic Art,' UCLA, Los Angeles, 10–13 May 1996.

7

Historical Introduction to Firuzabad, Palace City of the Deccan[*]

On the north bank of the Bhima River on India's Deccan Plateau lies the ruined city of Firuzabad, one of the most historically important yet unknown architectural legacies of medieval India. This city served as a royal palace and second capital for monarchs of the Bahmani kingdom (1347–1537), and in particular for its builder, Sultan Firuz Shah Bahmani (r. 1397–1422). Constructed between 1399 and 1406, Firuzabad remained in sporadic use by several of Firuz's successors through the end of the fifteenth century, after which it disappeared from recorded memory. The present essay examines the reasons for the establishment of the city, its fundamental character, the court life and activities that took place there, and the reasons for its abandonment.

The earliest surviving histories of Sultan Firuz Shah Bahmani's twenty-five year reign include the *Burhān-i maʾāthir*, composed between 1592 and 1596 by Saiyid 'Ali Tabataba, the *Tazkirāt al-mulūk*, written between 1608 and 1611 by Rafi' al-Din Ibrahim Shirazi, and the *Tārīkh-i Firishta*, written between 1606 and 1611 by Muhammad Qasim Firishta. Patronized by Indo-Muslim kings of the Deccan, all three chroniclers were immigrants from the Persian-speaking region of west Asia, as were many of the builders and inhabitants of Firuzabad. Although their histories were not recorded until a century after the collapse of the Bahmani dynasty and the abandonment of Firuzabad, the three men were all eminent scholars who based their work on oral traditions of their own day and on earlier histories, some of which are now lost.[1]

---

[1] Tabataba confined his study to the history of the Bahmani kingdom and the

[*] Reprinted from George Michell and Richard Eaton, *Firuzabad: Palace City of the Deccan*. Oxford Studies in Islamic Art, VIII, ed. Julian Ruby. Oxford: Oxford University Press, 1992.

These sources differ, however, in explaining why Firuzabad was built and how it was used. Since Firishta's is the most complete statement of the city's origins, we may begin by quoting in full the relevant extract from the *Tārīkh-i Firishta*:

Because Sultan Firuz Shah wished to possess the facility of language as lovely as fairies and as adorned as peacocks, he built on the banks of the Bhima River a city named Firuzabad, and made this place his royal residence [*takhtgāh*]. Its markets and shops achieved the acme of cleanliness and excellence, while its streets were both wide and straight. The city's citadel, constructed of plaster and stone, opened out onto the river on one side and canals carried water from the river into its interior.

Separate villas as lovely as the moon were also built, and each one was conferred upon one of the women of the sultan's harem. ... [In addition to Arabic- and Persian-speaking women], the sultan kept Turkish, European, Afghan, Rajput, Bengali, Gujarati, Telugu, Kanarese, and Marathi women in his harem, and knew the native language of each of them. Each day he would visit one of these apartments and comport himself in such a way that each woman considered herself the sultan's most beloved.[2]

According to Firishta, the sultan would seem to have built the city primarily for expanding his linguistic skills, and secondarily for indulging his appetite for female companionship. On this latter point, Firishta elsewhere noted that the sultan was so addicted to women that he was even compelled to modify his personal theology in order to legitimize his desires in the eyes of Islamic Law.[3] Clearly, Firuzabad functioned

early history of one of its five successor states, the Nizam Shahi sultans of Ahmadnagar, under whose patronage the historian wrote. Shirazi, an Iranian adventurer and diplomat, confined his *Tazkirat al-mulūk* to the 'Adil Shahi dynasty of Bijapur. Firishta, who was patronized by the kings of the same dynasty, undertook a far more ambitious work than the other two historians, endeavoring to chronicle all Indo-Muslim history down to his own time. Concerning Firuzabad, Firishta relied upon several important chronicles that are now lost, in particular the *Tuḥfat al-salaṭin* by Mulla Da'ud Bidri, the *Sirāj al-tawārīkh* by Mulla Muhammad Lari, and the *Tārīkh* of Hajji Muhammad Qandahari. See Muhammad Qasim Firishta, *Tārīkh-i Firishta*, 2 vols. (Lucknow: Niwal Kishor, 1864–5), 1:307, 309.

[2] Firishta, *Tārīkh-i Firishta*, 1:308–9. My translation of this passage follows the original Persian somewhat more closely than does that of John Briggs in his *History of the Rise of the Mahomedan Power in India*, 4 vols. (London, 1829. Reprinted in 3 vols. Calcutta: Editions Indian, 1966), 2:227–8.

[3] The kingdom's chief minister, Mir Fazl Allah Anju, counselled Firuz that although polygamy was forbidden in the traditions of Sunni Islam, the sect to which the sultan belonged, in the Shi'i legal tradition the practice of taking multiple wives on a temporary basis, or *mut'a*, was perfectly lawful. Accordingly, Sultan Firuz elected to follow Shi'i custom in this one regard and forthwith called eight hundred

as a retreat for Sultan Firuz, as a place where the king was free to devote himself to scholarship, rest, and pleasure. Such an understanding of the city's basic purpose is also found in the work of Firishta's contemporary, Rafi' al-Din Ibrahim Shirazi, who noted that 'for a long time [Sultan Firuz] lived in that city in enjoyment and the gratification of his desires'.[4]

It would be a mistake, however, to understand from these remarks that the city served merely as a royal language lab or a multi-ethnic playpen.[5] References in other historical literature, the city's plan, and the nature of its monuments all belie such an interpretation. In the first place, we note Firishta's characterization of the city as a *takhtgāh*, which means 'throne-place,' or court. That Firuzabad served as the kingdom's ancillary capital is borne out by episodes known from its later history, as we shall see below. Secondly, one can infer from the massiveness of the city's walls and the enormous size of its Jami', or congregational mosque, that the city was intended to defend and accommodate a sizeable population. Completed probably in 1406,[6] the

---

women to his harem in a single day. See Firishta *Tārikh-i Firishta*, 1:307. One may legitimately question, however, whether the sultan's sexual prowess was so great. We know that Firishta was often given to exaggeration, and this is probably one such instance. Indeed, Shirazi wrote that the sultan had but one wife. See Rafi' al-Din Ibrahim Shirazi, *Taẕkirāt al-mulūk*. Pers. MS. (Hyderabad: Asafiyah Library, Tarikh no. 1081), fol. 9b. Cited in H. K. Sherwani, 'Taju'd-din Firoz and the Synthesis of Bahmani Culture,' *New Indian Antiquary* (July, 1943), 77n.

[4] Rafi' al-Din Ibrahim Shirazi, *Taẕkirāt al-mulūk* (Pers. MS) London: India Office Library, Persian MS 2838, fol. 11b. Partially translated by Wolseley Haig in *Indian Antiquary* 28 (July, 1899), 191.

[5] Excessive reliance on Firishta is seen in the only interpretive study of Firuzabad made to date, an essay written in 1955 by Klaus Fischer, who described the city as 'more a pleasure resort than a residence.' See Klaus Fischer, 'Firozabad on the Bhima and its Environs,' *Islamic Culture* 29 (1955), 246.

[6] The suggested date of the mosque's completion is derived from an inscription dated 30 Rajab 808 A.H., corresponding to 21 January, 1406, and which reads, 'This auspicious mosque was started and raised by the greatest and magnificent sultan, the most eminent among the sultans of Arabia and 'Ajam, Abu'l-Muzaffar Taju'd-Dunya wa'd-Din, Firuz Shah the Sultan, may Allah perpetuate his kingdom and sovereignty, on the last day of the auspicious month of Rajab, year eight and eight hundred.' The inscription even identifies the mosque's architect, Ahmad bin Husain al-Hisnkayfi. The inscription, however, is not at present located on the Jami' Mosque, but on a small mosque in the shrine of Khalifat al-Rahman, outside the city walls to the north. Akbaru'd-Din Siddiqi, who published this inscription, has argued that since it dedicates a mosque to the sultan, it more likely belonged originally to the great Jami' Mosque in the city, which has no inscription at

magnificent Jami' Mosque, which measures 343' by 202' (104.5 by 61.5 meters) and covers an area of 69,286 square feet (6,427 square meters), is the most imposing and impressive structure now remaining in Firuzabad. Nearly double the size of the royal mosque in the official capital of Gulbarga, the Firuzabad congregational mosque in its own day ranked among the largest in the subcontinent. More importantly, it was then the largest in the Deccan, the immediate point of reference for all sovereigns in the Indian peninsula.[7] A congregational mosque constructed on this grand scale, having as it did the function of accommodating the city's male Muslim population, suggests that Firuzabad was intended to be considerably more than simply a personal retreat for the sultan.

This conclusion is supported by the earliest surviving literary source for the history of Firuzabad, the *Burhān-i ma'āthir* by Saiyid 'Ali Tabataba. We have seen that Firishta discussed the building of Firuzabad only by way of illustrating certain features of the sultan's character, in particular his penchant for linguistic skills and women. Hence, his description of Firuzabad emerges as quite incidental to the history of the Bahmani kingdom, and the city's character appears almost frivolous. Tabataba, on the other hand, discusses the city in the context of the sultan's continual wars with his chief adversary and neighbor to the south, the great Vijayanagara empire, and of his concerns with the military defense of his kingdom. In fact, virtually all of Firuz's long reign was spent in warfare with Vijayanagara. Firishta records that Firuz led twenty-four campaigns against non-Muslims, meaning in particular Vijayanagara, which amounts to an average of exactly one campaign for each year of his reign.[8]

_____

present, and which can reasonably be expected to have had one. Arguing that the Jami' Mosque has a greater claim to this somewhat grandiose inscription than the more modest mosque outside the city's walls, Siddiqi has suggested that the inscription tablet was probably shifted at some time from the ruined Jami' Mosque to its present place in order to ensure its preservation. Akbaru'd-Din Siddiqi, 'Two Inscriptions of the Bahmani Period from Firozabad,' *Epigraphia Indica, Arabic and Persian Supplement* (1972), 41–42.

[7] The following is a list of the major mosques in the Deccan existing at the time Sultan Firuz built the Jami' Mosque at Firuzabad. Listed also are their approximate and probable dates of construction, their outside measurements, and their overall area. Daulatabad: 1318, 260' by 260', 67,600 sq. feet; Gulbarga: 1367, 216' by 176', 38,016 sq. feet; Firuzabad: 1406, 343' by 202', 69,286 sq. feet. The data for the Daulatabad and Gulbarga mosques are given in Z.A. Desai, 'Architecture: The Bahmanis,' in H. K. Sherwani and P. M. Joshi, eds, *History of Medieval Deccan (1295–1724)*, (2 vols, Hyderabad: Government of Andhra Pradesh, 1974), 2:229, 240.

[8] Firishta, *Tārīkh-i Firishta*, 1:309; Briggs, *Rise of the Mahomedan Power*, 2:228.

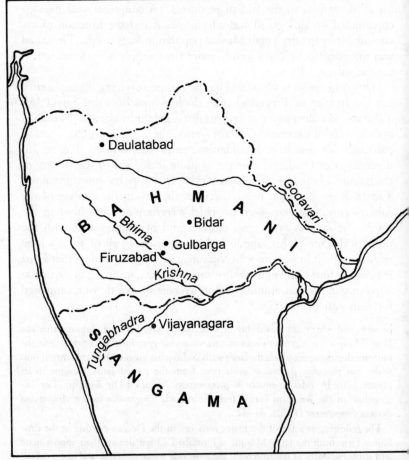

Map 3: Peninsular India at the beginning of the fifteenth century, showing the location of Fīrūzābād within the Bahmani kingdom, together with other important centres.

Source: George Michell and Richard Eaton, *Firuzabad: Palace City of the Deccan*, Oxford: Oxford University Press, 1992, p. 20 (Oxford Studies in Islamic Art, no. 8 ed. by Julian Ruby).

The perennial wars between the Bahmani kingdom and the Vijayanagara empire focused especially on access to and control over the agriculturally rich Raichur plain, or *dōāb*, which is formed by the Krishna and Tungabhadra rivers and which lay directly between the capital cities of Gulbarga and Vijayanagara (see map 3).[9] In the spring or summer of 1399, just a year after Firuz had assumed the Bahmani throne, internal rebellions and a foreign invasion tested the new sultan's mettle as a monarch.[10] Seizing the opportunity opened by the internal rebellions, the raja of Vijayanagara moved an immense force of 30,000 cavalry and a host of archers and foot soldiers across the Tungabhadra river and into the contested Raichur dōāb region. Firuz countered this by marching his own army of 12,000 cavalry out of Gulbarga and down to Sagar, just north of the Krishna river. The Vijayanagara army having moved northward over the Raichur dōāb by this time, the two forces now faced each other on either side of the Krishna river. While the two armies were camped and temporarily stalemated as the river was in full spate, Firuz resorted to a bold ruse. Under the cover of darkness, a small party of his forces crossed the river, stole into the heart of the Vijayanagara camp in the guise of musicians, and stabbed the crown prince while he was in a state of merry-making. The Vijayanagara army was thrown into such disarray that Firuz's soldiers were able to cross the river before dawn and, presenting themselves before their adversaries with swords drawn, forced the alarmed and demoralized raja to conclude a peace settlement favourable to the Bahmani sultan.[11]

Flushed by this victory and with his baggage trains full of booty captured from the Vijayanagara army, Firuz now retraced his steps northward toward his capital of Gulbarga. On his way, he passed again through Sagar, which he renamed Nusratabad, or 'City of Victory,' perhaps mocking the name Vijayanagara, which also means 'City of Victory'. Still moving northward, the sultan crossed the Bhima River

[9] See P. M. Joshi, 'The Raichur Doab in Deccan History—A Reinterpretation of a Struggle,' *Journal of Indian History* 36 (1958), 379–96.

[10] Firishta states that these events occurred in the year 801 A. H., which extended from 13 September 1398 to 3 September 1399. He furthermore stated that the armies became bogged down in the rains, which normally start in July. Elsewhere he says that the campaign was concluded several months before the beginning of 802, which commenced on 3 September 1399. Therefore the military campaigns must have begun during the preceding spring or summer, in 1399. See Firishta, *Tārīkh-i Firishta*, 1:309, 311; Briggs, *Rise of the Mahomedan Power*, 2:228–9, 232.

[11] Firishta, *Tārīkh-i Firishta*, 1:309–11; Briggs, *Rise of the Mahomedan Power*, 2:228–32.

and camped for several days on its northern bank. Then and there he determined to build a royal city named Firuzabad, or 'City of Firuz'. As to its purpose, wrote Tabataba, 'Anytime the king had the intention of waging war on the infidels of Vijayanagara, on the occasion of departure or returning he would stay several days in that glorious place for the purpose of resting in the paradisiac city. After he completed his stay at Firuzabad, the sultan would return to the capital to attend to the affairs of government.'[12]

Tabataba thus understood the city's essential character primarily in military terms, as a rallying point for the sultan's armies *en route* to do battle with the armies of Vijayanagara, and as a resting point for his armies returning from wars in the south. This interpretation is confirmed by the city's location. It lies seventeen miles (twenty-eight km.) due south of Gulbarga, on the northern side of the Bhima river separating the Bahmani capital from the Raichur doāb. Within easy access of Gulbarga, it was perfectly positioned to defend the Bahmani capital from direct attacks coming from the south. Moreover, as it lay directly on the route normally taken by Bahmani armies in their southern campaigns, Firuzabad could serve as a staging area for offensive strikes against Vijayanagara, just as Tabataba indicates. In these circumstances the city would have had to accommodate great numbers of soldiers, which would explain the large size of Firuzabad's congregational mosque.

We may conclude that Firuzabad served both as a military camp and as a personal retreat for Sultan Firuz Bahmani. We also know that while on campaign or tending to administrative affairs in Gulbarga, the sultan kept his family in Firuzabad. In September 1422, while lying on his deathbed in Gulbarga, Firuz summoned his brother Ahmad and read out to him his last will and testament. It seems that he had previously wished to be succeeded by his son Hasan Khan and had even arranged formal ceremonies in which the nobility paid homage to the son, but that in his final days the aged sultan changed his mind in favour of his younger brother Ahmad. Said Firuz to his brother, 'Go to Firuzabad and see to it that the rest of my family not deviate from this will of mine.'[13]

The city also seems to have figured prominently in the sultan's spiritual life. Some 1.3 miles (2 km.) north of its walls is the tomb and shrine of a Muslim holy man, locally known as Khalifat al-Rahman. Although we possess no authentic contemporary records concerning

[12] Tabataba, *Burhān-i maāthir*, 43.
[13] Tabataba, *Burhān-i maāthir*, 52.

the life of this saint,[14] there is little doubt that he played an important role in the spiritual life of both Firuzabad and its founder. Here one might recall that according to some traditions prevalent in India of Firuz's day, Indo-Muslim sultans were never endowed with the same degree of religious, or even political, legitimacy as were some Sufi shaikhs. In this view, temporal rulers had only been entrusted with a sort of temporary lease of power through the grace of Muslim shaikhs considered to have been especially well-endowed with *baraka*, or the grace of God. This is why we occasionally come across Sufis predicting who would attain political office, and for how long they would hold it. Many understood such predictions as virtual appointments.[15] Struck by the awesome spiritual powers commonly attributed to nearby Sufis, and believing in many cases that their own lease of power had been given them by such persons, Indo-Muslim monarchs typically sought their favour and patronized the construction of great edifices for them.

This is probably what happened in the case of Firuzabad's shrine of Khalifat al-Rahman, which appears to have been built by Sultan Firuz. Stylistically, the monument is contemporary with the other buildings of Firuzabad, and a nearby gravestone bears the date 1421.[16] Moreover, from what we know of Firuz's stormy relations with Saiyid

---

[14] See Akbaru'd-Din Siddiqi, 'Two Inscriptions,' 39. Muhammad Suleman Siddiqi reports finding a document, belonging to Firuz's reign, that records the donation of the whole of Firuzabad's revenues to Khalifat al-Rahman. The document also gives an account of a miracle that the Sufi purportedly performed in the sultan's presence, which leads Suleman Siddiqi to question the document's authenticity. See Muhammad Suleman Siddiqi, *The Bahmani Sufis* (Delhi: Idarah-i Adabiyat-i Delli, 1989), 76.

[15] An example will illustrate this point. It happened that in the early fourteenth century the future Sultan Ghiyath al-Din Tughluq, founder of the Tughluq dynasty of Delhi (1321–98), became one of many local notables attracted to the spiritual power and piety of a holy man in the Punjab named 'Ala al-Din Mauj Darya. The governor accordingly made frequent visits to the holy man, and on one such occasion brought along with him his son and his nephew, the future Sultans Muhammad bin Tughluq and Firuz Tughluq. All three were given turbans by the saint and told that each was destined to rule India. The length of each turban, moreover, exactly corresponded to the number of years each would reign. See Shams-i Siraj 'Afif, *Tārīkh-i Fīrūz Shāhī*, ed. Maulavi Vilayat Husain (Calcutta: Asiatic Society of Bengal, 1891), 27–8. In all likelihood Sultan Firuz Bahmani was familiar with this story. For not only was it related by an historian contemporary with Firuz, but it concerned the origins of Delhi's Tughluq dynasty of kings, from which the Bahmani house itself had sprung in 1347, and which remained in power down to the time of Firuz's accession.

[16] Akbaru'd-Din Siddiqi, 'Two Inscriptions', 44.

Muhammad Husaini Gisudaraz (d. 1422), perhaps the most famous Sufi of the Deccan, it seems very likely that the sultan patronized Khalifat al-Rahman and his shrine. According to Firishta, Sultan Firuz judged Gisudaraz deficient in learning and so withdrew royal favour from him. The sultan's brother Ahmad, on the other hand, lavishly patronized the shaikh by building a residence for him and by attending his meetings devoted to ecstatic practices. In 1415, Gisudaraz declined to endorse the sultan's selection of his son Hasan Khan to succeed him. Some eight years earlier, Firuz had ordered the shaikh to leave the city, on the pretext that his meetings with fellow dervishes were creating a public nuisance. Toward the end of the sultan's reign, when the question of his succession had driven a wedge between his son and his brother and their respective supporters, Saiyid Gisudaraz took a turban and divided it in two parts, placing one part on the head of the sultan's brother Ahmad, and another part on the head of Ahmad's own son, symbolically predicting the future sovereignty of both.[17] But as stated above, such 'predictions' were also understood as effective appointments.

Between 1415 and and his death in 1422, then, Firuz ruled his kingdom without the blessings of the most eminent shaikh in the realm. Worse still, those blessings had been given to his own brother and potential rival for the throne, Ahmad. It therefore seems likely that at some time after 1415, after having fallen out with Saiyid Gisudaraz, Firuz sought and found other Sufis on whom to lavish his patronage. We know from the chronicle of Rafi' al-Din Shirazi that he took as his spiritual advisor a certain Baba Kamal Mujarrad, whose tomb is supposed to have faced the sultan's own tomb in Gulbarga.[18] In the

---

[17] Firishta, *Tārīkh-i Firishta*, 1:316, 317; Briggs, *Rise of the Mahomedan Power*, 2:240, 242.

[18] Shirazi, *Tazkirat al-muluk* (India Office Library MS.), fol. 12 a. Trans. Wolseley Haig, *Indian Antiquary* 28 (July 1899), 192. Extant hagiographical literature does not record the name of this saint. Shirazi wrote that his tomb was an elaborate construction, that it faced the sultan's own tomb in Gulbarga, that it had beneath it a reservoir that the sultan had built during the saint's lifetime, and that in Shirazi's own day, i.e., 1611, the tomb's dome and the reservoir were still in existence. This saint may be Shah Kamal Mujjarad, whose tomb is built in the style of Firuz's period, and is accompanied by a mosque, a *sarāy*, and an unidentified structure. This complex faces Firuz's tomb, which is situated on the eastern edges of Gulbarga, but lies 0.6 miles (one kilometer) further east. On the other hand, the tomb of Baba Kamal might also be the as yet unidentified tomb lying to the immediate south of Sultan Firoz's tomb. See Desai, 'Architecture,' in Sherwani and Joshi, eds., *History of Medieval Deccan*, 2:237, 240.

same way, it would appear that Firuz had adopted still another spiritual advisor, Khalifat al-Rahman, whose impressive shrine he had built just outside the city.

In any event, it is certain that the character of Firuzabad underwent an abrupt change after the death of Sultan Firuz. Firishta recorded a rumor, current in the historian's day, that Ahmad had risen to power by having had his brother strangled to death.[19] Firishta's contemporary, Rafi' al-Din Shirazi, gave a detailed account of this same version, stating without reservations that Ahmad had arranged for his brother's death at the hand of an Abyssinian assassin.[20] This version conflicts with the earlier and probably more reliable account of Tabataba, according to which the two brothers reached a reconciliation just prior to Firuz's natural death. In any case, it is clear that politics in Gulbarga were for some time severely divided on the issue of Firuz's succession: Ahmad enjoyed the support of the respected shaikh, Saiyid Gisudaraz, and no doubt of the latter's numerous followers, while many nobles still supported the cause of Firuz's son, Hasan Khan. As a consequence of these deep political divisions, Ahmad, on becoming sultan, was advised by some of his counselors to confine, blind, or murder Hasan.[21] While not going so far as to murder his nephew, Ahmad did take immediate and vigorous steps to disentangle himself from the webs of intrigue that had surrounded his accession to power. For one thing, he shifted the Bahmani capital from Gulbarga, which had been the capital since the founding of the dynasty in 1347, to Bidar, a new site some sixty miles (96 km.) to the northeast. This symbolized his efforts to leave behind him the dangerous political world associated with the ancestral capital city.[22]

It seems to have been with the same political agenda in mind that the new sultan redefined the status of Firuzabad. Instead of murdering Hasan Khan as some of his advisors urged him to do, he made his nephew a noble (*amīr*) with the humble rank of 500 horses and assigned Firuzabad to him as a personal estate. But the unfortunate Hasan Khan was in effect placed under house arrest and made a prisoner in his father's palace city. There, as Firishta tells it, Hasan Khan was 'ordered' to live a life of ease, to which he was in any case naturally inclined,

---

[19] Firishta, *Tārīkh-i Firishta*, 1:319; Briggs, *Rise of the Mahomedan Power*, 2:245.

[20] Shirazi, *Tazkirāt al-mulūk* (India Office Library MS.), fol. 12b. Trans. Wolseley Haig, *Indian Antiquary* 28 (July 1899), 192.

[21] Firishta, *Tārīkh-i Firishta*, 1:320; Briggs, *Rise of the Mahomedan Power*, 2:247.

[22] H.K. Sherwani, *Bahmanis of the Deccan* (2nd edn, New Delhi: Munshiram Manoharlal, 1977), 122–3.

and was permitted to promenade or hunt only within an eight mile radius of the palace. Despite these measures, Sultan Ahmad still perceived his nephew as posing a real or potential threat to him, and subsequently had him blinded and kept confined to the Firuzabad palace until his death.[23]

Removed now to his new capital in Bidar, and busy with his many splendid construction projects there, Sultan Ahmad Bahmani (r. 1422–36) is not known ever again to have visited Firuzabad, which seems from the mid-1420s to have begun its decline. Not until 1461, when an eight-year old scion of the dynasty ascended the Bahmani throne as Sultan Nizam al-Din Ahmad III, do we again hear of the city. At this time several regents and the Queen mother shared power amongst themselves, but with no vigorous adult on its throne the kingdom was clearly weakened. Seeking to exploit the situation, in 1461–2 the sultan of Malwa invaded Bahmani domains with the apparent aim of laying seige to the capital. In these circumstances the Queen mother entrusted the defense of Bidar to one of her generals while she, together with the treasury and the women of the harem, retired with the young king to Firuzabad.[24] This suggests that as of 1461 Firuzabad no longer functioned as a permanent residence for either the harem, the treasury, or the king's family, and very likely had not been so used since the death of Firuz in 1422.

The last recorded reference to the city belongs to the unhappy events of 1481, when a combination of murderous internal conflicts and external invasions plunged the kingdom into rapid decline. On April 5 of that year Sultan Shams al-Din Muhammad III, in a drunken fit, ordered the execution of his talented and loyal minister, Mahmud Gawan. This execution, urged on the king by the minister's jealous enemies, drove the king into despair and the kingdom into confusion. Unable either to command the respect of his nobility or to find a suitable replacement for his trusted minister, the despondent sultan allowed his generals to disperse with their armies while he himself marched to Firuzabad.

There, in that city that had been built for, among other things, the pleasure of his great grandfather, a grief-stricken and remorseful Sultan Muhammad spent three months drowning himself in drink, which only hastened his decline. In what was perhaps the last government act effected in Firuzabad, the sultan, by this time very ill, entrusted the kingdom to his twelve-year old son, Prince Mahmud. As the document was being drawn up, the sultan was heard to lament: 'If they

[23] Firishta, *Tārīkh-i Firishta*, 1:320; Briggs, *Rise of the Mahomedan Power*, 2:247.
[24] Firishta, *Tārīkh-i Firishta*, 1:344; Briggs, *Rise of the Mahomedan Power*, 2:290.

do not obey me, who reigned gloriously for many years, and conquered nations with my sword, how will they submit to a child?'[25] The sultan then returned to Bidar where he died within several months, exactly one lunar year after the execution of his minister.

Firuzabad thus passed from historical memory. The city is not known to have been used again by any of the last Bahmani kings, nor by any kings of the dynasty's five successor states. In reality, the city's decline began at the death of its builder, since Firuz's brother Ahmad chose not to associate himself, his family, or his court with the place. Having banished his nephew there, Sultan Ahmad Bahmani seems to have allowed the city to languish in disrepair. Later, his successors made only desultory and temporary use of Firuzabad, considering it more a place of refuge than a royal court, as though the place were haunted by the ghost of its great builder.

In fact, there is evidence that, because of flooding and water damage, the city lay in partial ruins already in Firuz's day. Rafi' al-Din Shirazi observed that when the sultan was at Firuzabad, 'it chanced that at one time heavy rain fell, and the water of the river overflowed to such an extent that the country round for three or four *farsakhs* [ten to thirteen miles, or 16.1 to 20.9 km] was flooded, and much damage was caused. In the streets and bazaar of the city the water rose so high that the sultan and his family for seven days and nights had to live in the upper storey of the palace. The fortifications of the city still remain, but that building has not remained.'[26] Though written nearly two centuries after the death of Firuz, this extract suggests that politics may not have been the only cause of the city's abandonment.

To conclude, Firuzabad's brief apogee lasted only from 1406, the date the magnificent Jami' Mosque was probably completed, to Firuz's death in 1422. As the city was so thoroughly identified with a single monarch, it would be appropriate to conclude this essay, as we began it, with an extract from Firishta's estimate of the sultan. 'He used to say,' wrote the historian,

that kings should draw around them the most learned and meritorious persons of all nations, so that from their society they might obtain information, and thus reap some of the advantages acquired by travelling into distant regions of the globe. The King had so excellent a memory that he could converse in many languages; a practice he exercised, as far as practicable, towards foreigners.

[25] Firishta, *Tārīkh-i Firishta*, 1:361; Briggs, *Rise of the Mahomedan Power*, 2:319. Briggs's translation.

[26] Shirazi, *Taẕkirāt al-mulūk* (India Office Library MS.), fol. 11b. Trans. Wolseley Haig, *Indian Antiquary* 28 (July 1899), 191–2.

It was sufficient to hear a circumstance once related to enable him to retain it in mind ever after. He was a good poet, and often made extempore verses. He was well acquainted with several sciences, and particularly fond of natural philosophy. On Saturdays, Mondays, and Thursdays, he heard lectures on botany, geometry, and logic, generally in the day, but if business interfered, at night. It is said, that he even excelled Mahomed Toghluk in literary attainments.[27]

Like the Mughal Emperor Akbar (1556–1605), another great builder whom he preceded by two centuries, Sultan Firuz Shah Bahmani emerges as a man possessed of remarkable intellect. And like the builder of Fatehpur Sikri, Sultan Firuz chose the construction of an auxiliary capital as the vehicle for expressing and focussing his abundantly creative energies. The aptly named palace-city was the architectural manifestation of those energies.

---

[27] Firishta, *Tārīkh-i Firishta*, 1:308; Briggs, *Rise of the Mahomedan Power*, 2:227. Briggs's translation.

8

Sufi Folk Literature and the Expansion of Indian Islam[*]

The secondary literature on medieval Indian society frequently portrays the Sufis as a group that provided a vital link between Hindus and Muslims, to some extent mitigating the harshness of the Muslim military conquest of the subcontinent.[1] Many writers have advanced the argument somewhat further by identifying the Sufis as important agents in the conversion to Islam of a large segment of India's Hindu population, especially Hindus of lower castes.[2] But what is lacking in this literature is a satisfactory explanation of how an essentially esoteric mystical tradition might have filtered down to commoners in some sort of comprehensible and appealing form. It would be hard to imagine, for example, how depressed and illiterate Hindu castes such as the cotton cleaners or the barbers could have been attracted to an abstract system of mystical

[1] See H. K. Sherwani, 'Cultural Synthesis in Medieval India,' *Journal of Indian History* 41, no. 1 (April 1963), 256–7; Tara Chand, *Society and State in the Mughal Period* (Delhi, 1965), 96–100; Yusuf Husain Khan, 'Sufism in India,' *Islamic Culture* 30 (July 1956), 252; M. Yasin, *A Social History of Islamic India (1605–1748)* (Lucknow, 1958), 51.

[2] See T. W. Arnold, *The Preaching of Islam: A History of the Propagation of the Muslim Faith*, 2nd ed. (London, 1913), 270–1; Aziz Ahmad, *Studies in the Islamic Culture in the Indian Environment* (Oxford, 1964), 83–4; A. B. M. Habibullah, *The Foundation of Muslim Rule in India*, 2d ed. (Allahabad, 1967), 305–6; M. Mujeeb, *The Indian Muslims* (London, 1967), 22; K. A. Nizami, *Studies in Medieval Indian History and Culture* (Allahabad, 1966), 92; A. Rashid, *Society and Culture in Medieval India* (Calcutta, 1969), 192–3; A. L. Srivastava, *Medieval Indian Culture* (Agra, 1964), 78; M. T. Titus, *Islam in India and Pakistan* (Calcutta, 1959), 48–9.

[*] Reprinted from *History of Religions* 14, no. 2 (November 1974), 117–27.

stages and states requiring an immense degree of intellectual and spiritual discipline. Moreover, the Sufis of medieval India, as elsewhere, frequently stressed the elitist nature of their circles and the necessity of keeping their most esoteric knowledge to themselves. Indeed, one distinguished scholar has argued that Sufis in general felt a certain distrust of the common man and that this feeling was evidenced by their separation of the initiated Sufi from the noninitiated layman.[3]

One likely reason for the failure to explain the attraction of Hindu nonelites to Sufis has been the tendency among many scholars of Sufism to concentrate almost exclusively on the mystical literature, as opposed to the folk literature, as representing the sum and substance of the Sufi movement. The mystical literature, which can be said to represent the 'high tradition' of the Sufi movement in India and elsewhere, consisted of treatises on the abstract stages and states originally formulated by such mystical thinkers as Ibn al-'Arabi. This literature was written for the edification of fellow Sufis and does not seem to have circulated among the lower elements of Hindu India, nor was it intended to. Moreover in India, as in most of the non-Arab Muslim world, such literature was usually written in Persian, which was certainly not a vernacular language among the nonelite Hindu population. Hence if it is true, as R. A. Nicholson has noted, that 'Sufism is at once the religious philosophy and the popular religion of Islam,'[4] the link between the two has not been clearly established, at least as far as concerns Indian Islam.

Based on research on the medieval Deccan city-state of Bijapur (1490–1686), it is my opinion that such a link was supplied in at least one sector of the Indian subcontinent by the folk literature of certain local Sufis. Consisting of a number of short poems written in one of the vernacular languages of medieval Bijapur, Dakani, this literature employed indigenous themes and imagery for the propagation not of complex mystical doctrines of the sort mentioned above, but of a simpler level of Sufi and also of Islamic precepts. Written mainly in the seventeenth and eighteenth centuries by Bijapur Sufis belonging to the Chishti order, or by their descendants scattered elsewhere in the Deccan, this literature has been preserved in the oral tradition of Dakani-speaking villagers throughout the Deccan plateau. It has been suggested that until the twentieth century, when radio and cinema took its place, folk poetry of Sufi origin had occupied a dominant position in the folk culture

[3] Ann K. S. Lambton, 'Free Thinking and Individual Freedom,' in *Islam in the Modern World*, ed. Syed Ali Ahsan (Dacca, 1964), 82.

[4] R. A. Nicholson, *Studies in Islamic Mysticism* (Cambridge, 1967), 65.

of Deccan villages.[5] What, then, was the nature of this literature, to whom did it appeal, and what was its relation to Islam or to Sufism?

The bulk of the folk poetry written by Sufis was sung by village women while engaged in various household chores. The most common types included the *chakki-nāma*, so called because it was sung while grinding food grains at the grindstone or *chakki*, and the *charkha-nāma*, sung while spinning thread at the spinning wheel, or *charkha*. Other types of such folk poetry included the *lūñ-nāma* or lullaby, the *shādi-nāma* or wedding song, the *suhāgan-nāma* or married woman's song, and the *suhailā* or eulogistic song.[6] It is evident that most of these poetic forms appealed especially, and probably exclusively, to women. For in the villages of the Deccan it was the women who for centuries spun the cotton into thread, ground the *juwar* into meal, and rocked the children to sleep. Each of these activities involved a steady moving of the hands, which the singing of songs composed in a regular meter could easily assist. This is especially true for the chakki-nama and the charkha-nama, the most widespread forms of Dakani folk poetry, both of which involved the turning of a wheel by hand. Such village poetry appealed to women not only because it accompanied the household chores that they in particular performed, but also because its content was permeated with imagery especially meaningful to them. Female love and its manifestations were typical themes in this literature, and metaphors frequently drew on the two worlds of a young bride: the parental home she had left and her new father-in-law's home.[7]

The few studies that have been made of Dakani folk literature trace it to the efforts by Sufis to expand their teachings among the unlettered folk of the Deccan plateau.[8] This is no doubt true so far as the written tradition of this poetry is concerned. But it does not mean that Sufis originated the idea of singing songs while grinding *juwār* or while spinning thread. Some sort of folk poetry relating to work at the spinning wheel or the grindstone undoubtedly existed in the Marathi and Kannada oral traditions long before Islam penetrated the Deccan plateau and is probably as old as the ubiquitous grindstone or spinning wheel themselves.[9] What Sufis did was to adapt the simplest elements of Sufi doctrine

[5] Zinat Sajida, 'Dakani git,' *Majallai Osmania, Dakani Adab Number*, no. 65 (1963–4), 217.

[6] Abu'l-Hasan Qadiri, *Sukh anjan*, ed. Sayyida Ja'far (Hyderabad, 1968), 60–1 (passage quoted is from the editor's introduction to Qadiri's book).

[7] See Rafi'a Sultana, *Urdu nasr ka aghaz aur irtiqa* (Hyderabad, n.d.), 250.

[8] Sajida, 217–8; Sultana, 247–8; Ja'far, 60–1.

[9] The Marathi poems that village women of Maharashtra sing today while grinding

to the already existing vehicles of folk poetry and to substitute vernacular Dakani for vernacular Marathi or Kannada.[10] Since the Sufism injected into this literature carried with it the essentials of Islam, the Sufis' use of this vehicle may be said to represent a major development in the cultural history of the Deccan.

Sufi folk literature can be found today in both written and oral traditions. Despite the intrusion of modern media in the villages, folk poetry relating to household chores is still sung, though apparently less so today than formerly. In the written tradition, chakki-namas and charkha-namas have appeared in various cheap lithograph editions that can still be found in the Deccan countryside. There also exist manuscript versions of this poetry, of which some dozen, preserved in collections in Hyderabad, have come to my attention. These manuscripts indicate that most of the folk poetry discussed here originated with Bijapur Sufis of the Chishti order.

All eleven of these manuscripts, most of which are chakki-namas, are undated copies of poetry which, judging from the style of Dakani used, can be ascribed to the seventeenth or early eighteenth century. One chakki-nama is attributed to Amin al-Din A'la (d. 1675),[11] an important seventeenth-century Sufi and free thinking mystic. But this chakki-nama cannot be authentic, since it refers to events that occurred after Amin al-Din's death. Its style and content, however, clearly prove it to be the work of a Sufi, and probably a Sufi of Bijapur, since the scribe was himself a resident of that city.[12] Another chakki-nama closes with the name of Shah Hashim Khudawand Hadi (d. 1704–5),[13] one of Amin al-Din's closest initiates (*khalifa*) at Bijapur, and both internal and external evidence would support its authenticity. A third chakki-nama was written by a certain Faruqi,[14] a disciple (*murid*) of another

---

meal are functionally identical with the chakki-namas of the Sufis. Significantly, they, too, serve a devotional purpose, the object of their devotion being the deity Vithoba at Pandharpur (see G. A. Deleury, *The Cult of Vithoba* [Poona, 1960], 6).

[10] So far as I am aware, the Sufis of Bijapur used Dakani in all their popular literature. It is possible, however, that an exhaustive search in Deccan villages might turn up folk poetry written by Sufis in the Kannada, Marathi, or Telugu languages. The *qadi* of Kolhar, a town on the Krishna River directly south of Bijapur, informed me that he had some chakki-namas in the Dakani language but transliterated into the Kannada script (Akbar Khan, interviewed at the Hashim *dargah*, Bijapur, July 10, 1970)

[11] Hyderabad, Salar Jung Museum, Urdu MSS, Tasawwuf & Akhlaq no. 36.

[12] Ibid., fol. 6a.

[13] Hyderabad, Idara-e-Adabiyat-e-Urdu, no. 93B, fols. 126b–128a.

[14] Hyderabad, Idara-e-Adabiyat-e-Urdu, no. 657, fols. 1b–2b.

of Amin al-Din A'la's followers and hence most likely affiliated with the liberal tradition of Sufism that focused around Amin al-Din.[15] Two other chakki-namas in manuscript form are of more recent origin. One of them, catalogued as that of a certain Ghausi,[16] has recently been ascribed to a Sufi of Bijapur named Fi'l-Hal Qadiri (dates unknown).[17] The other is of a certain Shah Kamal,[18] or Shah Kamal al-Din (d. 1809–10), a Chishti Sufi from Belgaum who eventually settled in what is now Chittoor District and wrote the chakki-nāma at his wife's request.[19] There is also a manuscript copy of a *suhāgan-nāma*,[20] or married-woman's song, written by Shah Raju (d. 1681 or 1685), a Chishti of Bijapur who later migrated to Hyderabad.[21] A manuscript copy of a charkha-nama is attributed to a certain Salar,[22] but his place of origin is not known. Two other chakki-namas are attributed to the most famous Sufi of the Deccan plateau, Sayyid Muhammad Banda Navaz Gisudaraz (d. 1422) of Gulbarga.[23] These, however are of doubtful authenticity, first because they are signed 'Banda Navaz,' an epithet that the Sufi himself never used,[24] and second, because he lived a century and a half before the first authentic chakki-namas appeared, putting any such work of his in gross chronological isolation.

Certain conclusions emerge from this discussion. In the first place, there is no doubt that all of the above manuscripts, even those whose authorship is most dubious, are the work of Sufis. Devotion to God and respect for one's *pīr*, or spiritual guide, are their constant themes. Second, most of these manuscripts originated in Bijapur and are the work either of resident Sufis of the Chishti order or of lay members of the order who had studied there and then migrated elsewhere in the Deccan. Third, this popular literature was not the work of the

[15] See Muhiuddin Zore, *Tazkirah-e-makhtutat*, 5 vols (Hyderabad, 1957), 3:282.

[16] Hyderabad, Salar Jung Museum, Urdu MSS, Tasawwuf & Akhlaq no. 37, fols. la–3a.

[17] Ja'far, 62.

[18] Hyderabad, Salar Jung Museum, Urdu MSS, Pand & Nasayih no. 4.

[19] Sakhawat Mirza, 'Sayyid Shah Kamal al-Din,' *Urdu* (April 1939), 262–5; Zore, 3: 207.

[20] Hyderabad, Salar Jung Museum, Urdu MSS, Pand & Nasayih no. 144, fols. 1a–5a.

[21] 'Abd al-Jabbar Mulkapuri, comp., *Tazkira-yi auliya-i-Dakan*, 2 vols. (Hyderabad, 1912–13), 1:337–41.

[22] Hyderabad, Salar Jung Museum, Urdu MSS, Tasawwuf & Akhlaq no. 35.

[23] Hyderabad, Idara-e-Adabiyat-e-Urdu, MS no. 120B; Salar Jung Musuem, Urdu MSS, Tasawwuf & Akhlaq no. 37.

[24] Nasir al-Din Hashmi, 'Khwaja Banda Navaz ki Urdu sha'iri,' *Hindustan* (October 1934), 447.

great mystical writers of Bijapur—Shah Miranji Shams al-'Ushshaq (d. 1499), Shah Burhan al-Din Janam (d. 1597), or Shaikh Mahmud Khush Dahan (d. 1617)—but of their immediate spiritual descendants who lived in the second half of the seventeenth and early eighteenth centuries. But despite their separation in time by a generation or more, the mystical and popular writers were linked by close familial and doctrinal ties. In one of his works the mystic Burhan al-Din Janam alluded to the central symbol of the chakki-nama, the grindstone, in the same way that popular writers alluded to it: 'In the case of the chakki, some other power is required—somebody's hand must be applied to move the wheel. There are many people who use the chakki, yet only the power hidden in the hand actually turns the wheel. That hand is *'arif al-wujud* [knower of existence, i.e., God], and those who see that the power is in the hand are witnesses of the light; thereby they witness the essence, which is God.'[25]

If one analyses the content of the chakki-nama or the charkha-nama, three interwoven themes can be found:(1) an ontological link established between God, the prophet Muhammad, one's own pir, and the reciter herself; (2) the use of the grindstone or the spinning wheel, or the mechanical parts thereof, to illustrate the above; and (3) the use of the mystics' *zikr*, or spiritual exercise, to accompany and even to regulate the various phases of the woman's work.

In the following chakki-nama of Shah Hashim Khudawand Hadi the first theme, the ontological link between God, the Prophet, the pir, and the woman at the grindstone, is clearly stated. In this passage are also explicated in simplified form the essential elements of the Chishti theory of Creation and of God's relationship to the material world, a theory that can be traced directly to the writings of the great Spanish-Arabic mystic, Ibn al-'Arabi:

First was God's name,
And then His qualities.
In my mind I keep the name,
And with each breath
   (refrain): Say 'La-illah' [There is no god]
            Dwell in 'il-Allah' [But Allah]

God Himself from the hidden treasure
Has created the whole world artistically.
He has created it with His own power—
   (refrain): Say 'La-illah'

[25] Burhan al-Din Janam, *Kalimat al-haqayiq*, ed. M. Akbaruddin Siddiqi (Hyderabad, 1969), 53.

Dwell in 'il-Allah.'
God Himself came out from the hidden treasure
And showed Himself in the guise of the Prophet.
   (refrain)
In the presence of God, the Prophet is the chief
Whose teachings have given us support in both worlds.
   (refrain)
The Prophet's *khalifa* is 'Ali, who is dear to Him,
And whose disciples are our *pirs*.
   (refrain)
Allah, Muhammad, and 'Ali
Are our leaders whom we trust most
And obey as slaves.
   (refrain)
Our *pir* has taken our hands in his;
He has given us connections whole-heartedly.
May he keep this connection forever.
   (refrain): Say 'La-illah'
          Dwell in 'il-Allah.'[26]

The theology here is as simple as the language. The devotee is not asked to master either the doctrinal knowledge of the theologian or the fine points of the Sufi's esoteric knowledge, but only to feel comfort in God's unity and majesty.

These simple Islamic precepts were reinforced by parallels and metaphors drawn between them and the various parts of the grind-stone or spinning wheel at which the woman was working. 'As the chakki turns, so we find God,' concludes the above poem; 'it shows its life in turning as we do in breathing.'[27] Similar analogies are found in the charkha-nama:

Imagine that your body is a spinning wheel, oh sister.
   We should get rid of our negligence
   And give up worldly differences, oh sister.

The tongue is the unspun thread for the message of God;
   The tongue is the rim of the spinning wheel.
   Bring out the thread of breath and show it, oh sister.

Both of these memories should be in our throat:
   God has given us the ability to turn our hand,
   And it is that which moves the wheel, oh sister.

[26] Hashim Khudawand Hadi, *Chakki-nama 'Irfan*, Dakani manuscript (Hyderabad, Idara-e-Adabiyat-e-Urdu, no. 93B), fols. 126b–128a.
[27] Ibid., fol. 128a.

Faith must be for you what the drive-rope is for the wheel.
    Perhaps you know of the two wheels connected by the rope;
    Then you will know how the wheel turns, oh sister.[28]

A third feature of this literature is its incorporation of the mystical zikrs, which are the spiritual exercises intended to bring a Sufi closer to God. For practicing mystics the zikrs had a specialized use, certain ones being associated with certain stages on the traveller's path toward God. In the popular literature, however, the zikrs were largely divested of their mystical content and became more devotional. Although the various zikrs were still differentiated, they did not correspond to the stages of the path, as they did for the mystics, but to different functions being performed at the grindstone or the spinning wheel. Furthermore, all of the zikrs in this literature seem to be of a similar type—repetition of the names of God out loud—which in the mystic tradition would correspond only to the first and most elementary zikr, the *zikr-i-jali*. The following extract from a charkha-nama illustrates these points:

As you take the cotton, you should do *zikr-i jali*.
    As you separate the cotton, you should do *zikr-i qalbī*,
    And as you spool the thread you should do *zikr-i 'ainī*.
Zikr should be uttered from the stomach through the chest,
    And threaded through the throat.
The threads of breath should be counted one by one, oh sister.
    Up to twenty-four thousand.
Do this day and night,
    And offer this to your *pīr* as a gift.[29]

This passage best epitomizes the union of the high and low Sufi traditions, of Islam's religious philosophy and its popular religion. In it are found the main components of the Sufis' esoteric practice, merged with and adapted to a popular literary form, which would be repeated in many households each time cotton thread was spun. The result was quite comparable with the non-Muslim *bhakti* poetry of the contemporary Deccan—the Kannada *vacanas* of the Lingayats or the Marathi *abhangs* of the poet-saints of Pandharpur—in its use of a vernacular medium, its special appeal to women, and its devotional character.

    The role that this Sufi folk literature has played in the growth of Islam in the Deccan, though impossible to measure with precision, seems to have been related to the phenomenon of pir worship and the

[28] Salar, *Charkha-nama*, Dakani manuscript (Hyderabad, Salar Jung Museum, Tasawwuf & Akhlaq no. 35).
[29] Ibid.

devotionalism at pirs' tombs, which historically succeeded the worship of pirs themselves. One important reason that Sufis wrote the literature, apart from their general desire to expand their teachings among a constituency of commoners, was the object of securing for themselves the role of mediator between God and the people who used the literature. Typical is the closing line of the above-quoted charkha-nama: 'You are a maid-servant in your dervish's house. Say Allah and the Prophet's name on every breath.'[30] All available evidence indicates that in the seventeenth century a sizable nonelite constituency clustered around famous pirs, believing in their miraculous powers (*karāmāt*) and their ability to intercede with God, taking blessings from them, lighting candles at the *dargāhs*, or tombs, of departed pirs, and participating in festivals at the dargahs. This was the outer circle of a pir's following, as distinguished from his inner circle of murīds, or initiates, and it was to this outer circle that the folk literature seems especially to have appealed, serving as the litany of what may be called Indian folk Islam.

The dominant role played by women in this Indian folk Islam cannot be underestimated. One seventeenth-century account of a Sufi's conversations (*malfūẓāt*) noted that women were allowed to enter even the inner circle of a Sufi's followers.[31] This would mean that at one time women, along with men, were instructed in the religious exercises of living Sufis. Later, as the Sufis became replaced by their tombs as objects of popular veneration, women came to comprise the great majority of devotees at any given dargah in the Deccan. Their motivation for participating in the dargah's various functions seems to have been primarily votive in nature. That is, flowers, coins, or prayers would be offered up to the spirit of the pir buried at a particular dargah in the belief that the latter would redress some specific grievance or provide some specific fortune that had become associated with that dargah.[32]

---

[30] Ibid.

[31] *Maqsud al-murad*, comp. Shah Murad, manuscript (Hyderabad, Asafiyah Library, Tasawwuf no. 335), 129.

[32] This votive aspect of the dargahs is, of course, very much in keeping with indigenous traditions with respect to shrines and pilgrimages. With reference to Hindu, Buddhist, and Jain pilgrimages, Agehananda Bharati has written that '*vrata*, "vows" are often highly specific and they usually require a visit to one place only. It is the place where a deity specializes, as it were, in repairing damage, or balancing some need of the pilgrim who seeks remedy. The formulation of the *vrata* (vow), most generally put, is something like this: "If I gain x or overcome y or accomplish z, I shall make a pilgrimage to A"; or, "Because I have *not* gained x, etc., I shall make a pilgrimage to A in order to gain it, for A is known to specialize in granting x" ' ('Pilgrimage Sites and Indian Civilization,' in *Chapters in Indian Civilization*,

But whatever the special vows that became associated with individual dargahs, they were all generally associated with fertility. Indeed, the belief that visits to dargahs would in some measure enhance a woman's fertility is an obvious reason for their continuing popularity among rural women of the Deccan today.

Women originally attracted to the Sufis of the seventeenth century were probably of the same social origins as those presently participating in the social life of the dargahs. One could speculate that nonelite women living on the fringes of Hindu society would have gravitated towards Sufis and their tombs as places of religious refuge from any number of worldly concerns. These women would certainly have included widows of most castes, for whom organized Hindu society has little room. Then, too, one could expect that barren women of various castes would have been attracted to the dargahs because of the latter's association with fertility. What all such women probably shared in common was an eclectic religious attitude on account of which they would have perceived no great theological or social wall existing between Islam and Hinduism. For them the village dargah formed only one more facet of an already diffuse and eclectic religious life.[33]

The pervasive influence of women in the life of the dargahs provides an important clue in tracing the role of Sufi folk literature in the expansion of Islam in the Deccan. Judging from the content of the folk literature described above, it seems likely that the women who had come into contact with the culture of the dargahs transmitted this tradition to the children living in their households by constantly repeating the poetry. Children would be rocked to sleep at night or day by lullabies (*luñ-nāma*) that had originated in the dargahs; they would hear chakki-namas or charkha-namas recited daily in their own households each time grain was ground or thread was spun. Hence, just as one's first language is frequently termed one's 'mother tongue,' so also the mother—or indeed any household woman in the proximity of children—has doubtless been instrumental in the transmission of religious practices and attitudes at rural levels. Through this rather insidious medium, though perhaps not intended as such by its authors, Sufi folk literature invaded rural households and gradually gained an established place amidst the eclectic religious life of the rural Deccan

---

ed. Joseph W. Elder, 2 vols [Dubuque, Ia, 1970], 1:94).

[33] 'Indian Islam,' observed J. Spencer Trimingham, 'seems to have been a holy-man Islam. These (Sufi) migrants in the Hindu environment acquired an aura of holiness and it was this which attracted Indians to them, rather than formal Islam' (*The Sufi Orders in Islam* [Oxford, 1971], 22).

The above argument is that both the vehicle of folk literature originally penned by Sufis of the Deccan and the institution of the dargah have assimilated into the world of folk Islam various nonelite and predominantly female elements of the Deccan rural population from the seventeenth century to the present. However, this process should not be construed as 'conversion' to Islam, nor should the Sufis themselves be considered as Muslim 'missionaries,' though both terms have frequently been used in the general context of Sufis and the growth of Islam. The main problem is that both terms carry connotations of a nineteenth- and twentieth-century Christian movement in India, a context in which 'missionary' denoted a self-conscious propagator of the Christian faith and 'conversion' a self-conscious turning around in religious conviction. But the evidence concerning Bijapur's Sufis would not permit calling any of them missionaries in this sense. They made no conscious effort to gain non-Muslim followers, though it is true that many lower-caste non-Muslims were attracted to the Sufis' supposed supernatural power and entered, by gradual degrees, their outer and inner circles. The folk literature examined in this essay aimed primarily at committing its readers to a pir; the diffusion of Islamic precepts seems in the final analysis to have been a by-product of this effort.

Similarly, 'conversion' in the sense of a self-conscious, sudden, and total change of belief is an inadequate term to describe the process by which non-Muslims of the Deccan became attracted to certain Sufis, or later, to the dargahs. There are today several Muslim groups in Bijapur District whose ancestors are claimed to have been converted to Islam by one or another medieval Sufi. But ethnographic evidence indicates that these same groups, far from having suddenly 'converted' to Islam at any single point in time, have been and still are undergoing a gradual process of Islamic acculturation—reflected in dress, food, speech, etc.—which is not only gradual but uneven from one group to another.[34] While it is true that some Sufis seem to have initiated such a process by attracting non-Muslims to their fold, what they left behind them, namely, their folk literature and their tombs, have deepended and continued an on-going process of Islamic acculturation among nonelite groups in Deccan society.

---

[34] An ethnographic survey of Bijapur District conducted for the 1884 *Bombay Gazetteer* illustrates this point. The survey showed twenty-one Muslim 'castes' of Hindu origin, all in various stages of Islamic acculturation as measured by variables such as purity of Urdu speech, practice of circumcision, diet, attachment to Hindu deities and festivals, etc. (see *Gazetteer of Bombay Presidency: Bijapur District* 23 [Bombay, 1884]: 282–305).

SECTION 3
PUNJAB

9

The Political and Religious Authority
of the Shrine of Bābā Farīd[*]

In Islam the ultimate source of moral authority is unambiguous. As a guide to how individuals and society ought to be, the Qur'ān proclaims its moral authority on the basis of its being the very Word of God, for in Islam God revealed Himself not in any historical personage as in Christianity, but in a Book. The moral ideal thus established by the Qur'ān is at once objectively knowable, universally applicable to all peoples and times, and derived from a source external to humanity. These basic features of Islamic moral authority stand in contrast to Hindu-Buddhist ethical doctrines according to which reward and retribution operate on the self-fulfilling and self-regulating principle of *karma*, rather than on the judgment of a wholly transcendant, external god.

To Muslims literate in Arabic, the Qur'ānic source of moral authority presents no problems in terms of gaining access to that authority. But what could nonliterate, non-Arabic-speaking villagers or pastoralists make of such a religion? With reference to contemporary Morocco, Ernest Gellner has argued that to the unlettered Berber tribes of the Atlas, the lineages of holy men, saints, are not just interpreters of Islam for the tribesmen, nor mere representatives of a world religion. 'Koranic propriety emanates from their essence, as it were,' writes Gellner. 'Islam is what they do. They *are* Islam.'[1]

---

[1] Ernest Gellner, *Saints of the Atlas* (Chicago, 1969), 149. The emphasis is Gellner's.

[*] Reprinted from Barbara Metcalf ed. *Moral Conduct and Authority: The Place of Adab in South Asian Islam* (Berkeley: University of California Press, 1982), 333–56.

Another way in which the Book was conveyed to such peoples was through the vast shrines built over the tombs of saints. In India these shrines displayed, theatre-style and in microcosm, the moral order of the Islamic macrocosm. Although such shrines possessed important economic, political, and social ties with the masses of villagers who frequented them, their fundamental raison d'être was religious. For it was through its rituals that a shrine made Islam accessible to nonlettered masses, providing them with vivid and concrete manifestations of the divine order, and integrating them into its ritualized drama both as participants and as sponsors. Theologically, this involved interposing the spirit of the saint, sustained and displayed through the shrine institution, between the devotee and the supreme deity of the Qur'ān. For it was believed that the saint enjoyed a closer relationship with God than the common devotee could ever have, and that the saint's spiritual power (*baraka*) to intercede with God on the devotee's behalf outlasted the saint's mortal lifetime and adhered to his burial place. The latter therefore frequently evolved into a great centre of pilgrimage for persons seeking divine aid in their personal, matrimonial, or business affairs.[2]

In the nineteenth century, reformist movements such as that expressed by Maulānā Thānawī's *Bihishī zewar* vigorously opposed the entire culture of saints and shrines, the colourful pageantry they displayed, and above all the claims that they possessed an intermediate status between Man and God. Accordingly, supporters of these reformist movements sought to replace the shrine as the source of Islamic moral authority with a reassertion of the Book as the only such legitimate source. Theatre, in a word, was to be replaced by Scripture. Inasmuch as this was the case, an investigation of the formation and nature of this theatre-oriented Islam as represented by one such shrine, that of Bābā Farīd in Pakpattan, Punjab, would be appropriate in the present collection of essays.

The shrine of Shaikh Farīd ad-Dīn Ganj-i Shakar (d. A. D. 1265), known to his devotees as Bābā Farīd, lies on the right bank of the Punjab's most southeasterly river, the Sutlej, roughly halfway between

---

[2] The remarks of a British officer concerning the mediating role of Punjabi saints in 1911 are equally true of medieval shrines: 'The general idea of our riverain folk seems to be that the Deity is a busy person, and that his hall of audience is of limited capacity. Only a certain proportion of mankind can hope to attain to the presence of God; but when certain individuals have got there, they may have opportunities of representing the wishes and desires of other members of the human race. Thus, all human beings require an intervener between them and God,' Major Aubrey O'Brien, 'The Mohammedan Saints of the Western Punjab,' *Journal of the Royal Anthropological Institute* 41 (1911):511.

Ferozepore and Bahawalpur. The town in which the shrine is located, known since the sixteenth century as Pakpattan, is the ancient city of Ajudhan. As the principal ferry point on the Sutlej river, this town served from ancient times as a major nexus for east-west trade between the Delhi region and Multan. Ajudhan also lay fully exposed to the brunt of Turkish migration and invasions of India from the late tenth century onward. This process culminated in the thirteenth century when Mongol pressures forced waves of Turkish settlers into the sub-continent, many of them settling permanently in the urban centres of the Punjab, such as Lahore, Dipalpur, and Multan. Hence Bābā Farīd's decision to establish himself in Ajudhan was but one part of a larger process; it was the religious dimension of a very slow transformation of the Punjab's cities from a Hindu to a Turkish-Islamic orientation. Even when Bābā Farīd reached Ajudhan sometime in the early thirteenth century, a Jāmi mosque had already been established there, a resident *qāḍī* was there administering justice according to Islamic law, and the city was politically subordinate to a Muslim governor in neighbouring Dipalpur.[3]

This is not the place to discuss the tradition of Sufism as espoused by Bābā Farīd, which in any case has been superbly treated in the writings of K. A. Nizami.[4] Suffice it to say that two traditions of Islamic devotionalism developed at Ajudhan during Bābā Farīd's lifetime. One was the tradition of mystical endeavour practiced by full-time residents at Bābā Farīd's convent (*jamā'a khāna*), men who had been initiated into the Chishtī order, who lived a communal life of a strongly ascetic nature, and who, in short, had resolved to tread the arduous Sufi path to God. The second tradition was more popular-oriented and is the one with which the remainder of this essay is concerned. At the same time that Bābā Farīd instructed his elite group of initiates (khalīfas) in the mysteries of his order, he also handed out *ta'uīdh* or amulets to the common masses, who saw in these ta'widh a protection against evil, a boon for good fortune, or an agent for the cure of an illness. As is recorded in the contemporary hagiography by Amīr Hasan Sijzī,

Once when Shaikh Nizām ad-Dīn Auliyā' started for Ajodhan, a neighbor, Muhammad, who had a serious ailment, requested him to bring an amulet for him from Shaikh Farīd. When Nizām ad-Dīn placed Muhammad's request before his master, the latter asked him to write a *ta'uīdh* on his behalf. Shaikh

---

[3] Shaikh Jamālī Kamboh Dihlawī, comp.,*Siyar al-'ārifīn* (Delhi, 1893), 33-4.

[4] See his *The Life and Times of Shaikh Farid-ud Din Ganj-i Shakar* (Delhi, 1973) and his *Tārīkh-i mashā'ikh-i Chisht* (Islamabad, n.d.).

Nizām ad-Dīn wrote the following names of God on a piece of paper and presented it before the Shaikh who touched it, read it, and gave it back to him to be handed over to Muhammad.[5]

Huge crowds gathered daily at Bābā Farīd's convent to receive ta'wīdh, which, as in the case cited above, normally consisted of a scrap of paper on which were written the names of God or some Qur'ānic verses. The tediousness of writing out these ta'wīdh, however, compelled the saint to delegate much of the work to assistants. This aspect of Islamic devotionalism has not changed from the thirteenth century to the present; even now the successors of Bābā Farīd and his assistants, in common with those of other shrines in the Punjab, continue to write ta'wīdh for the masses.

When the ta'wīdh passed from the shrine to the devotee, the latter, or *murīd*, would frequently offer to the shrine some kind of gift, called *futūh*. This would typically be in the form of sweets,[6] but could be almost anything, and even in Bābā Farīd's own day the gift swelled to enormous proportions.[7] Bābā Farīd's giving of ta'wīdh, and the devotees' giving of futūh or gifts, provided the structural framework upon which the subsequent devotionalism of the shrine rested. In a religious sense the ta'wīdh-futūh system defined and sustained Bābā Farīd's intermediary status between the devotee and God, as a conduit through whose intercession with God one's wishes may be fulfilled. In a social and institutional sense, moreover, the ta'wīdh-futūh system required the shrine to adopt a certain degree of rational organization with respect to the distribution of material wealth. For it was Bābā Farīd's practice to distribute among his khalīfas and the common devotees the presents that other devotees had brought.[8] The *shaikh's* convent, and later his shrine, thus served as a nexus for the circulation and redistribution of a great deal of material wealth in the region.

In 1265 Bābā Farīd died, and with his death began the career of the vast shrine complex based on his tomb, in time encompassing a mosque, a welfare kitchen (*langar khāna*), and a number of related buildings. By the thirteenth century, it had become commonly believed in the Muslim world that a great shaikh's baraka adhered, after his death, to his familial descendants as well as to the place of his burial. Accordingly, the position of prime successor to Bābā Farīd, later called

---

[5] Amīr Hasan Sijzī, comp., *Fawā'id al-fu'ād* (Lucknow, 1884), 62. Cited in Nizami, *Life and Times*, 52n.

[6] Ibid., 127. Cited in Nizami, *Life and Times*, 53.

[7] Ibid., 124–5, 41. Cited in Nizami, *Life and Times*, 54.

[8] Mīr Khurd Kirmānī, comp., *Siyar al-auliyā'* (Delhi, 1885), 131.

the 'dīwān,' fell to his son, Badr ad-Dīn Sulaimān (1265–81).[9] The accession of Badr ad-Dīn as the Dīwān immediately set a pattern of hereditary religious leadership at the shrine. Amīr Khusrau mentioned the annual 'urs or death-date celebration on the occasion of the fiftieth anniversary of the shaikh's death and described in detail the 'urs celebration for the year 1315: the pilgrimage of pious persons to Ajudhan, the recitation of the saint's wonderful deeds, and the entertainments performed by an ensemble of *darweshes*.[10] The *Jawāhir-i Farīdī*, an important collection of biographies of Bābā Farīd's spiritual and lineal descendants compiled in 1623, records that all the major rituals of the shrine had become instituted in Badr ad-Dīn's day. These included the tying on of the turban (*dastār bandī*) indicating formal inheritance of Bābā Farīd's spiritual authority; the regularizing of ecstatic singing (*qawwālī*) at the shrine; the establishing of a public kitchen (langar khāna) from which the dīwān himself would, on formal occasions, direct the distribution of food and sweets; and the tradition of the dīwān opening the southern door (*bihishtī darwāza*) of Bābā Farīd's tomb on the occasion of the shrine's annual 'urs celebration, allowing the masses of common devotees to pass by the shrine's *sanctum sanctorum*, ritually entering heaven.[11]

The successorship of the second dīwān, Badr ad-Dīn's eldest son, Shaikh 'Alā' ad-Dīn Mauj Daryā (1281–1334), firmly established a tradition of hereditary religious leadership associated with Bābā Farīd's shrine and witnessed the spectacular growth of a popular cult that focused on the shrine. We find two dimensions of this growing cult: patronage by the Delhi court and the extension of mass devotionalism into the countryside. Although Bābā Farīd himself assiduously avoided contact with the mundane world of the court and its ministers,[12] and

---

[9] It is noteworthy that although every dīwān of the shrine down to the present has been the eldest son of his predecessor, Bābā Farīd's own first and second sons were passed over in favour of Badr ad-Dīn, who was the third son. Moreover, he was the only successor not to have received the office from his father and predecessor, as he was given the office directly by the Chishtī elders in Chisht, western Afghanistan. *Siyar al-auliyā'*, 188.

[10] Amīr Khusrau, *Rāḥa al-muḥibbīn*, Urdu edition (Lahore, 1957, 63–4. Cited in M. Abdullah Chaghatai, 'Pakpattan and Shaikh Farid,' *Iqbal Review* 9 (1968): 131.

[11] 'Ali Asghar Chishtī, comp., *Jawahar-i Farīdī* (Lahore, 1883–84), 298–300.

[12] Diyā ad-Dīn Baranī records that Bābā Farīd warned a certain Sufi who was then leaving Ajudhan for Delhi, in the following words: 'I give thee a bit of advice, which it would be well for thee to observe. Have nothing to do with maliks and amirs, and beware of their intimacy as dangerous; no darwesh ever kept up such

although the Khalajī sultans (1288–1321) do not seem to have been interested in the shrine, the whole picture changed with the advent of the Tughluq period (1321–98). It happened that in the late Khalajī times the governor of Dipalpur, the future Sultān Ghiyāth ad-Dīn Tughluq, became one of the many local notables attracted to the spiritual power and piety of Dīwān 'Alā' ad-Dīn Mauj Daryā.[13] He accordingly made frequent visits from Dipalpur, which was the administrative capital of the central Punjab, to nearby Ajudhan to pay respects to the dīwān. On one such occasion, according to the fourteenth-century chronicler Shams-i Sirāj 'Afīf, the governor brought along his son and nephew, the future sultans Muhammad bin Tughluq and Firoz Tughluq, and all three were given a turban by Dīwān 'Alā' ad-Dīn and told by him that each was destined to rule Hindustan.[14] Apart from rationalizing the subsequent patronage of Bābā Farīd's shrine by the leading Tughluq sultans, the story also weaves together the shrine's *dastār bandī* ceremony with succession to the royal throne in Delhi, effectively merging the symbols of the shrine and of the royal court.

Although hagiographic traditions refer to 'Alā' ad-Dīn's immense piety and his refusal to consort with royalty,[15] the renowned world traveller Ibn Battūta, certainly an impartial authority in this matter, wrote that Sultān Muhammad ibn Tughluq had bestowed the city of Ajudhan on the shrine.[16] This seems to be the earliest reference to the court's alienation of local revenues in favour of the shrine's support. Court patronage, however, was also expressed in other ways. The hagiographic tradition has it that Muhammad ibn Tughluq, who was also a disciple of Dīwān 'Alā' ad-Dīn,[17] expressed his desire to build a magnificent tomb for the dīwān, but the latter refused the offer, saying that if a tomb were built at all, this could be done only after

---

intimacy, but in the end found it disastrous.' *Tārīkh-i Firoz Shāhī*, abridged trans. in H. M. Elliot and Dowson, *History of India as Told by Its Own Historians* (Allahabad, 1964), 3:144.

[13] Ahmad Nabi Khan, 'The Mausoleum of Shaikh 'Ala al-Din at Pakpattan (Punjab): a Significant Example of the Tuqluq Style of Architecture,' *East and West* 24, nos. 3–4 (Sept.–Dec. 1974): 324–5.

[14] Shams-i Sirāj 'Afīf, *Tārīkh-i Firoz Shāhī*, ed. Maulavi Vilayat Husain (Calcutta: Asiatic Society of Bengal, 1891), 27–8.

[15] As Amīr Khurd recorded, 'In no way would he go anywhere except to the door of the Jāmi mosque, and if kings would come, he would not budge from his place.' *Siyar al-auliyā'*, 194.

[16] Ibn Battūta, *Rehla of Ibn Batuta*, trans. and ed. Mahdi Husain (Baroda, 1953), 20.

[17] *Siyar al-auliyā'*, 196.

his death.[18] Accordingly, soon after 'Alā' ad-Dīn's death in 1335, Sultān Muhammad commissioned two engineers to construct what proved to be one of the finest examples of Tughluq architecture in the subcontinent.[19] It is also the most imposing structure in the entire shrine complex, dwarfing by far Bābā Farīd's own tomb.

Once begun, the Tughluq court's patronage of the shrine continued to grow as 'Alā' ad-Dīn's successors proved more pliable to the court's will. In fact, his son and successor, Dīwān Mu'izz ad-Dīn, was even called to Delhi by Muhammad ibn Tughluq, placed in government service, and sent to Gujarat as deputy governor.[20] The dīwān's brother, meanwhile, was appointed to the office of Shaikh al-Islām of India.[21] Never were the affairs of the shrine more firmly welded to court interests. The shrine's leaders were now under Delhi's control, and the shrine became even more dependent economically upon court patronage. In Mu'izz ad-Dīn's brief successorship (1335–38), Muhammad ibn Tughluq granted an endowment or *mu'āf* in support of the shrine's public kitchen.[22] And Baranī recorded that Sultān Fīrūz Tughluq (1351–88) not only repaired the tomb of Bābā Farīd, but 'granted robes of honour to his descendants and confirmed them in possession of their villages and lands.'[23]

There was, however, a second and even more significant dimension of the shrine's institutionalization process, also clearly evident in the early fourteenth century. This was its growing popularity among the rural masses and its recognition even beyond the frontiers of India. In 1334, toward the end of 'Alā' ad-Dīn's fifty-four-year term as dīwān, Ibn Battūta visited the shrine and later recalled, 'We reached the city of Ajudhan, a small city belonging to the pious Shaikh Farid-ud-din of Badaun [sic] whom at Alexandria the holy and pious Shaikh Burhan-ud-din al-'Araj had foretold that I would meet.'[24] The man whom

---

[18] *Jawāhir-i Farīdī*, 307–8.

[19] Ibid. *Siyar al-auliyā*', 196. For a discussion of the architectural aspects of the magnificent tomb of 'Ala' al-Dīn Mauj Daryā, see Ahmad Nabī Khan, 'The Mausoleum of Shaikh 'Ala al-Dīn.' The date of construction of the tomb comes from an inscription on the tomb itself—Safar, 737, which corresponds to Sept./Oct., A.D. 1336.

[20] *Siyar al-auliyā*', 196. See also Barani, *Tārīkh-i Firoz Shāhī* (Calcutta, 1862), 347–8, 518.

[21] *Siyar al-auliyā*', 196.

[22] *Jawāhir-i Farīdī*, 308. '

[23] Baranī, *Tārīkh-i Firoz Shāhī* (Calcutta, 1862), 543. Cited in H. A. Rose, ed., *Glossary of the Tribes and Castes of the Punjab* (Patiala, 1970), 1:495.

[24] Ibn Battūta, *Rehla*, 20.

the famous traveller actually met was not Bābā Farīd, of course, but his grandson, Dīwān 'Alā' ad-Dīn Mauj Daryā. Nevertheless, the passage shows that Bābā Farīd, the saint, was now clearly identified with the physical shrine complex, and that his (its) fame had spread as far as Egypt.

It was also at about this time that small memorial shrines to Bābā Farīd began appearing, scattered throughout the countryside of central Punjab, and that the baraka and authority of Bābā Farīd became physically established over the land in much the same way that political/administrative authority was. As for the memorial shrines, what is significant is that they were built not by the Tughluq sultans as were the main structures of the Ajudhan complex, but by the common people themselves. Amīr Khurd, a contemporary of 'Alā' ad-Dīn Mauj Daryā, recorded that the dīwān had become so well known that

in the countryside around Ajudhan, Dipalpur, and in the hills toward Kashmir, the people out of love and belief have built structures and tombs in the name of his shrine [i.e., the shrine of Bābā Farīd] and they go to these villages for alms and devotions.[25]

The appearance of these shrines shows that a certain tract of the Punjab had become identified with Bābā Farīd's *wilāyat*, or spiritual kingdom, which to his devotees was perceived as having specific geographic boundaries that bordered the wilāyats of other saints. Thus we read in an early-sixteenth-century hagiography that Bābā Farīd's spiritual power protected a certain 'Abd Allāh Rūmī from highway robbers as he travelled southwest from Ajudhan to Multan, for the saint had told the traveller that 'from here [Ajudhan] to such-and-such a village is in my charge, and from such-and-such a reservoir is the frontier of Shaikh Bahā' ad-Dīn Zakariyā [beyond which] is in his charge.'[26] This passage clearly demonstrates how closely the notion of spiritual sovereignty could parallel, in spatial terms, that of political sovereignty, and represents one of several ways in which the shrine of Bābā Farīd fused religious and political categories of authority.

Who were the rural folk who frequented the main shrine in Ajudhan and also the memorial shrines in the surrounding countryside? It is well known that in the mid-thirteenth century, Balban, in order to build a defensive bulwark against Mongol incursions, pursued the policy of strengthening and populating certain cities in the Punjab with large

---

[25] *Siyar al-auliyā'*, 193.
[26] *Siyar al-ārifīn*, 115.

garrisons of Turkish elements.[27] The effect of these measures was to augment considerably the pattern of Muslim settlement in the urban centres of the Punjab, including not only the soldiers but also thousands of refugees fleeing before the advancing Mongols—artisans, merchants, petty officials, and the like. Although Ajudhan was not one of these garrisoned cities, the large size of its Jāmi' mosque originally constructed before Bābā Farīd's arrival and now part of the shrine complex,[28] attests to the presence of a substantial Muslim population at that time.

Behind and beyond these urban centres of the western Punjab, all of which were economically based on intensive cultivation of food crops along the flood plains of the rivers, lay a vast tract of sparsely populated land, the *barr* country between the five rivers. This area, though possessing excellent natural soils for agriculture, was but little cultivated owing to the very scanty rainfall that has always characterized the western Punjab. The barr country could and did, however, support an ecological system less demanding of the land than peasant agriculture. This was a type of pastoral nomadism based primarily on the herding of goats and camels.[29] Unlike the nomadism of Baluchistan or Afghanistan, where pastoral tribes move between plains in the wet winter season and the mountains in the dry season, the pastoralists of the western Punjab 'moved only down to the riverain [sic] in the hot dry months and returned to the barr and *thāl* after rains, never leaving the Punjab plains and covering at the most a distance of less than one hundred miles.'[30] This pattern placed the peoples of the barr country in a symbiotic relationship with the settled peoples of the riverine area. The pastoralists needed access to the rivers for their herds, which placed them in a position of potential conflict with the riverine peoples, but they were nevertheless dependent upon the agrarian-based urban centres for trade. Moreover, and this is an important theme to which I shall return shortly, they were also dependent upon the riverine peoples for providing the rituals and belief structures that made up their religious system.

---

[27] Barani, *Tārīkh i Firoz Shāhī*, in Elliot and Dowson, *History of India*, 3:107, 109. See also Briggs, *Rise of the Mahommedan Power*, 1:143–5. Garrisoned cities included Lahore, Multan, Sirhind, Bhatinda, and Dipalpur.

[28] Chaghatai, 'Pakpattan and Shaikh Farid,' 134–5.

[29] For an excellent discussion of the ecology of the western Punjab, see chapter 1 of Emily Hodges' dissertation, in progress (University of California, Berkeley, Department of History).

[30] Ibid., 22.

The pastoralists to which I refer were primarily Jat groups that had been moving up from Sind into the Multan area between the seventh and eleventh centuries. The seventh-century Chinese traveller Hsuan Tsang wrote of river groups in Sind who 'gave themselves exclusively to tending cattle and from this derive their livelihood,' 'have no masters,' and possess 'an unfeeling temper' and a 'hasty disposition'.[31] The eighth-century *Chāch–nāma* styled these groups 'Jatts', located them in the wastes of the Indus valley in Sind, and noted an absence among them of social hierarchy.[32] This evidence all points to the conclusion that these Jat pastoralists, before their entry into the Punjab, had not yet been integrated into Hindu society. Indeed, there is evidence that in the eighth century, when Arabs replaced Brahmans as rulers of Sind, the new rulers merely continued the earlier practice of requiring the Jats to associate themselves with dogs—unclean to Muslims as well as to Hindus—and in this way to affirm their lowly status.[33]

In the eleventh century, Jats were fighting Mahmūd of Ghaznī in the Multan region, though their social standing was still miserably low at that time, as al-Bīrūnī referred to them as 'cattle-owners, low Sudra people'.[34] By the time of Bābā Farīd, however, in the 1260s, we find the first mention of Jats occupying the Punjab proper, specifically the Bet Jullundur and Bari doabs—i.e., the Sutlej-Beas barr and the Beas-Ravi barr.[35] In describing the success of Balban's governor of Lahore and Dipalpur in resisting the Mongols, the historian Baranī referred to the governor's campaigns against the 'Jats, the Khokhars, the Bhattis, the Minas, the Mandahars, and other similar tribes'.[36] In 1519 and

---

[31] Cited in Irfan Habib, 'Jatts of Punjab and Sind,' in Harbans Singh and N. G. Barrier, eds, *Punjab Past and Present: Essays in Honour of Dr. Ganda Singh* (Patiala, 1976), 94.

[32] See ibid.

[33] Y. Friedmann, 'A Contribution to the Early History of Islam in India,' in Myrian Rosen-Ayalon, ed., *Studies in Memory of Gaston Wiet* (Jerusalem 1977), 332.

[34] Edward Sachau, ed., *Alberuni's India* (New Delhi, 1964), 1:401.

[35] See map of Punjab, circa 1605. In our period the Beas River did not, as it does now, end at the point where it joins the Sutlej. Rather, after joining the Sutlej above Ferozepur it again split off from it in a southwesterly direction until it joined the Chenab below Multan. In the 1790s the old Beas bed below Ferozepur dried up, so that what had formerly been two doabs below Ferozepur, the Bet Jullundur and the Bari, now became one, the Bari Doab between the Sutlej and the Ravi. See Herbert Wilhelmy, 'The Shifting River: Studies in the History of the Indus Valley,' *Universitas* 10, no. 1 (1968): 53–68.

[36] Baranī, *Tārīkh-i Fīroz Shāhī*, in Elliot and Dowson, *History of India as Told by*

again in 1525 Bābur described Jat pastoralist groups in the Sind Sagar doab and Sialkot regions, giving us good descriptions of Jat relations with the dominant Rajput groups in the former region.[37] The northward movement of Jat clans and their settlement in the grazing tracts of the Punjab is thus well supported by contemporary evidence.

By the end of the sixteenth century, the Jats had multiplied prodigiously and spread throughout the Punjab, as is vividly reflected in the *A'īn i Akbarī's* statistics for the Lahore and Multan *sūbas*, compiled about 1595. For each *pargana*, Abū al-Faḍl listed the dominant *zamīndār* caste, together with its assessed revenue. If the number of zamīndārs listed by Abū al-Faḍl as 'Jat' is added to that of other named castes listed as Jat by the British ethnographers Ibbetson and Rose,[38] it appears that of the total 186 Punjabi parganas whose dominant zamīndārs are known, fully 82, or nearly half, were controlled by Jat groups.[39] Only in the extreme western Punjab, in the Sind Sagar doab, where the Janjua Rajputs and Ghakkars dominated, were the Jats conspicuously absent as zamīndārs. Thus from being the pastoralist 'low Sudras' described by al-Bīrūnī in the eleventh century, the Jats had clearly risen in social position, having become the dominant agrarian caste in nearly half of the Punjab. This rise was occasioned by a gradual transformation from nomadic pastoralism to peasant agriculture which, though not complete in Abū al-Faḍl's day, was sufficiently dramatic that by the 1650s, as today, the very word 'Jat' had become virtually synonymous with peasant agriculturalist.[40] The economic explanation for this change, argues Irfan Habib, lay in the introduction of the Persian wheel in the Punjab and its extensive use by Bābur's time both in the riverine lands and in the tracts between the riverine area and the grazing zone, thereby making much of the arid western Punjab's naturally rich soil capable of supporting the cultivation of food crops.[41]

Its Own Historians, 3:109.

[37] John Leyden and William Erskine, trans., *Memoirs of Zehir-ed-Din Muhammad Babur* (London, 1921), 2:93–5, 102, 163–4.

[38] See Rose, ed., *Glossary of the Tribes and Castes*, vols 2 and 3.

[39] From Abū al-Fadl 'Allāmī, *A'in i Akbarī*, trans. H. S. Jarrett, 2nd ed. (Calcutta, 1949), 2:320–5 passim.

[40] *Dabistān-i madhāhib* (Calcutta, 1809), p. 276. The author of this work wrote that in Punjabi 'Jat' meant 'villager' (*dihistānī, rūstāʾī*.

[41] Habib, 'Jatts,' 98. See also idem, 'Presidential Address,' *Indian History Congress Proceedings* (1969), 153–4. In describing the Persian wheel as an ingenious irrigation device, which he had apparently never seen before, Babur specifically mentioned the Bet Jullundur and Bari Doabs ('Lahore, Dipalpur, Sirhind, and the neighbouring districts'), where it was prevalent; *Memoirs of . . . Babur*, 2:296–7. In 1832

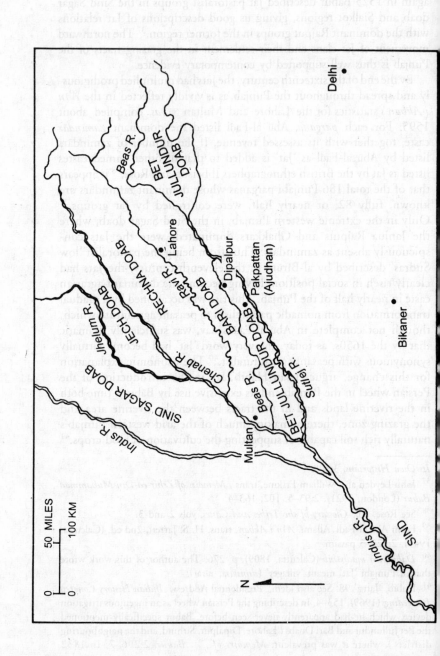

All of this discussion of the Jats—their migration north from Sind to Punjab, their rise in social status from low Sudras to zamīndārs, and their gradual transformation from pastoralists to farmers—would be irrelevant were it not that yet another important change accompanied those already mentioned: many of them also converted to Islam. Moreover, of those Jat and Rajput groups that became Muslim in the medieval period, the vast majority of them claim to have been converted either by Bābā Farīd or by his contemporary, Baha' al-Haqq Zakariyā (d. 1263), whose tomb is in Multan city. Table 9.1 lists some of the Punjabi Muslim clans that traditionally claim Bābā Farīd as the agent of their conversion. But as Mohammad Habīb notes, converting non-Muslims was not a function of the early shaikhs of the Chishtī order, Bābā Farīd included;[42] and the earliest primary sources on Bābā Farīd make no mention of his having converted anyone. Indeed, it is probable that many if not most of these clans, in the course of their northward migrations up the rivers of the Punjab, had not yet reached the Ajudhan area during Bābā Farīd's lifetime.

Table 9.1 Some Clans Claiming to Have Been
Converted by Bābā Farīd

Clan	Source
Bhattī	*Jawāhir-i Farīdī*, 323
Chhīna	Rose, *Glossary*, 1, 168
Dhudhī	*Jawāhir-i Farīdī*, 323
Dogar	*Rawāj-i 'Amm*, 1860s
Gondal	Rose, *Glossary*, 1, 302
Gondāl	Ibid.
Hāns	*Jawāhir-i Farīdī*, 323
Jo'iya	Rose, *Glossary*, 1, 412
Khokhar	*Jawāhir-i Farīdī*, 323
Siyāl	Rose, *Glossary*, 2, 417
Tiwāna	Sir 'Umar Hayāt Khān
Wattū	Rose, *Glossary*, 2, 491
Kharral	Oral tradition
Arā'in	Oral tradition

Captain Wade, who led the earliest English expedition down the Sutlej valley, noted the remains of an extensive irrigation system based on the Persian wheel. See F. Mackeson, 'Journal of Captain Wade,' *Journal of the Asiatic Society of Bengal* 6 (1837):181, 187–8, 194.

[42] Mohammad Habib, 'Shaikh Nasirrudin Mahmud Chiragh-i Delhi as a Great Historical Personality,' *Islamic Culture* (April 1946): 140.

On the other hand, we need not, because of these hagiographic and chronological problems, dismiss outright the claims of the clans. If one were to hypothesize that the agent of the clans' conversion, instead of Bābā Farīd himself, was the shrine of Bābā Farīd as a highly complex religious and social institution, a number of problems fade away. Bābā Farīd resided in Ajudhan only sixteen or twenty-four years,[43] which is a very short time span for the many eponymous clan founders or *māliks* who are claimed to have met him actually to have been there. The shrine, on the other hand, has been there all along, sustaining the powerful baraka of the saint through its line of dīwāns. The identification of the shrine with the spirit of Bābā Farīd has been so thorough, in fact, that by the sixteenth century the very name of the city containing the shrine, Ajudhan, became known as Pakpattan ('the holy ferry'), in honour of Bābā Farīd's memory. Under these circumstances it would hardly be surprising that the clans, in reconstructing the story of their own conversion to Islam, should recall the name of the saint himself and not that of any particular dīwān.

Moreover, throughout the period when Jat groups moved up the riverine region and on to the *barr* country, there were several nonreligious ways in which the shrine patronized the clans and thus integrated them into its wide orbit of social and political influence, paving the way for the Jats' gradual integration into its ritual and religious structure. In Clifford Geertz's terms, the shrine provided the tribes with a tiny 'theatre-state' of their own;[44] that is, it displayed throughout the ceremonies and celebrations that marked its liturgical calendar the pageantry of both the court of God and the court of Delhi, albeit on a microcosmic scale. The shrine thus gave clan leaders and their followers not only access to Islam, but the honour of participating in the reflected splendour of the Sultanate or Mughal courts without actually being directly subservient to the authorities in Delhi.

As an intermediary institution in both a religious and a political sense, the shrine of Bābā Farīd was itself patronized by Delhi. We have seen how, since the third dīwān, the Delhi court lavished the revenues of towns and villages in support of the shrine and its attendants. No major ruler passed by the area without showing deference to its spiritual power. For instance, in October 1398 Tīmʿur, amidst his plundering of northern India, took the time to visit the shrine.[45] Likewise,

---

[43] *Siyar al-auliyā'*, 63.

[44] Clifford Geertz, *Islam Observed: Religious Development in Morocco and Indonesia* (Chicago, 1971), 38.

[45] Emperor *Tīmūr*, *Malfūzāt-i Tīmūñ*, abridged trans. in Elliot and Dowson, eds,

Akbar, in March 1571, opened his sixteenth regnal year in Pakpattan, where he implored strength at Bābā Farīd's shrine.[46] And in 1629 Shāh Jahān issued a *farmān* indicating precisely what his and his predecessor's policy was vis-à-vis the shrine:

The sacred town of Pak Pattan with all its dependencies is by old agreement held in grant from the preceding emperors for the 'Langar' expenses of the shrine of the revered saint Baba Shekh Fureed Shukur Gunj by Shekh Moham-mad, Sujjadah Nasheen of the shrine, a descendant of the Baba, and the proceeds thereof are applied to his own maintenance and to that of the Durveshes and Khadims attached thereto, as well as to the feed of Travellers and the repair and adornment of the building. Continue the whole 'Muhal' [i.e., *pargana*] in endowment to the shrine.[47]

In return for this royal patronage, the dīwāns of Pakpattan performed several functions for the Mughal government. Above all, on certain tracts of land they received the government's share of all crops on which revenue was levied in kind, whereas the tax on cash crops such as cotton, indigo, or tobacco had to be paid in cash and went straight to revenue officials without passing the dīwān.[48] It was therefore in the dīwān's interest as a de facto *chaudhrī*, first, that agriculture be expanded at the expense of pastoralism, for the dīwān derived no cattle tax from the *barr* clans, and secondly, that food crops be sown instead of cash crops. Although there is no corroborating evidence to this effect, these circumstances suggest that the dīwāns might have been promoters of peasant agriculture, and might explain the *Jawāhir–i Farīdī*'s seeming approval of peasant agriculture as a way of life for the shrine's dependent clans.[49]

As the Delhi court patronized the shrine, so also the shrine patronized

---

History of India, 3:421. Like any other of Bābā Farīd's millions of devotees, Tīmūr implored the saint's intercession with God for the attainment of worldly concerns—in his case, victory in battle. With or without Bābā Farīd's help, Tīmūr's prayers were certainly answered.

[46] Abū al-Fadl 'Allāmī, *Akbarnāma*, trans. H. Beveridge (Delhi, n.d.), 2:525–6.

[47] West Pakistan Board of Revenue, Lahore. File 131/6/24/24.

[48] *Punjab District Gazetteers*, vol. 18-A. *Montgomery District, 1933* (Lahore, 1935), 38.

[49] In enumerating the shrine's *mund* clans, the *Jawāhir-i Farīdī* records: 'so these clans—Adhank, Valank, and Sipan—are all farmers in Pākpattan, and are descendants of the aforesaid Makh, and are commonly known as Bughutis, Daks, and Sapan. The Baritis are originally Jats.... They live in Pakpattan and practice agriculture. Then there are the Jakh, whose descendants are called Jhakarwalis. The Dikan, Dahkan, Sipan, Baritis and Bughutis are all farmers.' *Jawāhir-i Farīdī*, 397.

the agricultural clans, in some ways even mimicking the symbols of the larger court. For example the very word for 'shrine' used in the subcontinent, 'dargāh,' is also the word for a royal court. More significantly, the special title of Bābā Farīd's chief successor, a personage who at other shrines was designated simply *sajjāda nishīn* ('one who sits on the prayer carpet'), at Pakpattan was and is 'dīwān,' a term taken directly from the lexicon of Indo-Islamic royal courts, and possibly alluding to the man's revenue-collecting function mentioned above. Similarly, the *dastār bandi* ceremony, tying on a turban symbolically bestowing legitimate authority on someone, has obvious parallels with a coronation ceremony. Thus in the hagiographic literature reconstructing the story of Bābā Farīd's sending off the Siyāl chief to settle and populate the Chenab-Ravi area, he gave the chief a frock and a turban,[50] thus combining a specifically Sufi symbol of authority (the frock) with a symbol conferring authority in both courtly and Sufi contexts (the turban).

The clan's attachments to the shrine were far more than merely symbolic, however. The *darweshes* and *khādims* (i.e., 'servants') mentioned in Shāh Jahān's *farmān* as receiving royal support comprised the many hundreds of lineal descendants of Bābā Farīd living in the Pakpattan region.[51] So numerous were these descendants that they literally formed a separate zamīndār caste in the area, the 'Chishtī' caste, possessing both economic privileges and ritual status vis-à-vis the local clans. An 1897 British Assessment Report for this area described the Chishtīs as 'a semi-religious Mussalman tribe' having 'considerable local influence,' who 'are not working agriculturalists, but depend for cultivation entirely on tenants.'[52] It is probable that the Chishtīs enjoyed the same sort of proprietary rights in relation to their tenant clients from a very early date.

More interesting is the well-documented fact that the clans swore allegiance not to Bābā Farīd but to his family—i.e., the Chishtī caste of Pakpattan. Our early-seventeenth-century source, the *Jawāhir-i Farīdī*, states the matter quite clearly: 'The Khokhars, Bhattīs, Dhudhīs, and Hāns are found in the environs of Pakpattan, and all the clans take *bai'at* with this family and have become *murīds*.'[53] Elsewhere the same

[50] Ibid., 324.

[51] It was on account of this vast proliferation of descendants that even in the seventeenth century Bābā Farīd himself was called 'the Second Adam'. G. A. Storey, *Persian Literature, a Bio-bibliographical Survey* (London, 1927–71), 2:986.

[52] Patrick J. Fagan, *Assessment Report for Pakpattan Tahsil* (Lahore, 1896), 50.

[53] *Jawāhir-i Farīdī*, 323.

source mentions that 'these clans serve the *progeny* of Bābā Farīd.[54] Now, bai'at means a compact of allegiance, which in early Sufism meant spiritual allegiance only, but which among the unlettered Jat clans carried political as well as ethical obligations. In fact, one passage of the *Jawāhīr-i Farīdī* suggests that even military obligations were involved in the taking of bai'at:

And in these environs [Pakpattan] the Khokhars, Dhudhīs, Jo'iyas, Bhattūs, Wattūs and other groups who became Muslim from the time of Bābā Farīd, until now are busy in prayer and fasting [i.e., they conform to the outward observances of Muslim law]. For they are the possessors of dignity in the environs of Pakpattan. They can place ten thousand cavalry and foot soldiers in his [Bābā Farīd's] service, and have complete faith in Bābā Farīd and his descendants, and are their *murīds*.[55]

The above account having been written during Jahāngīr's reign, when the Mughals enjoyed effective authority in the Punjab, we do not hear that the dīwān's Jat murīds were actually called upon to do battle in service of the shrine. In the mid-eighteenth century, however, Mughal decline had allowed various local powers to assert their independence and to expand their holdings at their neighbour's expense. Thus in 1757 Dīwān 'Abd as-Subhān (1752–66) gathered an army of his Jat murīds, attacked the raja of Bikaner, and thereby expanded the shrine's territorial holdings for the first time to the east of the Sutlej.[56] Then, however, he had to face the expanding Sikh power to the north, in particular the Nakkai *mithl* headed by Hīra Singh. Supported mainly by his Wattu murīds,[57] the dīwān successfully defended a Sikh attack on Pakpattan around 1776 in which Hīra Singh was killed, and then pursued the retreating Sikhs with four thousand cavalry, killing a great number of them.[58] In 1810 the shrine's extensive holdings were seized by Ranjīt Singh, and the dīwāns of Pakpattan, their brief period of political independence now at an end, reverted to their former status of political intermediaries.[59]

What bound the clans to the shrine even more powerfully than

[54] Ibid., 396. Emphasis added.

[55] Ibid., 397–8.

[56] *Montgomery District Gazetteer* (1933), 38.

[57] Ibid., 35.

[58] Syad Muhammad Latif, *History of the Punjab* (Lahore, n.d.), 312.

[59] To be sure, it was under much worse terms than under the Mughals. Ranjīt Singh allowed the dīwān and his retainers only Rs. 1,000 a year for their maintenance, derived from the town duties of Pakpattan, in addition to a fourth share of four small villages nearby. *Journal of the Asiatic Society of Bengal,* 6 (1837): 193.

economic or political ties were the ties of kinship and intermarriage established between dependent Jat and Rajput groups and the dīwān's family. The significant point here is that the latter groups gave their daughters to the dīwāns and their immediate family, whereas Chishtī daughters were evidently kept within the caste. In traditional Indian kinship terms, client-patron relations among castes are often structured by the direction of bride-giving, the bride-giving groups normally being clients of the bride-receiving group. In fact, the kinship relations of the dīwān and the clans immediately call to mind those of the Mughal court and its subordinate Rajput clans, except that in the case of the dīwāns religious as well as political patronage was involved.

The *Jawāhir-i Farīdī* not only lists the clans that, as of 1623, had entered into a bride-giving relationship with the dīwān and his family, but even names the groom and the bride's father in such alliances. Accordingly, we find that of the thirteen marriage alliances between the Khokhars and the shrine, seven of the Khokhar brides were daughters of clan *māliks*, or chiefs. And on the other side of the contract, we find that of these same thirteen alliances, three brides went to the dīwāns themselves and six went to sons of various dīwāns. The earliest instance of this Khokhar-dīwān connection was that of a Khokhar bride given to a son of Dīwān Ahmad Shāh, who was dīwān of the shrine from 1452 to 1474.[60] Similar data exist for other groups, namely the Bhattīs, Hāns, and Dhudhīs. Of five exchanges involving the Bhattīs, two brides were daughters of Bhattī chiefs and three grooms were sons of dīwāns, the earliest alliance dating back to the late 1400s.[61] Of four alliances mentioned between the dīwān's family and the Hāns and Dhudhī tribes, one involved a chief's daughter and two others involved granddaughters, and on the other side one alliance involved a dīwān and the other three, sons of dīwāns.[62]

Paralleling these economic, political, and kinship ties between the shrine and its neighboring clans, the latter gradually became integrated into the shrine's ritual functionings, to the point that they eventually came to define themselves in religious terms the same way the shrine so defined itself—in Muslim terms. As argued above, it seems reasonable to discount the clan's claims that their eponymous founder or some other early migrant from Sind or Rajasthan actually met Bābā Farīd and was converted to Islam by his suasion. The evidence presented below further indicates that at no time, whether in Bābā Farīd's day

[60] *Jawāhir-i Farīdī*, 323–4.

[61] Ibid., 324.

[62] Ibid.

or later, were the tribal murīds of the shrine converted to Islam en bloc. On the contrary, the conversion process seems to have been remarkably slow.

In his discussion of conversion to Islam in Iran, Richard Bulliet has suggested an objective index for measuring the overall rate of change from any given religion toward Islam in a specified region—namely, the frequency with which Muslim given names were bestowed on males. Observing that 'the naming of children is an act of free choice such as most individuals do not often have in their lifetime,' Bulliet notes that in selecting names,

one overriding motivation in many instances is the specific desire either to display group membership in a name, or to conceal group membership. Unless there is some peculiar reason for doing so, parents are generally loath to burden their children with names that will cause them to be ostracized. In other words, naming for many parents is an act that reflects, usually unconsciously, their view of the society around them at that particular point in time.[63]

According to both the shrine's hagiographic accounts[64] and the earliest known history of the clan,[65] the Siyāls of Jhang District were introduced to Islam by Bābā Farīd himself, who converted Rāy Siyāl, the clan's founder. After this event, according to these accounts, all Siyāls presumably, were Muslim. A very different picture emerges, however, if—as I have done in Table 9.2—one applies Bulliet's methodology to the fourteen genealogical charts of prominent Siyāl families given in the *Tārīkh-i Jhang Siyāl*. These charts record twenty generations of leading Siyāls from Rāy Siyāl to the time of the book's composition in 1862. Knowing, as we do, the dates of the Siyāl chiefs in the ninth and seventeenth generations, we can estimate the approximate date of each generation by using the rule-of-thumb of three generations per century. This would place Rāy Siyāl's life in the early thirteenth century, not far, in fact, from Bābā Farīd's lifetime.

As the table indicates, however, all masculine given names through the sixth generation remained Punjabi secular names; it was only in the early fifteenth century that specifically Muslim names began appearing at all. Gradually, between then and the early seventeenth century, the incidence of Muslim given names edged up from 10.24 per cent of the total to 39.21 per cent, not achieving parity with Punjabi secular

63 Richard W. Bulliet, 'Conversion to Islam and the Emergence of Muslim Society in Iran,' in N. Levtzion, ed., *Conversion to Islam* (New York, 1979), 43.

64 *Jawāhir-i Farīdī*, 324, 397.

65 Maulawī Nūr Muhammad, *T'arīkh–i Jhang Siyāl* (Meerut, 1862), 4–7.

names until about the middle of that century. It was not until the early eighteenth century that Muslim names became clearly preponderant (81.81 per cent). After that time our data become skewed because of the shrinking data base, but nonetheless indicate a total disappearance of Punjabi secular names by the early nineteenth century. The whole conversion process thus involved a period from the sixth to the nineteenth generation, or from the late fourteenth to the early nineteenth centuries.

Table 9.2. Changes in Names of Males of the Siyal Clan,
circa 1217 to 1862

Generation	Year	Total names recorded	Number of Punjabi secular names	Number of Muslim names	Percent of Muslim names to total
1	ca. 1217	1	1	0	0
2	ca. 1250	3	3	0	0
3	ca. 1283	13	13	0	0
4	ca. 1316	11	11	0	0
5	ca. 1349	9	9	0	0
6	ca. 1382	15	15	0	0
7	ca. 1415	39	35	4	10.25
8	ca. 1448	27	20	7	25.19
9	Mal Khān (d. 1481)	51	45	6	11.76
10	ca. 1514	51	38	13	25.49
11	ca. 1547	53	41	13	24.52
12	ca. 1580	61	42	18	29.50
13	ca. 1613	51	31	20	39.21
14	ca. 1646	34	15	19	55.88
15	ca. 1679	12	5	7	58.33
16	ca. 1712	22	4	18	81.81
17	Walīdād Khān (d. 1749–50)	12	3	9	75.00
18	ca. 1782	8	3	5	62.00
19	ca. 1815	10	0	10	100.00
20	1862	8	0	8	100.00

Source: Maulawī Nūr Muhammad, *Tārīkh–i Jhang Siyāl* (Meerut, 1862), 15–28.

If these data on the Siyāls are at all indicative of the conversion pattern for the other clans that had taken baiʿat with Bābā Farīd's shrine, or for that matter with any other shrine, then we may conclude that religious conversion among Punjabi clans was very slow indeed—not only slow, but probably unconscious as well. This was, after all, a period long before either British census officials or zealous reformers began urging Indians to place themselves into sharply differentiated religious categories. Accordingly, murīds of Bābā Farīd's shrine probably saw themselves less in terms of adherents of the Book and more in terms of clients and sponsors of a theater-shrine that displayed the wondrous baraka of its saint through its pageantry, festivals, and ceremonies. As Miles Irving wrote in 1911,

To the ordinary Montgomery cattle-thief who comes once a year to Pakpattan to obtain remission for the enormities of the past twelve months, Baba Farid is the mediator by whose merits he obtains forgiveness, assurance of which he obtains through the presence in the flesh of the descendant of the saint.[66]

Contemptible as this form of Islam may have been to nineteenth- and twentieth-century reformers, the shrine in the medieval period had managed gradually to give the clans an identity which, to their own satisfaction at least, was Islamic. In both the Sultanate and Mughal periods a long tradition of economic, political, and social patronage by the dīwāns had absorbed into the shrine's orbit of ritual influence groups which, as former pastoralists who had only recently achieved a settled way of life, had not formerly been integrated into anything approaching urban culture. It was the shrine's historical function to incorporate local systems of culture into a larger cultural system, to connect rustic clans politically with Delhi and religiously with Islam. This process, however, did not involve for newly incorporated groups a change from a Hindu to a Muslim identity, for at the time of the clans' first contact with Bābā Farīd's shrine these groups had not yet become integrated into the Hindu ritual or social structure. Although the precise nature of the Jats' pre-Muslim religion is as yet unclear, they seem to have had a deep-rooted tradition of social egalitarianism. Hence their rise in status from low Sudras to agrarian zamīndārs could more easily find ideological/ritual expression in Islam than within the highly stratified Hindu social system via the process of 'Sanskritization'.[67]

CONCLUSION

Although I have argued that the shrine of Bābā Farīd integrated local systems of culture into a larger one, the shrine nonetheless remained

---

[66] Miles Irving, 'The Shrine of Baba Farid Shakarganj at Pakpattan,' *Journal of the Panjab Historical Society* 1 (1911–12):73. It was, of course, Irving's imperial-administrative viewpoint that caused him to judge most clans of the barr country as 'cattle-thieves' and their actions as 'enormities'.

[67] In fact, it is just this dynamic, as Irfan Habib has suggested, that lay behind the attraction of other Jat tribes, in another part of the Punjab, to the equally egalitarian creed of Sikhism. See Habib, 'Jatts,' 99–100.

a local manifestation of that larger culture. The Chishtī brotherhood of Sufis, of which Bābā Farīd was himself one of the most renowned spokesmen, was historically the first great order of Sufis in the Indo-Muslim capital of Delhi. This meant that the tombs of these Sufis—e.g., of Muʿīn ad-Dīn Chishtī at Ajmer, Nizām ad-Dīn Auliyāʾ at Delhi, and Bābā Farīd at Pakpattan—became the first Muslim holy places *within* India. As such, they assumed immense importance, for it meant that South Asian Muslims were no longer compelled to look exclusively to the Middle East for spiritual inspiration.[68] Shrines like that of Bābā Farīd made a universal culture system available to local groups, enabling such groups to transcend their local microcosms.

In carrying out this role there evolved a distinctive code of conduct, or *adab*, of the shrines, just as medieval Indo-Muslim culture had evolved an equally distinctive adab of the court, i.e., a highly elaborated code of etiquette and pageantry that both dazzled and integrated into its structure the subjects of the kingdom. At Pakpattan this adab comprised the whole set of rituals and symbols that became institutionalized almost immediately after Bābā Farīd's death and that served progressively to assimilate various groups into its social and religious world. Consider, for example, the symbolic power of the turban. Precisely because the shrine of Bābā Farīd assimilated people religiously as well as politically and socially, the tying of the turban (*dastār bandī*) possessed a great symbolic repertoire: it defined relations of kinship between the shrine and subordinate clans, it symbolically conferred legitimacy on actual rulers in Delhi, and it conferred spiritual discipleship at the shrine itself. Another aspect of the shrine's adab was its carefully defined formula for achieving religious transcendence, namely, the practice of passing through its Gate of Paradise (*bihishtī darwāza*), enabling all who did so to ritually enter paradise.

Yet the adab of the shrine, like that of the court of Delhi, also established and sustained a hierarchic principle: in descending rank there was the dīwʿan, the dīwʿan's family, the khalīfas and shrine functionaries, the Chishtī caste, the clan leaders, and the common Jat agriculturalists. Even while integrating diverse peoples into a common religious culture, the shrine's highly elaborated code of conduct sorted, arranged, and held such peoples in a graded hierarchy that has persisted for centuries.

[68] We find, for example, early hagiographic manuals declaring that a certain number of pilgrimages to certain Sufi shrines in India would be equivalent in moral value to a single pilgrimage to Mecca.

10

Court of Man, Court of God
Local Perceptions of the Shrine of Bābā Farīd, Pakpattan, Punjab*

In his important book *The Cult of the Saints*, Peter Brown discusses how, between the third and the sixth centuries, a Christian cult of saints—the 'invisible friends in invisible places,' as he calls them—grew up in the great cemeteries that lay outside the cities of the Roman world. The tombs of these saints were privileged places, Brown writes, precisely because they were considered places 'where the contrasted poles of Heaven and Earth met,' for 'the saint in Heaven was believed to be "present" at his tomb on earth'.[1] In this sense, the world of Christian late antiquity, argues Brown, can be seen as a reversal of classical Greek thought, in which the boundaries between gods and humans were firm and unbridgeable. With the rise of the cult of the saints, such boundaries melted away.

Looking at post-thirteenth century Islam as it was naturalized beyond the Arab world, one finds a strikingly similar phenomenon. Here, too, there arose a cult of saints—many cults, actually—which had the effect of softening if not erasing the stark boundary separating Heaven and Earth as posited by Islam in its formal or legalistic sense. Many scholars of Islamic civilization have made this observation in a general way. But what has been lacking is any careful study of how Islam after the thirteenth century was mediated to whole societies and was sustained

---

[1] Peter Brown, *The Cult of the Saints: Its Rise and Function in Latin Christianity* (Chicago: University of Chicago Press, 1981), 3.

* Reprinted from Richard C. Martin, ed., *Islam in Local Contexts*, vol. 17 of *Contribution to Asian Studies*, Leiden: Brill, 1982, 44–61.

by any one of these tomb cults; and, above all, how Islam and the cult were viewed from the local perspective, that is, by those believers who were integrated into the religious and social world of one of these shrines.

The aim of this essay is to address just this topic by analysing the local perceptions of devotees of the shrine of Shaikh Farīd al-Dīn Ganj-i Shakar, a thirteenth-century Sufi whose tomb and shrine are located in the town of Pakpattan, in Pakistani Punjab. Popularly known simply as Bābā Farīd, this saint has remained for many centuries an immensely popular 'invisible friend' among millions of villagers inhabiting the southwestern Punjab.

Just as the immediate beneficiaries of legal disputes are lawyers, historians are perhaps the ultimate beneficiaries. In December 1934, Sa'īd Muḥammad, who was the religious head of the shrine of Bābā Farīd, died, leaving behind him his eleven-year-old son, Qutb al-Dīn, as his chosen successor. Only four months later, however, a local group of devotees at the shrine, who like Sa'īd Muḥammad were genealogical descendants of Bābā Farīd, filed a legal plaint in the nearby District Court in which they not only disputed Qutb al-Dīn's claim to the shrine's leadership, but substituted a rival claimant, Ghulām Rasūl, for this post. In order to fortify their respective cases, lawyers for both sides of the dispute solicited the testimony of a large number of the shrine's devotees, most of them common villagers, as to their views of the shrine's religious practices. Between 6 April 1935, when Ghulām Rasūl filed his plaint, and 2 December 1938, when a District Court judge decided the case in favour of the defendant, Qutb al-Dīn, no less than 159 oral depositions were filed on behalf of the plaintiff and 172 on behalf of the defendant, covering in all over 836 typed pages. In addition, both sides filed nearly three hundred documents with the Court. As a body, the depositions, submitted for the most part by local peasant-devotees from the district of Montgomery (now Sahiwal), Bahawalpur and Lyallpur, provide a remarkable sampling of the shrine's local constituency, documenting how the latter viewed the shrine's relationship to God, to Islamic Law, to the British government that ultimately ruled them, and to their own daily lives. As such, they afford an intimate look at how Islam, as sustained and mediated by this shrine, was popularly perceived in one locality of the Muslim world.[2]

---

[2] The past tense is used here and in the following discussion because the data on which the discussion is based belong to the period 1935–8. It is fair to assume, however, that the most general aspects of the shrine as described here hold as true for the present day as for the 1930s.

THE SHRINE AND THE EXCHANGE OF RELIGIOUS GOODS

In the minds of his many devotees, called *murīds*, Bābā Farīd was an 'invisible friend' not only to them; he was also a 'friend of God,' or *walī*. It is in this capacity to serve as a friend both of God and murīd, to join as it were the opposing poles of Heaven and Earth, that we see the basic religious role not only of Bābā Farīd, but also of his shrine and its religious leader. Called the *sajjāda-nishīn, gaddī-nishīn*, or most commonly the 'Dīwān,' the shrine's religious leader was a direct lineal descendant of the saint and was believed to be Bābā Farīd's living representative. Both the Diwan and the shrine itself, a magnificent marble edifice constructed in the fourteenth century, are perceived to be carriers of Bābā Farīd's *baraka*, i.e., the spiritual power that enabled the saint to intercede with God on behalf of the devotees. Hence both the Diwan and the shrine functioned as intermediaries for an intermediary, as on-going vehicles of the saint's mediative power.

Underlying and reinforcing this conceptual world was an exchange of 'religious goods' between the shrine's patrons and its clients—the chief patron being the Diwan, and the clients being the masses of murīds. For their part, the murīds made donations, usually cash contributions, that were called *nazrāna*. As one cultivator from Lyallpur District put it, 'We give nazrānas to Dewan Sahib out of love, respect and regard for the Pir and to invoke his blessings for the good of the murīd'.[3] In practical terms, this meant that murīds regularly made religious vows or 'contracts' with Bābā Farīd, as a mediator between them and God, in hopes of receiving any number of concrete favours, such as female fertility, good crops, relief from illness, etc. Though the vow was made with the saint, the donations went to one of the saint's on-going representatives, namely, either the Diwan or the shrine as a whole. For this reason the manner in which nazrāna was given varied somewhat. Some murīds testified that, having made the pious visit to Pakpattan, they would 'earmark' their nazrāna to go either in support of the shrine's public kitchen, or to the Diwan.[4] Others gave their nazrāna to the Diwan when he visited them in their villages. The amount of nazrāna varied, of course, with the means of the devotee.

If the nazrana represented the flow of religious goods from the devotee inward to the shrine, the opposite flow, from the shrine outward to the devotees, took place in several ways. One of these was through

---

[3] *Lahore High Court, Regular First Appeal No. 93 of 1939: Dewan Ghulam Rasul vs. Ghulam Qutab-ud-din*, 5 vols (Lahore, 1940), 2: 239.

[4] Ibid., 1:55; 2:28, 239.

the *langar*, or the public kitchen that the shrine housed and administered. Located in the shrine's courtyard just opposite Bābā Farīd's tomb, the langar was a vast operation, daily providing physical sustenance to the many pilgrims who came to pay respects and devotions at the shrine. One former worker in the kitchen estimated that between 240 and 320 lbs. (i.e. 3 or 4 *mans*) of wheat were consumed there every day, along with commensurate amounts of *dāl*, or split pea.[5]

Murīds also received religious goods of a more symbolic sort, consisting of sugar[6] or turbans, distributed only by the Diwan, and only on the occasion of particularly important shrine rituals at which he officiated. In part, the distribution of sugar represented the outward flow of Bābā Farīd's bounty and blessings. Symbollically, too, it linked both the Diwan and the murīds with their spiritual ancestor, Bābā Farīd, whose best-known epithet, Ganj-i Shakar, or 'treasury of sugar,' was associated with legends concerning the saint's severe austerities taken in pursuit of ascetic virtue.[7] The distribution of turbans—a powerful symbol of religious authority to be considered at greater length below—likewise served to connect murīds to the Diwan, and both of these parties to Bābā Farīd himself, whose spiritual authority at a very early period in the history of the shrine's cult came to be represented by his turban.[8]

THE SHRINE'S PLACE IN TIME AND SPACE

From the data recorded in the legal depositions, it does not appear that the murīds of the shrine saw any abrupt conceptual break between

[5] Ibid., 2:256.

[6] Ibid., 1:133.

[7] 'By continuous fasting,' noted a British gazetteer in 1884, 'his body is said to have become so pure that whatever he put into his mouth to allay the cravings of hunger, even earth and stones, was immediately changed into sugar, whence his name Shakar-Ganj, or sugar store. Another version of the story is that the saint, when hungry, used to tie a wooden cake (*chappati*) or a branch of wooden dates to his stomach, and that this composed his sole nourishment for thirty years. The truth of the story is vouched for by the preservation of the identical cakes and dates to this very day. They are kept at his shrine....' *Punjab District Gazetteers. Montgomery District* (Lahore, 1884), 184.

[8] The *Jawāhir-i Farīdi*, an important collection of the lives of Bābā Farīd's spiritual and lineal descendants completed in 1623, records that all the major rituals associated with the shrine, including those dealing with Bābā Farīd's turban, had become instituted in the generation following the saint's death, that is, in the late thirteenth century. See *Jawāhir-i Farīdi*, comp. 'Ali Asghar Chishti (Lahore, 1883–4), 298–300.

the life of Bābā Farīd, who died at the age of ninety in A.D. 1265, and the life of the shrine built over his grave. Indeed, many murīds referred to the saint and his shrine in the same terms, sometimes defining themselves as murīds of Bābā Farīd, and sometimes referring to themselves as murīds of the gaddī, or shrine. By conceptually fusing the saint and his shrine, murīds were able to understand the shrine as linking not only Heaven and Earth, but also past and present. The shrine *was* Bābā Farīd.

On the other hand, these same murīds had a very clear sense of their own tribal ancestors having, at some point in the historical past, been converted to Islam by Bābā Farīd. According to the depositions, this claim was made by many of the major endogamous clans that are spread throughout the southwestern Punjab, mainly as peasant agriculturalists. These clans, or *birādarīs* (brotherhoods), include the Wattu, the Siyal, the Dogar, the Kathia, the Bhatti, and the Tiwana.[9] Typical of their statements is this by a fifty-four-year-old cultivator from Lyallpur District: 'Our Tiwana tribe was converted by Baba Farid. Since then our relation of discipleship has been continued with the *gaddī*.'[10] Similar is this statement by another Lyallpur farmer: 'Baba Farid converted us Bhattis into Islam. Since that time we are the followers of the *gaddi* and respect the *gaddinashin* [i.e., sajjāda-nishīn, or Diwan] in office.'[11] Now we know that most of those Jat or Rajput clans claiming conversion at the hand of Bābā Farīd were not in fact anywhere near the Pakpattan region in the thirteenth century when Bābā Farīd himself was living, meaning that in any literal sense such an event could not have occurred. But since, as is clear from these depositions, saint and shrine are conceptually fused in terms of religious function, no real contradiction exists. As the tribes were converted at some point in medieval history by the agency of the shrine, so also were they converted by Bābā Farīd.

As for conceptions of religious space, the murīds appear to have seen the shrine of Bābā Farīd as occupying one in a network of sacred *wilāyats*, or territories under the spiritual authority of one or another *pīr* (saint), which dot all of North India. Moreover, these shrines were perceived as related to each other in terms of a ranked hierarchy, with the shrine of Bābā Farīd being the supreme shrine of the Punjab, to which others were subordinate. The *sajjāda-nishīn* of one of these shrines listed the following as among the shrines subordinate to that of Bābā Farīd in Pakpattan: that of Shaikh Jamāl al-Dīn of Hansi,

---

[9] *Lahore High Court*, 1:124, 138, 188, 225; 2:80, 87.

[10] Ibid., 2:87.

[11] Ibid., 2:80.

Hissar District, of Muḥammad Shāh in Basi Nau, Hoshiarpur District, of Niẓām al-Dīn Auliyā' in Delhi, Piran Kaler in Saharanpur District, Golra Sharīf in Rawalpindi District, Taunsa Sharīf in Dera Ghazi Khan District, Mukhan Sharīf and Basal Sharīf in Campbellpore District, Uch Sharīf in Bahawalpur State, and the shrines of Kasur and Lakhneke in Lahore District, Kastiwala in Gurdaspur District, and Panipat in Karnal District.[12] Although one shrine located in the nearby town of Dipalpur had been given land by an earlier Diwan of Pakpattan and for this reason saw itself as subordinate to Bābā Farīd's shrine,[13] most of the 'daughter' shrines of Bābā Farīd in the Punjab were founded by family descendants of Bābā Farīd, and hence they looked upon the shrine at Pakpattan as their spiritual superior. As we shall see below, this ranked hierarchy was ritually acted out according to an unwritten etiquette governing the attendance of shrine rituals by the sajjāda-nishīns of other shrines.

The spiritual potency, or baraka, of Bābā Farīd's shrine thus flowed out over the Punjab, infusing a series of subordinate shrines with sanctity. But the saint's baraka was seen as continuing to flow not only through the medium of such shrines, but also through living pīrs who likewise traced their spiritual, if not familial, descent from Bābā Farīd. Consider in this context how a fifty-four-year-old man from the neighbouring town of Dipalpur, who was himself both a common cultivator and a pīr, identified himself: 'I am a *ghulam* ['slave'] of Baba Farid's *silsila* ['spiritual order']. I am Watuzai Pathan and my ancestor of the 16th degree higher up was a disciple of Baba Farid. I am personally a pir of my tribe.'[14] This pīr's authority, in other words, stemmed from his descent not from Bābā Farīd's family, but from one of the saint's disciples. By this means Bābā Farīd's *spiritual* following spread out over many ethnically distinct groups, yet was sustained within such groups by living pīrs such as this gentleman, who served as a spiritual guide only for members of his own clan. Like the main shrine in Pakpattan, such pīrs also received cash payments from their murīds,[15] who readily identified the pīrs residing in or near their villages as their links with the shrine of Bābā Farīd in Pakpattan.[16] In fact, the very term 'pīr' as used among the murīds in this court case could refer to a living saint related to Bābā Farīd, as well as to the shrine of the saint or of one of his

---

[12] Ibid., 1:180.
[13] Ibid., 2:51.
[14] Ibid., 2:13.
[15] Ibid., 2:164.
[16] Ibid., 1:193.

descendants. Both pīr and shrine, after all, performed the same function—to sustain and transmit the blessings and intercessional power of Bābā Farīd.

THE SHRINE'S RELATIONSHIP TO 'THIS WORLD'

Where did the devotees place the shrine's status in the political universe of the Punjab in the 1930s? The case vividly illustrates the nature and contradictions of British imperial jurisprudence. Here was an Anglo-Indian civil court deciding, according to British legal procedures, a dispute between two Muslims over which one of them, according to Islamic Law as well as local custom, should legitimately succeed to the leadership of a Muslim shrine. In fact, religious considerations so permeated this dispute that one of the major points of contentions that emerged was whether or not the former Diwan, Sa'īd Muhammad, had received a dream in which Bābā Farīd revealed to him that his son Qutb al-Dīn should succeed him as Diwan.

This situation implied two things, one respecting the proper jurisdiction of the Anglo-Indian legal system, and the other respecting the popular perception of the shrine's status in the political as well as religious world of the Punjab. As to the former, by being drawn into disputes such as was represented by this case, the Anglo-Indian courts were forced to make decisions that were strictly religious in nature: for example, that the former Diwan did in fact have a revelation from Bābā Farīd.[17] The case would seem, therefore, to have posed theoretical difficulties for a ruling British government that professed to steer clear from interference with India's religious matters.

More central to the purpose of this essay, the resolution of the shrine's internal conflicts in an Anglo-Indian court of law seemed to promote the popular perception of the shrine as a religious institution *only*, and to diminish perception of it as a political institution. Formerly, in the history of medieval Punjab, the Diwans of Pakpattan had frequently played important political roles, enjoying close relations with the sultans and Mughal emperors of Delhi. And during the decline of Mughal authority, the Diwans' political roles even outweighed their religious roles. As one important functionary of the shrine observed, from the early 1700s the Diwans of Pakpattan 'were inclined to make conquests, to maintain armies, and to build forts. They themselves

[17] In his final judgment, delivered on 2 December 1938, Judge Guru Datta ruled, *inter alia*: 'I decide that the defendant has sufficiently succeeded in proving that Diwan Said Muhammad had received revelation and that the defendant's nomination was made on the strength of that.' Ibid., 3:290.

stopped giving spiritual education and employed Maulvīs, Imāms, Khaṭībs and Mubālighs for the purpose.'[18] Lesser folk, murīds of the shrine, tended to see the Diwan's traditional function as both religious and political, and some murīds during the trial actually characterized the current Diwan as a pīshwā, or leader, 'who leads us on the material and spiritual lines'.[19]

But now that a non-Muslim foreign power was ruling India—a situation brought home by the fact that this dispute was being tried in an Anglo-Indian court—other murīds sensed a sharp separation between the Diwan's religious and political authority, and saw the Diwan and the shrine as greatly reduced in their political authority. One Jat murīd from Bahawalpur wistfully looked back upon the early days of Islam, when the first four caliphs combined political with religious authority, and contrasted that period with this own: 'The Khulafa-i Rashedin, who were four in number, were both political and spiritual and religious heads. After Khulafa-i Rashedin, the Khalifas [caliphs] became the heads of [the] political department and the religious side became separate. On the political side, there is now no Khalifa in British India, only the British Government governs the country. The spiritual system was taken up by Baba Farid Shakar Ganj who was one of the various heads.'[20] The fact that 'only the British Government governs the country' had as its natural corollary, then, the enhancement of the shrine's *religious* status in the eyes of its devotees.[21]

THE SHRINE AND ITS RELATIONSHIP TO FORMAL ISLAM

What was, then, this religious status? One of the basic issues that emerged in the course of the litigation of this case—basic because it touched on the means of determining legitimate succession—was whether the shrine was to be understood fundamentally as a local institution, which governed its affairs according to its own customs, or whether it was to be understood fundamentally as an Islamic institution, governing its affairs according to Islamic Law, the sharī'a. The defendant, Quṭb al-Dīn, had been named Diwan by his father Fa'īd Muḥammad

[18] Ibid., 2:278.

[19] Ibid., 2:240-1.

[20] Ibid., 2:288.

[21] For a perception discussion of the intrusion of British power in Punjabi shrines and the implications this had for the modes of shrine leadership, see David Gilmartin, 'Shrines, Succession, and Sources of Moral Authority', in Barbara Metcalf, *Moral Conduct and Authority: The Place of Adab in South Asian Islam* (Berkeley and Los Angeles: University of California Press, 1984), 221–40.

just before the latter died, and the defendant's lawyers vigorously argued that this kind of de facto primogeniture accorded with the shrine's traditional custom with respect to succession. It was logical, then, that because the sharī'a is not generally interpreted as sanctioning primogeniture, the defendant's lawyers argued bluntly that 'this *Gaddi* follows custom and not Mohammadan Law'.[22] They also marshalled a wealth of historical evidence showing that previous Diwans had succeeded to the shrine's leadership as minors, though according to most interpretations the sharī'a would not have sanctioned such succession.

On the other hand the plaintiff claimed to have been 'elected' Diwan by the Chishti *birādarī*, which is the brotherhood of family descendants of Bābā Farīd, and he supported his arguments with pious appeals to early Islamic precedent. 'The *gaddi* in dispute is an Islamic *gaddi*,' the plaintiff argued. 'It is governed by Mohammadan Law and not by custom. We are bound by *Shariat*, ever since the time of Holy Prophet, Hazrit Mohammad. What has happened ever since the time of [the] Holy Prophet is this, that those who claim to succeed to the *gaddi*, the disciples and the other rightful persons collect together and select one of them, who is considered to be the fittest person. The present *gaddi* is governed by the same rule of succession, as was in vogue during the time of *Khulafa-i Rashedin*. We, the descendants of Baba Farid, claim to be the descendants directly from Hazrit Umar, the second Caliph.'[23] The issue of the shrine's Islamic character thus proved to be central to the entire case. But in soliciting opinions from sajjāda-nishīns of other shrines on this question, the Court failed to find much agreement: some argued that Muslim shrines could not follow local custom when it violated Islamic Law,[24] others that Islamic Law recognizes the use of local custom,[25] and one of them adopted the view that the sajjāda-nishīn is an autocrat, essentially above both custom and the sharī'a[26] The Court's final ruling on this question was an interesting compromise which saw the shrine basically as a local institution governing its affairs by its own traditional custom, but that, conveniently, this traditional custom happened to coincide with the sharī'a since 'Muhammadan Law itself reserves [customary] usage as

---

[22] *Lahore High Court*, 1:12.

[23] Ibid., 2:93.

[24] Ibid., 3:65, 121, 151, 212.

[25] Ibid., 3:86, 97.

[26] 'It depends on the sweet will of the *sajjada nashin*,' argued the sajjāda-nishīn of the shrine of Jamāl al-Dīn Hansawī, 'He can do about the shrine whatever he pleases.' Ibid., 3:140.

the primary rule for governing succession to a religious institution'.[27] The Court went on to cite several texts on Islamic jurisprudence to show that the sharī'a even allows a shrine's leader to name his own successor.[28]

The Court, in other words, had it both ways. It saw the shrine at once as a local institution that ruled by its own custom, and as a Muslim institution whose traditions conformed with Islamic Law. In retrospect, this formula would seem to have provided the Court with a practical means of settling the dispute: the shrine could continue using its own customary practices, which the ruling authorities would simply declare as conforming with Islamic Law. In 1938, with the forces of Islamic reform and Muslim separatism rising on all sides in British India, the government could hardly have taken the politically dangerous step of declaring that the most popular Islamic shrine in the western Punjab was not, after all, Islamic.

Moreover, the vast majority of the shrine's murīds seemed to see the issue in much the same way. 'The *gaddi* in dispute is bound by custom,' said one fifty-two-year-old villager: 'The *gaddi* in dispute is [an] Islamic *gaddi*, but is governed by custom. The *gaddinashin* [Diwan] must be of his father's caste, the mother's caste is immaterial. A Dewan can appoint whether he receives a revelation or not. But a revelation is generally received.'[29] Here again we see a view of the shrine that found no basic conflict between customary practice and Islamic Law. This view would seem to have allowed devotees to follow familiar religious practices without facing the disturbing thought that they were in any way violating the dictates of the sharī'a. On the other hand many of the urban 'ulamā', for whom the whole culture of shrines and saints smacked of idolatry, would have flatly rejected this position. But this was 1938, the very twilight of British India. And though the demand for Pakistan was becoming increasingly strident, the 'ulamā' were not yet in positions of effective power.[30]

THE SHRINE AND GRADED HIERARCHIES

The shrine's religious status must be viewed, however, not only from the perspective of its position *vis-à-vis* formal Islam. One of the primary

[27] Ibid., 3:254.

[28] Ibid.

[29] Ibid., 2:138.

[30] For a discussion of how the Government of Pakistan has dealt with the culture of shrines and saints since 1947, see Kathy Ewing, 'The Politics of Sufism: Redefining the Saints of Pakistan,' *Journal of Asian Studies* 42, no. 2 (Feb. 1983), 251–68.

religious roles of the shrine that emerges from the many depositions of its devotees is one of establishing and maintaining a graded, spiritual hierarchy descending from God through the Prophet Muḥammad and Bābā Farīd to the Diwan and from him to his khalīfas (spiritual adepts) and murīds (spiritual affiliates). One also detects a perceived flow of grace, or baraka, from God to the murīd in which process the shrine is critical since it represents the visible, tangible point at which this grace is localized. It is in Pakpattan, a town that lay within easy reach of only several days' travel in the Punjab, that God's grace was made concrete and accessible, that Heaven and Earth met. It remains, then, to examine how each component of this spiritual hierarchy was perceived by the devotees themselves.

Although the murīds seldom mentioned the Prophet Muḥammad in their depositions, he seems to have been visualized through the prism of the Islamic mystical tradition. One fifty-seven-year-old villager stated that Islam consisted of four principles—ṭarīqat, sharīʿat, ḥaqīqat and maʿrifat—and that it was the Prophet Muhammad who had laid them down, using the following words: *Shariat* is my word, *Tariqat* is my actions, *Haqiqat* is my conditions, and *Maʿrifat* is my mystery.'[31] Ironically, though Muḥammad the Prophet was here cast generally in a Sufi light, Bābā Farīd the historical Sufi was cast as an infallible revealer of God's essence and a commander of God's Law. 'I believe in the sanctity of the sayings, commands, or revelations of Baba Farid,' said a forty-year-old landholder from Ferozepore District; 'Baba Farid's command can never be incorrect. As the *Sajjada Nashin* in office is a representative of Baba Farid, the same sanctity and reverence is shown to the *Gaddi Nashin* as is shown to Baba Farid.'[32]

The above quotation and others previously cited illustrate decisively that the Diwan was seen above all as Bābā Farīd's living representative. Some murīds, such as the one quoted in note 20, seem to have viewed him as a sort of local caliph of Islam, though one lacking political authority since the British ruled the land. One witness even referred to the first four successors to the Prophet Muḥammad as 'gaddī-nishīns' and not as caliphs,[33] a perception suggesting the extent to which the religious culture of the shrine permeated a murīd's general outlook on Islam and Islamic history.

As for how the murīds viewed themselves in relation to the sociology of the shrine, they seem generally to have understood their inferior

---

[31] *Lahore High Court*, 2:43.

[32] Ibid., 1:220.

[33] Ibid., 1:150.

rank in the institution's hierarchy. When, for example, a fifty-five-year-old Jat peasant was asked why he did not sign a petition witnessing the installation of the plaintiff as Diwan, he replied, 'Prominent persons were made to sign, and we smaller people were not asked to sign.'[34] Moreover, the murīds almost without exception identified themselves not as individuals but in terms of a collective group, be that their kin group (barādarī) or the collective mass of murīds. Reflecting such kin-group identity, one villager belonging to the Wattu clan explained, 'Khewa, one of my ancestors, was converted into Islam by Baba Farid, and since that time we have been following the *gaddi* in dispute.'[35] Another murīd simply used as his reference point 'we Jat people'.[36] The other variety of collective identity transcended the kin group and tended to view all rural Muslims as devotees of Bābā Farīd. 'All the Mohammadans are the *Murids* of Baba Farid,' stated one villager, 'and so is my family.'[37]

At the bottom of the shrine's social hierarchy, then, were the peasant murīds, 'we smaller people,' belonging for the most part to Jat agricultural clans in southwestern Punjab. At the top, of course, was the Diwan, the supreme patron of all ritual functions at the shrine and the chief dispenser of Bābā Farīd's blessings. In between these was an endogamous clan of family descendants of Bābā Farīd, the Chishti clan (named after the Sufi brotherhood to which the saint had belonged), which possessed both economic privileges and ritual status *vis-à-vis* the local clans defining themselves as murīds of the shrine. An 1897 British Assessment Report for the Pakpattan region described the Chishtis as a 'semi-religious Mussalman tribe' having 'considerable local influence' and who 'are not working agriculturalists, but depend for cultivation entirely on tenants'.[38] As these tenants were drawn from among Jat clans whose members were murīds of the shrine, what we see here is a system embracing two tiers of lineages: an upper tier comprising the Chishti clan, and a lower tier comprising a number of subordinate lineages linked religiously to the shrine as murīds, and economically to the Chishti clan as tenant farmers.[39]

---

[34] Ibid., 1:148.

[35] Ibid., 2:64.

[36] Ibid., 2:31.

[37] Ibid., 1:205.

[38] P. J. Fagan, *Assessment Report for Pakpattan Tahsil, Montgomery District,* 1897 (Lahore, 1898), 50.

[39] Away from the immediate area around Pakpattan, this connection was probably religious only, and not economic, since the dominant Chishti clan, many of whose

The Chishti clan was thus socially quite distinct from non-Chishti clans whose members were devotees of the shrine. In fact, the essential purpose of the trial of 1935–8 was to judge the plaintiff's claim that the prerogative to select a new Diwan belonged to the Chishti clan and not to the previous Diwan. Neither side in this case argued that the murīds should have had any say in the matter, and in fact the evidence shows that the murīds were clearly outside the decision-making process. As one villager testified, 'the [Chishti] *biradri* was at first consulted about the appointment of the plaintiff. The murīds were never consulted, they only said *Amin* to the *biradri's* election.'[40] Even though the plaintiff lost this case, it is clear that the Chishti brotherhood—or certainly a substantial portion of it—claimed the status of the shrine's governing elite, and that many murīds acquiesced in this claim.

The claimed superior status of the Chishti clan was further enhanced by traditional marital practices that aimed at maintaining the clan's genealogical purity. So concerned with this issue was the Chishti clan that the leaders of a substantial faction of it—the faction supporting the plaintiff's cause—issued the following document on 16 February 1921:

Be it noted by all people in general that the revered descendants of Hazrat Shah Ala-ud-Din Mauj Darya ... grandson of Hazrat Baba Sahib ... are the most honourable and distinguished of all the descendants of Farid (be he blessed), and have been contracting matrimonial relations among themselves, and that though they took girls of other families in marriage, yet they did not give away their daughters in marriage in other families for the last five or six centuries.... Whoever of the descendants of Mauj Darya gives his daughter in marriage in another family, should be excommunicated from the brotherhood, and it is also improper to maintain connections of any sort with him.[41]

It is well known that a rigid control over marital contracts, especially with respect to bride-giving, is a key mechanism by which the Hindu social order maintains its system of endogamous castes ranked in a graded hierarchy. The influence of Hindu social concepts on the functioning of the Chishti clan's social relations is therefore obvious. What is even more remarkable about this policy statement was that it appealed to Islamic Law for its justification. Although 'all the descendants of Farid (be he blessed) are undoubtedly equal in lineal nobility,' the document continued, 'there are many traditions from the holy Prophet

---

members were landholders, were traditionally clustered around the town of Pakpattan.
[40] *Lahore High Court*, 2, 18–19.
[41] Ibid., 4:27.

(peace be on him) in regard to prohibition from abandonment of one's own family in matters of matrimonial relations.'[42]

In sum, it is evident from the documents of the Court's proceedings that the shrine had the objective function of establishing and maintaining not only a spiritual hierarchy, but also a social hierarchy as between the Diwan and his innermost family, the Chishti clan, and the many agricultural clans who as murīds constituted the shrine's lay affiliates and traditional supporters. But these hierarchies were maintained not just by the fact of birth-ascribed kin groups or the marital policies of elite groups at the shrine. A series of elaborate initiatory and com-memorative rituals had the effect of reinforcing existing hierarchal ar-rangements, while at the same time providing expressive meaning and cognitive order in the religious world of the shrine's devotees.

RITUALS AND SYMBOLS AT THE SHRINE

Question: 'What is the aim and object of the *Dastar bandi* performed on the fortieth day?'
Answer: 'So that all may come to know that such and such person has suc-ceeded.'[43]

The above extract from the Court's proceedings hints at what is perhaps the most important on-going business of the shrine, namely, the projec-tion of a dramatized image of the sacred order into this world. In Clifford Geertz's terms, the shrine provided its client clans of murīds with a tiny 'theatre-state' of its own.[44] Through the ceremonies and celebrations that marked its liturgical calendar, the shrine displayed the pageantry, order and beauty of the Court of God, albeit on a microcosmic scale. To the extent that religion itself can be understood as systems of symbols by means of which societies apprehend and comprehend the sacred order, Bābā Farīd's shrine provides the very stuff of religion.

The most common ritual that took place at the shrine was the initiation rite by which ordinary folk were formally made its spiritual

---

[42] Ibid. As the judge shrewdly observed in his final judgment, the fact that the former Diwan had given his own daughter in marriage outside the lineage constituted one of the ultimate causes of the entire dispute, since that act had touched off the profound discord within the Chishti barādarī that erupted only after the former Diwan died in 1934. See *Ibid.*, 3:298.

[43] Ibid., 3:110.

[44] Clifford Geertz, *Islam Observed: Religious Development in Morocco and In-donesia* (Chicago: University of Chicago Press, 1971), 38. 'See also his *Negara: The Theater State in Nineteenth-Century Bali* (Princeton University Press, 1980), especially chapter four.'

devotees. Belonging to a kin group that at some distant point in time had been converted to Islam by Bābā Farīd did not automatically make one a murīd of the shrine. One still had to participate in a formal initiation ceremony during which one made a solemn oath, known as bai'at, swearing spiritual allegiance to Bābā Farīd and his spiritual descendants, including of course the incumbent Diwan. One devotee said that this ceremony properly occurred but once in one's lifetime,[45] and other testimony suggests that murīds generally were young when initiated. Of those about whom we have information, one was age twenty-eight, one eighteen, one fourteen or fifteen, one ten or twelve, and one said simply that he was a young child when he took bai'at.[46] The bai'at ceremony itself was described in the following words: 'I was made [a] disciple some 18 years back. I was made to go through the following ceremonies:—my hand was placed in the hand of the *Gaddi Nashin.* I offered *Nazrana,* and I was given spiritual instructions to lead a truthful and noble life. I was also given a "Wazifa" for my recitation.'[47] In this context the term *wazīfa* referred to a prescribed liturgical formula, often a verse from the Qur'ān, which pīrs customarily gave their murīds to recite in order to aid them in spiritual concentration. Three other murīds reported having their forelocks (*lat*) clipped by the Diwan as part of their bai'at ceremony.[48] This practice follows a basic Indian paradigm of religious initiation in which such clipping symbolizes for the initiate an avowal of an ascetic way of life. Since murīds did not literally adopt ascetic vows when becoming devotees of the shrine of Bābā Farīd, the cutting of their forelocks must either be a remnant from earlier times when the bai'at compact actually did involve such vows (Bābā Farīd himself was a renowned ascetic), or, as is more likely the case, it was borrowed from Hindu-Buddhist initiatory practices which, ancient as well as modern, associate the cutting of hair with the adoption of ascetic vows.

The *dastār-bandi,* or 'turban-tying' ceremony, was one of the great religious dramas that took place at the shrine, since it was the ceremony by which a new Diwan was formally installed in office. Its purpose, as indicated in the quoted extract introducing this section, was to give public notice of the fact that Bābā Farīd had a new successor as his representative, a new spiritual custodian of his shrine. In many ways the ceremony mirrored the bai'at ceremony for murīds, since it too

---

[45] *Lahore High Court,* 2:39.

[46] Ibid., 1:109, 199, 160, 222, 186.

[47] Ibid., 1:109.

[48] Ibid., 1:160, 162.

was concerned essentially with initiation, though of course on a far grander scale. For example, if in a bai'at ceremony the murīd's forelocks were clipped, in the dastār-bandī ceremony the candidate's whole head was shaved.[49] The timing of the ceremony—the fortieth day after the death of the previous Diwan—coincided with the chehlum, which is a traditional day of mourning a person's death in Islam, thereby balancing the grief over the loss of a departed Diwan with the joy over the installation of a new one.

In the foreground of the dastār-bandī ceremony—or on the 'stage', to follow the metaphor of the theatre—were the most august figures associated with the shrine: the family of the Diwan, the most respected members of the Chishti clan, resident mystics living at the shrine, and sajjāda-nishīns of all of Bābā Farīd's 'daughter' shrines in the Punjab. The central ritual of the dastār-bandī ceremony at Bābā Farīd's shrine, as in others, was the placing of a special turban on the head of the new successor, symbolizing the legitimate succession of the saint's representative in the present time. Only somebody of equal or higher spiritual rank than the new sajjāda-nishīn could perform this ceremony, just as only a pīr, or someone of a spiritual rank higher than that of a murīd, could perform a bai'at ceremony. But since there was no one within the shrine's own hierarchy possessing a higher rank than that of the Diwan-elect, this ceremony was normally performed by the head of an outside shrine having at least equal if not more spiritual authority than the one sponsoring the ceremony. In this way, while the heads of subordinate shrines attended a dastār-bandī ceremony as honoured guests, only a head of a superior shrine actually performed it. Accordingly, on 1 February 1935, the eleven-year-old Quṭb al-Dīn, son of the recently deceased former Diwan, had the turban of succession placed on his head by the sajjāda-nishīn of the preeminent Chishti shrine of British India, that of Shaikh Mu'īn al-Dīn Chishtī in Ajmer, Rajasthan.[50] True, Bābā Farīd's is the preeminent shrine of the Punjab. But the Ajmer shrine is the most eminent of all Chishti shrines in India since its patron saint, Mu'in al-Dīn Chishtī (d. 1236), founded the Chishti order of Sufis in India and was the pīr of Bābā Farīd's own pīr. At one level, then, the dastār-bandī ceremony provided an opportunity for inter-shrine hierarchies to be acted out and confirmed.

In the background of the dastār-bandī ceremony, forming as it were the off-stage audience, throngs of murīds assembled in the shrine's spacious courtyard in front of Bābā Farīd's tomb where the ceremony

---

[49] Ibid., 1:170.
[50] Ibid., 3:215; 2:163.

was performed. But it was not just for the Jat villagers, murīds of the shrine, that the pageantry was performed. Hindu civic leaders and wealthy merchants also attended, and even participated. Accordingly, Ganpat Rai, a businessman and representative of a large market in Pakpattan, testified that 'on the *dastarbandi* of the defendant *nazranas* were paid us on behalf of the *Mandi* [market].'[51] In the same way, a certain Devi Bakhsh, a member of the Khatri caste, attended the ceremony and offered the new Diwan a turban and twenty-one rupees cash.[52] And Ram Rakha Mal, another Khatri and a member of Pakpattan's District Board, attended the ceremony, offering a turban and eleven rupees.[53] As Hindus, these gentlemen were probably not offering *nazrāna* out of expectations consonant with the Muslim-oriented conceptual structure of the shrine, but out of respect for a local institution of great repute, and perhaps also out of a sense of civic responsibility. As one Hindu remarked, 'there was a large number of persons including *Zamindars* [landholders], the gentry, and the *sajjadanashins* present.'[54] Nonetheless, the presence of Hindus participating in this event suggests how, in the past, generations of people of various castes and creeds had become integrated into the public aspects of the shrine's activities.[55]

While the dastār-bandī ceremony properly occurred only when a new Diwan was installed, the anniversary of Bābā Farīd's death was celebrated in a vast pageant known in 1938 as the Bihishti *melā*. At other Indo-Muslim shrines, the anniversaries of the deaths of great saints are similarly celebrated, and done with a joyous air that would befit a wedding ceremony. This is no coincidence, of course, since this is the *'urs* celebration, which means 'marriage with God'. As such, it commemorates not the saint's death so much as his everlasting union with God, and hence his spiritual survival for purpose of passing on his grace, or baraka, to his devotees. But in the Bihishti melā the theme of salvation through loving devotion was made far more explicit than in most other Indo-Muslim shrines, since it was literally acted out by all participants. Called the *bihishtī darwāza*, or 'Gate of heaven,' the south door of Bābā Farīd's tomb remained closed on all days of the year until the date of Bābā Farīd's *'urs*, the fifth of Muharram. On

---

51 Ibid., 2:174.

52 Ibid., 2:224.

53 Ibid., 2:223.

54 Ibid.

55 This integrative aspect of the shrine constitutes one of its oldest and historically most significant roles. See my essay, 'The Political and Religious Authority of the Shrine of Baba Farid in Pakpattan, Punjab,' in the present volume.

that day the Diwan personally unlocked and opened the gate, passed through it, and was then followed by throngs of murīds estimated to number between fifty and sixty thousand.[56] All through the night and in states of intense religious ecstasy, the devotees filed through this 'Gate of Heaven' and past Bābā Farīd's flower-bedecked tomb, thereby both commemorating and ritually reenacting the ascension of their patron saint to heaven. A description of this ceremony noted by a European visitor a century earlier, in 1833, vividly illustrates the salvation aspect of the ritual. When the gate is opened, the visitor observed,

> numbers of pilgrims, both Hindus and Mussalmans, come to visit the shrine, and all who pass through this doorway are considered saved from the fires of perdition. The door-way is about two feet wide, and cannot be passed without stopping, and the apartment itself is not capable of containing thirty people crowded together.... A superlative heaven is allotted to those who are first to enter the tomb on the day mentioned. The rush for precedence may, therefore, be better imagined than described. The crowd of pilgrims is said to be immense, and as they egress from the sacred door-way, after having rubbed their foreheads on the foot of the saint's grave, the air resounds with their shouts of Farid! Farid![57]

It is worth noting that because only the Diwan opened the gate, it was only through his agency that devotees gained access to Bābā Farīd, and only through the saint's agency that they gained access to Heaven. More than that, it seems that in the minds of the murīds, a fixed order of precedence existed with respect to entering the 'Gate of Heaven,' despite the rush mentioned by the European visitor in 1833. 'Dewan Sahib first opens the Bahishti Gate,' explained a certain Khan Muhammad in his deposition of August, 1938; 'he enters the gate and thereafter his companions pass through that gate. The companions number about 100–125. After that, the pass-holders pass through it, they are about 400–500; after that, the *darveshes* of the *Hujra* [i.e., resident mystics], who number 1,000–1,200. After them the plaintiff, Ghulam Rasul and his party, pass through the Bahishti Gate, after that the *sajjadanashins* of other institutions pass, and so on.'[58] The great masses of common devotees, included among the 'and so on' in the above quote, were allowed to enter through the gate only after the other dignataries had done so. The Gate of Heaven, after all, is a narrow one, and can be

---

[56] *Punjab District Gazetteers. Montgomery District* (Lahore, 1884), 185.

[57] Lieut. F. Mackeson, 'Journal of Captain C. M. Wade's Voyage from Lodiana to Mithankot by the River Satlaj on His Mission to Lahor and Bahawalpur in 1832–33,' *Journal of the Asiatic Society of Bengal* 6 (1837): 192.

[58] *Lahore High Court*, 2:249.

entered only one by one, in single file. All this suggests that the Bihishti ceremony served to act out and confirm the sense of spiritual hierarchy that pervades the whole ethos of the shrine.

We also see that certain core symbols pervaded the initiatory and commemorative rituals of the shrine. Some were associated with medieval Indian royalty and served to emphasize the Diwan's supreme religious and administrative position. Thus when the Diwan would visit the shrine of Bābā Farīd's son-in-law in Pakpattan, Badr al-Dīn Ishāq, on the occasion of that shrine's *'urs* ceremony, the Diwan was carried on a palanquin (*palkī*). This means of conveyance, consisting of a litter borne on the shoulders of men by means of poles, was from ancient times traditionally reserved for persons of privileged status. One villager simply explained that on the occasion of Badr al-Dīn's *'urs* it is necessary for the *sajjadanashin* to go there in a *palkī*.[59] Once there, moreover, gifts presented by the Diwan to Badral-Dīn's descendant further suggested the style and magnanimity associated with Indo-Muslim nobles—100 rupees in cash, a horse, and a silver saddle.[60]

One symbol in particular, the turban, perhaps transcended all others in importance. Associated with traditional Sufi lore but also having ambiguous associations with the crown and thereby with royalty, the turban served as a vehicle both for religious legitimacy and for the distribution of Bābā Farīd's grace. As to the former, the depositions are full of evidence indicating that a proper successor to Bābā Farīd's shrine had to be 'crowned' with a turban representing the saint's own turban, i.e., the dastār-bandī ceremony. Both disputants in this case accordingly went through such 'turban-tying' ceremonies by way of laying claim to legitimate succession as Diwan. In the case of the defendant, who claimed that only a former Diwan could choose his successor, his own father, Diwan Sa'īd Muhammad, had placed a turban on the boy's head during the course of the Bihishti melā of 1933.[61] Later, on the occasion of the fortieth day after his father's death, the boy had a second dastār-bandī ceremony during which the sajjāda-nishīn of the Ajmer shrine placed the turban on the boy's head. As for the plaintiff, who claimed that a new Diwan must be elected by the Chishti clan, a special dastār-bandī ceremony was held at which representatives of the whole clan placed a turban on his head.[62]

[59] Ibid., 2:153.
[60] Ibid.
[61] ibid., 2:181, 193.
[62] Ibid., 1:47.

It further appears that the headgear used in the dastār-bandī ceremony, a special saffron-coloured turban reserved only for the Diwan, was physically touched to the saint's tomb before being placed on the candidate's head.[63] This act decisively served ritually to link the new successor with Bābā Farīd himself, and rested in the popular belief that Bābā Farīd had used his own turban as a symbol of spiritual authority. One villager, for example, testified that the second Diwan, 'Alā' al-Dīn Mauj Daryā (1281–1334), became Diwan by placing Bābā Farīd's very turban on his head when he was a child.[64] This seems to be a truncated version of a story given in more detail by another villager, to the effect that as a child, 'Alā' al-Dīn had one day playfully put Bābā Farīd's turban on his head. When a servant objected, Bābā Farīd, then an old man, pardoned the child's behavior saying that the boy would one day be his successor anyway.[65] Still another witness testified that when the first Diwan died and a dispute arose over who should succeed him, the great saint of Delhi, Khwāja Niẓām al-Dīn Auliyā', came to Pakpattan to arbitrate. At his instance, the story continued, 'the turbans of all the rival claimants were emersed in water. The turban of Dewan Alau-ud-Din Mauj-i Darya came out coloured, consequently, the *Bradari* accepted Dewan Alau-ud-Din Mauj-i Darya as the proper *Gaddi Nashin* to the exclusion of all other claimants.'[66] In all of these versions we find the common assumption that the turban, used in the proper ritual context, was uniquely empowered to endow the wearer with Bābā Farīd's own spiritual authority.

A second use of the turban was as a carrier in distributing Bābā Farīd's grace among his devotees. As one sixty-year-old villager remarked. '*pechas* [turbans] are distributed at the annual urs only by [the] *sajjadanashin* and nobody else. At that time, [the] *sajjadanashin* has hundreds of *pechas* with him. He must distribute those *pechas* personally.'[67] Yet turbans were passed in the opposite direction, too. We have seen that oftentimes nazrāna given to the Diwan by devotees, or simply by well-wishers, consisted of turbans in addition to cash. In this sense, we find the turban employed as a symbol of a shared cultural

---

[63] Ibid., 2:55, 169, 181. Since the plaintiff was not given access to the shrine for his dastār-bandī ceremony, this aspect of the rite had to be omitted in his case.

[64] Ibid., 1:170.

[65] Ibid., 1:102–3. The same witness added that Bābā Farīd also placed saliva from his own mouth into that of the boy 'in order to impart spiritual light from himself to the boy.' See *Ibid.*, 1:103.

[66] Ibid., 1:158.

[67] Ibid., 2:104.

heritage. Since it got passed to and from persons otherwise occupying different positions in the social hierarchy, the *pecha* or 'honourary' turban promoted egalitarian feelings of a shared, common tradition. On the other hand the word dastār referred to the turban that served to separate Bābā Farīd's legitimate successor from the common crowd, thereby having the opposite effect of maintaining hierarchy. Indeed, it is in the turban's rich symbolic repertoire that we see its capacity to express and sustain values, so central to the shrine, that might otherwise appear mutually antagonistic, i.e., a hierarchy of religious status and a commonality of cultural inheritance.

COURT OF GOD, COURT OF MAN

To conclude, the shrine of Bābā Farīd in Pakpattan provides a striking example of how Islam, the religion par excellence 'of the Book,' has been mediated among common villagers most of whom were illiterate. For them it was the shrine, and less so the Book, which manifested the juncture 'where the contrasted poles of Heaven and Earth met'. Through its elaborate rituals, grand processions and colorful pageantry, the shrine displayed a sense of divine magnificence and mercy. It displayed, in short, the Court of God. Not that Bābā Farīd himself was confused with God. This would of course have been blasphemous idolatry, as was fully understood by one old cultivator who declared, 'doing *sajda* [prostration] to the tomb of Baba Farid under Mohammadan Law is not permissible'.[68] Rather, though the Court of God as a cosmological construct seemed to lie beyond the devotee's immediate grasp, he did have a 'friend in court,' as it were, who represented his interests there. This 'friend in court,' this special pleader, was Bābā Farīd.

In the years 1935 to 1938 this Court of God conception of the world was contrasted by a conception made manifest in the town of Montgomery, some 25 miles down a dusty road from the hallowed marble domes of Pakpattan, in the court of the senior subjudge of the Montgomery District, British Punjab. In the Court of Man, the world is held together not by an unseen Presence, but by principles, or 'laws,' which are whatever men state them to be. In British India, the effect of such laws was to render state sanction to whatever local customs the courts judged were already being practiced by a majority of the people. Accordingly, in the Court of Man superhuman evidence such as a revelation from Bābā Farīd was inadmissible. As the District Court

[68] Ibid., 2:39.

Judge commented in his final verdict, 'Whatever weight an argument as to revelation may be entitled to in a purely religious or metaphysical discussion, it cannot, I think, prevail ... in a Court of law at the present day.'[69]

The case examined here might therefore appear to have represented a clash of two conceptual systems. But did they really clash? As we have seen, the District Court in the end merely ratified what it deemed to be the customary practice with regard to succession at the shrine, and then declared its judgment to be in conformity with Islamic Law. To the masses of devotees in Pakpattan, however, the little drama unfolding in the district courthouse in Montgomery was apparently irrelevant to their religious concerns. 'I am a follower of the *Gaddi Nashin* whosoever may be occupying it,' stated one of Bābā Farīd's murīds.[70] Though they could choose whom they wanted as Diwan, this sentiment seems to suggest, the actions of the learned lawyers of Montgomery could not really affect what this shrine was all about. In the last analysis, the Court of God quite transcended the Court of Man in the eyes of the shrine's common devotees.

---

[69] Ibid., 3:289. Nonetheless, it is a measure of the genius of human institutions that on the very next page, this same judge made a ruling on the fact of Bābā Farīd's revelation. See above, footnote 17.

[70] *Lahore High Court*, 1:138.

SECTION 4
BENGAL

11

Who are the Bengal Muslims?
Conversion and Islamization in Bengal*

A striking feature of Islam in pre-modern Bengal is the cleavage that emerged between a folk Bengali variant, which was built upon indigenous roots, and a variant practiced and patronized primarily by urban-dwelling, *ashrāf* classes. This divide lay behind the nineteenth century reform movement and contributed to the twentieth century upheavals that led first to the inclusion of eastern Bengal in the state of Pakistan, and ultimately to its secession from that state. The present essay examines the evolution of the Bengal Muslims between the sixteenth and eighteenth centuries, a period when evidence of the religious culture of both ashrāf and non-ashrāf communities is especially well-documented. It also explores why and how Islam became the dominant religious tradition in Bengal but not in upper India, the epicentre of Indo-Muslim political culture, and in the eastern, but not the western, portion of the Bengal delta.

In the Bengali context, the ashrāf generally included those Muslims claiming descent from immigrants from beyond the Khyber—or at least from beyond Bengal—who cultivated high Perso-Islamic civilization and its associated literatures in Arabic, Persian, and Urdu. Soon after the Turkish conquest of the delta in 1204, Muslim immigrants from points west settled in cities like Gaur, Pandua, Satgaon, Sonargaon, and Chittagong, principally as long-distance traders, administrators, soldiers, and literati. But from 1342 to 1574, under the rule of a succession of independent Muslim dynasties, Bengal became isolated from north India, and immigration from points west was largely curtailed. In the wake of the Mughal conquest of 1574, however, Muslim immigrants from north India once again settled the delta, in such numbers

---

* From Rafiuddin Ahmed, ed., *Understanding Bengali Muslims: Interpretive Essays* (New Delhi: Oxford University Press, 2000)

that it was their understanding of Islam that came to define ashrāf religious sensibilities in modern Bengali history.

Although the Mughals had originated in fifteenth century Central Asia, by the time they conquered Bengal in the late sixteenth century they had already assimilated the political traditions of north India, a process accelerated by Akbar's policy of admitting Rajputs into his ruling class. In fact, they had become virtual Rajputs themselves. In the early seventeenth century, for example, we already hear of Muslim officers in Bengal indulging in the Rajput practice of *jūhar*, the destruction of women and children as an alternative to suffering their capture by an enemy.[1] The Mughals in Bengal also preferred Ayurvedic medical therapy to the Yunani system inherited by medieval Islamic civilization. Islam Khan, the first governor to establish permanent Mughal dominion in the delta, sent for an Indian physician when he fell terminally ill in 1613. As one was not available, the Governor only reluctantly accepted the services of a Muslim healer (*ḥakīm*), who was later blamed for having administered the wrong treatment and unnecessarily killing him.[2] Reliance on Indian systems of medical theory in the face of fatal illness, and on Rajput customs when faced with immanent annihilation in battle—both of them life-threatening situations—suggests the degree to which Indian, and especially Rajput, values had penetrated Mughal culture by the early seventeenth century.

Conversely, from the Mughal-Rajput perspective Bengal was a distinctly alien land. Abu'l-fazl, Akbar's chief counselor and ideologue, described the region as 'a house of turbulence' (*bulghāk-khāna*). As he wrote in 1579, shortly after Akbar's armies had seized the province from its Afghan rulers,

The country of Bengal is a land where, owing to the climate's favouring the base, the dust of dissension is always rising. From the wickedness of men

---

[1] Mirza Nathan, *Baharistan-i Ghaybi*, Persian MS. Paris: Bibliothèque Nationale, Pers. Sup. 252, fols. 203b–204a. Trans. M. I. Borah, *Baharistan-i Ghaybi*, 2 vols. (Gauhati: Government of Assam, 1936), 1:440. Mirza Nathan, the author of one of the most important literary sources for early seventeenth century Bengal, was a junior officer who accompanied Bengal's first governor, Islam Khan Chishti (1608–13), out to Bengal in 1608 and participated in many if not most of the political and military engagements that marked Bengal's consolidation into the Empire during the years 1608–18. During this time Nathan kept a careful account of his operations in Bengal, as well as those of his colleagues and adversaries. The *Baharistan* is especially valuable for our present purposes since its author, a Punjabi Muslim, saw Bengal from both a north Indian and an imperial perspective.

[2] Mirza Nathan, *Baharistan*, text fol. 140b; tr., 1:256.

families have decayed, and dominions ruined. Hence in old writings it was called Bulghāk-khaña (house of turbulence).[3]

In effect, we have here a theory of socio-political decay: an enervating climate corrupts men, corrupted men ruin sovereign domains and, implicitly, ruined domains pave the way for conquest by more virile, 'manly' races. In its linking of Bengal's climate with the debased behaviour of the people exposed to it, Abu'l-fazl's theory of decay at once recalls similar views later adopted by British colonial officials.[4]

The Mughals' alienation from the land was accompanied by feelings of superiority or condescension toward its people. Especially in matters of language, dress, or diet, officials newly-arrived to the delta experienced profound differences from the North Indian culture to which they had been accustomed. The Bengali diet of fish and rice, for example, contrasted sharply with the wheat and meat diet of the Punjab and seems to have posed a special stumbling block for immigrants.[5] At the same time, Mughal officers associated Bengalis with fishing, a mode of life they despised. Around 1620 two Mughal officers, aiming to belittle the martial accomplishments of one of their comrades, challenged the latter with the words: 'Which of the rebels have you defeated except a band of fishermen who raised a stockade at Ghalwapara?' In reply, the other observed that even the Mughals' most formidable adversaries in Bengal, 'Isa Khan and Musa Khan, had been fishermen. 'Where shall I find a Dawud son of Sulayman Karrani to fight with, in order

---

[3] H. Beveridge, tr., *The Akbar Nama of Abul-Fazl*, 3 vols, 2nd repr. (Delhi: Ess Ess Publications, 1977), 3:427; text, 3:290.

[4] Typical were those of Robert Orme, written in 1763: 'The abundance of advantages peculiar to this country,' he wrote, 'through a long course of generations, have concurred with a languor peculiar to the unelastic atmosphere of the climate, to debase all the essential qualities of the human race, and notwithstanding the general effeminacy of character which is visible in all the Indians throughout the [Mughal] empire, the natives of Bengal are still of weaker frame and more enervated disposition than those of any other province.' Robert Orme, *History of the Military Transactions of the British Nation in Indostan* (repr., Madras: Pharaoh, 1861), 2:4–5.

[5] Written in 1786, the *Riyaz al-salatin* reads almost like a colonial British manual on how to survive 'amongst the natives': 'And the food of the natives of that kingdom, from the high to the low, are fish, rice, mustard oil and curd and fruits and sweetmeats. They also eat plenty of red chilly and salt. In some parts of this country, salt is scarce. The natives of this country are of shabby tastes, shabby habits and shabby modes of dress. They do not eat breads of wheat and barley at all. Meat of goats and fowls and clarified butter do not agree with their systems.' Ghulam Husain Salim, *Riyazu-s-Salatin: A History of Bengal,* trans. Abdus Salam (repr. Delhi: Idarah-i Adabiyat-i Delli, 1975), 21.

to please you?' he asked rhetorically, and with some annoyance, adding that it was his duty as an imperial officer to subdue all imperial enemies in Bengal, 'whether they are *Machwas* [fishermen] or Mughals or Afghans'.[6] This exchange reveals the notion that the only opponents truly worthy of the imperial forces were Mughal rebels or Afghans like the recently-defeated Karranis; Bengalis, being fishermen, apparently occupied a separate category of less worthy adversaries.

Mughal officials thus saw themselves as the land's natural rulers, distinguished from Bengalis not only as tax-receivers as opposed to tax-payers, but as north Indian fighting men as opposed to docile fishermen. On one occasion Governor Islam Khan's chief naval officer, Ihtimam Khan, expressed resentment that the Governor had treated him and his son like 'natives'.[7] The idea that ashrāf Muslims occupied a social category altogether separate from the 'natives' was echoed in the observation of an outside observer, Fray Sebastien Manrique, who in 1629 described Bengal's population as composed of three groups—'the Portuguese, the Moors, and the natives of the country'.[8] According to this system of social classification, Muslims were, by definition, foreigners to the land. The idea that 'natives' could also be 'Moors'—that is, that there could be Bengali Muslims—was, from the perspective of members of the urban, Mughal ruling class whom Manrique met, conceptually impossible.

Regarding the religion of the Mughal ashrāf, three features stand out: (a) a special link with the pan-Indian Chishti order, (b) a conceptual separation of religion and state, and (c) a disinclination to convert Bengalis to Islam. Most Muslims in the imperial corps brought to Bengal styles of Islamic piety that had already evolved in north India during the preceding century. We can glimpse a profile of this piety from the remarks of Mirza Nathan, a middle-level imperial officer whose unofficial memoir is filled with references to witchcraft, astrology, and notions of the paradisiac afterlife associated with Mughal soldiers he called *ghāzīs*. All of these elements were well integrated into his

---

[6] Mirza Nathan, *Baharistan*, text fol. 278b; trans. 2:650–51.

[7] Ibid., text fol. 18a; trans. 1:51. Since the Persian term used here, *ahl-i Hind*, means simply 'Indian', one might expect to find it used only by those members of the ruling class who had immigrated from beyond India. But Ihtimam Khan was himself an Indian Muslim from the Punjab; hence his use of the term *ahl-i Hind* in a pejorative sense suggests he had adopted ashrāf attitudes as a result of serving in a power structure in which such attitudes were dominant.

[8] Fray Sebastien Manrique, *Travels of Fray Sebastien Manrique, 1629–1643*, trans. E. Luard and H. Hosten, 2 vols (Oxford: Hakluyt Society, 1927), 1:40.

worldview.[9] Above all, Nathan's religion was characterized by a vivid sense in which Allah mediated his blessings to believers through the agency of saints. These, however, were not the village *pīrs* who played such important roles in the world of rural Bengalis, but shaikhs belonging to the Chishti order of Sufism, the order most clearly associated with Mughal, and before that, Tughluq imperialism. This was also the most authentically Indian of Sufi brotherhoods, its wealth and power centred on the enormous cults based on the tomb-shrines of north Indian saints such as Muin al-Din Chishti (d. 1236) in Ajmer, Rajasthan; Nizam al-Din Auliya (d. 1325) in Delhi; or Farid al-Din Shakarganj (d. 1265) in Pakpattan, Punjab. Since the Tughluq period, this order enjoyed a very special status among Delhi's rulers, who lavishly patronized the descendants of the great Chishti shaikhs with magnificent tombs and considerable tax-free land. Mirza Nathan was himself a 'faithful disciple' (*murīd-i bandagī*) of Farid al-Din Shakarganj, probably because the writer's ancestors had come from the Punjab where Baba Farid's cult was especially prominent.[10] Moreover Islam Khan, Bengal's first permanent governor (1608–13) and the man most responsible for consolidating Mughal rule in Bengal, was the grandson of Akbar's chief spiritual guide, Shaikh Salim Chishti. It was on this account that the Governor on one occasion referred to Sufism as 'our ancestral profession' (*faqīrī ki kasb-i buzurgān-i māst*).[11] One feature of ashrāf piety, then, was a close and enduring connection with the Chishti order.

Second, ashrāf Muslims conceptually distinguished religion and state, which was reflected, among other ways, in a functional specialization of their cities. As a provincial capital and administrative centre, Dhaka was primarily devoted to revenue collection, administration, politics, and military reviews. The city was also involved in considerable trade

---

[9] Thus he remarked on the efficacy of witchcraft, as in the ability of Muslim practitioners to cause blood spontaneously to appear from the throat and stomach of victims. Both Muslim and Hindu astrologers counseled Mughal commanders against inauspicious activities such as moving armies northward on Tuesdays or Wednesdays. And reflecting his understanding of the afterlife, Nathan wrote the following in describing a particularly bloody battle in which many Muslim warriors died: 'The houris of the highest heaven were waiting with the cups of heavenly drink in their hands watching which of the brave heroes, with their eyes fixed on the Unique and the Incomparable God, will make his journey to the heavenly kingdom in the most glorious way so that they might embrace him and satiate him with a drink of the pure wine from the reservoir of *Kawsar* (the river of paradise).' *Bahāristan*, text fols. 286a, 180a, 190a; trans. 2:671–72, 1:367, 397–8.

[10] Ibid., text fol. 302b; trans. 2:716.

[11] Ibid., text fol. 60a; trans. 1:152.

and money-making. Fray Manrique, who was there in 1640, wrote that merchants of Dhaka 'have raised the city to an eminence of wealth which is actually stupefying, especially when one sees and considers the large quantities of money which lie principally in the houses of the Cataris [Khatri], in such quantities indeed, that, being difficult to count, it is usually commonly to be weighed.'[12] In short, Dhaka was a secular city. Even its most imposing mosques, such as the Satgumbad Mosque (ca. 1664–76) or the mosques of Haji Khwaja Shahbaz (1679) and Khan Muhammad Mirza (1704), bear the stuccoed stamp of their north Indian patrons, and seem intended more to display imperial power than to inspire piety.

On the other hand the ancient capitals of Gaur and Pandua, denied any political significance under the Mughals, emerged under their rule as Islamic sacred centres. The sanctity of Gaur focussed in part on the Qadam Rasul, a reliquary established by Sultan 'Ala al-Din Husain Shah in 1503, containing a dais and black marble stone purporting to bear the impression of the Prophet's footprint.[13] But the shrines most lavishly patronized by the Mughals were the older and more important shrines in nearby Pandua—the tombs of Shaikh 'Ala al-Haq (d. 1398) and Shaikh Nur Qutb-i 'Alam (d. 1459). Both shaikhs were members of the Chishti order; in fact, they were the most prominent Chishtis ever to have settled in Bengal. The shrine of Nur Qutb-i 'Alam had been the object of state patronage ever since the son and successor of Sultan Jalal al-Din Muhammad (r. 1415–32), Sultan Ahmad (r. 1432–33), became a disciple of the famous shaikh. By the end of the fifteenth century it had become the focus of annual pilgrimages performed by Sultan 'Ala al-Din Husain Shah (r. 1493–1532).[14] A century later, in 1609, the Mughal officer Mirza Nathan made a three-day pilgrimage to the shrine, having vowed to do so should his father

---

[12] Manrique, *Travels*, 1:44.

[13] Shamsud-Din Ahmed, ed. and trans. *Inscriptions of Bengal*, vol. 4 (Rajshahi: Varendra Research Museum, 1960), 163. In 1609 Mirza Nathan, while in the midst of Mughal military operations in northwestern Bengal, paid his respects at this shrine, noting that the marble footprint had been purchased and brought from Arabia by one of the sultans 'so that the people of Bengal and everybody else, who were destined to come there, might attain eternal blessing by kissing the holy footprint.' Mirza Nathan, *Baharistan*, text fol. 58a; trans. 1:146.

[14] 'Abd al-Rahman Chishti, *Mirat al-asrar*, Persian MS, composed 1654, copied 1806 (Patna: Khuda Bakhsh Library, Pers. MS no. 204), fol. 517b; Khwajah Nizamuddin Ahmad, *Tabaqat-i-Akbari*, trans. Brajendranath De, ed. Baini Prashad, 3 vols (1939; repr. Delhi: Low Price Publications, 1992), 3:443.

recover from an illness.[15] And on the occasion of his own marriage, he made a pilgrimage to Gaur's Qadam Rasul and Pandua's shrine of Shaikh 'Ala al-Haq.[16] Later, while in Bengal in 1624, the future emperor Shah Jahan distributed Rs 4,000 at Nur Qutb-i 'Alam's shrine, his largest cash contribution in all of Bengal.[17]

Thirdly, ashraf Muslims in Bengal adopted a strictly hands-off policy toward the non-Muslim society that surrounded them everywhere. Unlike the contemporary Ottoman Empire where non-Muslim military recruits were converted to Islam as part of their assimilation into the ruling class, in India non-Muslims were given full admission into the Mughal officer corps as non-Muslims. What bonded together Mughal officers of diverse cultures was not a common religion, then, but the ideology of 'salt,' the ritual eating of which served to bind people of unequal sociopolitical rank to mutual obligations: the higher-ranked person swore to protect the lower, in return for which the latter swore loyalty to the higher. Such bonds of loyalty among Mughal officers not only ran across religious or ethnic communities, but persisted over several generations.[18] At the same time, when making vows or swearing oaths, members of the imperial corps appealed to different deities according to their particular religious identities. On one occasion, a copy of the Qur'an and a black geode worshiped in the form of Vishnu (*sālagrām*) were brought to a mixed group of Mughal officers about to swear on oath. Placing their hand on the Qur'an, the Muslim officers took solemn oaths in the name of Allah; while the Hindu officers, placing their hand on the geode, did the same in the name of Vishnu.[19]

The invocation of a Hindu deity in this political ritual shows that unlike the early Sultans of Bengal, Mughal officials did not patronize Islam as a state religion. Except for a brief episode of anti-Hindu persecution

---

[15] Mirza Nathan, *Baharistan* text fol. 15a-b, trans. 1:42–3.

[16] Ibid., text. fol. 58a, trans. 1:145.

[17] Ibid., text fol. 299b; trans. 2:707.

[18] When Mirza Nathan donned the garb of the Sufi in his protest against Governor Islam Khan, several Hindu officers obstinately stood by Nathan and even suffered imprisonment and flogging for their loyalty to him. When brought before the Governor to explain their behaviour, one of the Hindus, Baikuntha Das, was interrogated with the words, "'You are a Hindu; why did you join this rebellion?" He replied, "God forbid! No rebellion will ever be raised either by Ihtiman Khan or his son [Mirza Nathan]. But as from my childhood, my father, at the request of his father, has given me to serve him and as I have been equally sharing his prosperity and adversity from my early life, so I can not leave his company.'" *Baharistan*, text fol. 60b, trans. 1:153.

[19] Ibid., text fol. 219b; trans. 2:476–7.

in the early 1680s,[20] Bengal's rulers maintained a strictly non-interventionist position in religious matters, despite pressure from local religious functionaries (*mullās*) and Sufis to support Islam over other religions.[21] This point is seen most dramatically in the way local judges adjudicated disputes between Hindus and Muslims. In August 1640, a Bengali Muslim was brought before the judge (*shiqdār*) of Naraingarh in modern Midnapur District, having been accused of violating the religious sensibilities of nearby Hindu villagers by killing and eating a couple of peacocks. Turning to the accused, the judge, himself a Bengali Muslim, asked, 'Art thou not, as it seems, a Bengali and a Musalman...? How then didst thou dare in a Hindu district to kill a living thing?' The judge then explained that sixty-six years earlier, when the Mughals conquered Bengal, Akbar had given his word 'that he and his successors would let [Bengalis] live under their own laws and customs: he [the judge] therefore allowed no breach of them.' With that, the judge ordered the accused to be whipped.[22] The larger point, of course, is that the Mughals were determined not to allow religion to interfere with their administration of Bengal.

[20] In 1679 Emperor Aurangzeb (r. 1658–1707), the most controversial of Mughal emperors, imposed the religion-sanctioned *jizya* tax on all non-Muslims of the Empire. Theoretically required of all non-Muslims in return for state protection, the *jizya* had never previously been imposed or collected in Bengal. But in early 1681 Dutch observers noted that imperial officials had begun collecting the *jizya* from the Hindus of Dhaka 'ever so strictly.' *Dagh-Register gehouden int Casteel Batavia vant passerende daer ter plaetse als over geheel Nederlandts-India* (Batavia: C. Kolff, 1928), 1680:121. In Qasimbazar, at that time the centre of Bengal's flourishing textile industry, officials forcibly demanded the *jizya* from Hindu silk workers, which disrupted the local textile production business and drove the city's 'little people' into the interior. Bengal's dīwān, or chief revenue officer, demanded that even resident European officials of the Dutch East India Company, as non-Muslims, pay the tax. *Generale missiven van gouverneurs-generaal en raden aan Heren XVII der Verenigde Oostindische Compagnie* (The Hague: Martinus Nijhoff, 1960), 4:391, 445, 564.

[21] Fray Manrique, who was in Dhaka in 1640, wrote that mullās and Sufis—that is, members of both the official and unofficial Muslim establishments—had urged the Mughal government in Dhaka to prosecute European Christian missionaries on grounds that they had been encouraging Muslims to break Islamic injunctions against taking pork and wine. But both Shah Jahan and the governor rejected these appeals. 'These attempts at persecution,' he observed, 'would have succeeded had the [Christian] Brethren not obtained the support of the Emperor and consequently of the Nababo [Governor].' Manrique, *Travels*, 1:46–7.

[22] Ibid., 2:95–115.

One consequence of this hands-off policy was that Mughal officials refused to promote the conversion of Bengalis to Islam. Islam Khan is known to have discouraged the conversion of Bengalis and on one occasion actually punished one of his officers for allowing it to happen. In 1609 when the Governor's army was moving across the present Bogra region subduing hostile chieftains, one of his officers, Tuqmaq Khan, defeated Raja Ray, the landholder (*zamīndār*) of Shahzadpur. Shortly after this, Tuqmaq Khan employed the son of the defeated raja as his personal servant and at the same time converted him to Islam. This news deeply annoyed the Governor, who punished Tuqmaq Khan by transferring him from his *jāgīr*.[23] Clearly, the Governor did not view government service as a reward for conversion to Islam; to the contrary, in this instance the man responsible for causing the conversion was censured and transferred. Moreover, it was not only Islam Khan who opposed the conversion, but also 'the other officers of the State,' suggesting that the hands-off policy was a general one.

This observation points to one of the great paradoxes of Bengali history, namely, that although Muslim regimes had ruled over Bengal since the early thirteenth century, a noticeable community of Muslim cultivators did not emerge there until the late sixteenth century, under a regime that did nothing to encourage the conversion of Bengalis to Islam and in fact opposed such conversions. Communities of Muslim cultivators were first reported in the Dhaka region in 1599, at a time when the balance of power in that region was gradually shifting from powerful zamīndārs like 'Isa Khan and the other so-called 'twelve chieftains' (*bāra bhūyān*), to Mughal imperial authorities.[24] Communities of Muslim cultivators were first reported in the Noakhali region in the 1630s, and in the Rangpur region in the 1660s.[25]

It is significant that the areas where communities of Muslim cultivators were first noticed—Dhaka, Noakhali, Rangpur—are located in the eastern half of the Bengal delta, and not the western delta. The reasons for this appear related to the extraordinary economic growth that the eastern delta was then experiencing relative to the west. Prior to the sixteenth century, eastern Bengal had been a heavily forested region that, being isolated from the main centres of Brahmanic culture, had

---

23 Mirza Nathan, *Baharistan*, text fol. 10b; trans. 1:32.

24 H. Hosten, 'Jesuit Letters from Bengal, Arakan and Burma (1599–1600),' *Bengal Past and Present* 30 (1925), 59.

25 S. H. Askeri, 'The Mughal-Magh relations down to the time of Islam Khan Mashhadi,' *Indian History Congress, Proceedings,* 22nd session (1959), 210. Kazim b. Muhammad Munshi Amin, *'Alamgir-nama,* ed. Khadim Husain and 'Abd al-Hai (Calcutta: Asiatic Society of Bengal, 1868), 677.

been only lightly touched by Indo-Aryan civilization. Archaeological data on the distribution and relative size of Bengal's ancient urban centres show that, between the Mauryan and Sena periods (fourth century BC–AD twelfth century), the western delta was more densely populated than the east.[26] Greater urbanization suggests greater occupational specialization and social stratification. As a result, prior to the Turkish conquest of 1204, western Bengal had become far more deeply penetrated by Indo-Aryan civilization generally, and in particular by Brahman settlement and the diffusion of Brahmanic notions of hierarchical social organization and caste specialization. Around 1590, the poet Mukundaram, a native of Burdwan, described the highly elaborated caste society that by that time had appeared in western Bengal.[27] No such evidence exists for the east.

Two major obstacles inhibited the advance of Brahmanical society into the eastern delta: heavy forestation, and an absence of direct riverine contact with upper India. Today, West Bengal gets about 55 inches of rain annually, whereas central and eastern Bengal get 60 inches to 95 inches, with the mouth of the Meghna receiving from 100 inches to 120 inches and eastern Sylhet about 150 inches.[28] Assuming this climatic pattern held in ancient times, the density of vegetation in the

[26] Barrie Morrison has made comparative calculations of the total area in square feet of ancient Bengal's six principal royal palaces: Pundranagara, 22,555,000; Pandua, 13,186,800; Gaur, 10,000,000; Kotivarasha, 2,700,000; Vikrampur, 810,000; and Devaparvata (at Lalmai), 360,000. The four largest of these were located in cities in Varendra, or northwestern Bengal, whereas Vikrampur and Devaparvata, located in the east and southeast respectively, were many times smaller than the others. See Barrie Morrison, *Lalmai, a Cultural Center of Early Bengal: An Archaeological Report and Historical Analysis* (Seattle: University of Washington Press, 1974), 124.

[27] Mukundaram gives detailed lists of Hindu communities, divided into four tiers of occupationally differentiated endogamous groups, or *jātis*. The first tier included Brahmans, Kayasthas, and Baidyas. The second included productive classes such as cultivators, herders, iron smiths, potters, weavers, gardeners, barbers, candy makers, spice merchants, brass smiths, gold merchants, and so on. The third tier was composed of ritually less pure castes: fisherman, oil pressers, woodcutters, launderers, tailors, molasses makers, carpenters, ferrymen, and beggers. At the end of the list, compelled to live outside the poet's imaginary city, were the grass cutters, leather-workers, prostitutes, and Dom tribals, who were scavengers and sweepers. Mukundaram, *Kavikaṅkaṇa Caṇḍī*, ed. Srikumar Bandyopadhyaya and Visvapati Chaudhuri (Calcutta: University of Calcutta, 1974), 355–61.

[28] O. H. K. Spate and A. T. A. Learmonth, *India and Pakistan: A General and Regional Geography*, 3rd edn (London: Methuen, 1967), 575.

delta's hinterland, formerly covered with thick forests of *śāl*,[29] would have increased dramatically as one moved eastward. Cutting and clearing the land would have required much more labour and organization, even with the aid of iron implements, than was the case in the less densely forested westerly regions. The other obstacle to economic growth in the east was its isolation from the great Ganges river system. In ancient times, the Ganges flowed down the delta's western corridor though the present Bhagirata-Hooghly channel, emptying into the Bay near Calcutta, where the river is still known as the Adi-Ganga, 'original Ganges'. This left eastern Bengal disconnected from the Ganges system. Due to continual sedimentation, however, the Ganges in very early times began to spill out of its former river-bed and find new channels to the east[30]—the Bhairab, the Mathabhanga, the Garai-Madhumati, the Arialkhan—until finally, in the late sixteenth century, it linked up with the Padma, enabling its main course to flow directly into the heart of East Bengal.[31] European maps dated 1548, 1615, 1660, and 1779 clearly show this riverine movement.[32]

The implications of the Ganges's eastward migration, moreover, were far-reaching. For one thing, it linked eastern Bengal's economy with wider markets since it opened up a heavily forested and formerly isolated region to direct commercial contact with upper India. More importantly,

[29] Anil Rawat, 'Life, Forests and Plant Sciences in Ancient India,' in *History of Forestry in India*, ed. Ajay S. Rawat (New Delhi: Indus Publishing Co., 1991), 246.

[30] See R. K. Mukerjee, *The Changing Face of Bengal: A Study of Riverine Economy* (Calcutta: University of Calcutta, 1938), 3–10; S. C. Majumdar, *Rivers of the Bengal Delta* (Calcutta: University of Calcutta, 1942), 65–72; Kanangopal Bagchi, *The Ganges Delta* (Calcutta: University of Calcutta, 1944), 33, 58; N. D. Bhattacharya, 'Changing Course of the Padma and Human Settlements,' *National Geographic Journal of India*, 24/1–2 (March–June 1978), 63–5.

[31] Already in 1567 the Venetian traveler Cesare Federici noted that ships were unable to sail north of Satgaon (near modern Calcutta) on the old Ganges, and seven years later Abu'l-fazl, Akbar's principal ideologue, recorded that the Ganges had divided into two branches at Tanda, with one branch flowing south to Satgaon and the other flowing east toward Sonargaon and Chittagong. By 1666, the deterioration of the former Ganges had progressed to the point that it had become altogether unnavigable. Cesare Federici, 'Extracts of Master Caesar Frederike his Eighteene Yeeres Indian Observations,' in Samuel Purchas, *Hakluytus Posthumus, or Purchas his Pilgrimes* (1625; repr. Glasgow: James MacLehose & Sons, 1905), 10:113; Abu'l-fazl 'Allami, *Ain-i Akbari*, vol. 3 trans. H. S. Jarrett, ed. Jadunath Sarkar, 2nd edn. (1927; repr. New Delhi: Oriental Books Reprint Corp., 1977–8), 3:153. Jean Baptice Tavernier, *Travels in India*, ed. V. Ball (1889; repr. Lahore: al-Biruni, 1976), 1:125.

[32] See the sequence of four maps 'Changing Courses of Bengal Rivers, 1548–1779'.

Map 5. Changing courses of Bengal rivers, 1548–1779

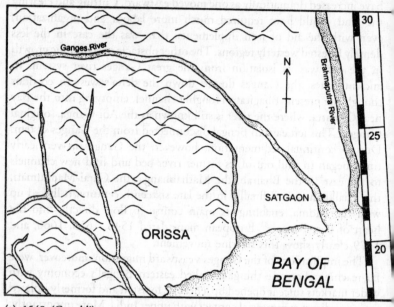

(a) 1548 (Gastaldi)

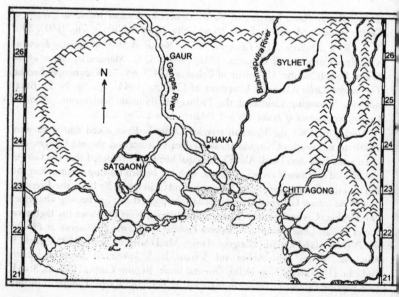

(b) 1615 (de Barros)

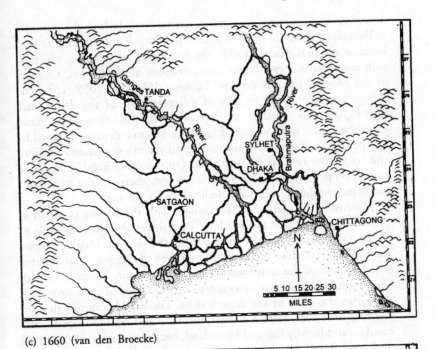

(c) 1660 (van den Broecke)

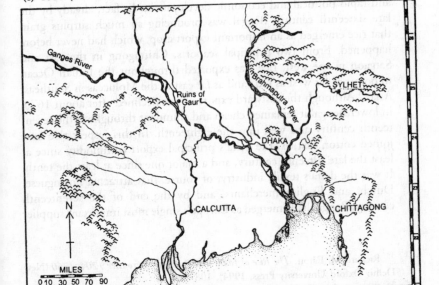

(d) 1779 (Rennell)

however, the great river's eastward migration carried with it the epicentre of Bengali civilization, since its annual flooding deposited the immense loads of silt that made possible the cultivation of wet rice, which in turn could sustain ever larger concentrations of population. Changes in the Mughal revenue demand between 1595 and 1659 reflect the changes in the relative fertility of different parts of the delta, since such figures were based on the capacity of the land to produce grain. Over the course of those sixty-four years, revenue demand jumped by 117 per cent in the delta's most ecologically active southeastern region, and by 97 per cent in the northeast. On the other hand, it increased by only 54 per cent in the less active southwest, whereas in the ecologically moribund northwest it actually declined by 13 per cent.[33]

Moreover, the merger of the Ganges with the Padma occurred at the very moment that the whole of Bengal was absorbed into one of the largest imperial systems ever seen in South Asia—the Mughal Empire under Akbar. Unlike earlier Muslim rulers of Bengal, who situated their capitals in the northwestern delta (i.e., Gaur, Pandua, Tanda), the Mughals in the early seventeenth century planted their provincial capital in the heart of the eastern delta, Dhaka. This meant that for the first time ever, eastern Bengal, formerly an underdeveloped, inaccessible, and heavily forested hinterland, became the focus of concerted and rapid political and economic development. In fact, already by the late sixteenth century Bengal was producing so much surplus grain that rice emerged as an important export crop, which had never before happened. From two principal seaports, Chittagong in the east and Satgaon in the west, rice was exported throughout the Indian Ocean to points as far west as Goa and as far east as the Moluccas in Southeast Asia.[34] Although the eastward export of rice declined after about 1670, in lower Bengal it remained cheap and abundant throughout the seventeenth century and well into the eighteenth. In this respect rice now joined cotton textiles, the delta's principal export commodity since at least the late fifteenth century, and a major one since at least the tenth. It was the delta's textile industry, of course, that attracted Portuguese, Dutch, and English merchants, and by the end of the seventeenth century, Bengal had emerged as Europe's single most important supplier

---

[33] Richard M. Eaton, *The Rise of Islam and the Bengal Frontier 1204–1760* (New Delhi: Oxford University Press, 1994), 198–9.

[34] François Pyrard, *The Voyage of François Pyrard of Laval to the East Inde, the Maldives, the Moluccas and Brazil,* ed. and trans. Albert Gray (Hakluyt Society, 1st ser., nos 76, 77, 80, 1887–90; repr. New York: Burt Franklin, n.d.), 2:327.

of goods in all of Asia.[35] In exchange for manufactured textiles, both European and Asian merchants poured into the delta substantial amounts of silver which, minted into currency, fueled the booming agrarian frontier by monetizing the local economy.[36]

In the ecologically active portions of the delta, and more particularly on the cutting edge of East Bengal's agrarian frontier, the pivotal figure was the forest pioneer, tied economically to the land and politically to the expanding Mughal state. Concerned with bringing stability to their turbulent and undeveloped eastern frontier, the Mughals did more than plant their provincial capital in the heart of the eastern delta. They also granted favourable or even tax-free tenures of land to industrious individuals who were expected to clear and bring into cultivation undeveloped forest tracts. The policy was intended to promote the emergence of local communities that would be both economically productive and politically loyal. Every recipient of such grants, Hindu or Muslim, was required to support his dependent clients and to pray for the long life of the Mughal state.[37] Hundreds of Mughal records dating from the mid-seventeenth century down to the advent of British power in 1760 document these pioneers' steady push into virgin jungle and their recruitment of local peoples to clear the jungle and bring the land into rice cultivation.[38] Because they mobilized local labour for these purposes, these men played decisive roles in the socio-economic development of the eastern delta. Through their agency, much of this region witnessed either the introduction or an intensification of wet rice cultivation, while local communities formerly engaged mainly in

[35] Om Prakash, *The Dutch East India Company and the Economy of Bengal, 1630–1720* (Princeton: Princeton University Press, 1985), 75. The notion that the influx of silver was primarily a European and maritime phenomenon has been vastly overstated in the literature. Even as late as the mid-eighteenth century, Asian traders—especially Gujaratis, Armenians, and Punjabis—played a more important role in Bengal's commercial economy than did Europeans. See Sushil Chaudhury, *From Prosperity to Decline: Eighteenth Century Bengal* (New Delhi: Manohar, 1995), esp. chapters seven and eight.

[36] Eaton, *Rise of Islam*, 200–7.

[37] The earliest of such grants issued from Chittagong, dated 2 September 1666, transferred to a certain Shah Zain al-'Abidin 166.4 acres of jungle land, which he was required to bring into cultivation. The order issuing the grant also stipulated that 'he must assiduously pray for the survival of the powerful state.' Chittagong District Collectorate Record Room, 'Kanun Daimer Nathi,' No. 1, bundle 59, case no. 3863.

[38] See Eaton, *Rise of Islam*, ch. 9.

hunting, fishing, or shifting agriculture began devoting more time to full-time wet-rice peasant agriculture.

These pioneers also played decisive roles in the religious development of the region, since one of the conditions for obtaining a grant was to build on the land a mosque or temple, to be supported in perpetuity out of the wealth produced on site. Grants made out to Hindu institutions (e.g., *brahmottar, devottar, vishnottar, śivottar*) tended to integrate local communities into a Hindu-ordered cultural universe, whereas grants authorizing the establishment of mosques or shrines tended to integrate such communities into an Islamic-ordered cultural universe. Subsequent demographic patterns evolved from these earlier processes.[39] Since most pioneers were Muslims, however, mosques comprised the majority of institutions established, with the result that the dominant mode of piety that evolved on East Bengal's economic frontier was Islamic. To be sure, the mosques themselves were not architecturally comparable with the great stone or brick religious monuments that the Mughals built in the cities. They were, rather, humble structures built of thatching and bamboo.

Nonetheless, such simple structures exercised considerable influence among the indigenous peoples of the eastern delta. For one thing, long after the founding pioneer died, the mosque he had built would continue to diffuse Islamic religious ideals amongst local communities, since Qur'an readers, callers to prayer, and preachers were also supported in perpetuity according to terms specified in the foundational grants. Furthermore, by the Mughal period the peoples of rural eastern Bengal, unlike those of the more Hinduized western delta, had not yet been integrated into a rigidly-structured caste society informed by Brahmanical notions of hierarchy and order. That is, they were not yet 'Hindu,' meaning that in much of the eastern delta rice agriculture and Islam were introduced simultaneously and grew together, both of them focused on these humble mosques. As a result, many pioneers who had obtained the land grants, mobilized labour, and founded these institutions passed

---

[39] In 1898, a time when the colonization of some of the Sylhet forest was still within living memory, a Muslim gentleman of northern Sylhet recalled that whenever a new village was founded, a temple to the goddess Kali was built if the founding landlord were a Sakta Hindu, and a temple to Vishnu if he were a Vaishnava. If a majority of the village were Vaishnava, they would build a shrine (*ākhṛā*) to Radha and Krishna. If the area were infested with snakes, the patron deity was the snake goddess Manasa, and if the village were founded by Muslims, a shrine to some Muslim pīr would be established. P. N. Bhattacharjee, 'Folkcustom and Folklore of the Sylhet District of India.' *Man in India* 10/1 (January–March, 1930), 133.

into subsequent memory as powerful saints, or *pīrs*. In not a few cases, tomb cults grew up on their gravesites.

The religious authority possessed by the hundreds of tiny mosques and shrines that sprang up along the eastern frontier was further enhanced by the simultaneous diffusion of papermaking technology.[40] Traceable to the fifteenth century and unmistakably identified with Islamic civilization—the ordinary Bengali for 'paper' (*kāgaj*) and 'pen' (*kalam*) are both Perso-Arabic loan words—the new technology fostered attitudes that endowed the written word with an authority qualitatively different from oral authority. With the proliferation of books and the religious gentry in the countryside, a 'culture of literacy' began to spread far beyond the Mughal state's bureaucratic sector or the delta's urban centres. Contemporary government documents confirm that Qur'an readers were attached to rural mosques and shrines as part of their endowments,[41] while Bengali sources dating from the fifteenth century refer to the magical power popularly attributed to the Qur'an.[42] In particular, the culture of literacy endowed the cult of Allah with a kind of authority—that of the unchangeable written word—that the delta's preliterate forest cults had theretofore lacked. For, apart from those areas along the older river valleys where Hindu civilization had already made inroads among indigenous peoples, most of the eastern hinterland was populated by communities lightly touched, if touched at all, by Hindu civilization and its own 'culture of literacy'. In the east, then, Islam came to be understood as a religion, not only of the axe and the plough, but also of the book.

Thus, although the Mughal government does not appear to have intended to Islamize the East Bengali countryside, such an outcome

[40] Jeremiah P. Losty, *The Art of the Book in India* (London: British Library, 1982), 10–12, 113; W. W. Rockhill, 'Notes on the Relations and Trade of China with the Eastern Archipelago and the Coast of the Indian Ocean during the Fourteenth Century,' *T'oung Pao* 16/2 (1915), 440.

[41] 'Qur'an readers' were titled *Qur'ān-khwānī* or *tilāwat*. See 'Kanun Daimer Nathi,' Chittagong District Collectorate Record Room, No. 65, bundle 73, case no. 4677; No. 72, bundle 63, case no. 4100; No. 113, bundle 35, case no. 2296.

[42] Writing in 1494 in the Barisal region, Vijaya Gupta speaks of 'a teacher of the Qādī named Khālās ... who always engaged himself in the study of the Qur'an and other religious books.... He said, if you ask me, I say, why are you afraid of demons [*bhūt*], when you have got the religious books. Write (extracts) from the book and hang it down the neck. If then also the demons (implying snakes) bite, I shall be held responsible.' Abdul Karim, *Social History of the Muslims of Bengal (down to AD 1538)* (Dacca: Asiatic Society of Pakistan, 1959), 171. Karim's translation. Cf. Vijaya Gupta, *Padma Purāṇa* (Calcutta: University of Calcutta, 1962), 140.

nonetheless resulted from its land policies. Seen from a global perspective, moreover, at the very time that the region became integrated politically with the Mughal Empire—that is, from 1574—it was also becoming integrated economically with the whole world, since silver originally mined in South or Central America and shipped to Spain ultimately ended up fueling the eastward push of Bengal's economic frontier. This occurred when silver imported to pay for Bengal's textile exports was coined into Mughal currency and locally invested, as when Hindu financiers advanced capital to Muslim pioneers, who in turn organized local labour for cutting forested regions and founded mosques around which new agrarian communities coalesced.[43] All of this fostered a kind of cultural authority that was in the first instance Mughal, but ultimately Islamic. Ironically enough, Europe's early modern economic expansion in the 'New World' contributed to the growth of Islam in the 'Old World,' and especially in Bengal, which by the end of the seventeenth century had become one of the most dynamic economic zones in all Eurasia.

It is true, of course, that deltaic peoples had been transforming forested lands to rice fields long before the Mughal age. What was new from at least the sixteenth century on, however, was that this process had become particularly associated with Muslim holy men, or perhaps more accurately, with industrious and capable forest pioneers subsequently identified as holymen. In popular memory, some of these men swelled into vivid mythico-historical figures, saints whose lives served as metaphors for the expansion of both religion and agriculture. They have endured precisely because, in the collective folk memory, their careers captured and telescoped a complex historical socioreligious process whereby a land originally forested and non-Muslim became arable and predominantly Muslim. For this reason, one finds evidence of medieval Bengal's socio-economic and religious transformations not only in Mughal revenue documents, but also in contemporary Bengali literature.

---

[43] Already in the late sixteenth century, the poet Mukundaram had linked mobile cash with the process of forest clearing and agricultural operations. In the *Candī-Maṅgala*, the goddess Chandi orders the poem's hero, Kalaketu, to sell a valuable ring and use the money thus obtained to clear the forest so that a city may be built in her honour. Once the land was prepared for agriculture, Kalaketu was to advance his men rice, seeds, and cash, thereby facilitating their establishment on newly claimed lands. Mukundaram, *Kavikankaṇa Candī*. Ed. Srikumar Bandyopadhyay and Visvapati Chaudhuri (Calcutta: University of Calcutta, 1974), 290, 295–6, 354–5.

For example the *Caṇḍī-Maṅgala*, composed around 1590 by the poet Mukundaram, celebrates the goddess Chandi and her human agent, the hunter Kalaketu. In this poem the goddess entrusts Kalaketu with temporal sovereignty over her forest kingdom on the condition that he, as king, renounce the violent career of hunting and bring peace on earth by promoting her cult. To this end Kalaketu is enjoined to oversee the clearing of the jungle and to establish there an ideal city whose population will cultivate the land and worship the king's benefactor, Chandi. The poem can thus be seen as a grand epic dramatizing the process of civilization-building in the Bengal delta, and more concretely, the push of rice-cultivating civilization into virgin forest. It is true that the model of royal authority that informs Mukundaram's *Caṇḍī- Maṅgala* is unambiguously Hindu. The king, Kalaketu, is both a devotee of the forest goddess Chandi and a raja in the classical Indian sense, while the peasant cultivators in the poem show their solidarity with the king by accepting betel nut from his mouth, an act drawing directly on the Hindu ritual of devotion performed for a deity, that is, *pūja.* Yet the principal pioneers responsible for clearing the forest, the men who made it possible for both the city and its rice fields to flourish, were Muslims. 'The Great Hero [Kalaketu] is clearing the forest', the poet proclaimed,

Hearing the news, outsiders came from various lands.
The hero then bought and distributed among them
    Heavy knives (*kāṭh-dā*), axes (*kuṭhār*), battle-axes (*ṭāngī*), and pikes (*bān*).
From the North came the Das (people),
    One hundred of them advanced.
They were struck with wonder on seeing the Hero,
    Who distributed betel-nut to each of them.
From the South came the harvesters,
    Five hundred of them came under one organizer.
From the West came Zafar Mian,
    Together with twenty-two thousand men.
Sulaimani beads in their hands,
    They chanted the names of their *pīr* and the Prophet.
Having cleared the forest,
    They established markets.
Hundreds and hundreds of foreigners
    Ate and entered the forest.
Hearing the sound of the axe,
    The tiger became apprehensive and ran away, roaring.[44]

---

[44] Ibid., 299–300.

Muslim pioneers in this poem are associated with three interrelated themes: (a) subduing a tiger, that is, taming Bengal's untamed wilderness, (b) clearing the jungle, thus preparing the land for the cultivation of rice, and (c) establishing markets, that is, introducing commerce and a cash economy into a theretofore undeveloped hinterland. Moreover, these men are said to have come from the west, suggesting origins in upper India or beyond, in contrast to the aboriginals who came from the north and the harvesters who came from the south, that is, from within the delta. In point of numbers, the twenty-two thousand Muslims far surpassed the other pioneers. We also see that the Muslims were led by a single man, 'Zafar Mian,' evidently the chieftain or the organizer of the Muslim workmen. Finally, these men practiced a style of Islamic piety that focussed on chanting the name of a pīr, who quite possibly was Zafar Mian himself.[45] Although the narrative cannot be understood as an eyewitness account, it probably had some basis in what was happening in Mukundaram's own day. Even if there had been no historical 'Zafar Mian,' the poet was clearly familiar with the theme of thousands of Muslims entering and transforming the forests under the leadership of capable chieftains or charismatic pīrs.

Similar themes are seen in the legend of Shaikh Jalal al-Din Tabrizi, found in another sixteenth century text, the *Sekaśubhodayā*.[46] Although the events described in Mukundaram's poem take place in a 'time-out-of-time,' those described in the *Sekaśubhodayā* are set in the period just prior to the Turkish conquest; indeed, its author purports to have been the minister of Lakshmana Sena, the Hindu king defeated by the Turks in 1204. Both poems belong to a genre of pre-modern Bengali literature, the *mangala-kāvya*, which typically glorified a particular deity and promised the deity's followers bountiful auspiciousness in return for their devotion. But the hero of the *Sekaśubhodayā* is not a traditional Bengali deity, but Shaikh Jalal al-Din Tabrizi, a figure said to have come from somewhere west of Bengal. He was instructed by *Pradhān-puruṣa* ('Great Person,' i.e., God) to go to 'the eastern country,' where he would meet Raja Lakshmana Sena, in whose kingdom he would build a 'house of God' (*devasadana*), or mosque. The shaikh did as

---

[45] It is possible that this Zafar Mian represents a hazy memory of Zafar Khan, the historical pioneer who in 1298 patronized the constructions of a *madrasa* at Tribeni, not distant from Mukundaram's home in Burdwan. See Shamsud-din Ahmed, ed. and tr., *Inscriptions of Bengal*, 4 vols (Rajshahi: Varendra Research Museum, 1960), 4:18–21.

[46] Sukumar Sen, ed. and trans. *Sekasubhodaya of Halayudha Misra* (Calcutta: Asiatic Society, 1963), ix–xi.

he was told. Walking on the Ganges River with his magical shoes, Shaikh Tabrizi reached the Senas' capital at Pandua, and upon meeting Raja Lakshmana Sena he challenged the king to cause a nearby heron to release a fish caught in its bill. When Lakshmana Sena declined, the shaikh merely glanced at the bird, which at once dropped the fish. Seeing this, the astonished king asked for the shaikh's grace (*prasād*) and vowed to remain his steadfast devotee.

Shaikh Tabrizi then set about building the mosque. After Lakshmana Sena donated some forest land for the purpose, the holyman prepared the site by clearing the area of demons and offering handfuls of holy water to *Pradhānpuruṣa*, to the Himalayas, and to various other personages. This done, Shaikh Tabrizi 'invited people from the country and had them settled in that land'. Here we see a clear division of labour between the Hindu monarch and the Muslim holyman: the former donates forest land for the mosque while the latter performs the ritual feats necessary to establish the institution and invites local people to settle a formerly forested land. The shaikh issued formal documents of settlement to these men, who now cultivated the fields whose income would be used to support the mosque.[47]

As with 'Zafar Mian' in Mukundaram's poem, we should not hope to recover in this text the historical 'Shaikh Tabrizi'. Rather, both men represent metaphors for changes experienced by people all over the delta, and in particular, the gradual cultural shift—well under way by the sixteenth century—from a Bengali Hindu world to a Bengali Muslim world. The *Sekaśubhodayā* accomplished this by presenting the new in the guise of the familiar: Shaikh Tabrizi radiated a 'glow of penance,' or *tapahprabhāb*, the power acquired through the practice of ascetic austerities; the 'grace' he gave to the king was *prasād*, the food a Hindu deity gives a devotee; the shaikh's consecration of the mosque followed a ritual program consistent with that of a temple, and the shaikh's patron deity, 'Allah,' was given the generic and hence portable name *Pradhānpuruṣa*, 'Great Person'. Shorn of its fabulous embellishments, the text presents us with a model of patronage—a mosque linked economically with the hinterland and politically with the state—that was fundamental to the historical expansion of Muslim agrarian civilization throughout the delta. The *Sekaśubhodayā* and the *Caṇḍī-Maṅgala* thus present us with literary versions of a process of socio-economic and cultural change that confirm the evidence of such change found in administrative documents of the period.

[47] Ibid., 135–7, 179, 217–18, 220, 222–4.

A more complex and self-consciously 'Islamic' work is Saiyid Sultan's great epic poem, the *Nabī-Baṃśa*. Composed in the Chittagong region and also dating to the late sixteenth century, this ambitious work seeks to carve out a theological space for Islam amidst the various religious traditions already nested in the Bengal delta. For example, the work treats the major deities of the Hindu pantheon, including Brahma, Vishnu, Śiva, Rama, and Krishna, as successive prophets of God, followed in turn by Adam, Noah, Abraham, Moses, Jesus, and Muhammad. By commenting in this way on Vedic, Vaishnava, and Śaiva divinities, in addition to biblical figures, the *Nabī-Baṃśa* fostered the claim that Islam was the heir, not only to Judaism and Christianity, but also to the religious traditions of pre-Muslim Bengal. In this way, rather than repudiating those older religious traditions, Saiyid Sultan's epic served to *connect* Islam with Bengal's socioreligious past, or at least with that part of it represented in the high textual tradition of the Brahmans. But it would be wrong to characterize the work as merely 'syncretic'; on fundamental points of theology, the poet clearly drew on Judeo-Islamic and not on Indic thought. For example, although the author freely interchanges the Arabic term *nabī* with the Sanskrit *avatāra*, his meaning is not the Indic conception of repeated incarnations of the divine, but rather the Judeo-Islamic 'once-only' conception of prophethood. Similarly, the epic does not view cosmic time as oscillating between ages of splendour and ages of ruin in the cyclical manner characteristic of classical Indian thought. Rather, as religion in the time of each *nabī/avatāra* became corrupt, God sent down later prophets with a view to propagating belief in one god, culminating in the last and most perfect *nabī/avatāra*, Muhammad. Already in the four Vedas, the poet states, God ('*Kartār*') had given witness to the certain coming of Muhammad's prophetic mission.[48]

It is in its characterizations of Adam and Abraham, however, that the epic poem's agrarian dimension comes through most clearly. Adam, for his part, made his first earthly appearance on Sondwip Island, off Bengal's southeastern coast. There the angel Gabriel instructed him to go to Arabia, where at Mecca he would construct the original Ka'ba.[49] When this was accomplished, Gabriel gave Adam a plough, a yoke, two bulls, and seed, addressing him with the words, 'Niranjan [God] has commanded that agriculture will be your destiny.' Adam then planted

---

[48] Saiyid Sultan, *Nabī-Baṃśa*, ed. Ahmed Sharif, 2 vols (Dhaka: Bangla Academy, 1978), 1:24–5.

[49] Ibid., 1:88, 98, 103.

the seeds, harvested the crop, ground the grain, and made bread.[50] Similar ideas are found in the poet's treatment of Abraham, the supreme patriarch of Judeo-Christian-Islamic civilization. Born and raised in a forest, Abraham is said to have travelled to Palestine, where he attracted tribes from nearby lands, mobilized local labour to cut down the forest, and built a holy place, Jerusalem's Temple, where prayers were offered to Niranjan.[51] Clearly, the main themes of Abraham's life as presented here—his sylvan origins, his recruitment of nearby tribesmen, his leadership in clearing the forest, and his building a house of prayer—mirrored rather precisely the careers of the hundreds of pioneers who, during the sixteenth to eighteenth centuries, had been given state land-grants for the purpose of mobilizing local clients in the Bengali countryside for just such activities.

Here, then, was a remarkable fit between social reality and religious thought. To be a good Muslim, so it was believed, one must cultivate the earth, as Adam did. Present-day Muslim cultivators attach a similar significance to Adam's career. Cultivators of Pabna District identify the earth's soil, from which Adam was made, as the source of Adam's power and of his ability to cultivate the earth. In their view, farming the earth successfully is the fundamental task of all mankind, not only because they themselves have also come from (i.e., were nurtured by the fruit of) the soil, but because it was God's command to Adam that he reduce the earth to the plough. It was by farming the earth that Adam obeyed God, thereby articulating his identity as the first man and as the first Muslim. Hence all men descended from Adam, in this view, can most fully demonstrate their obedience to God—and indeed, their humanity—by cultivating the earth.[52] A 1913 village survey in Dhaka District noted that Muslims there 'entirely fall upon agriculture as their only source of income, and unless driven to the last stage of starvation they never hire themselves for any kind of service, which is looked upon with contempt on their part.'[53] In 1908 the gazetteer for

[50] Ibid., 1:107–9.

[51] Ibid., 1:348, 420–1.

[52] John P. Thorp, 'Masters of Earth: Conceptions of "Power" among Muslims of Rural Bangladesh' (Ph. D. diss., University of Chicago, 1978), 40–54. Although Adam's career as a tiller of the soil is also found in the Book of Genesis (3:23), such an association is not made in the Qur'an. In the Muslim world, the perception of Adam as the first cultivator, and of his cultivating the earth at the command of God, may therefore be a uniquely Bengali variant. On the other hand, the notion that God fashioned Adam from clay is common to both Genesis (2:7) and the Qur'an (15:26).

[53] Dhaka District Collectorate, Record Room. Mauza Notes, Rupganj, vol. 1.

Khulna District noted that the Muslim masses 'are descendants of semi-Hinduized aborigines, principally Chandals and Pods, and of low caste Hindus, who were converted to Islam. ... [They] do not, however, know or admit that they are the descendants of converts to Islam; according to them they are the tillers of the soil, while the Ashraf do not cultivate the land with their own hands.'[54]

The last phrase in this passage takes us back to the socio-religious cleavage referred to at the outset of this essay. I have argued that what defined ashrāf identity was the cultivation of high Perso-Islamic civilization and a claimed descent from immigrants from west of Bengal. But this fails to go far enough. What served most profoundly to distinguish Bengali Muslim cultivators from ashrāf classes, as the evidence cited above suggests, was the plough. Whereas farmers defined their Muslim identity around cultivating the soil, the ashrāf disdained the plough and refused to touch it. A 1901 survey among Muslims of Nadia District found that 'the Ashrafs will not adopt cultivation for their living. They consider cultivation to be a degraded occupation and they shun it for that reason.'[55] And in the Census for the same year H. H. Risley wrote that 'like the higher Hindu castes, the Ashraf consider it degrading to accept menial service or to handle the plough.'[56] After all, the bulk of the Turks, Afghans, Iranians or Arabs who had migrated to India from the eleventh century onward no more saw themselves taking up agriculture than did English servants of the East India Company. Like the British, foreign-born Muslims saw themselves

---

Agla, No. 1063.

[54] L.S.S. O'Malley, *Bengal District Gazetteers: Khulna* (Calcutta, 1908), 65.

[55] 'Reports on the Religious and Social Divisions amongst the Mahomedans of Bengal,' London: India Office Library, Risley Collection, Eur. MSS E 295, 9:88.

[56] E. A. Gait, 'Muhammadan Castes and Tribes,' in *Census of India, 1901*, vol. 6, 'The Lower Provinces of Bengal and their Feudatories', pt. 1, Report, 439. These turn-of-the-century observations are echoed in more modern studies of Bengali Muslim society. In 1960 a village study conducted in Comilla District by the Pakistan Academy for Rural Development found that 'the Muhuri Bari claimed greater respect because of their [Pathan] ancestry in the village. ...For them, working in the field was considered beneath one's dignity, as was true with the Khondkars, the Mirs and others who received formal education. ... The Khondkars who are a sort of religious leaders are held in respect. Cultivation with their own hands is considered taboo. ... the "Mirs" whose title generally signifies dignity of a great lineage came to this village three generations ago. Apparently the first to settle had little land. Cultivation was repugnant to this family, too. It initially thrived on trade and service.' S. A. Qadir, *Village Dhanishwar: Three Generations of Man-Land Adjustment in an East Pakistan Village* (Comilla: Pakistan Academy for Rural Development, 1960), 52–4.

as having come to India to administer a vast empire whose wealth they would appropriate, and not to participate with Indians as fellow cultivators.

CONCLUSION

Over the past fifteen centuries, Islam has been continuously redefined, reinterpreted, and contested, as competing social groups have risen or fallen in prominence and influence. To the historian, the challenge is to identify those groups and, by situating them in their unique historical contexts, to determine how they constructed the religion in the particular way they did. From this perspective, it becomes unproductive, or simply wrong, to speak of one group's understanding of Islam as 'orthodox' and another's as 'unorthodox,' or of one variant as 'fundamentalist' and another as 'syncretic,' or whatever. Such rhetorical labels may help in identifying and sorting out competing social classes in a given historical situation, or in determining who is on whose side in a particular debate. But as analytical tools they are quite useless.

In the same way, it would be wrong to view Islam as a monolithic essence that simply 'expanded' across space, time, and social class, in the process assimilating great numbers of people into a single framework of piety. In Bengal as elsewhere, Islam was continuously reinterpreted as different social classes in different periods became its dominant carriers, spokesmen, or representatives. Thus, in the thirteenth century, Islam had been associated with the ruling ethos of the delta's Turkish conquerors, and in the cities, at least, such an association persisted for several centuries, sustained especially by Sufi shaikhs of the Chishti order. Later, the Mughal conquest permitted an influx of a new elite class of ashrāf Muslims—immigrants from points west of the delta, or their descendants—who were typically administrators, soldiers, mystics, scholars, or long-distance merchants. For them, a rich tradition of Persian art and literature served to mediate and inform Islamic piety, which most of them subordinated to the secular ethos of Mughal imperialism. In particular, the ashrāf classes refused to engage in agricultural operations, and some Mughal officers even opposed the Islamization of native Bengalis who did. By the seventeenth and eighteenth centuries, however, owing principally to phenomenal levels of agrarian and demographic expansion in East Bengal, the dominant carriers of Islamic civilization in the delta were no longer the urban ashrāf, but peasant cultivators of the eastern frontier, who in extraordinary ways had assimilated Islam to their agrarian worldview.

What made this possible was that in the Mughal period, Bengal's agrarian and political frontiers had collapsed into one. From Sylhet through Chittagong, the government fused the political goal of deepening its authority among dependent clients rooted on the land with the economic goal of expanding the state's arable land area. This was achieved by issuing grants aiming at the agricultural development of the forested hinterland, most of whose recipients were petty *mullās*, pilgrims returned from Mecca, preachers, charismatic pīrs, and local chieftains seeking tax-free land. These men oversaw, or undertook to oversee, the clearing of forests and the construction of mosques or shrines, which in turn became the nuclei for the diffusion of Islamic ideals along the agrarian frontier.

Above all, the local communities that fell under the economic and religious influence of these institutions do not appear to have perceived Islam as alien, or as a closed, exclusive system to be accepted or rejected as a whole. Although today one habitually thinks of world religions as self-contained and complete systems with well-defined borders, such a static or fixed understanding does not apply to Bengal's premodern frontier, a fluid context in which Islamic superhuman agencies, typically identified with local superhuman agencies, gradually seeped into local cosmologies that were themselves dynamic. This 'seepage' occurred over such a long period of time that one can at no point identify a specific moment of 'conversion,' or any single moment when peoples saw themselves as having made a dramatic break with the past.[57] Islam in Bengal absorbed so much local culture and became so profoundly identified with the delta's long-term process of agrarian expansion, that the cultivating classes never seem to have regarded it as 'foreign'—even though some Muslim and Hindu literati and foreign observers did, and still do.[58]

---

[57] As late as the early twentieth century, Muslim cultivators retained indigenous names like Chand, Pal, and Dutt. J. E. Webster, *Eastern Bengal and Assam District Gazetteers: Noakhali* (Allahabad: Pioneer Press, 1911), 39.

[58] In 1629, when Sebastien Manrique divided Bengal's population into three groups, 'the Portuguese, the Moors, and the natives of the country,' he anticipated by several centuries the thinking of later observers who, informed like Manrique by normative understandings of what constitutes proper Islam, had difficulty understanding how Bengal's 'natives' could also be 'Moors'. In particular, during the nineteenth and twentieth centuries, British imperialists and both Hindu and Muslim reformers, each for their own reasons, stressed Islam's 'foreignness,' which further contributed to the notion that there was a certain tension between being Bengali and being Muslim. For further discussion, see Joya Chatterji, 'The Bengali Muslim: A Contradiction in Terms? An Overview of the Debate on Bengali Muslim Identity,' *Comparative Studies of South Asia, Africa, and the Middle East* 16/2 (1996), 16–24.

In the context of premodern Bengal, then, it would seem inappropriate to speak of the 'conversion' of 'Hindus' to Islam. What one finds, rather, is an expanding agrarian civilization, whose cultural counterpart was the growth of the cult of Allah. This larger movement was composed of several interwoven processes: (a) the eastward movement and settlement of colonizers from points west, (b) the incorporation of frontier tribal peoples into the expanding agrarian civilization, and (c) the natural population growth that accompanied the diffusion or the intensification of wet rice agriculture and the production of surplus food grains. Because this growth process combined natural, political, economic, and cultural forces, we find in eastern Bengal a remarkable congruence between a socioeconomic system geared to the production of wet rice and a religious ideology that conferred special meaning on agrarian life. It is testimony to the vitality of Islam—and one of the clues to its success as a world religion—that its adherents in Bengal were so creative in accommodating local socio-cultural realities with the norms of the religion.